AQA Religious Ethics for AS and A2

AQA Religious Ethics for AS and A2 is an ideal textbook for students of Advanced Subsidiary or Advanced Level courses, structured on the AQA specification. The book covers all necessary topics of the Religious Ethics A level specification in an enjoyable student-friendly fashion, and is split into four parts:

- What is ethics?
- AS Ethics
- A2 Ethics
- Ways of moral decision making.

Each chapter includes:

- A list of key issues, to introduce students to the topic
- AQA specification checklist
- Explanations of key terminology
- Exam practice questions
- Self-test review questions
- Helpful summaries.

To maximise students' chances of exam success, the book includes a section dedicated to answering examination questions. The book comes complete with lively illustrations, a comprehensive glossary and full bibliography.

The author:

Jill Oliphant teaches Religious Studies at Angley School in Cranbrook, Kent. She is also an experienced examiner.

The editors:

Jon Mayled has been Chief Examiner for Religious Studies. He is author and editor of many popular books for the GCSE specifications.

Anne Tunley is Head of Religious Studies at Gateways School in Leeds and an experienced examiner.

AQA Religious Ethics for AS and A2

JILL OLIPHANT

EDITED BY JON MAYLED AND ANNE TUNLEY

Routledge
Taylor & Francis Group

LONDON AND NEW YORK

First published in 2011
by Routledge
2 Park Square, Milton Park, Abingdon, OX14 4RN

Simultaneously published in the USA and Canada
by Routledge
270 Madison Ave., New York, NY 10016

Routledge is an imprint of the Taylor & Francis Group, an informa business

© 2011 Jill Oliphant, Jon Mayled and Anne Tunley

Typeset in Charter by
Keystroke, Station Road, Codsall, Wolverhampton
Printed and bound in Great Britain by
MPG Books Group, UK

British Library Cataloguing in Publication Data
A catalogue record for this book is available from the British Library

Library of Congress Cataloging in Publication Data
A catalog record for this book has been requested

ISBN 13: 978–0–415–54933–2 (pbk)
ISBN 13: 978–0–203–83021–5 (ebk)

This book is dedicated to Hannah, Lucinda and Miranda.

Contents

List of Illustrations   ix
Acknowledgements   xi
How to Use this Book   xiii
Answering Examination Questions   xv
Timeline: Scientists, Ethicists and Thinkers   xviii

1 What Is Ethics?   1

AS UNIT A RELIGION AND ETHICS 1   **5**

2 Utilitarianism   7
3 Situation Ethics   28
4 Religious Teaching on the Nature and Value of Human Life 42
5 Abortion   63
6 Euthanasia and the Right to Life   85

AS UNIT B RELIGION AND ETHICS 2   **101**

7 Kant   103
8 Natural Law   121
9 Religious Views of the Created World   136
10 Environment, both Local and Worldwide   146

A2 UNIT 3A RELIGION AND ETHICS   **173**

11 Libertarianism   175
12 Virtue Ethics   206
13 Religious Views on Sexual Behaviour and Human Relationships 226
14 Science and Technology   250

UNIT 4C 279

15 Ways of Moral Decision Making 281

Glossary 306
Bibliography 316
Index 323

List of illustrations

2.1	The quantity of happiness	11
2.2	The quality of happiness	13
2.3	A pig . . .	14
4.1	War cemetery	53
5.1	Sperm fertilising egg	65
5.2	Ultrasound image of human foetus	66
5.3	The quality of life	72
6.1	A syringe	89
7.1	Immanuel Kant	104
7.2	Duty: a charity collection box	108
8.1	Purpose	123
8.2	Reason – the *School of Athens*	123
8.3	Eternal Law	125
8.4	Divine Law	125
8.5	Natural Law	126
8.6	Human laws	126
10.1	Gaia – Earth from space	162
11.1	Child development	183
11.2	The fall of dominoes	194
11.3	Behaviourism – white laboratory rats	197
12.1	Playing a musical instrument	210
13.1	*The Kiss*	228
14.1	DNA helix	253
14.2 and 14.3	Two diagrams of stem cell research	260
15.1	Moses and the Ten Commandments	283

Acknowledgements

I am very grateful to the many people who have helped me prepare this book, particularly to Lesley Riddle of Taylor & Francis for commissioning me to write this text. I much appreciate the support I have received from Taylor & Francis staff. I also wish to thank greatly the people who have read drafts of the book and made so many helpful suggestions, particularly Lesley Riddle, Amy Grant, Gemma Dunn, Katherine Ong, Moira Taylor, Anne Tunley and Jon Mayled for all their assistance and support, not to mention their patience while waiting for parts of the text. I am also very grateful to the friends and family members who have supported and encouraged this project. I would like to thank in particular the sixth-form students of Angley School who read early drafts of the book, especially Emma Whittall, who did the drawings for the chapter on genetic engineering.

We are indebted to the people and archives below for permission to reproduce material. Every effort has been made to trace copyright-holders. Any omissions brought to our attention will be remedied in future editions.

TEXT

Extracts from specification details are produced by the kind permission of AQA.

Scripture quotations are from *The New Revised Standard Version of the Bible*, Anglicised Edition, © 1989, 1995 by the Division of Christian Education of the National Council of the Churches of Christ in the United States of America. Used by permission. All rights reserved.

IMAGES

Sperm fertilising egg (digital composite) – Sarah Jones (Debut Art)/Getty Images

Ultrasound image of human foetus (digital enhancement) – Kallista Images/
Getty Images

Portrait of Immanuel Kant (1724–1804) (oil on canvas) by German School
(eighteenth century) © Private Collection/The Bridgeman Art Library

Aristotle and Plato: detail from *The School of Athens* in the Stanza della
Segnatura, 1510–11 (fresco) (detail of 472) by Raphael (Rafaello Sanzio
of Urbino) (1483–1520) © Vatican Museums and Galleries, Vatican City,
Italy/The Bridgeman Art Library

White laboratory rats (*Rattus* sp.) in laboratory, close-up – Jonathan Selig/
Getty Images

The Kiss, 1888–98 (marble) by Auguste Rodin (1840–1917) © Musée Rodin,
Paris, France/Philippe Galard/The Bridgeman Art Library

DNA helix, blue glow 2 (microscopic) – 3D Clinic/Getty Images

Moses Receives the Tablets of the Law from God on Mount Sinai (colour litho)
by French School (nineteenth century) © Private Collection/Archives
Charmet/The Bridgeman Art Library

How to Use this Book

This book has been written for AQA students but it will be of use to all AS and A2 level Religious Studies students, as well as students taking the Moral Philosophy section of AS/A2 Philosophy and Scottish National Examinations at Higher Level.

The book is designed for students to use in class and at home. Every chapter provides an overview of the major themes and issues of Religious Ethics on the AQA specification for Religious Studies. The following features are designed to help you make the most effective use of the book:

1 **'The issues arising' section**
   This highlights the key issue or issues you should think about while studying each chapter.

2 **AQA checklist**
   The box about the AQA specification tells you which topics from the AS/A2 Religious Studies course are covered.

3 **Essential terminology box**
   You should be able to use this terminology accurately in examinations.

4 **Examination questions practice**
   This section contains advice about answering examination questions on the topic, with a sample question or questions.

5 **Review questions**
   The review questions are designed to test your understanding of topics discussed in the chapter. Make use of this section as a way to assess your learning about and from the issues in the chapter.

6 **Thought points**
   These offer additional ideas, questions and case studies.

7   **Biographical notes**

These are provided as useful background information but the information is not required for the examination.

8.   **Further reading**

Lists of suggestions for further reading for each chapter are to be found on the associated Routledge website: www.routledge.com/textbooks/9780415549332.

Stretching and challenging are important aspects of Advanced Level criteria, and opportunities are provided throughout the text to stretch students beyond the requirements of the AQA specification.

Answering Examination Questions

To be successful in Advanced Level Religious Studies you must learn examination techniques. Some advice to guide you is given below, but there is no substitute for practising writing examination questions. There are example questions at the end of the chapters in this book, and your teacher will give you plenty of other questions with which to practise. Some important aspects to answering examination questions are explained below.

All questions are written using the two Assessment Objectives in the QCA Subject Criteria for GCE Religious Studies:

- AO1 Select and demonstrate clearly relevant knowledge and understanding through the use of evidence, examples and correct language and terminology appropriate to the course of study. In addition, for synoptic assessment, A Level candidates should demonstrate knowledge and understanding of the connections between different elements of their course of study.
- AO2 Critically evaluate and justify a point of view through the use of evidence and reasoned argument. In addition, for synoptic assessment, A Level candidates should relate elements of their course of study to their broader context and to aspects of human experience.

SUBJECT KNOWLEDGE

At both AS and A2 level the majority of marks are given for your demonstration of a good understanding of the topic the question is examining. It is important not only that you learn the work you have studied, but also that you are able to select the knowledge that is relevant to an answer. For example, if the question is (AS level) *Explain how a follower of Natural Law might approach the issue of abortion*, your answer should be focused on the Natural Law approach to abortion, not writing everything you know about Natural Law or abortion.

When preparing for examination questions, it is a good idea to think about not only what a question is asking but also what material you have studied that is relevant to the question.

Selecting the correct information

Think about how you would answer the two questions below. Make a list of the topics and information you need to include in any answer. Be specific – for example, do not just say 'Utilitarianism' for question 1.

1   Explain Mill's approach to Utilitarianism.
2   Explain the main strengths of Utilitarianism.

TIMING

It is very important that you learn how to complete questions in the time available. In an examination the time available is very limited. It is a good idea to practise timing yourself writing answers to examination-style questions. You will get a low mark if a question is incomplete, as this limits the maximum level your answer can reach. Always try to spend equal amounts of time on each whole question you answer, as each question is worth the same number of marks.

Practise writing answers

It is very important that you practise answering questions for Religious Studies examinations by handwriting answers. In an examination you have very little time to write answers and you have to write not type. This takes practice; try to avoid typing answers when you practise doing examination questions at home.

UNDERSTANDING THE QUESTIONS

It is also very important that you think carefully about what a question is asking you. The table opposite focuses on some of the common instruction words used in AQA questions and what they mean.

Instruction word	Example question	Explanation
Explain	Explain Kant's theory.	When a question uses the word **explain**, it is telling you to demonstrate your knowledge of the topic in the question, and your ability to select and show understanding of relevant information and to use technical terms accurately. Thus, in the example question, you would need to demonstrate what you know about Kant's theory of duty, such as the categorical imperative, universability and the importance of good will, and to give examples.
Discuss	People are not free to make moral decisions. Discuss.	The word **discuss** in a question is telling you that you should examine the strengths and weaknesses of arguments for and against the statement in the question. You need to consider whether arguments in favour of and against the statement are successful. To do this, you will need to demonstrate an accurate understanding of one or more philosophers' views and the strengths and weaknesses of these views.
	Kant's ethical theory is too harsh. Discuss.	You would need to state (not explain in detail) one or more arguments in agreement with the statement, such as Kant's lack of consideration for consequences, the conflict of maxims, and the importance of universal and unchanging principles, and present reasons for and/or against the claim.
Assess	Assess a Utilitarian approach to the environment.	This means that you should first explain the issue you are being asked to assess and second present arguments for and against the issue you have been asked to assess. Part of your assessment should present reasons analysing the strengths and weaknesses of arguments supporting or disagreeing with the issue. You should finish your answer with a conclusion which presents the result of your assessment.
		In the case of the example question, you would need to explain clearly and precisely the anthropocentrism of Utilitarianism and the application of the principle of utility. Second, you should present philosophers' and theologians' arguments for and against a Utilitarian approach. You should analyse the strengths and weaknesses of the philosophers' and theologians' arguments concerning a Utilitarian approach to the environment.
To what extent	To what extent should conscience be considered to be the voice of God?	The question asks why some philosophers and theologians might hold this view. Next, you need to assess the strengths and weaknesses of reasons for holding these views and compare the strengths of the different reasons for holding this view with each other. The **extent** will be limited or defined by the strongest view you have considered. In the example question you need to explain the strengths and weaknesses of reasons philosophers and theologians give when discussing the ways conscience comes from God. The extent of the role of God in forming conscience will be decided by comparing the different reasons and arguments you present and deciding which one is strongest.

Timeline
Scientists, Ethicists and Thinkers

This timeline gives the names and dates of people whose great ideas are discussed within the book. However, it is not a comprehensive list of every important or significant ethicist of Western civilisation. The people at the end of the list declined to give their date of birth.

Protagoras (c.480–c.411 BCE)
Socrates (c.470–c.399 BCE)
Plato (428–347 BCE)
Aristotle (384–322 BCE)
Epicurus (341–270 BCE)
Cicero (106–43 BCE)
Jesus of Nazareth (c.3 BCE –30)
Saul of Tarsus/Paul (9–67)
Eusebius (c.260–c.340)
Ambrose of Milan (c.340–397)
Augustine of Hippo (354–430)
Pelagius (c.360–c.420)
St Francis of Assisi (1182–1226)
Thomas Aquinas (1225–1274)
John Duns Scotus (c.1266–1308)
William of Ockham (1280–1349)
Francisco de Vitoria (1480–1546)
John Calvin (1509–1564)
Francisco Suárez (1548–1617)
Francis Bacon (1561–1626)
Hugo Grotius (1583–1645)
René Descartes (1596–1650)
Baruch Spinoza (1632–1677)
John Locke (1632–1704)
Isaac Newton (1642–1727)
Gottfried Wilhelm Leibniz (1646–1716)
Joseph Butler (1692–1752)
David Hume (1711–1776)

Emerich de Vattal (1714–1767)
Paul-Henri Thiry (Baron) d'Holbach (1723–1789)
Immanuel Kant (1724–1804)
Jeremy Bentham (1748–1832)
Pierre Laplace (1749–1827)
John Henry Newman (1801–1890)
John Stuart Mill (1806–1873)
Charles Robert Darwin (1809–1882)
Søren Kierkegaard (1813–1855)
Henry Sidgwick (1838–1900)
Ivan Petrovich Pavlov (1849–1936)
Sigmund Freud (1856–1939)
Clarence Darrow (1857–1938)
Pope Pius XI (1857–1939)
H.A. Prichard (1871–1947)
Bertrand Russell (1872–1970)
G.E. Moore (1873–1958)
W.D. Ross (1877–1971)
John B. Watson (1878–1958)
Albert Einstein (1879–1955)
Karl Barth (1886–1968)
Aldo Leopold (1887–1948)
Reinhold Niebuhr (1892–1971)
Jean Piaget (1896–1980)
Pope Paul VI (1897–1978)
Erich Fromm (1900–1980)
Werner Heisenberg (1901–1976)

Alan Marshall (1902–1984)
B.F. Skinner (1904–1990)
Joseph Fletcher (1905–1991)
Jean-Paul Sartre (1905–1980)
Dietrich Bonhoeffer (1906–1945)
Rachel Carson (1907–1964)
C.L. Stevenson (1908–1979)
A.J. Ayer (1910–1989)
Richard Brandt (1910–1997)
Aarne Naess (1912–)
Paul Ramsay (1913–1988)
Thomas Merton (1915–1968)
Hans Jürgen Eysenck (1916–1997)
J.L. Mackie (1917–1981)
John Hospers (1918–)
G.E.M. (Elizabeth) Anscombe
    (1919–2001)
R.M. Hare (1919–2002)
James Lovelock (1919–)
Philippa Foot (1920–2010)
John Rawls (1921–2002)
Lawrence Kohlberg (1927–1987)
Annette Baier (1929–)
Germain Gabriel Grisez (1929–)
Martin Luther King Jr (1929–1968)
Alasdair MacIntyre (1929–)
Judith Jarvis Thomson (1929–)
Bernard Williams (1929–2003)
Enda McDonagh (1930–)

Richard Holloway (1933–)
Ted Honderich (1933–)
Richard Sylvan (Routley) (1935–1996)
Walter Wink (1935–)
Keith Ward (1938–)
John Finnis (1940–)
J. Baird Callicott (1941–)
Richard Dawkins (1941–)
Jonathan Glover (1941–)
James Rachels (1941–2003)
Michael Slote (1941–)
Peter Van Inwagen (1942–)
Rosalind Hursthouse (1943–)
Roger Scruton (1944–)
Peter Singer (1946–)
Robert Louden (1953–)
Steven Pinker (1954–)
Robert Song (1962–)
Julia Annas
Joseph Boyle
Celia Deane-Drummond
Helga Kuhse
David Lyon
Vincent MacNamara
Jack Mahoney
Timothy O'Connell
Vernon Ruland
Mary Anne Warren

1 What Is Ethics?

Essential terminology

Deduction
Definition
Factual statement
Logic

Ethics is the philosophical study of good and bad, right and wrong. It is commonly used interchangeably with the word 'morality', and is also known as moral philosophy. The study of ethics requires you to look at moral issues such as abortion, euthanasia and cloning, and to examine views that may be quite different from your own. You need to be open-minded, you need to use your critical powers, and above all learn from the way different ethical theories approach the issues you study for AS and A2.

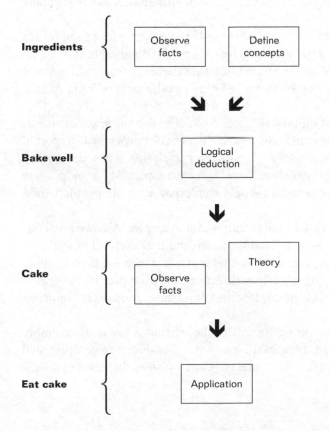

Ingredients

Observe facts

Define concepts

Bake well

Logical deduction

Cake

Theory

Observe facts

Eat cake

Application

Ethics needs to be applied with logic so that we can end up with a set of moral beliefs that are supported with reasons, are consistent and reflect the way we see and act in the world. Ethical theories are constructed logically, but give different weights to different concepts. However, it is not enough to prove that the theory you agree with is true and reasonable; you must also show where and how other philosophers went wrong.

FALLACIES

With the possible exception of you and me, people usually do not have logical reasons for what they believe. This is especially true for ethical issues. Here are some examples of how not to arrive at a belief. We call them fallacies. Here are some common beliefs:

* a belief based on the mistaken idea that a rule which is generally true is without exceptions; for example: 'Suicide is killing oneself – killing is murder, I'm opposed to euthanasia'
* a belief based on peer pressure, appeal to herd mentality or xenophobia; for example: 'Most people don't believe in euthanasia, so it's probably wrong'
* a belief in fact or obligation simply based on sympathy; for example: 'It's horrible to use those poor apes to test drugs, I'm opposed to it'
* an argument based on the assumption that there are fewer alternatives than actually exist; for example: 'It's either euthanasia or long, painful suffering'
* an argument based on only the positive half of the story; for example: 'Animal research has produced loads of benefits – that's why I support it'
* hasty generalisation: concluding that a population has some quality based on a misrepresentative sample; for example: 'My grandparents are in favour of euthanasia, I would think that most old people would agree with it'
* an argument based on an exaggeration; for example: 'We owe all of our advances in medicine to animal research, and that's why I'm for it'
* the slippery slope argument: the belief that a first step in a certain direction amounts to going far in that direction; for example: 'If we legalise euthanasia this will inevitably lead to killing the elderly, so I'm opposed to it'
* an argument based on tradition: the belief that X is justified simply because X has been done in the past; for example: 'We've done well without euthanasia for thousands of years, we shouldn't change now.'

IS–OUGHT FALLACY

David Hume (1711–1776) observed that often when people debate a moral issue they begin with facts and slide into conclusions that are normative; that is, conclusions about how things ought to be. He argued that no amount of facts taken alone can ever be sufficient to imply a normative conclusion: the is–ought fallacy. For example, it is a fact that slavery still exists in some form or other in many countries – that is an 'is'. However, this fact is morally neutral, and it is only when we say we 'ought' to abolish slavery that we are making a moral judgement. The fallacy is saying that the 'ought' statement follows logically from the 'is', but this does not need to be the case. Another example is to say that humans possess reason and this distinguishes us from other animals – it does not logically follow that we ought to exercise our reason to live a fulfilled life.

Ethics looks at what you ought to do as being distinct from what you may in fact do. Ethics is usually divided into three areas: meta-ethics, normative ethics and applied ethics.

1. *Meta-ethics* looks at the meaning of the language used in ethics, and includes questions such as: are ethical claims capable of being true or false, or are they expressions of emotion? If true, is that truth only relative to some individual, society or culture?
2. *Normative ethics* attempts to arrive at practical moral standards that tell us right from wrong, and how to live moral lives. These are what we call ethical theories. This may involve explaining the good habits we should acquire, looking at whether there are duties we should follow, or whether our actions should be guided by their consequences for ourselves and/or others.
3. *Applied ethics* is the application of theories of right and wrong and theories of value to specific issues such as abortion, euthanasia, cloning, foetal research, and lying and honesty.

Normative ethics may be further divided into deontological and teleological ethical theories.

- *Deontological ethics*. Deontological ethical theories claim that certain actions are right or wrong in themselves regardless of the consequences. Examples of deontological theories considered in this book are: Natural Law, Kantian ethics and Divine Command theory.
- *Teleological ethics*. Teleological ethical theories look at the consequences or results of an action to decide if it is right or wrong. Examples of teleological theories considered in this book are Utilitarianism and Situation ethics.

Ethics is not just giving your own opinion, and the way it is studied at AS and A2 is very like philosophy: it is limited to facts, logic and definition. Ideally, a philosopher is able to prove that a theory is true and reasonable on the basis of accurate definitions and verifiable facts. Once these definitions and facts have been established, a philosopher can develop the theory through a process of deduction, by showing what logically follows from the definitions and facts. The theory may then be applied to controversial moral issues.

ETHICAL THEORIES

If we are to have valid ethical arguments then we must have some normative premises to begin with. These normative premises are either statements of ethical theories themselves or statements implied by ethical theories.

The ethical theories that will be examined in this book are:

- *Utilitarianism*: An action is right if it maximises the overall happiness of all people.
- *Kantian ethics*: Treat other people the way you wish they would treat you, and never treat other people as if they were merely objects.
- *Cultural relativism*: What is right or wrong varies according to the beliefs of each culture.
- *Divine Command*: Do as the creator tells you.
- *Natural Law*: Everything is created for a purpose, and when this is examined by human reason a person should be able to judge how to act in order to find ultimate happiness.
- *Situation Ethics*: Based on agape (see p. 28) which wills the good of others.
- *Virtue Ethics*: Agent-centred not act-centred. Practising virtuous behaviour will lead to becoming a virtuous person and contribute to a virtuous society.

AS UNIT A
RELIGION AND
ETHICS 1

2 Utilitarianism

Essential terminology

Act Utilitarianism
Consequentialist
Hedonic calculus
Hedonism
Preference
Utilitarianism
Principle of utility
Qualitative
Quantitative
Rule Utilitarianism
Teleological
Universalisability

WHAT YOU WILL LEARN ABOUT IN THIS CHAPTER

- The principle of utility, the hedonic calculus, Act and Rule Utilitarianism.
- Classical forms of Utilitarianism from Bentham, Mill and Sidgwick; modern versions from Hare and Singer.
- The strengths and weaknesses of Utilitarianism.
- How to apply Utilitarianism to ethical dilemmas.

THE AQA CHECKLIST ✔

The general principles of Utilitarianism:

- Consequential or teleological thinking in contrast to deontological thinking
- Bentham's Utilitarianism, Act Utilitarianism, the hedonic calculus
- Mill's Utilitarianism, Rule Utilitarianism, quality over quantity
- The application of Bentham's and Mill's principles to **one** ethical issue of the candidate's choice **apart from abortion and euthanasia.**

ISSUES ARISING

- What are the strengths and weaknesses of the ethical systems of Bentham and Mill?

- Which is more important – the ending of pain and suffering, or the increase of pleasure?
- How worthwhile is the pursuit of happiness, and is it all that people desire?
- How compatible is Utilitarianism with a religious approach to ethics?

WHAT IS UTILITARIANISM?

You have probably heard someone justify their actions as being for the greater good. Utilitarianism is the ethical theory behind such justifications.

Utilitarianism is a teleological theory of ethics. Teleological theories of ethics look at the consequences – the results of an action – to decide whether it is right or wrong. Utilitarianism is a consequentialist theory. It is the opposite of *deontological* ethical theories that are based on moral rules, on whether the action itself is right or wrong.

The theory of Utilitarianism began with Jeremy Bentham as a way of working out how good or bad the consequence of an action would be. Utilitarianism gets its name from Bentham's test question: 'What is the use of it?' He thought of the idea when he came across the words 'the greatest happiness of the greatest number' in Joseph Priestley's *An Essay on the First Principles of Government; and on the Nature of Political, Civil, and Religious Liberty* (1768). Bentham was very concerned with social and legal reform and he wanted to develop an ethical theory which established whether something was good or bad according to its benefit for the majority of people. Bentham called this the principle of utility. Utility here means the *usefulness* of the results of actions. The principle of utility is often expressed as 'the greatest good of the greatest number'. 'Good' is defined in terms of *pleasure* or *happiness* – so an act is right or wrong according to the good or bad that results from the act, and the good act is the most pleasurable. Bentham's theory is quantitative because of the way it considers a pleasure as a quantifiable entity.

THE ORIGINS OF HEDONISM

The idea that 'good' is defined in terms of pleasure and happiness makes utilitarianism a hedonistic theory. The Greek philosophers who thought along similar lines introduced the term *eudaimonia*, which is probably best translated as the harmonious well-being of life. Both Plato and Aristotle agreed that 'good' equated with the greatest happiness, while the Epicureans stressed 'pleasure' as the main aim of life. The ultimate end of human desires and actions, according to Aristotle, is happiness and, though pleasure sometimes accompanies this, it is not the chief aim of life. Pleasure is not the same as

Teleological

According to teleological theories, moral actions are right or wrong according to their outcome or *telos* (end).

happiness, as happiness results from the use of reason and cultivating the virtues. It is only if we take pleasure in good activities that pleasure itself is good. This idea of Aristotle's is taken up by John Stuart Mill, as we will see later.

JEREMY BENTHAM'S APPROACH

Jeremy Bentham developed his ethical system around the idea of pleasure and it is based on ancient hedonism, which pursued physical pleasure and avoided physical pain. According to Bentham, the most moral acts are those that maximise pleasure and minimise pain. This has sometimes been called the 'utilitarian calculus'. An act would be moral if it brings the greatest amount of pleasure and the least amount of pain.

Pain v. pleasure

Bentham said: 'The principle of utility aims to promote happiness which is the supreme ethical value. Nature has placed us under the governance of two sovereign masters, *pain* and *pleasure*. An act is right if it delivers more pleasure than pain and wrong if it brings about more pain than pleasure' (*An Introduction to the Principles of Morals and Legislation*). By adding up the amounts of pleasure and pain for each possible act we should be able to choose the good thing to do. Happiness equals pleasure minus pain.

The hedonic calculus

To help us choose the good thing to do and work out the possible consequences of an action, Bentham provided a way of measuring. This is the hedonic calculus. It has seven elements:

1. the intensity of the pleasure (how deep)
2. the duration of the pleasure caused (how long)
3. the certainty of the pleasure (how certain or uncertain)
4. the remoteness of the pleasure (how near or far)
5. the chance of a succession of pleasures (how continuous)
6. the purity of the pleasure (how secure)
7. the extent of the pleasure (how universal).

This calculus gave Bentham a method of testing whether an action is morally right, in that if it was good it would result in the most pleasurable outcome,

Consequentialist
Someone who decides whether an action is good or bad by its consequences.

Jeremy Bentham (1748–1832)

Jeremy Bentham was born in London on 15 February 1748. He could read scholarly works at 3, played the violin at 5, and studied Latin and French at 6. At the age of 12 he went to Oxford and trained as a lawyer. Bentham was the leader of the Philosophical Radicals who founded the *Westminster Review*. He died in London on 6 June 1832. His body was dissected and his clothed skeleton is in a glass case in University College, London.

Bentham advanced his theory of Utilitarianism as the basis for general political and legal reform.

having weighed up all the elements. Whatever is good or bad can be measured in a quantitative way.

How to operate the hedonic calculus:

- Consider those who are most directly affected.
- Weigh up the balance of pleasure and pain for each possible action.
- The larger amount is the morally right course of action.

This applies for what is called *private utility* (when only a few people are involved), but some ethical decisions are in the area of *public utility* (when many people are involved – e.g. political decision): then criterion number 7, extent, must be used. The average happiness of all the people in the group must be estimated and then multiplied by the number of people in the group.

To popularise the hedonic calculus, Bentham composed the following mnemonic:

> *Intense, long, certain, speedy, fruitful, pure –*
> Such marks in *pleasures* and in *pains* endure.
> Such pleasures seek, if *private* be thy end:
> If it be *public*, wide let them *extend*.
> Such *pains* avoid, whichever be thy view:
> If pains *must* come let them *extend* to few.
> (*An Introduction to the Principles of Morals and Legislation*, 1789)

Principle of utility

The theory of usefulness – the greatest happiness for the greatest number.

Hedonism

The view that pleasure is the chief 'good'.

Epicurus (341–270 BCE)

Epicureans are followers of Epicurus. Epicurus was born on the island of Sámos. In 322 he began teaching in Colophon. In 311 he founded a philosophical school in Mitilíni on the island of Lésvos and then became head of a school in Lampsacus. He returned to Athens in 306 and taught his group of followers there.

Epicurus developed a system of ethics but later thinkers have used his philosophy as an equivalent to hedonism, teaching that pleasure or happiness is the chief good, which people should aim to achieve.

Thought Point

Make your own mnemonic to remember the hedonic calculus:

I
D
C
R
S
P
E

The quantity of happiness

Hedonism

Bentham's Utilitarianism is a universal hedonism – the highest good is the greatest happiness for the greatest number. Actions are judged as a *means to an end*. What is right is that which is calculated to bring about the greatest balance of good over evil, where good is defined as pleasure or happiness. Bentham's view is described as Act Utilitarianism.

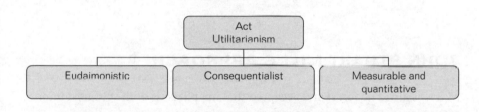

Bentham argued that we should be guided by the principle of utility and not by rules. However, it may be necessary to use rules of thumb based on past experience, especially if there is no time to work out the consequences.

Hedonic calculus
Bentham's method for measuring the good and bad effects of an action.

Quantitative
Looking at the quantity of the happiness.

Act Utilitarianism
A teleological theory that uses the outcome of an action to determine whether it is good or bad.

Qualitative
Looking at the quality of the pleasure

Thought Point

1. What would be the problems if everyone acted as an Act Utilitarian all the time?
2. Are all actions only good because they have good results?
3. Suppose a rape is committed that is thought to be racially motivated. Riots are brewing that may result in many deaths and long-term racial antagonism. You are the police chief and have recently taken a man into custody. Why not frame him? He will be imprisoned if found guilty and this will result in peace and safety. Only you, the innocent man and the real rapist (who will keep quiet) will know the truth. What is the morally right thing to do? Look at all the consequences of any action.
4. Suppose a surgeon could use the organs of one healthy patient to save the lives of several others. Would the surgeon be justified in killing the healthy patient for the sake of the others?
5. You are an army officer who has just captured an enemy soldier who knows where a secret time bomb is planted. If it explodes it will kill thousands. Will it be morally permissible to torture the soldier so that he reveals the bomb's location? If you knew where the soldier's children were, would it also be permissible to torture them to get him to reveal the bomb's whereabouts?

JOHN STUART MILL'S APPROACH

Mill was also a hedonist and accepted that happiness is of the greatest importance. He stressed happiness rather than pleasure.

The Greatest Happiness Principle

Mill said: 'The Greatest Happiness Principle holds that actions are right in proportion as they tend to promote happiness, wrong as they tend to produce the reverse of happiness. By happiness is intended pleasure, and the absence of pain; by unhappiness, pain and the privation of pleasure.'

The quality of happiness

The quality of pleasure

Having affirmed his agreement with the principle of utility, Mill then modifies Bentham's approach, especially the quantitative emphasis. He says: 'Some kinds of pleasures are more desirable and more valuable than others, it would be absurd that while, in estimating all other things, quality is not also considered as well as quantity.'

According to Mill, quality of pleasure employs the use of the higher faculties. Here he is answering the objection to Bentham's approach that utilitarians are just pleasure-seekers. For example, consider the case of the Christians and the Romans: many Romans get a lot of pleasure from seeing a few Christians eaten by lions – here the greatest happiness (that of the Romans) is produced by an act (Christians being eaten by lions) that is surely quite wrong. Mill says that the quality of pleasure that satisfies a human is different from that which satisfies an animal. People are capable of more than animals, so it takes more to make a human happy. Therefore, a person will always choose higher quality, human pleasures, and reject all the merely animal pleasures. As Mill puts it:

> Few human creatures would consent to be changed into any of the lower animals for a promise of the fullest allowance of the beast's pleasures. . . . It is better to be a human being dissatisfied than a pig satisfied; better to be Socrates dissatisfied than a fool satisfied. And if the fool or the pig are of a different opinion, it is because they only know their side of the question.
>
> (*Utilitarianism*)

So since the Romans are only enjoying 'animal' pleasure, it does not matter that they are getting a lot more of it than the Christians – it is the quality not the quantity of the pleasure that really counts. For Mill, it is intellectual pleasures (e.g. reading poetry or listening to music) that really count and are more important than such pleasures as eating, drinking or having sex. Happiness, he argues, is something that people desire for its own sake, but we need to look at human life as a whole – happiness is not just adding up the units of pleasure but rather the fulfilment of higher ideals.

A pig . . .

Universalisability

Universalisibility
What is right or wrong for one person in a situation is right or wrong for all.

Mill next develops the argument that in order to derive the principle of the greatest good (happiness) for the greatest number we need the principle of universalisability. He says: 'Each person's happiness is a good to that person, and the general happiness, therefore, is a good to the aggregate of all persons' (*On Virtue and Happiness*). This means:

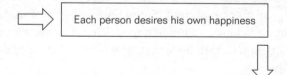

Each person desires his own happiness

Therefore each person ought to aim at his happiness

Therefore everyone ought to aim at the happiness of everyone

As you can see, the last proposition does not follow logically from the previous one. To move from each person to everyone is a fallacy. Mill makes this move because he wants to justify 'the greatest number'. This can mean that Utilitarianism demands that people put the interests of the group before their own interests, and Mill compares this to 'the Golden Rule of Jesus of Nazareth'. Mill has a positive view of human nature and thinks that people have powerful feelings of empathy for others which can be cultivated by education and so on. Mill also separates the question of the motive and the morality of the action. There is nothing wrong with self-interest if it produces the right action.

Rule Utilitarianism

Another aspect of Mill's approach is the idea that there need to be some moral *rules* in order to establish social order and justice – but the rules should be those which, if followed *universally*, would most likely produce the greatest happiness. Mill has been seen as a Rule Utilitarian in contrast to Bentham's Act Utilitarianism – though Mill never discussed Act or Rule Utilitarianism in these terms.

Rule Utilitarianism
Establishing a general rule that follows utilitarian principles.

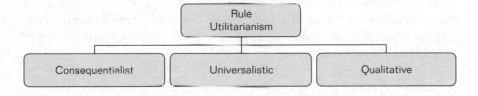

Comparing Bentham and Mill

Bentham	Mill
'The greatest good [*pleasure*] for the greatest number'	'The greatest *happiness* for the greatest number'
Focused on the *individual* alone	We should protect the common good, *universalistic*
Quantitative – hedonic calculus	*Qualitative* – higher/lower pleasures
Act Utilitarianism	*Rule Utilitarianism*
In search of maximisation of happiness	
Consequentialist	Consequentialist

HENRY SIDGWICK'S APPROACH

Another important Utilitarian was Henry Sidgwick. In *The Methods of Ethics* he argues that the balance of pleasure over pain is the ultimate goal of ethical decisions. His argument is closer to Bentham than to Mill, as he questions how it is possible to distinguish between higher- and lower-order pleasures, and how we can distinguish one higher-order pleasure from another. However, Sidgwick does argue that the process of deciding is *intuitive* – we make self-evident judgements about what we ought to do.

Justice

Sidgwick was concerned with justice in society and, like Mill, he had a positive view of human nature, hoping that the future would bring a growth in human empathy and moral motivation. He argued that justice is the similar and injustice the dissimilar treatment of similar cases: 'whatever action any of us judges to be right for himself, he implicitly judges to be right for all similar persons in similar circumstances'. It cannot be right for Jack to treat Tom in a manner in which it would be wrong for Tom to treat Jack, simply on the grounds that they are two different individuals and without there being any difference in their circumstances or their natures. This argument that we must act according to just laws raises the issue of which laws are just, and the whole issue of justice seems to sit uncomfortably with the principle of utility and the Act Utilitarian position.

SIDGWICK AND BENTHAM

There are obvious differences between Bentham and Sidgwick, but both may be described as Act Utilitarians – moral actions are judged not only by their consequences but also by how they benefit the welfare of people. The act that brings happiness to the greatest number is a right act. Sidgwick's approach to Utilitarianism is the starting point for modern-day approaches to this ethical theory.

ACT AND RULE UTILITARIANISM

Before looking at modern approaches to Utilitarianism, it is important that you fully understand the two variations – Act Utilitarianism and Rule Utilitarianism. The distinction is to do with what the principle of utility is applied *to*.

- According to Act Utilitarianism the principle is applied directly to a particular action in a particular circumstance.
- According to Rule Utilitarianism the principle is applied to a selection of a set of rules which are in turn used to determine what to do in particular situations.

ACT UTILITARIANISM

You must decide what action will lead to the greatest good in the particular situation you are facing and apply the principle of utility directly. You need to look at the consequences of a particular act and what will bring about the greatest happiness.

Flexibility

Since the same act might in some situations produce the greatest good for the greatest number, but in other situations not, Utilitarianism allows moral rules to change from age to age, from situation to situation. There are no necessary moral rules except one: that we should always seek the greatest happiness for the greatest number in all situations. Act Utilitarianism is linked to Bentham's form of Utilitarianism.

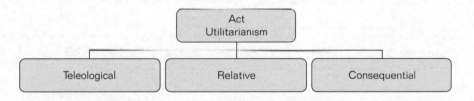

- *Teleological* – aims for a maximisation of pleasure for the majority. It has an end aim or goal.
- *Relative* – no notion of absolute right or wrong. No external source of truth. Nothing in itself is right or wrong.
- *Consequential* – the consequences of an act alone determine its rightness or wrongness.

Weaknesses of Act Utilitarianism

- It is difficult to predict the consequences.
- There is potential to justify any act.

- There is difficulty in defining pleasure.
- There is no defence for minorities.
- It is impractical to say that we should calculate the morality of each choice.

RULE UTILITARIANISM

Rule Utilitarians believe that rules should be formed using Utilitarian principles for the benefit of society. Your action is judged right or wrong by the goodness or badness of the consequences of a rule that everyone should follow in similar circumstances. Rule Utilitarianism enables us to establish rules which will promote the happiness of humanity and will generally be right in most circumstances (e.g. telling the truth, keeping your promises).

Strong Rule Utilitarians believe that these derived rules should never be disobeyed.

Weak Rule Utilitarians say that although there should be generally accepted rules or guidelines, they should not always be adhered to indefinitely.

There may be situations where the better consequence might be achieved by disregarding the rule (e.g. where it might be better to tell a lie).

Rule Utilitarianism is commonly linked with Mill.

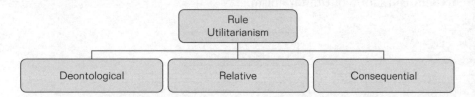

- *Deontological* – rules take priority.
- *Relative* – what is right or wrong is established as the maximisation of pleasure for the particular community or society within which it operates.
- *Consequential* – the overall consequences determine its rightness or wrongness.

Weaknesses of Rule Utilitarianism

- It is difficult to predict the consequences.
- It is difficult to define what constitutes happiness.
- There is no defence for minorities.
- To invoke rules means that the approach becomes deontological not teleological.

- Followers of Rule Utilitarianism can either be strict rule-followers or rule-modifiers, but neither seems satisfactory. Strict rule-followers can be irrational: obeying the rule even when disobeying it will produce more happiness. Rule-modifiers can end up being no different from Act Utilitarians.

PREFERENCE UTILITARIANISM

Preference Utilitarianism is a more recent form of Utilitarianism and is associated with R.M. Hare, Peter Singer and Richard Brandt. An Act Utilitarian judges right or wrong according to the maximising of pleasure and minimising of pain, a Rule Utilitarian judges right or wrong according to the keeping of rules derived from utility, but a Preference Utilitarian judges moral actions according to whether they fit in with the preferences of the individuals involved. This approach to Utilitarianism asks: 'What is in my own interest? What would I prefer in this situation? Which outcome would I prefer?' However, because Utilitarianism aims to create the greatest good for the greatest number, it is necessary to consider the preferences of others in order to achieve this.

Preference Utilitarianism
Moral actions are right or wrong according to how they fit the preferences of those involved.

Thought Point

1   Suppose that you were God, and, because you are omnibenevolent, you want your creatures to be as happy as possible across time (i.e. you believe in Utilitarianism). If you were choosing a moral code to teach your created people that would make them all happy, what code would you teach them?

2. Explain the distinction between Act and Rule Utilitarianism and why Rule Utilitarianism came about.

3.   The country is threatened with drought, so people are urged to conserve water and hosepipe bans are in force. Joe lives in an isolated part of the country and nobody ever drives past his house. The water company has forgotten Joe exists and so he is never billed for his water. Joe knows about the hosepipe ban, but he really wants a green lawn. His lawn is tiny, so he knows he will not be harming anyone if he waters it and the small amount he uses will not affect the drought. Joe continues to use water. What would an Act Utilitarian say about this? What would a Rule Utilitarian say? Give reasons.

R.M. Hare's approach

Hare argues that in moral decision making we need to consider our own preferences and those of others. He says that 'equal preferences count equally, whatever their content'. People are happy when they get what they prefer, but what we prefer may clash with the preferences of others. Hare says we need to 'stand in someone else's shoes' and try to imagine what someone else might prefer. We should treat everyone, including ourselves, with impartiality – he also argues for universalisability.

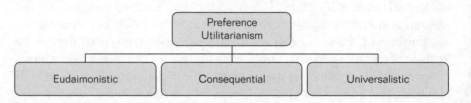

Peter Singer's approach

Peter Singer (1946–)

Peter Singer was born on 6 July 1946 in Melbourne. He studied at Melbourne and Oxford. In 1999 he was appointed DeCamp Professor of Bioethics at the University Center for Human Values, Princeton University. Singer's system is based on reason and not on self-interest or social conditioning. His work deals with issues such as embryo experimentation, genetic engineering, surrogacy, abortion and euthanasia. Singer's best-known work is *Animal Liberation* (1975). He is a vegetarian and donates the royalties from his books to international aid and animal liberation. He gives between 10 and 20 per cent of his income to the poor.

Singer also defends Preference Utilitarianism and suggests that we should take the viewpoint of an *impartial spectator* combined with a broadly utilitarian approach. He says that 'our own preferences cannot count any more than the preferences of others' and so, in acting morally, we should take account of all the people affected by our actions. These have to be weighed and balanced and then we must choose the action which gives the best possible consequences for those affected. For Singer, the 'best possible consequences' means what is in the *best interests* of the individuals concerned – this is different from Bentham, Mill and Sidgwick, as he is not considering what increases pleasure and diminishes pain.

This principle of equal consideration of preferences or interests acts like a pair of scales – everyone's preferences or interests are weighed equally. So, in Singer's view, killing a person who prefers to go on living would be wrong and not killing a person who prefers to die would also be wrong. Racism is wrong, as it goes against the principle of acknowledging other people's interests or preferences and gives greater value to the preferences of one's own race.

Singer did not attempt to suggest that this weighing up of preferences should occur every time someone has to make an ethical decision, but is the basis for deciding how one should live life and make ethical decisions in general. Otherwise it is difficult to decide whose preferences should be considered; for example, whether those of a child towards whom I have a duty of care because I have given birth to and raised the child count as much as those of a child I do not know. Singer makes it clear that newborn babies are not persons as they are not autonomous – therefore central to Preference Utilitarianism is defining what is meant by a person so that their interests may be taken into account.

Richard Brandt's approach

Richard Brandt was one of the leading Utilitarian philosophers of the twentieth century. He defended a version of Rule Utilitarianism, but later, in his book *A Theory of the Good and the Right* (1979), he talks about the preferences you would have if you had gone through a process of cognitive psychotherapy and explored all the reasons for your preferences and rejected any you felt were not true to your real values. He argued that the morality you would then accept would be a form of Utilitarianism – with your preferences free from any psychological blocks and you in full possession of all the facts. Such a person would not, therefore, be influenced by advertising.

STRENGTHS OF UTILITARIANISM

- It is straightforward and based on the single principle of minimising pain and maximising pleasure and happiness. A system which aims to create a happier life for individuals and groups is attractive.
- It relates to actions which can be observed in the real world (e.g. giving to charity promotes happiness for poor people and is seen to be good, whereas an act of cruelty is condemned as bad).
- Its consequentialism is also a strength, as when we act it is only natural to weigh up the consequences.
- Utilitarianism's acceptance of the universal principle is essential for any ethical system. It is important to go beyond your own personal point of view.
- The idea of promoting the 'well-being' of the greatest number is also important – this is the basis of the health care system: care is provided to improve the health of the population and, if more money is spent on the health service, people are healthier and therefore happier.
- Preference Utilitarianism also gives us the valuable principle of being an impartial observer or, as Hare puts it, 'standing in someone else's shoes'. It is important to think about others' interests or preferences as long as one also includes behaving justly.

WEAKNESSES OF UTILITARIANISM

- It is good to consider the consequences of our actions, but these are difficult to predict with any accuracy.

- Utilitarianism can also be criticised because it seems to ignore the importance of *duty*. An act may be right or wrong for reasons other than the amount of good or evil it produces. The case of the dying millionaire illustrates this. The millionaire asks a friend to swear that on their death the friend will give all their assets to the local football club. The millionaire dies and the friend sets about fulfilling these last wishes, but sees an appeal to save a million people who are dying of starvation. Should the friend keep the promise or save a million people? However, some promises may be bad and should not be kept. Duty does not stem from self-interest and is non-consequential – is motive more important than outcomes? Should promises be kept, the truth told and obligations honoured? W.D. Ross thought that the role of duty had some importance and advocated prima facie duties as more acceptable.

- Utilitarianism can also advocate injustice, as in the case above where the innocent man is unjustly framed for rape to prevent riots.

- Another weakness is the emphasis on pleasure or happiness. If I seek my own happiness it is impossible for me to seek general happiness and to do what I ought to do.

- The qualitative and quantitative approaches also pose problems, as all we can really do is guess the units of pleasure – how do we measure one pleasure against another? Should we try to maximise the average happiness or the total happiness (e.g. should the government give tax cuts for the minority with the lowest income or spread the cuts more thinly across all taxpayers?). Bentham would allow an evil majority to prevail over a good minority and the exploitation of minority groups – does this not go against what we would consider ethical behaviour?

- Utilitarianism does not consider motives and intentions and so rejects the principle of treating people with intrinsic value. Utilitarianism does not take any notice of personal commitments but only considers the consequences of an action. Bernard Williams said that we should not ignore integrity and personal responsibility for moral actions, and he uses the story of Jim and the Indians to illustrate this and argues that people need to retain their integrity even if this leads to unwelcome consequences (B. Williams, 'A Critique of Utilitarianism' in Smart and Williams, *Utilitarianism: For and Against*, Cambridge, Cambridge University Press, 1973).

- John Rawls also argues that Utilitarianism is too impersonal and does not consider the rights of individuals in its attempt to look for the 'greater good'.

Jim and the Indians
Either Jim can order the death of a whole group of Indians or he can follow his Captain's suggestion and chose one to sacrifice and so save the rest. There are two approaches from which this can be judged: rule-based action or end-based action.

Utilitarianism has some major weaknesses as far as duty, justice, motives, intentions and consequences are concerned, and the principles of 'the greatest good for the greatest number' and 'treating people as a means to an end' are rather dubious moral principles. The principles of seeking to act in a benevolent way, trying to apply universality and a consideration of consequences (even if only estimated) are principles that may be used with other, more deontological principles such as duty and integrity. Perhaps we need to combine the best principles from both the teleological and deontological approaches to ethics.

UTILITARIANISM AND RELIGIOUS ETHICS

Utilitarianism has a teleological approach to ethics, focusing on the outcome of actions, and Christian ethics seems more deontological as shown in the absolutes of the Ten Commandments.

Natural Law is very different from Utilitarianism, as it maintains that by using our reason we can arrive at moral knowledge and does not believe that the ends justify the means. However, Natural Law does look beyond this world and sees the ultimate purpose as union with God which is teleological, even if it is not aiming, as Utilitarianism is, to achieve a democratic state of 'happiness' in this world.

Jeremy Bentham reacted against the rule-based morality of his time, with certain actions being perceived as intrinsically right or wrong. He was therefore dismissive of the Bible, conscience or Natural Law as a means of knowing right from wrong. As an empiricist he believed that knowledge had to come from the senses, and he tried to make a scientific basis for morality. People should measure the rightness or wrongness of an action in terms of how many units of pain or pleasure it produced – these could be measured quantitatively using the hedonic calculus. Bentham's view on religious ethics cannot be divorced from his social and political views which found their basis in the continental liberalism of Descartes, Voltaire and Rousseau. This liberalism demanded emancipation from all prejudice and all beliefs that could not be rationally justified – rules and laws should be founded on reason. Mill called Bentham 'the great questioner of all things established'; however, Bentham did not have the political naivety of the continental philosophers and recognised the role and use of government. Bentham was not a committed atheist, and advocated religious freedom rather than enforced belief or non-belief. Utilitarianism is a way of improving the lives of most people, and religious ethics also aims to act out of compassion and love to improve the lives of others.

John Stuart Mill calculated pleasure in a qualitative way, regarding intellectual pleasures as superior to merely physical ones. He also thought

Sir Bernard Williams (1929–2003)

Bernard Williams was born in Southend-on-Sea and studied at Balliol College, Oxford. In 1967 he was made Knightbridge Professor of Philosophy at the University of Cambridge. In 1988 he moved to the USA. He was Professor at Berkeley, California, and White's Professor of Moral Philosophy at Oxford until his retirement in 1996.

He was very interested in politics and sat on several government committees, including those on gambling, drugs and pornography.

John Rawls (1921–2002)

John Rawls was known for his theory of 'justice as fairness'. He taught at Cornell University and Massachusetts Institute of Technology, then moved to Harvard.

He is known for *A Theory of Justice* (1971) and *Political Liberalism* (1993).

that most ordinary people should stick to some traditional rules based on utilitarian principles rather than calculate what they should do in each situation. He likened the principle of utility to Jesus' Golden Rule: 'You shall love your neighbour as yourself' (Matthew 22:39); 'do to others as you would have them do to you' (Matthew 7:12). He saw Utilitarianism as universal benevolence, doing good to others and denying self-love. In fact, Bentham thought that Christianity would support Utilitarianism as God is supposed to be benevolent.

Situation ethics is accused of being Utilitarian, and Joseph Fletcher recognised the similarity between the two theories. Both are relativist in approach and Fletcher saw love as 'justice distributed' – justice means working out the most loving thing to do for all – which simply replaces the 'good' of Utilitarianism with 'agape'.

Natural Law is very different from Utilitarianism, as it sees certain actions as intrinsically wrong, regardless of the consequences. Both Utilitarianism and Situation ethics fail to see that love is not always about the collective good, but also about the individual. Love that cares about the individual will not sacrifice the few for the sake of the majority without any attention being given to their particular needs and welfare. Utilitarianism ignores the idea that some actions are intrinsically wrong (e.g. murder).

The empiricism of Utilitarianism results in a very particular understanding of human nature as only motivated by pleasure or pain. The value of a person, and humanity as a whole, is measured only in terms of experiences with no room for the idea of a human made in the 'image of God' with intrinsic value and rights. The teachings and life of Jesus do not fit with Utilitarianism, except for the manner of his death: 'it is expedient for you that one man should die' (John 11:15a). According to the New Testament Christian ethics, others should always be placed first; we should turn the other cheek, forgive unto seventy times seven and real happiness comes in serving others – how can this be measured using the hedonic calculus?

In Utilitarian ethics motives and character are unimportant compared to the consequences. Unlike Virtue Ethics (see p. 206), the act is more important than the agent. In Christian ethics, moral decision making is about habitual actions, not one-off acts – the virtuous person becomes virtuous by practice. In Galatians 5:22–3 the fruits of the Spirit are shown by the characteristics of Christian living: love, joy, peace, patience, kindness, goodness, faithfulness, gentleness, self-control. Living a Christian ethical life involves modelling one's character on that of Christ.

APPLICATION OF UTILITARIANISM TO AN ETHICAL DILEMMA – EMBRYO RESEARCH

Utilitarianism does not accept the principle that human life has absolute value which should be promoted whatever the consequences. It attempts to assess the individual situations on their own merits and promote the greatest happiness for all concerned. Utilitarianism would consider embryo research a good thing as long as the good effects outweighed the bad.

Utilitarianism may consider that, as spare embryos from IVF treatment would be destroyed, they might as well be put to a good use. However, Utilitarianism works only if it is actually possible to assess the results of embryo research and decide whether the research would be of benefit to all concerned. In practice this is difficult as we cannot predict the consequences. All Utilitarians can say is that, from their point of view, it is better to save many lives in the future through embryo research at the cost of a few embryos now.

Peter Singer thinks that life ends when your brain dies, so it could be argued that life must begin when the brain starts working – embryo research up to the lawful fourteen days allowed by the Human Fertilisation and Embryology Authority (HFEA) would not be a problem. Questions of personhood and sentience also need considering as the hedonic calculus can be applied only to those who suffer. Our present stage of knowledge presumes that the early embryo does not feel pain and so embryo research can not be measured using the hedonic calculus. However, the benefits of embryo research can be measured using the hedonic calculus – the pleasures brought about by finding a cure to a disease such as Parkinson's outweigh the cost to the embryo. Utilitarianism would consider it acceptable to use the embryo as a means to an end.

Mill's version of Utilitarianism can be applied also to embryo research. The actual research itself and the knowledge gained through the research would be considered a higher pleasure of the mind – Mill would consider it a duty to use knowledge. However, the effects of embryo research on improved health may not be so well-regarded as Mill might consider them to be lower pleasures of the body.

Utilitarianism would also consider the practicalities of embryo research for the majority – such as the cost and the likelihood of success.

REVIEW QUESTIONS

Look back over the chapter and check that you can answer the following questions:

1   Explain the main principle of Utilitarianism.
2   Explain the Utilitarianism of Bentham.
3   Explain the Utilitarianism of Mill.
4   Explain the differences between Act and Rule Utilitarianism.
5   Complete the following diagram:

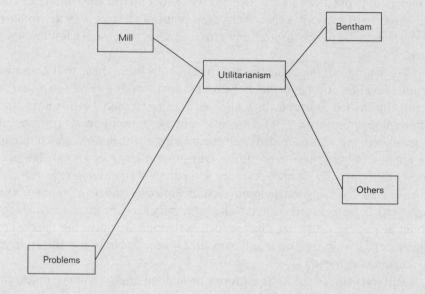

Terminology

Do you know your terminology?

Try to explain the following key ideas without looking at your books and notes:

* Consequentialist
* Teleological ethics
* Act Utilitarianism
* Rule Utilitarianism
* Preference Utilitarianism

SAMPLE EXAMINATION QUESTIONS

(a) Outline the general principles of Utilitarianism, and explain the strengths and weaknesses of these. (30 marks)

- You need to briefly explain the principles behind utilitarianism. You might mention the 'Greatest Happiness Principle' and the hedonic calculus, and you should consider the idea of 'weighing up' each situation. You might decide to focus on Bentham or Mill or both.
- You should consider some of the strengths and weaknesses of Utilitarianism, e.g. the debate over quality v. quantity, the cumbersomeness of applying the calculus, the lack of emotion, the logic of the calculus, Mill's amendments, and the importance of consequences.

The highest levels cannot be awarded if you have not addressed both demands of the question.

(b) 'Religion is a much better guide to resolving ethical issues than Utilitarianism.' Assess how far you agree with this claim. (15 marks)

You might answer this question from the perspective of any one religion or from religion in general.

- You should debate the advantages and disadvantages of both systems, e.g. religion considers individuals but could be seen as out-of-date; Utilitarianism treats everyone equally but is focused on unforeseen consequences which are thus unpredictable.

Essential terminology

Agape
Antinomianism
Consequentialism
Deontological
Legalism
Situationism
Teleological

3 Situation Ethics

WHAT YOU WILL LEARN ABOUT IN THIS CHAPTER

- How Situation Ethics is different from traditional Christian ethics.
- The principles of Situation Ethics and how it is applied.
- The strengths and weaknesses of Situation Ethics.

THE AQA CHECKLIST

The general principles of Situation Ethics: the middle way between legalism and antinomianism; the idea of situation; conscience – what it is and what it is not; the emphasis on making moral decisions rather than following rules:

- Fletcher's six fundamental principles and the understanding of Christian love
- Fletcher's four presumptions: pragmatism, contextual relativism, positivism, personalism
- The application of Situation Ethics to **one** ethical issue of the candidate's choice **apart from abortion and euthanasia**.

ISSUES ARISING

- Strengths and weaknesses of Situation Ethics as an ethical system
- Does Christian love allow people to do anything, depending on the

context, and how far is it true that love should be the highest Christian law, overruling all others when necessary?

* How practical is Situation Ethics?
* How compatible is Situation Ethics with other Christian approaches to moral decision making?

JOSEPH FLETCHER

Joseph Fletcher developed Situation Ethics in the 1960s in reaction to Christian legalism and antinomianism (which is the belief that there are no fixed moral principles, but that morality is the result of individual spontaneous acts). Fletcher's ethics were influenced by a variety of scholars from William Temple to Paul Tillich, and in turn has influenced the views of modern ethicists such as Richard Holloway. Many of the ideas that seemed outlandish and almost heretical at the time have now become mainstream within Christianity, so much so that they no longer stand out but are part of the way many Christians think today and how they put these beliefs into practice.

Many Christian thinkers such as Paul Ramsay say that the Church should not be making specific judgements on issues affecting society, but should, after analysing the situation in the light of fundamental Christian principles, seek to illuminate decisions about courses of action. Much of Christian ethics today attempts to respond to the changing needs of society and the ethical issues that arise by following the ideas of William Temple, whose strong sense of personal responsibility led him to believe in a just inclusive society, but seemed to resist any attempt to make detailed recommendations. This is one of the most important legacies of Situation Ethics – that Christians make their own moral decisions; as John Robinson put it, Situation Ethics is 'an ethic for humanity come of age'.

However, Situation Ethics did not arise in a vacuum but was a product of its time. It is not coincidence that Fletcher's book *Situation Ethics* was published in 1966, as the 1960s were a time of social change – characterised by the hippies and 'free love' and influenced by existentialist philosophy culminating in the events of May 1968 in Paris. For Fletcher, Christian ethics were summed up in the phrase 'You shall love your neighbour as yourself'. Both Bishop John Robinson and William Temple saw this as essential – Fletcher aimed to find an ethical system that would enable people to put this into practice.

Fletcher argues that each individual situation is different and absolute rules are too demanding and restrictive. The Bible shows what good moral decisions look like in particular situations, but it is not possible to know what God's will is in every situation. Fletcher says: 'I simply do not know and

> **Joseph Fletcher (1905–1991)**
>
> Fletcher was an American professor who founded the theory of Situation Ethics in the 1960s. He was a pioneer in bioethics and was involved in the areas of abortion, infanticide, euthanasia, eugenics and cloning.
>
> Fletcher was an Episcopalian priest, but later renounced his belief in God and became an atheist.

cannot know what God is doing.' As it is not possible to know God's will in every situation, *love* or *agape* is Situation Ethics' only moral 'rule'. So it is not just the situation that guides what you should do but the principle of agape and the guiding maxims of the Christian community: 'Do not commit murder', 'Do not commit adultery', 'Do not steal', 'Do not lie'. Situation Ethics is midway between legalism and antinomianism, and Fletcher's book, which was published in 1966, reflected the mood of the times – Christians should make the right choices without just following rules and by thinking for themselves.

According to Fletcher there are three different ways of making moral decisions.

Legalism – the idea that there are fixed moral principles that are to be obeyed at all times. Legalism, according to Fletcher, is abstract and impersonal, and its rigidity means that it cannot respond to the complex ethical decisions that people are required to make during their lives. He sees the Catholic following of Natural Law as falling into this category, as does the Protestant adherence to biblical teachings.

Antinomianism – the idea that there are no rules that need to be obeyed. Moral decisions have no basis in any ethical systems, but are simply spontaneous, responding to the moment. This can seem to be truly free and creative, but Fletcher sees it as anarchic and nihilistic (there is no God and one can do anything one wishes). Everyone is a law unto themselves and so antinomianism has no principles to govern decisions, and so does not provide a sound basis for ethics.

Consequentialism
The belief that the rightness or wrongness of an act is determined by its consequences.

Situationism – this puts people before rules, love and community before principles. Situationism does not ignore tradition, but is not bound by it – if what has been said about a particular moral situation in the past is helpful at the time and assists in doing the right thing for the right reason it should be followed if 'love is best served', but rejected if it will not bring about the most loving consequence. Right actions depend on the circumstances at the time, on the consequences as far as they can be seen.

Christians should base their decisions on one single rule – the rule of agape. This love is not merely an emotion but involves doing what is best for the other person, unconditionally. It is reciprocal, and neighbour-regarding – neighbour meaning 'everybody', even an enemy. Fletcher explained that 'Christian love is will, disposition; it is an attitude not a feeling'. Agape is not an easy option; it may require self-sacrifice, and is concerned with what is best for others, irrespective of one's own personal interest or gain.

Although not exclusive to Christianity, Fletcher did associate agape with Christian love – Jesus' call to 'love one another as I have loved you' (John 13:34). This means that other guiding maxims could be ignored in certain situations if they do not serve agape; for example, Fletcher says it would be right for a mother with a thirteen-year-old daughter who is having sex to break the rules prohibiting underage sex and insist her daughter uses contraception – the right choice is the most loving thing and it will depend on the situation. However, the situation can never change the rule of agape which is always good and right regardless of the circumstances. This is the one absolute obligation.

Fletcher's Situation Ethics depends on four working presumptions and six fundamental principles. The four working presumptions are as follows.

1. *Pragmatism* – what you propose must work in practice. Situation Ethics is interested in the practical application of agape to particular situations, so it rejected the European approach which emphasised reason, theories and systems of thought.

Equally Joseph Fletcher believed that what was important was not the dogma (beliefs of the official Church) but how the spirit of Jesus' message was applied to everyday living.

2. *Relativism* – words like 'always', 'never', 'absolute' are rejected. There are no fixed rules, but all decisions must be relative to agape.

Love relativises the absolute, it does not absolutise the relative.
(Joseph Fletcher)

The law of love is the ultimate law because it is the negation of law; it is absolute because it concerns everything concrete. The absolutism of love is its power to go into the concrete situation.
(Paul Tillich, *Systematic Theology*)

Tillich claims that the sole intrinsic good of agape can be universally applied because agape has the flexibility to be applied in different ways depending on the particular demands of the situation.

One of the strengths of Situation Ethics is that it avoids the rigidity and legalism of other deontological theories of ethics, such as Natural Law, Kantian ethics, and Divine Command theory.

3. *Positivism* – a value judgement needs to be made, giving the first place to Christian love. God is the foundation for love, that is to say: 'God is love.'

Paul Tillich's expression, '*Love is an ontological dimension of the universe*' is another way of saying the same thing – love is a feature of the existence of the universe ('ontological' simply meaning existence or being). Tillich is saying that it makes sense for a Christian to live life in a loving way as God, the creator of the universe, has made this a real possibility as a way of living.

4. *Personalism* – people are put in first place, morality is personal and not centred on laws. In many ways this is similar to Kant's maxim 'Treat people as ends, never as a means to an end'. Both Kant and Fletcher value people, though for somewhat different reasons. This principle also stresses that God is personal, and that we are created in his image for a relationship of love.

The six fundamental principles

These are used not as rules, but to shed light on the situation. *'Only one thing is intrinsically good; namely love: nothing else at all'* (Fletcher, *Situation Ethics* (1966 ed.) p. 56).

1. Love (agape) is the only absolute. It is the only thing which is intrinsically 'good' and 'right', regardless of the situation. Love alone is *always* good and right in every situation. It is the only intrinsic good and the only universal – this idea of agape is similar to Kant's idea of the Good Will. Agape though is not about being, it is about doing. Fletcher says that one cannot assign good and bad to actions, e.g. killing is a bad action, but actions are only as loving as their consequences.

    > *The ruling norm of Christian decision is love: nothing else.*
    > (Fletcher, *Situation Ethics* (1966 ed.) p. 69)

2. This love is self-giving love, which seeks the best interests of others but allows people the freedom and responsibility to choose the right thing for themselves. Situation Ethics stresses the importance of making free moral decisions. Here Fletcher is stressing that love **is** the law, not in the sense of what people understand as 'laws', but love overrides all laws. This does then give permission to kill, to steal if it is seen as the most loving thing in the situation. He writes:

    > *The plain fact is that love is an imperious law unto itself. It will not share its power. It will not share its authority with any other laws.*
    > (Fletcher, *Situation Ethics* (1966 ed.) p. 85)

    > *Love and justice are the same, for love is justice distributed, nothing else.*
    > (Fletcher, *Situation Ethics* (1966 ed.) p. 87)

3. Justice will follow from love, because 'justice is love distributed'. If love is put into practice, it can only result in justice. Justice is concerned with giving everyone their due – its concern is with neighbours, not just our neighbour. One cannot love someone and see them treated unfairly. A good example of this is to be found in restorative justice, such as Desmond Tutu's Truth and Reconciliation Commission which was set up to heal the wounds of apartheid in South Africa. However, this equation of love with justice can also be seen as Utilitarian – the right thing to do is the greatest amount of love to the greatest amount of people.

> *Love wills the neighbour's good, whether we like him or not.*
> (Fletcher, *Situation Ethics* (1966 ed.) p. 103)

4. Love has no favourites and does not give those whom we like preferential treatment – it is good will which reaches out to strangers, acquaintances, friends and even enemies. Joseph Fletcher wrote:

> *Agape is giving love – non-reciprocal, neighbour regarding – 'neighbour' meaning 'everybody', even an enemy.*
> (Fletcher, *Situation Ethics* (1963 ed.) p. 79)

However, this can be seen to ignore the duties we have to our families and friends.

> *Only the end justifies the means, nothing else.*
> (Fletcher, *Situation Ethics* (1963 ed.) p. 120)

5. Love must be the final end, not a means to an end – people must choose what to do because the action will result in love, not be loving in order to achieve some other result.

> *Love's decisions are made situationally, not prescriptively.*
> (Fletcher, *Situation Ethics* (1963 ed.) p. 134)

6. The loving thing to do will depend on the situation – and, as situations differ, an action that might be right in one situation could be wrong in another. This is quite different from traditional Christian ethics and is far more relativistic, having just one moral rule – agape.

Strengths of Situation Ethics

*   Situation Ethics is easy to understand and can be constantly updated for new problems and issues as they arise, such as genetic engineering and foetal research.
*   It is flexible and can take different situations into account, but it is based on the Christian concept of love.
*   It focuses on humans and concern for others – agape.
*   Situation ethics allows people to take responsibility for their own decisions and make up their own minds about what is right or wrong. Bishop John Robinson called it 'an ethic for humanity come of age'.

Weaknesses of Situation Ethics

- Situation Ethics can be seen as arrogant in rejecting thousands of years of Christian history and tradition which is based on love. This method of decision making was condemned in 1952 by Pope Pius XII, who said it was wrong to make decisions based on individual circumstances if these went against the teaching of the Church and the Bible. After all the Church does teach love as central – it simply assists people by offering guidance for moral behaviour.
- It is not possible to determine the consequences of actions – how do we know that the result will be the most loving for all concerned?
- Situation Ethics has just one moral rule – agape or unconditional love – and it is relative in that it accepts that different decisions will be right or wrong according to the circumstances. It can be seen as too subjective, placing too much responsibility on the individual.
- Situation Ethics has been criticised for being utilitarian and simply substituting love for pleasure, and Fletcher is thought to be rather vague; values and situations are so variable that we cannot easily see all the ramifications, past, present and future.
- Humanity has not come of age as John Robinson thought – the twentieth century was proof of that with more wars and bloodshed than ever before. Situation Ethics may work in a community of saints but it is hard, if not impossible, to put into practice in a community of sinners. It is just too utopian and no use in our modern meritocratic and egotistical society.

Thought Point

These examples are taken from William Barclay's *Ethics in a Permissive Society* (1971). Barclay wants you to agree with the actions; can you see other ways of acting?

1. Suppose in a burning house there is your aged father, an old man, with the days of his usefulness at an end, and a doctor who has discovered a cure for one of the world's great killer diseases and who still carries the formulae in his head, and you can save only one – whom do you save? Your father who is dear to you, or the doctor in whose hands there are thousands of lives? Which is love?
2. On the Wilderness trail, Daniel Boone's trail, westward through Cumberland Gap to Kentucky, many families in the trail caravans lost their

lives to the Indians. A Scottish woman had a baby at the breast. The baby was ill and crying, and the baby's crying was betraying her other three children and the rest of the party; the party clearly could not remain hidden if the baby continued crying; their position would be given away. Well, the mother clung to the baby; the baby's cries led the Indians to the position, the party was discovered, and all were massacred. There was another such occasion. On this occasion there was a Negro woman in the party. Her baby too was crying and threatening to betray the party. She strangled the baby with her own two hands to stop its crying – and the whole party escaped. Which action is love?

3. What about the commandment that you must not kill? When T.E. Lawrence (1888–1935, a British Army officer who had a very important liaison role in the Arab Revolt against Ottoman Turkish rule in 1916–1918) was leading his Arabs, two of his men had a quarrel and in the quarrel Hamed killed Salem. Lawrence knew that a blood feud would arise in which both families would be involved, and that one whole family would be out to murder the other whole family. What did Lawrence do? He thought it out and then with his own hands he killed Hamed and thus stopped the blood feud. Was this right? Was this action that stopped a blood feud and prevented scores of people from being murdered an act of murder or of love?

4. Ethically, has humanity come of age, as Bishop John Robinson suggested in 1966?

5. To what extent is love compatible with human nature?

6. Why might critics of Situation Ethics argue that it is really Utilitarianism under a different name?

7. Explain why some critics have questioned whether Situation Ethics is really Christian.

Christianity and Situation Ethics

Can Situation Ethics be considered Christian? It certainly puts love at the centre, but there are many differences among Christians about what exactly love is and how it is shown. Fletcher's examples are all exceptional cases: the last blood plasma to be given to a skid-row drunk or a mother of three; the resistance fighter priest who refused to surrender in spite of the death of hostages; Mrs Bergmeier (she was taken prisoner by the Russians during the Second World War: later, her family tried to find her; she could leave the Prisoner of War camp only if she was pregnant so she arranged for a guard to make her pregnant so that she could rejoin her family). Fletcher's idea of love is not exactly the same as that of Jesus, who individualised love; take, for example, the woman with the haemorrhage, or the healing of the centurion's servant – not a very popular act of love. Fletcher either reinterprets Jesus' actions or dismisses them, so it is hardly surprising that in later life religion played no part in his life and he ceased to describe himself as a Christian Situationist.

The Catholic Church also criticised Situation Ethics:

Conscience thus formulates *moral obligation* in the light of natural law; it is the obligation to do what the individual, through the workings of his conscience, *knows* to be good he is called to do *here and now*. The universality of the law and its obligations are acknowledged, not suppressed, once reason has established the law's application in concrete present circumstances. The judgement of conscience states 'in an ultimate way' whether certain particular kind of behaviour is in conformity with the law; it formulates the proximate norm of the morality of a voluntary act, applying the objective law to a particular case.

(Veritas Splendor 1993)

The instruction in this encyclical is based on 'Instruction on "Situation Ethics" *Contra Doctrinam*' (2 February 1956).

Another criticism came from the late Anglican theologian Professor Gordon Duncan, who wrote: 'It is possible to forgive Professor Fletcher for writing this book, for he is a generous and lovable man. It is harder to forgive SCM Press for publishing it.'

Proportionalism

Proportionalism approaches ethics from the view that many situations are complex and unique so it is not always easy to decide on the right thing to do. Situation Ethics argues that love is the only intrinsic good and, though rules and principles can be helpful in that they shed light on things, they cannot tell us what to do – we must apply love to a particular situation. If rules or principles conflict with love they must be discarded. Many critics have found Fletcher's theory unacceptable and vague – it is not enough to say that 'love will tell you what to do in a situation'; though many will also agree that it is important to consider the situation and the consequences.

So we are left with a dilemma: on the one hand is the teleological theory of Situation Ethics and on the other the deontological theory of Natural Law. Bernard Hoose suggests Proportionalism as a middle way between these two views. Proportionalism attempts to take into account all the goods and evils involved in making a judgement about the rightness or wrongness of an action. Proportionalism arose among Catholic ethicists about the same time as Situation Ethics – in the 1960s. Unlike Situation Ethics it is rooted in Natural Law, but recognises that Natural Law is not rigid and static. It recognises that what it means to be human and what we understand by human flourishing can change and develop – so moral laws must also change and develop.

However, Proportionalism can be seen as merely consequentialist and it is impossible to foresee all the results of an action. Proportionalism still requires people to weigh up values against one another – this means you could justify telling a lie to save a life. For proportionalists, judgements have to be made on the basis of comparisons of values, and, unlike followers of Situation Ethics, they will accept that the accumulated wisdom and traditions of society do provide good moral norms for governing behaviour – with some exceptions. It is these exceptions that make Proportionalism inconsistent as a theory.

The role of conscience

How does Joseph Fletcher consider the role of conscience in ethical decision making? In the New Testament Paul refers to conscience as the law written on the heart (2 Corinthians 1:12). For Fletcher it is linked to the ideas of agape and personalism. However, the main problem with this is that Jesus does not give precise rulings on certain situations such as war, abortion, euthanasia, etc., but he did radically challenge accepted rules and customs, e.g. in his teaching on the Sabbath, his attitude to the poor, outcasts, immoral women, etc.

Personalism
A philosophical school of thought which describes the uniqueness of a human being in the world of nature.

If conscience just follows the laws of love, can we work out the correct thing to do through reason? Or is conscience the innate knowledge of right and wrong and is God's moral law put into the heart of human beings as Augustine says? Augustine says that laws are revealed through Christianity but also to each individual directly by God. This 'voice of God' speaks directly to humans, but God's grace is necessary for humans to act in the right way. However, Augustine did argue that unless the motive was right the action could not be right, the motive was always the love of God and the desire to become closer to God. This is a totally different approach to that of Fletcher, who saw the love of neighbour as most important. However, it must be pointed out that this approach is bound to be flawed as people inevitably see things from their own perspective and so it is difficult to assess what is actually the loving thing to do. With no clear rules, favouritism and selfishness can creep in, but Fletcher, in saying that love justifies anything, is in fact stressing personal responsibility for decisions. This does not mean necessarily discarding all the ethical maxims of his community or heritage but being prepared to set them aside if love seems better served by doing so.

APPLICATION OF SITUATION ETHICS TO AN ETHICAL DILEMMA – IVF

There are different forms of reproductive technologies:

- *AIH* – artificial insemination by the husband, where the husband's sperm is injected into the wife's reproductive tract
- *AID* – where donor sperm is used
- *IVF* – in-vitro fertilisation – outside the human body using the sperm of a husband or donor, and the egg of the wife or a donor egg.

When applying Situation Ethics to an ethical dilemma such as IVF it is helpful to understand a more deontological Christian approach. In 1987, nine years after the birth of the first 'test-tube' baby, Louise Brown, the Catholic Church published the document *Donum Vitae*. The Church welcomed Louise Brown as a gift and as a unique person, but expressed doubts about the process of IVF and the resulting science of human embryology.

The creation of a surplus of human embryos in a laboratory made it possible to experiment on them – many embryos would never be transferred to a womb as Louise was.

The Catholic Church sees human life as sacred, with the parents as co-creators of new life – the baby is the result of the love the couple have for each other. IVF takes the new baby away from that expression of love and becomes simply part of a process.

IVF and ET (embryo transfer) are brought about outside the bodies of the couple through actions of third parties whose competence and technical activity determine the success of the procedure.

The Church sees the life of the embryo as entrusted to doctors, and technology as dominant in creating new life. The Catholic Church also sees every human life from the first moment of conception and at every stage of development, however early, as worthy of protection.

The Catholic Church does not approve of IVF, or of the destruction of human embryos, or of the freezing of embryos, or of surrogacy; however, the Church does not disapprove of experiments on human embryos that are therapeutic and will assist the embryo to overcome the effects of disease.

Some Protestant ethics see the question of IVF differently. Paul Ramsay has a Christocentric approach and opposes AID, as it 'means a refusal of the image of God's creation in our own'. Reproduction should be only within marriage, as that is the only way to remain faithful to God, since the love between husband and wife should reflect the love of Christ for the Church.

Joseph Fletcher, on the other hand, was not negative towards IVF or even AID. His Situation Ethics was person-centred and saw that there were higher values in a couple's relationship than their biological relationship to their children. Fletcher did not see a third person as personally involved in the sexual relationship – what mattered was the outcome: pregnancy. Using IVF means that humans are using their technologies and creative skills for compassionate reasons.

This, however, is just a general overview of IVF, and when applying Situation Ethics to this issue it is necessary to explain that it does not give a very clear answer. Although it may be in favour of IVF as it is the most loving thing to do for an infertile couple, the issue needs to be examined in more detail.

The first fundamental principle of Situation Ethics – that only love is intrinsically good – makes us consider whether a couple seeking IVF are really acting out of unconditional love for one another or whether they are being selfish.

The second principle implies that Christians are required not simply to love others but to do so to the extent that they sacrifice part of themselves in doing so: the couple would need to consider what would be the consequences of having IVF – destruction of spare embryos, whether reproduction is a right and whether the IVF process is in fact in their best interests as a couple. They would also need to look at the issue pragmatically – how likely is it to succeed if IVF works only for every fourth or fifth couple? Is it worth the heartache of failure, perhaps many failures?

The third principle says that love and justice are the same – this love needs to support the whole community. How much unconditional love will be the outcome of choosing IVF? Who has the right to IVF? Married couples and possibly unmarried couples would head the list. However, what if the couple divorced or separated or, as in the case of Diane Blood, one partner died? Does the right then no longer exist? Would homosexual couples be allowed IVF? IVF uses considerable medical resources that could otherwise be used to treat those with more serious illnesses, and so one solution might be to limit the use of IVF to those whose reproductive ability has been damaged by medical treatments or by exposure to dangerous working conditions. Would this be more just?

The fourth principle that love has no favourites means that it may be more loving to consider another solution, such as adoption.

The fifth principle says that only the ends justify the means – but does this mean ignoring the cost involved, other people's feelings or concerns, religious teaching and laws, the concept of the Sanctity of Life, etc.?

The sixth principle requires that love's decisions are made situationally, not prescriptively – and so we are back where we started: that Situation Ethics allows a couple to have a child using IVF for loving and compassionate reasons, but the answer is not clear-cut and ultimately depends on the best interests of the couple involved.

REVIEW QUESTIONS

Look back over the chapter and check that you can answer the following questions:

1. What did Fletcher mean by agape?
2. What is the difference between legalism, antinomianism and situationalism?

ACTIVITIES

Create a spider diagram or mind map of Situation Ethics, with examples.

Make a chart of the strengths and weaknesses of Situation Ethics.

Terminology

Do you know your terminology?

Try to explain the following terms without looking at your books and notes:

- Legalism
- Antinomianism
- Situationism
- Consequentialism
- Teleological
- Deontological
- Agape

SAMPLE EXAMINATION QUESTIONS

(a) Explain how Fletcher understood the concept of Christian love, with reference to his six fundamental principles. (30 marks)

The main focus here is the explanation of Christian love. In unpacking this concept, you should refer to Fletcher's principles. You do not need to consider all of them. You may refer to agape, self-sacrifice ('No one has greater love than this, to lay down one's life for one's friends' (John 15:13)), free will, justice, loving one's neighbour.

(b) Assess how far it is true to say that love is the highest Christian law. (15 marks)

You might debate the merits of following rules based upon love as opposed to other rules, such as the rules of the religion, obedience (to God and humanity), justice, truthfulness, forgiveness, etc.

Essential terminology

Autonomous being
Exclusivist
Inclusivist
Just War
Original Sin
Pluralist
Predestination
Speciesism
The Fall

4 Religious Teaching on the Nature and Value of Human Life

WHAT YOU WILL LEARN ABOUT IN THIS CHAPTER

- The religious teachings on human nature.
- Ideas of fatalism and free will.
- Religious teachings about equality.
- The value of human life.
- The ethical implications of these perspectives.

THE AQA CHECKLIST ✔

Candidates will be expected to have studied the teaching of **one** of the six major world religions, but, where appropriate, may refer to more than one religion in their answers.

- Nature of humanity and the human condition: what it means to be human
- Fatalism and free will: to what extent human beings are able to influence their own life and destiny
- Equality and difference: religious teaching about equality with particular reference to race, gender and disability
- The value of life: religious teachings about the value of life with particular reference to the quality of life, self-sacrifice and non-human life including the relative importance of human and non-human life.

ISSUES ARISING

- How far must a religious view of life be fatalistic?
- How far can religion support the idea of equality?
- Human life must be given priority over non-human life and some human lives are more valuable than others – how far could religion accept this view?

CHRISTIAN TEACHING ON HUMAN NATURE AND THE HUMAN CONDITION

Christians have a particular view of human life and how humans interact with the rest of creation. In order to look at the question of whether there is such a thing as human nature we need to consider what it might consist of and what it is that makes humans different from other living things, what it means to be a person and whether humans have free will.

When looking to understand human nature Christians would look to the Bible, but this seems to offer a limited idea of what is meant by human nature. Genesis 1:26–8 describes human beings as created in the image of God (*imago Dei*); but this description has given rise to many different theological interpretations. Traditionally only human beings are in the image of God: because they are moral and spiritual beings, this confers on them 'personhood'. However, in recent times this traditional understanding has been challenged by philosophers: Peter Singer sees a person as a sentient being that interacts with others and has preferences about continued life, while for John Harris a person is any being who is capable of valuing their own life.

These approaches imply that to be a human you must have an advanced brain: so there are a number of human beings who would not qualify as persons – foetuses, new-born babies and infants, those with brain abnormalities, dementia and some psychiatric illnesses – whereas many mammals such as chimpanzees and dolphins might be seen as persons. Those who meet these criteria of personhood have moral rights and, for Singer, to make moral distinctions on the basis of human nature or personhood is to be guilty of 'speciesism'. Singer seems to replace discrimination by species with discrimination by cortical functioning – so is human nature defined by what a human being can do, by having a functioning brain, by thinking and choosing, or is there something else?

Most ancient and medieval Christian theologians interpreted the 'image of God' as an ability to reason, and it was this that distinguished us from other living beings. Irenaeus of Lyons made a further distinction between the image and the likeness of God, as both terms are used in Genesis 1, and this led later theologians to argue whether or not humans are still in the image of God after the Fall, or are now merely in God's likeness, with the image being restored by the redeeming action of Christ.

After the Reformation the idea of the 'image of God' was again reinterpreted. Martin Luther and later Karl Barth saw it in terms of human relations with God, and later during the European Enlightenment of the eighteenth century, and particularly after Schleiermacher, the 'image of God' was often understood as the human capacity for self-consciousness. Today many modern theologians continue to be influenced by these two interpretations, added to the influence of science which stresses human continuity with nature through our evolutionary heritage and our increased understanding and knowledge of animals; so Langdon Gilkey and Gregory R. Peterson argued that all of nature should be understood as being in the 'image of God'.

The dominant idea of our human nature is understood by Christian thought in terms of our relationship with God, and this is what makes humans unique and different from other species. Being made in the 'image of God' means that we remind each other of God and we take care of God's creation as his stewards. Humans are responsible to God for creation, yet are at the same time part of creation: made of the dust of the earth and ultimately returning to that dust. We exist because God breathed life into us and the Bible shows that human life depends on the continuous activity of God; however, there is no idea of humans being body and soul as the Greeks understood it, as this idea entered Christian theology much later. In the Hebrew Bible human nature is seen as a whole – the body is just as important as the soul or heart.

This view was challenged when Christianity began to dialogue with other philosophies, especially Greek thought, and the whole idea of what it meant to be made in the 'image of God' was rethought. Augustine of Hippo developed the ideas of Plato, emphasising the rationality and the eternity of the human soul, whereas Thomas Aquinas was influenced by the ideas of Aristotle which put humans on the same level as the rest of nature, but with rationality. For Aquinas consciousness – that is, feeling, thought and sentience of some sort – will exist without the body as we are in the 'image of God' and God has no body. The human person, as Keith Ward puts it, 'seems to have a dual nature, having both a physically observable body and brain and a rich, colorful, value-laden inner world of experience and thought' (2008 p. 161).

Christians see human nature as being in the 'image of God' because it has reason and free will and is able to be its own master.

In St Paul's letter to the Galatians he wrote: 'For freedom Christ has set us free. Stand firm, therefore, and do not submit again to a yoke of slavery' (Galatians 5:1). Redemption in Christianity is seen as freedom from bondage, from original sin and from fallenness to salvation. Human nature is seen as imperfect and so needs to be saved. This teaching of original sin has had a major influence on Christianity and again has been interpreted in a variety of ways. Traditional Christian teaching is that original sin is a result of Adam and Eve's disobedience to God when they ate the forbidden fruit in the Garden of Eden. This had the effect of separating humans from God and bringing dissatisfaction and guilt into their lives; original sin is a condition and not something that people do. It is only by accepting God's grace and love and forgiveness that people can be saved. The doctrine of original sin was largely devised by Augustine of Hippo, in contrast to some of his contemporaries who taught that humans were not born into a sinful state and that we had free will. Augustine's triumph in the ensuing debate meant that humanity became polarised into the saved and the damned.

So how exactly did Augustine interpret the first chapters of Genesis? His starting point was the perfection of the first man Adam who he said was free from physical ills, had the liberty not to sin and was devoted to obeying God. Adam's fall was entirely his own fault and, because his will was completely free, his sin was more serious than any other sin and had consequences for the whole of humanity: condemnation for all humans as all sinned in Adam.

The result of this is that we no longer have the moral and physical perfection of Adam and are slaves to a search for pleasure. We can no longer avoid sin without God's help. However, the narrative in Genesis 2–3 is not interested in describing the situation before the Fall, rather in explaining the condition of humanity – why we suffer toil, pain and death. The stories in Genesis do not tell of a historical Fall from grace but describe our present situation. According to Westermann (1984) these stories are not historical but are simply stories illustrating how people can choose to rebel against God and the terrible effects this can have. So for Westermann, people's sinfulness is an aspect of their human nature. They are still free to serve God if they want to or rebel and pay the price.

Modern theologians accept that the stories of the creation of a perfect world and the Fall are mythical, and evolution suggests that the world is changing and becoming more diverse so that humanity should concentrate not on a past fall from grace but on becoming more ethical beings and so making the world better.

CHRISTIAN TEACHING ON FREE WILL AND FATALISM

What is meant by free will? It does not mean willing without motives or arbitrarily choosing anything. Humans are considered to be rational beings and so always attracted by what they see as good. Having free will does not mean that we are constantly using this power all the time, any more than being a rational creature means that we are always reasoning. Most of the things we do each day – getting up, eating, studying, work, etc. – are almost automatic acquired habits that we do not think about. However, they may still be free as we freely acquired these habits. It is only when we are put in a position that we need to choose, sometimes between right and wrong but often between two things that seem good (for example, stay in and study or go to the pub with our friends) that we are aware that we are choosing freely.

The Christian teaching that God created humans and commanded them to obey the moral law with its resulting reward and punishment for their actions made the question of free will vitally important. Unless people are really free they cannot be justly held responsible for their actions. Augustine of Hippo addressed this question, clearly teaching the importance of both free will and the necessity of grace. He also stressed the absolute rule of God over our wills because God is both omnipotent and omniscient, so his fore-knowledge includes our motives. Augustine's teaching was important as it formed the basis of all Christian teaching on free will and has been interpreted in various ways, sometimes including a form of predestination that is little different from fatalism.

Thomas Aquinas developed the teachings of Augustine and saw that humans can freely choose but that God knows all our future actions. For Aquinas, God does not exist in time, and so both the future and the past are one to God. Aquinas explains this with the idea of a man sitting on a mountain top seeing in one glance everything that those walking up the winding mountain path see only as a series of successive experiences – in a similar way God sees our future.

CHRISTIAN TEACHING ON EQUALITY AND DIFFERENCE

For Christians equality seems to be central as we are all created in the image of God and Christians believe that God loves all regardless of race, colour or sex. However, as always the biblical texts are open to a variety of interpretations – did God create men and women as different and separate, or are they equal as he made them both of the same stuff, or is man superior as he was made first?

Bible teachings also seem inconsistent regarding racism and equality. While God is said to love everybody, some other passages seem to suggest that God prefers one sex (male) and one race (the Jews) above all others. Some Christians have, in fact, used passages from the Bible to justify racism, sexism and other forms of prejudice. The Dutch Reformed Church in South Africa used Genesis 9:18–27 to justify the apartheid system, as it had been previously used to justify slavery. They believed that Black people were not equal to Whites and that God was the 'Great Divider'. In 1985 the Kairos Document was published by other South African Christians stating that these claims were untrue, and the Dutch Reformed Church later publicly repented of this teaching. There are many examples in the Bible which challenge the idea that racism is acceptable – in Matthew 22:39 Jesus says 'love your neighbour as yourself' and in the story of the Good Samaritan Jesus made it clear that racism is wrong.

Christians have responded to this by reinterpreting the more negative passages and teaching a God who loves the oppressed – giving rise to Liberation Theology, Feminist Theology and Black Theology.

The epistles of Paul, however, do seem to teach equality:

> As many of you as were baptized into Christ have clothed yourselves with Christ. There is no longer Jew or Greek, there is no longer slave or free, there is no longer male and female; for all of you are one in Christ Jesus.
>
> (Galatians 3:27–8)

This would seem to say that all Christians are equal before God and that God does not see any differences between the sexes, but in practice Christianity has differing attitudes towards the roles of men and women within the Church. Historically women have not been treated as equals, either within society as a whole or within the Church. Traditional roles meant that women were expected to bring up children, run a Christian home and submit to their husbands, though husbands were expected to love their wives (Ephesians 5:22–4, 33) and there was no church leadership role for women (1 Corinthians 14:34, 1 Timothy 2:11–13). This is still the view taken by the Roman Catholic Church, Eastern Orthodox Church and some Protestant churches who will not allow women to become priests, as priests are believed to be the successors of the twelve apostles and, as Jesus only appointed men, this role is not open to women. However, in the twentieth century many Protestant churches allowed women to become priests and ministers, not only in response to the changes in society but also on a sound biblical basis that male and female were both created in God's image and are to use the God-given gifts for the service of all.

There is a similar confused account when it comes to disability. In both the Old and New Testaments disease and disability can be seen as punishment for sin and so somehow deserved, but suffering can be accepted by linking it to the redemptive suffering of Christ. Christians believe that Jesus came to heal the effects of sin and restore humanity to oneness with God. In breaking the boundaries that separated humanity and God, Jesus broke the boundaries of his time by reaching out to those marginalised by society by healing the lame, the blind and deaf and the lepers. Whether these healings are interpreted literally, seen as myths or psychological phenomena, the healing miracles still show the power of God through Jesus reaching out to those shunned by the rest of society. The Christian churches have been slow to speak out for the disabled, but, as understanding of disability issues grew within society as a whole, so Christian teaching on the rights and dignity of disabled people became clearer. Documents from the Catholic Church from 1981 (International Year of the Disabled) reflected this as the Church called for a just wage and the right to work to be applied to people with disabilities.

There is still, however, an element of the 'cross-bearing' approach and the offering up of suffering. The danger of this misunderstanding of the theology of suffering, which fails to accept suffering as the evil it really is, can lead to a glorification of suffering and see the disabled as 'objects of pity and mission' only, without recognising their innate dignity as people made in the 'image of God' and so somehow different from the able-bodied. The New Testament view of God as the 'wounded healer' leads to seeing the disabled as equal to the able-bodied as all people are wounded in some way. So the disabled are as necessary to the whole of humanity as the non-disabled. 1 Corinthians 12:21–7, and the book of Job teach that bad things just happen to good people.

Any cursory study of Christianity will see that, for most of their history, Christians have not challenged inequality in society, and those who did are often found on the fringes of the Church. One famous example is the fourteenth-century priest John Ball (1338–1381), who held that as we are all descended from Adam and Eve there is no basis for class or social division, and he acted on this belief by leading the first poll tax revolt which was advocated by the then Archbishop of Canterbury.

During the Civil War the ideas of equality were promoted by the Quakers who believed that all had the 'light within' and could come to know Christ without the help of a 'learned priest'. For them God was the 'great Leveller', and so they treated all as equal, refusing to remove their hats when in the presence of their 'superiors' and using the familiar 'thee' and 'thou' form of address to all. Both Religious Society of Friends (Quaker) and Leveller women argued their equality with men. A further offshoot known as the Diggers set up communities based on common ownership, encouraging people to see that sharing the land was the only way to achieve a just and fair society.

The teachings behind these actions can be seen in the 1960s when both Vatican II and the World Council of Churches spoke of the Church as a sign of the coming unity of humankind and an instrument for its achieve-ment: Christians see this unity when they come together to celebrate Holy Communion – in the sharing of bread and wine they anticipate and celebrate the future 'kingdom' when human distinctions of wealth, status and power will be levelled.

The teaching of equality is also seen in the way in which Christianity approaches other religions. Most Christian churches agree that there should be religious freedom and that everyone should have the right to follow their own faith: however, their interpretation of what this means exactly varies.

Thought Point

Research the different Christian views on the role of women in the Church.

- What other groups could be seen as marginalised by the Church – e.g. disabled people, homosexuals – and what are the results for the Christian community?
- What gives people human dignity? What does having human dignity mean in practice?

Some Christians believe that only Christianity has the full truth and that there is only one true religion. Those Christians who follow this approach are called exclusivists: possibly the most well known is the Swiss theologian Karl Barth, who wrote that the only truth is revelation and therefore only Christianity is true insofar as it embodies revelation: 'And the Word became flesh' (John 1:14a). However, Barth did admit to the possibility that God might reveal himself outside Christianity. Some Christians believe that only Christianity has the full truth, but that it is possible to come to God through other religions. This inclusivist approach sees God as a God of love, and so people of good will are included in God's saving grace regardless of their religion. This was the view of the German theologian Karl Rahner, who called people who were adherents of other religions, living good moral lives, 'anonymous Christians'. The Roman Catholic Church also follows this view, as Vatican II also said that salvation is possible for people of other religions. A few Christians are pluralists and believe that all religions are equal and are just different ways of finding God, so all religions lead to salvation.

CHRISTIAN TEACHING ON THE VALUE OF HUMAN LIFE

The fact the humans are made in the 'image of God' is the basis for their belief in the importance and value of human life. This is seen in Christian approaches to life issues such as abortion and euthanasia, which are dealt with elsewhere in this book, but also in the Christian teaching on war. There are two main responses to the taking of life in war – pacifism and Just War.

Neither of these approaches allows the taking of life for reasons such as revenge, conquest or economic interest; both stress the unconditional value of human life, and that, being made in the 'image' of God, we are all valued by God – saint and sinner alike. This is the foundation of the commandment not to murder and of Jesus' command to love our enemies.

Thought Point

1. What would make anyone want to go to war?
2. Under what circumstances would you be prepared to go to war?
3. Under what circumstances would you not be prepared to go to war?
4. Is the 'war against terrorism' truly a war?
5. Can you think of any circumstance in which someone would be justified in killing another person?
6. Why does it always appear that the enemy's justification for war is weaker than our own?

The preference for pacifism underlies all Christian responses to the use of violence. In the West, pacifism is rooted in Christianity and was particularly strong in the early Church. It looked to the Gospels, which record that Jesus called his followers not to violence but to sacrificial love. Jesus taught that we must love our enemies and do good to those who hate us, and 'Blessed are the peacemakers' (Matthew 5:9). These themes are rooted in the Jewish prophetic tradition, and followers of Jesus see both his ministry and his sacrificial death as a continuation and a fulfilment of that tradition, which must be carried on by his followers. The early Christians saw Jesus' commands as a prohibition on the bearing of arms, and so they refused to join the Roman army. A profound change in the Christian attitude to war came at the time of the emperor Constantine, and from this time pacifism has been a minority view within the Christian Church.

However, there have been influential peace churches which continue the original Christian position, such as the Religious Society of Friends (Quakers), the Mennonites, the Amish, the Bruderhof Brethren (a community now living in East Sussex) and the Doukhobors (originally from Russia, but now living mainly in Canada).

The Quakers are the most familiar group in the UK and, having been founded at the time of the Civil War, they consider that violence leads only to more violence, and also that it is important that each person should actively work to overcome anything which causes conflict between peoples.

Most of these pacifist Christian communities were not against state military service, or the idea that a state should be able to defend itself, as they saw the state as a necessary vehicle for social order, but they themselves would not serve in the military. These Christian pacifists follow the teaching of Paul in Romans, where he wrote: 'Let every person be subject to the governing authorities; for there is no authority except from God, and those authorities that exist have been instituted by God' (Romans 13:1).

Paul saw those in authority thus: 'It is the servant of God to execute wrath on the wrongdoer' (Romans 13:14b). The state seems permitted to use force, but not the individual Christian. Peace churches see a complete separation between the 'church' and the 'world', and take the stance of conscientious objectors, often being persecuted by the authorities who do not share their view. However, this pacifism does not mean doing nothing, but often encompasses non-violent direct action. The most well-known example of this was Martin Luther King Jr, who used forceful language, non-violent resistance, strikes, peaceful protest and civil disobedience, eventually culminating in his assassination, in the struggle for racial equality in the USA. He was influenced by the campaign for Indian independence led by Gandhi, who advocated *ahimsa* or non-violence and *satyagraha* or zest for truth. Other examples include the transformation of Polish society by the Solidarity movement led by Lech Wałęsa. However, whether such action will work in a war situation is another question.

Christian pacifism is not, however, limited to small Protestant groups but is followed by many in mainstream Christian denominations. Influential among these was the Catholic monk Thomas Merton, who influenced many with his prolific writings. He renounced violence as a way to peace and wrote that the task of the Christian is to work for the total abolition of war. Merton advocated non-violence as a realistic alternative to violence and killing; the task was to try to win people's minds instead of destroying their bodies. In the Preface of his autobiography he wrote:

> It is my intention to make my entire life a rejection of, a protest against the crimes and the injustices of war and political tyranny which threaten to destroy the whole human race . . . and the world with it.
>
> By my monastic life and vows I am saying NO to all the concentration camps, the aerial bombardments, the staged political trials, the judicial murders, the racial injustices, the economic tyrannies and the whole socio-economic apparatus which seems geared for nothing but global destruction in spite of all its fair words in favour of peace.

Merton was censored by his superiors, but partly because of him Catholic pacifism is now more common and is even supported by the Vatican as an appropriate faith response to issues of war.

On the mainstream Protestant side Walter Wink criticises Augustine's support of violence to defend the innocent, and the whole Just War theory, as it has led Christians to be one of the most warlike factions on Earth. He says that Christians should be non-violent pacifists who resist evil, but reject any idea of Just War.

However, though the early Church generally taught against violence or military service, the Church also taught that the government was responsible for maintaining order, so when the Roman empire became officially Christian the Church found itself having to reconcile the response of self-sacrifice to the value of human life on the one hand, and God's justice for the protection of human life on the other hand. Ambrose and Augustine, and later Thomas Aquinas, began to put forward principles by which war might be justified in the eyes of God. These were divided into two: *Jus ad bellum* – just principles for going to war; and *Jus in bello* – just principles for the conduct of the war.

Jus ad bellum contains:

Principle of just cause	only for the protection of innocent life
Principle of just authority	only when authorised by the proper authority (e.g. the ruler or government)
Principle of right intention	to protect innocent life and not for revenge
Principle of last resort	all other attempts to protect the innocent must have been tried
Principle of proportionality	only when the good that results from the war outweighs the harm that is inflicted
Principle of probability of success	only when there is a reasonable chance that it will be successful in protecting innocent life.

Jus in bello contains:

Principle of proportionality	only when the good that results from the war outweighs the harm that is inflicted
Principle of discrimination (non-combatant immunity)	only against those who threaten innocent life.

Later Christians added *Jus post bello* – just principles for after the war. The Just War teachings always attempt to stress the value and sanctity of human life.

War cemetery

Thought Point

1. Is it morally defensible to have rules for war?
2. What problems can you see with the following imaginary press release? 'During a recent action against terrorism, the ground troops called up air support who carried out a targeted strike using smart missiles. Collateral damage was kept to a minimum, with the loss of a few to friendly fire. There were few casualties.'

REVIEW QUESTIONS

Look back over the chapter and check that you can answer the following questions:

1. Explain how Christians understand the concept of free will.
2. Explain the different Christian approaches to the roles of men and women in the Church and in society.

3. Make brief bullet point notes on each of the following:

    *   *Jus ad bellum*
    *   *Jus in bello*

4. Make a chart of the strengths and weaknesses of Just War theory in protecting innocent life.
5. Make a chart of the strengths and weaknesses of pacifism in protecting innocent life.

BUDDHISM

Human nature and the human condition

Unlike most religious traditions Buddhism does not emphasise the value of the individual person. In fact, it teaches that the more a person is attached to the self the more they seek gratification and become self-centred, ignore others and bring about suffering.

This teaching of non-atman or 'not self' does not mean that individualism is denied but that people are linked by common factors. The suffering of an individual is the suffering that all people experience. Because all beings are part of the cycle of birth and rebirth this idea of suffering applies to all sentient beings and is very influential in regard to ethical issues and the taking of life.

One of the most important Buddhist teachings is to follow the 'Noble Eightfold Path' which can lead to enlightenment. The eight parts of the path are: right view; right intention; right speech; right action; right livelihood; right effort; right mindfulness and right concentration. All these steps can lead to moral virtue and therefore are sometimes seen as more akin to Virtue Ethics than to a deontological or teleological approach. Each step of the path can lead the individual towards *nibbana*.

Free will and fatalism

Unlike other forms of life, human beings have the possibility of reaching enlightenment and eventual nibbana (sometimes spelled *nirvana*). Humans have the freedom to choose and therefore to shape the *kamma* (sometimes spelled *karma*)which will follow them into their next rebirth. Buddhism has no idea of fatalism as humans can choose to make their own moral and spiritual progress.

Equality

All human beings are on the cycle of rebirth and therefore all can choose being good and bad acts and the resulting kamma. Therefore Buddhism holds that all human beings are equal and should be treated equally. The Buddha rejected the Hindu idea of being born into a caste, maintaining that caste was the result of actions not of birth.

Buddhist teachings of equality do not, however, necessarily extend to gender in the same way. Many traditions teach that women cannot become a Buddha but must be born as a man first. There are stories of female Bodhisattvas being somehow transformed into men and then becoming Buddhas. However, both the main traditions, Theravada and Mahayana, have recognised female Buddhas in the past. Similarly, Bhikkunis (female monks) have been seen as junior to the Bhikkus (males).

Disability is often viewed as the consequence of bad kamma from a previous life. This is logical within Buddhist belief as the aim of existence is to achieve enlightenment and eventual nibbana.

The value of human life

For Buddhists the value of human life is the opportunity to achieve enlightenment. Nevertheless, human life is still the most precious in the world and must be protected by not causing suffering or death to it. To kill another human intentionally will create bad kamma.

HINDUISM

The value of human life

All Hindu teaching about the value of life is based on the idea of the *atman*, which is the divine 'soul' which is continually reborn in the cycle of *samsara*. Everything has a beginning and end to its life which is part of the way in which the world is structured. However, human beings are a particularly important part of this re-creative process and therefore human life may be seen as having a special value. The ultimate goal of the atman is to achieve final union with Brahman, the eternal spirit and the end of samsara.

Free will and fatalism

Unlike animals, humans have free will and are able to decide between good and evil. A good life, lived according to a person's *dharma*, can then lead to the creation of good *karma* so that the next rebirth may bring the atman nearer to nirvana and the escape from samsara. It is necessary for the atman to be reborn into human form in order to have the possibility of reaching *nirvana*.

As well as a spiritual form, the human body has a material nature. This must be cared for and the decision made to keep the body pure by, for example, exercising self-control and practising virtuous behaviour. This self-control is necessary to avoid damaging the material nature by, for example, gluttony or drunkenness.

People may feel that they have little control of their life because they are, in some ways, the product of the karma of a previous life. However, the possession of free will means that they are in a position where they can influence the karma of this life and so the future fate of the atman.

Human nature and the human condition

Humans have the possibility of reaching the final goal of nirvana and the reuniting of the atman with Brahman. Human life traps the atman in the cycle of rebirth and is exposed to suffering and, ultimately, death. Therefore people should live their lives according to their dharma and work for others by good acts, liberation and righteousness.

It is not possible to make absolute statements about the nature of Hindu belief because of the enormous diversity found within the faith. However, there is one clear difference between the ways in which Hinduism and Western thinking view the individual. Because of the belief in samsara, humans are seen as part of this universal family rather than the Western stress on the individual.

Equality and difference

A further difference between Hinduism and Western philosophies lies in the complexity of humanity. Any person of either sex and of any role in life may be virtuous. However, a person's identity is greatly influenced by the caste into which they are born. The caste system has received much criticism from people over the centuries such as the founder of Sikhism, Guru Nanak Dev Ji and Mohandas Gandhi in the twentieth century. Nevertheless it remains a very important part of Hindu life. Those people without caste, now self-identified as Dalits (oppressed), number more than 200 million in India. The continued existence of the caste system is sometimes justified by the belief that samsara and the personal ability to live a good life offer the chance of rebirth into a higher caste.

Although there are many prominent women within Hinduism, they are often still seen as primarily having a domestic role. Although they have a duty in charge of religion in the home and the religious nurture of children, they play little part in public worship.

The practice of killing female babies still continues in some areas because of the preference for boys to continue the family line and, despite the practice of sati being banned in the twentieth century, some widows are still burnt on their husband's funeral pyre.

ISLAM

Human nature and the human condition

The Qur'an teaches that humanity is distinct:

> We have honoured the sons of Adam; provided them with transport on land and sea; given them for sustenance things good and pure; and conferred on them special favours, above a great part of our creation.
>
> (Surah 17:70)

All humanity is born with a dignity bestowed by God and not earned. This is not the result of behaviour or deeds. All people of all religions have this dignity which must be respected.

Free will and fatalism

Although there is within Islam a view that God does know the future and the future actions of humanity, this is not viewed as predestination and does not limit the free will of the individual. In fact free will is a necessary aspect of being human: as people must choose to follow God's teachings as found in the Qur'an, there would be no virtue in humans who performed good acts without the choice to do otherwise. It is part of human dignity to have free will and to be able to exercise a personal conscience. This does not mean that there are not actions which are subject to punishment whether in life or after death.

The Muslim scholar al-Ash'ari (874–936) argued that, as all power lies with God, then God wills everything to happen and therefore has foreknowledge of everything. However, although this appears fatalistic, he continued that each individual has the responsibility over how an act is performed and should pray before each act. Muslims believe that God will not allow them to be tempted beyond what they can resist.

Equality and difference

The distinctness of the creation of humanity is seen in God's instructions to the angels and to Iblis (Shaytan) to bow down before Adam. It was Iblis' refusal to obey this command which led to his exile. Humanity is distinct and made in the image of God; therefore humans have higher powers than those given to animals.

In understanding the Muslim view on gender equality it is important to consider what is the teaching of the Qur'an and of the Prophet and what is due to different societies. Both men and women have an equal duty to follow the way of Islam. To treat women differently and argue that this is Islamic teaching would be untrue to Islam. Muhammad ﷺ changed the way in which women and orphans were treated when he settled in al-Madinah, and many of these rights then given to women were not reflected in Western societies until the twentieth century. Women have the right to own property, to own businesses, to control their own money, to keep their maiden name and the right to education.

The value of human life

Human life has infinite value and is sacred. All life comes from God and should be taken only by God unless there is justification which would be approved by God. There may be occasions when to protect self or the community proportionate force may be used in defence – this is Lesser Jihad. However, recognition of the dignity of the individual means that care must always be shown to civilians and the vulnerable, and physical abuse is not acceptable.

JUDAISM

Human nature and the human condition

According to the book of Genesis, humanity was a distinct and different part of creation being made in 'imago dei' – the image of G-d. Because of this unique aspect of humanity, Jews believe that they must strive to live their lives in such a way that they show this G-dlike image in their behaviour. In fact, it is unclear as to exactly what this expression means. Some people choose to view it in an almost literal way suggesting a physical image, others may consider that humans have a divine quality within them, while some may consider that humans have the ability to act in a G-dlike way towards others. Humans have the ability to love rather than hate, and this is seen as a G-dlike attribute.

Free will and fatalism

Judaism teaches that the uniqueness of humanity which separates it from all other life is the quality of G-dliness. It is not simply that humans are more intelligent than other life forms but importantly that they can use this intelligence to decide between good and evil.

It is clear within Jewish teaching that humans have free will. Nevertheless this does not mean that they will necessarily choose good over evil. The fact that they can make this choice is part of their uniqueness and an important aspect of their creation. Judaism stresses that it is not desire which is wrong but it is the way in which moral responsibility is exercised in the pursuit of desire which can lead to good or evil.

Equality and difference

Judaism stresses equality but it must be acknowledged that gender equality is still an issue within some communities.

The creation account in Genesis 1 says that G-d created men and women at the same time. The earlier account, found in Genesis 2, is often interpreted as suggesting that the woman was created from the side of the man. In fact the first creation – the 'man' – has no gender and the difference between men and women does not appear until after this second creation from the rib. It is also clear that, although generally referred to as 'he', G-d is not seen as having one exclusive gender and contains both male and female aspects.

In the Jewish scriptures there are many examples of very strong women, of women in leadership positions and female prophets. However, there are still arguments today as to whether women can be rabbis, the physical separation of men and women in the synagogue and the legal rights of women over issues such as divorce. In many communities women are seen as equal to men but different.

The value of human life

Jews believe that they have a special role as G-d's chosen people. However, this can be seen as an obligation rather than a blessing. All Jews have a duty to bear witness to G-d and to demonstrate how G-d wishes humanity to live. This is part of the Covenants which G-d made with the Jews.

Judaism teaches that human life has a special dignity and value. Jews are told to worship G-d, to love their neighbour and that murder is a sin. Building on these principles is the idea that human life must always be preserved and protected, Jewish and non-Jewish.

SIKHISM

Human nature and the human condition

Sikhism teaches that the aim of human life is to achieve escape from rebirth and to unite the atman with God (Waheguru). A Sikh must turn away from being self-centred towards being God-centred. In doing this it is possible to avoid the damaging evils of lust, attachment and anger and to move towards kindness and, most importantly, caring for others (*sewa*).

Free will and fatalism

Being born a Sikh places a person in the best position to create good karma and achieve union between the atman and God after death. However, practising evil and producing bad karma leads back to the cycle of rebirth.

All life was created by Hukam (Divine Will) and God is therefore involved in human life. This does lead to a suggestion of predestination but this is seen not as a judgement made from the beginning of a person's life but as the consequence of the sort of life they choose to lead.

By His Command, bodies are created; His Command cannot be described.

By His Command, souls come into being; by His Command, glory and greatness are obtained.

By His Command, some are high and some are low; by His Written Command, pain and pleasure are obtained.

Some, by His Command, are blessed and forgiven; others, by His Command, wander aimlessly forever.

Everyone is subject to His Command; no one is beyond His Command.

(*Guru Granth Sahib Ji*; Sardar p. 1)

Equality

The teachings on equality of Guru Nanak Dev Ji show that all humanity, male and female, should be treated as one group. He rejected the Hindu caste system, teaching that human value came from moral behaviour and the possibility of enlightenment. Sikhism teaches that because of this possibility the human body must be preserved and protected, thus enabling it to serve others most effectively. This protection includes abstaining from alcohol, drugs, tobacco and, for some, meat.

The last human Guru – Guru Gobind Singh Ji (1666–1708) – had great concern for people with disabilities and encouraged them to overcome them whenever possible. Sikhism teaches that disability has no bearing on reaching enlightenment.

The value of human life

The value of humanity lies in the good that people can do and in the possibility of reaching union with God. Sikhism permits violence to protect the vulnerable and weak and religious freedom but it sees human beings as having value because everyone has the possibility of reaching union with God and all humans can do good for others.

Terminology

Do you know your terminology?

Try to explain the following key ideas without looking at your books and notes:

- Autonomous being
- Exclusivist
- Inclusivist
- Just War
- Original Sin
- Pluralist
- Predestination
- Speciesism
- The Fall

SAMPLE EXAMINATION QUESTIONS

(a) Examine the teaching of one religion about the concept of self-sacrifice. (30 marks)

In your answer, you must answer with *specific teaching* from *one* religion. Teaching includes scripture, comments from religious leaders and individual interpretation of scripture.

- *Buddhism*: any activity has consequences, could be seen as 'Right Action', fulfils many of the ten perfections (*paramitas*), is the ultimate form of loss of attachment, could (adversely) affect kamma, could be seen as causing harm to life.
- *Christianity*: any activity has consequences, only God has the right to take life, do not murder, yet seen as 'the Greatest Love', agape, Jesus sacrificed himself on the cross.
- *Hinduism*: any activity has consequences, could be seen as part of the maintenance of balance and harmony (*rita*), could be seen as 'duty' (*dharma*), could be seen as a form of ahimsa (avoiding harm to others); on the other hand could be against ahimsa.
- *Islam*: any activity has consequences, only God has the right to take life, humans are God's most noble creation (Surah 95:4), concept of accountability, may be seen as God's will.
- *Judaism*: any activity has consequences, only G-d has the right to take life, do not murder, not showing respect for G-d's creation, told to 'choose life'; however, primary commandment is to save life.
- *Sikhism*: any activity has consequences, Guru Gobind Singh Ji challenged Sikhs to be prepared to die for their faith, concept of martyrdom (*shahidi*), could be a form of *seva* (service), concept of daya; however, could affect one's karma.

(b) Assess the idea that self-sacrifice means that human life is not important. (15 marks)

Religious views can be included in this answer, but do not have to be.

For

- The concept of giving up your life does imply that human life is not important.
- Humans should be focused on the afterlife, not on the 'here and now'.
- If God requires it of his followers, then the implication is that human life is dispensable.
- Suicide bombers and others seem to regard human life as dispensable.

Against

- Religions (notably Christianity) teach that to give up one's life voluntarily is supremely important.
- One is giving up one's own life for another's, therefore showing how important life is.
- It is possibly the greatest action one person could do for another.

Further information on world faiths can be found at: http://subknow.reonline.org.uk/.

5 Abortion

Essential terminology

Abortion
Consciousness
Doctrine of double
  effect
Embryo
Ensoulment
Foetus
Hippocratic Oath
Ordinary and
  extraordinary means
Personhood
Primitive streak
Quality of life
Sanctity of life
Viability

WHAT YOU WILL LEARN ABOUT IN THIS CHAPTER

- The idea of the sanctity of life and how it applies to abortion.
- Ideas of personhood and the status of the foetus.
- The rights of all those involved.
- The approaches of different ethical theories to abortion.

THE AQA CHECKLIST ✔

Abortion: definitions for the start of human life, including: potentiality, conception, primitive streak, viability, birth.

- The value of potential and real life
- Mother's versus child's life, double effect
- Ethical issues involved in legislation about abortion
- Arguments for and against abortion with reference to religious and ethical teachings.

Study hint

Many of the issues of medical ethics are shifting all the time as science and technology move forward. To keep up with these issues it is a good idea to keep a folder of relevant newspaper cuttings and to annotate them with how you think the different ethical theories would react to the issue.

ISSUES ARISING

- Does the definition of human life stop abortion being murder?
- Can abortion ever be said to be 'good'?
- Do humans have a right to life?

WHAT IS ABORTION?

Abortion is the induced termination of a pregnancy to destroy the foetus. In the UK, abortion is legal up to the 24th week of the pregnancy. After that time an abortion can be carried out if there is a serious threat to the life of the mother or the foetus is severely disabled. According to the current law, at present a woman must have the agreement of two doctors for the termination. The 24-week rule was introduced in 1991, as it was established then that babies born at 24 weeks are viable and with intensive care can survive. The principle behind this ruling is that, whatever the reasons for an abortion, a foetus should be given legal protection if it is possible for it to survive outside the womb. Medical science has now moved on, and there is some pressure to lower the time to 20 weeks, but as yet this has not happened.

Abortion raises some important moral questions:

- What is a person?
- Is all human life intrinsically valuable or sacred?
- Is all intentional killing of people always wrong?
- Is it always a duty to preserve innocent life?
- When does life begin?

When does life begin? – The value of potential and real life

At what point does human life have moral status? Is it at conception, at a particular point in development or at birth? Does a potential human life have the same moral status as an actual human life? This question is central to the abortion debate but the answer is vital, as, once you have decided this is a human being, you need to give that individual rights and protection under the law.

At conception

According to the teaching of the Catholic Church, life begins at conception and at this moment the genetic materials of both parents mix and form a biologically distinct entity. This is an attractive view as it is so clear-cut, and marks a definite moment when the foetus becomes a human being.

In 1869 Pope Pius XI in his encyclical *Casti Connubi* stated that the foetus is a human person from the moment of conception and the life of an unborn child is as sacred as that of its mother; this was reinforced by Pope Paul VI in his encyclical *Humanae Vitae* in 1968 and again stated in the *Catechism of the Catholic Church* (1994):

Human life must be respected and protected absolutely from the moment of conception. From the first moment of his existence a human being must be recognised as having the rights of a person – among which is the inviolable right of every innocent being to life.

There are several biblical quotations which suggest that life begins before birth:

Before I formed you in the womb I knew you.

(Jeremiah 1:5b)

For it was you who formed my inward parts; you knit me together in my mother's womb.

(Psalm 139:13)

For as soon as I heard the sound of your greeting, the child in my womb leaped for joy.

(Luke 1:44)

> ### Pope Paul VI (1897–1978)
>
> Paul VI was born Giovanni Battista Montini on 26 September 1897 at Concesio, Italy. He became Pope in 1963 during the Second Vatican Council. He died on 6 August 1978 at Castel Gandolfo.

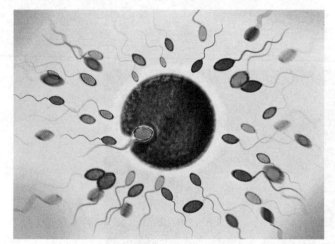

Sperm fertilising egg (digital composite)

Taxi Sarah Jones (Debut Art) Getty Images

After conception

According to the Human Fertilisation and Embryology Act of 1990, the foetus is given legal protection from 24 weeks if it is possible for it to survive outside the womb. This is the legal point of viability: however, to take this time as the moment life begins is problematic, as modern technical advances mean that the foetus can survive outside the womb before this time. Supporters of the argument that life begins at some point after conception say there is a difference between *potential* and *actual* life. Some would also add that life begins at the moment of implantation in the womb (about six or seven days after conception), others when the heart starts beating or there are signs of brain activity. Others would say that at 14 days after conception the primitive streak can be identified, and from this point a person can be said to exist. Until that point it is not certain which cells will form the placenta and which the embryo, or indeed whether there will be more than one embryo.

Primitive streak

According to the biologist Lewis Wolpert the primitive streak, which appears at a time about two weeks after fertilisation, when a groove forms on the surface of the growing embryo, is the most important point in the development of a human being. The primitive streak is an outward sign of a massive reorganisation of the embryo from a sphere into a multi-layered organism, in a process called gastrulation. From this point the body plan of the future foetus is established, and, once the streak is fully developed, it thickens at one end to form Hanson's node, which produces chemicals that cause the formation of the nervous system. It is also the beginning of individuality, and some would say of personhood as, if the fertilised egg turns into twins, it almost always happens before this point.

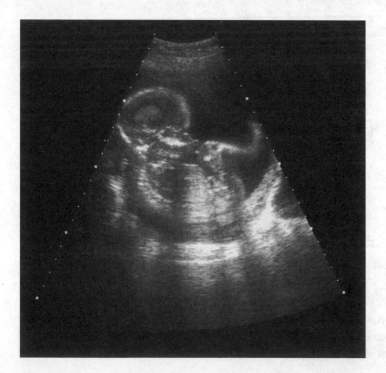

Ultrasound image of human foetus (digital enhancement)

The Image Bank (SMC Images) Getty Images

At birth

Thus far there are two clearly defined views of when human life begins – at conception or some time after conception. However, for centuries it was established that birth was the point at which life began and the deliberate killing of a baby after birth was regarded as murder. Some still follow this line; for example, Mary Anne Warren argues that birth is the time when the baby no longer relies totally on the mother for its survival. Jonathan Glover rejects this, as there are no major differences between a late foetus and a new-born or premature baby. He therefore argues for a more flexible time as the beginning of life.

THE LIFE OF THE MOTHER VERSUS THE LIFE OF THE CHILD

This issue asks whether one life should be saved in preference to another: is one life more sacred, more valuable than another, or does one life have more right to life than another?

Thought Point

1. What would your reaction be to the following:

   - A suicide bomber who kills many people in a crowded marketplace
   - A man who shoots an intruder in his house
   - A soldier who kills in war
   - A compulsive serial killer.

2. Do we think some lives are more valuable than others? (For example, how do we justify spending money on fertilisation treatment for a couple when the money could be used to improve the quality of life of the sick and elderly? Or justify allowing thousands to die of starvation in Africa? Or think it more tragic if a young person dies than if an old person dies?)

However, it is now very rare that a choice has to be made between the life of the foetus and the life of the mother. Many would say that saving the life of the mother is not abortion and would use the doctrine of double effect (see p. 70) to argue this. The right to life of the foetus has recently been argued

Jonathan Glover (1941–)

Jonathan Glover teaches ethics at King's College, London. He argued that to call a foetus a human person was to stretch the term beyond its natural boundaries. He is quoted as saying: 'Our entanglements with people close to us erode simple self-interest. Husbands, wives, lovers, parents, children and friends all blur the boundaries of selfish concern. Francis Bacon rightly said that people with children have given hostages to fortune. Inescapably, other forms of friendship and love hold us hostage too. . . . Narrow self-interest is destabilized.'

Sanctity of life
The belief that human life is valuable in itself.

for in the case of late abortions. A Church of England curate caused a stir in the media by challenging the lawfulness of late abortion (Jepson v. The Chief Constable of West Mercia Police Constabulary 2003). Ms Jepson had been reading through the abortion statistics for 2001 when she came across the abortion of a 24-week-old foetus which had been diagnosed as suffering from a bilateral cleft lip and palate. Ms Jepson, who was born with a serious facial abnormality, later remedied by surgery, argued that a cleft lip and palate cannot amount to a serious handicap, and so the abortion was unlawful. However, no criminal charges were brought against the two doctors in this case as they were deemed to have acted in 'good faith'.

At the time concern was expressed that the impact on the life of the mother in having a handicapped child was greater than the lethal impact on the life of the baby: the rights of the mother were deemed by law to be greater than those of the unborn child. This case does seem to open up the need for a further debate about rights and the legal status of the foetus. Such discussion might need to extend beyond the rights of the mother and the foetus, to consider welfare and economic rights, the encouragement of male sexual responsibility and the development of more assistance to enable women to be supported by society in making decisions about abortion.

RELIGIOUS APPROACHES TO THE SANCTITY OF LIFE

For religious believers, however, any talk of rights is secondary to the most important teaching of all – on the Sanctity of Life. The teaching on the Sanctity of Life holds that all life is sacred, worthy of respect and reverence, and intrinsically worthwhile. People therefore have a duty to preserve life, and yet we have very mixed reactions to this idea. Do we actually see some lives as being more valuable than others? Within the Christian tradition the views may be roughly divided into strong and weak Sanctity of Life arguments.

Those who hold a strong Sanctity of Life stance are often called *pro-life* and appeal to the biblical basis of their ideas: God is the giver and creator of life and people have no right to destroy what he has given. People are seen as created in the 'image of God' – imago Dei – so humans are set apart from other animals and have a 'spark' of divinity within them: the breath of life was breathed by God into Adam.

The incarnation, according to Christian teaching, reaffirms the sanctity of human life as God himself became human:

So God created humankind in his image.

(Genesis 1:27a)

God blessed them, and God said to them, 'Be fruitful and multiply, and fill the earth and subdue it; and have dominion over the fish of the sea and over the birds of the air and over every living thing that moves upon the earth.'

(Genesis 1:28)

And the Word became flesh and lived among us, and we have seen his glory, the glory as of a father's only son, full of grace and truth.

(John 1:14)

And if God is the creator of life it is down to him to say when it should start and end. A person does not have the freedom to decide to end his or her own or anyone else's life.

He said, 'Naked I came from my mother's womb, and naked shall I return there; the Lord gave, and the Lord has taken away; blessed be the name of the Lord.'

(Job 1:21)

Throughout the Bible there is also the command not to take life, and the biblical writers saw this as part of the covenant with God and his people: 'You shall not murder' (Exodus 20:13).

This idea of the Sanctity of Life is also part of the teaching of Natural Law which underlies the ethical teaching of the Catholic Church. Taking life is seen as intrinsically evil, and unborn life must be protected. Natural Law states that preserving the innocent is a primary precept and there are no exceptions which make it right. Natural Law does not look at the people involved in a decision about abortion, or the consequences of the action; instead, Natural Law considers the act of abortion itself. Reproduction is a primary precept and abortion goes against this, as it stops the purpose and outcome of procreation. In addition, if you consider the foetus to be a human person from conception, then abortion also goes against the primary principle to preserve innocent life.

In real life, however, issues are not quite as clear-cut and even in this day and age, in a developed country, pregnancy can be dangerous. In cases such as ectopic pregnancy, when the fertilised egg remains in the fallopian tube, the decision is clear, as continuing with the pregnancy will result in two deaths, but existing conditions in the mother such as heart complaints, high blood pressure, thrombosis and eating disorders can also cause serious problems. The most serious condition affecting pregnancy is cancer in its various forms. Here a decision must be made about treatment – after 12 weeks when the organs have formed, chemotherapy will not harm a foetus; however, radiotherapy will kill it especially in the first half of pregnancy. An expectant

Ensoulment

The moment when the soul enters the body – in traditional Christian thought this was at 40 days for boys and 90 days for girls. The Church now believes that life begins at conception.

Doctrine of double effect

An action where the main intention is to do good, but which may have a bad side-effect. The good intention makes the action right.

Embryo

The developing bundle of cells in the womb up to eight weeks' gestation.

Ordinary and extraordinary means

According to Natural Law, moral duties apply in ordinary situations. A patient may refuse certain treatments on the grounds that they are 'extraordinary' (i.e. over and above the essential).

woman has to make difficult decisions about treatment, as it is impossible to know what a safe interval between diagnosis and treatment may be, because diseases are different in different individuals.

In cases such as this, abortion may be justified using the doctrine of double effect; for example, in the event of an ectopic pregnancy (where the embryo has not implanted in the womb but is developing in the fallopian tubes) it is considered all right to remove the embryo, as the intention is to save the life of the mother rather than to kill the foetus. The death of the foetus is simply an unfortunate side-effect. This teaching does not mean that the abortion can be seen as the lesser of the two evils. This principle is also held by those who hold a weak sanctity of life stance. They realise that the advances of medical science have meant that the boundaries between life and death are far more flexible than previously thought and so would allow exceptions to the general sanctity of life position. They would appeal to extra-ordinary means as a justification for killing, and would apply the Christian principle of love and compassion. However, a major criticism of this view is that, like the doctrine of double effect, it is difficult to assess or know true intentions.

Weak Sanctity of Life is also the basis for other Christian responses to abortion; for example, the Church of England's report of 1965, *Abortion: An Ethical Discussion*, expresses overriding compassion for the needs of the mother, especially where there is a threat to her mental or physical health. This view was reinforced in a more recent document, *Abortion and the Church*, in 1993:

We do not believe that the right to life, as a right pertaining to persons, admits of no exceptions whatever; but the right of the innocent to life

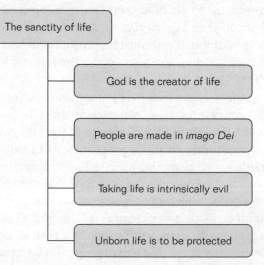

admits surely of few exceptions indeed. Circumstances exist where the character or location of the pregnancy renders the foetus a serious threat to the life and health of the mother, in such circumstances the foetus could be regarded as an 'aggressor' on the mother. The mother would be entitled to seek protection against the threat to her life and health which the foetal life represented.

Strengths of the Sanctity of Life argument

- It values *all* human life equally, regardless of status or gender.
- It states clearly that killing is always wrong and respects the individual's future.
- It gives everyone equal dignity.
- It avoids too much group pressure and power (e.g. to abort a disabled foetus).

Weaknesses of the Sanctity of Life argument

- Charles Darwin challenged the biblical view of imago Dei with his theory of natural selection.
- Kant saw no reason to link vital signs to valuing life – but he did link the possession of reason to valuing life.
- Peter Singer stated that to treat human life as having a special priority over animal life is 'speciesism'. So we ought to value all life and not just human foetuses.
- The Sanctity of Life view cannot cope with conflicts of duty – which life is more sacred: that of the mother or that of the foetus?

THE QUALITY OF LIFE

Some scholars think that those who hold a Sanctity of Life position as regards abortion make it work only by including quality of life arguments. The quality of life view allows the value of life to vary with its quality and may factor in the immanence of death, constancy of pain, an ability to think, an ability to enjoy life and make rational choices. However, when considering the foetus there is always the question of who benefits and whose quality of life is being judged: that of the foetus, the parents or society as a whole?

There is a danger here of 'playing God', and the quality of life approach may be seen as paternalistic, as it allows others to make decisions. Above all there is the fear that it fails to treat the foetus with dignity and could lead down a 'slippery slope' to genocide.

Quality of life
The belief that human life is not valuable in itself; it depends on what kind of life it is.

However, Peter Singer and Helga Kuhse both say that there is confusion, and that it would be better to drop the Sanctity of Life teaching and work out a quality of life ethic instead. This idea is based on what it means to be a person.

The quality of life

Is the foetus a person? Does the foetus have a right to life?

It has been argued that a person has to possess a concept of self – a person is self-aware; however, young babies are not self-aware and most people would agree that killing babies is killing human beings. Other possible criteria also need to be considered:

- A person has to be conceived by humans.
- A person has to have a human genetic structure.
- A person has to look like a human.
- A person has a soul.
- A person is viable – it can survive birth.
- A person has a future like ours.

Self-consciousness
Awareness of self as an independent being, the ability to feel pain and pleasure.

Personhood
Definition of a human being as a person – having consciousness, self-awareness, ability to reason and self-sufficiency.

Thought Point

1. What do you think makes a human life a person? This question is vital, as the answer depends on whether or not it is right to end the life of the foetus, and the answer is crucial for evaluating the following argument:

    *   The foetus is an innocent person.
    *   It is wrong to end the life of an innocent person.
    *   Therefore, it is wrong to end the life of a foetus.

2. So is a foetus a person, at which stage does it become a person and what are the necessary criteria for personhood?

Mary Anne Warren suggests the following criteria:

*   *sentience* – the ability to have conscious experiences
*   *emotionality* – the ability to feel happy, sad, loving
*   *reason* – the ability to solve new and complex problems
*   *the capacity to communicate*
*   *self-awareness* – awareness of oneself as an individual and as a member of a social group
*   *moral agency* – the ability to regulate one's actions through moral principles.

She goes on to say that it is not necessary to have all these attributes – many people do not meet all the criteria for personhood and are still considered persons. A foetus, however, does not have any of these attributes and is not a person, though some do develop in later foetuses (e.g. the ability to feel pain). One solution she considers is to regard the foetus as a *potential person*; she rejects this as a basis for giving the foetus a right to life.

Others think this is a significant idea, as if you kill a person the most important thing you take away from them is their future, and the same could be said for a foetus – they and others will never be able to enjoy and benefit from their potential talents. Looking at the foetus as a potential person also removes the difficult speculations about when the foetus has a soul or develops consciousness. However, at what point does a foetus become a potential person? In addition, is it right to judge a foetus by what it might be?

It is also possible to argue that, even though the foetus is a person, abortion may be morally justified. This is the view of Judith Jarvis Thomson, who disputes the idea that 'It is wrong to end the life of an innocent person'. She says that even if a foetus has the same right to life as any other human being, women are not morally obliged to complete every unwanted pregnancy. She bases her argument on the following analogy:

> But now let me ask you to imagine this. You wake up in the morning and find yourself in bed with an unconscious violinist. He has been found to have a fatal kidney ailment, and the Society of Music Lovers has canvassed all available medical records and found that you alone have the right blood type to help. They have therefore kidnapped you, and last night the violinist's circulatory system was plugged into yours, so that your kidneys can be used to extract poisons from his blood as well as your own. The director of the hospital now tells you 'Look we're sorry, the Society of Music Lovers did this to you – we would never have permitted it if we had known. But still, they did it, and the violinist now is plugged into you. To unplug him would be to kill him. But never mind, it's only for nine months. By then he will have recovered from his ailment, and can safely be unplugged from you.' Is it morally incumbent on you to accede to the situation?
>
> (Judith Jarvis Thomson, 'A Defense of Abortion')

Viability

Where a foetus is considered capable of sustaining its own life, given the necessary care.

This story raises a number of moral issues about rights and duties, but Judith Jarvis Thomson concludes that unwilling persons should not be required to be extremely Good Samaritans, whether towards violinists or towards foetuses, and suggests that there is a great gap between the claim that a human being has a right to life and the claim that other human beings are morally obliged to do whatever is necessary to keep anyone alive.

As we have seen, a potential life cannot have rights and obligations – sperm and an egg have the potential to become a human being, yet nobody would claim that the sperm and egg are a human being and should be treated as such. However, when a couple voluntarily cause an egg to be fertilised by a sperm with the intent of creating another life, there is a right to be born. What if the fertilisation was involuntary (rape) or accidental? This is what Judith Jarvis Thomson is examining – even if it is agreed that the embryo has the right to be kept alive, the mother cannot be obliged to carry this unwanted embryo. In addition, does the embryo have the right to use the mother's body and resources in order to sustain its own life?

A further problem about when a foetus becomes a person is the question of twins and the stage at which an embryo might divide into two or more individuals. Conception is not a single act but a process, and until about the fourteenth day it is not possible to say whether there will be a single or a multiple birth. Is it, then, possible to say that the single genetic identity established at conception is the basis for personhood? The Warnock Committee, whose recommendations were the basis for the 1990 Human Fertilisation and Embryology Act, chose the fourteenth day to distinguish the individual human embryo from a collection of cells and allowed them to be used for experimentation up to this stage. Jonathan Glover also argues that to call a foetus a person from conception stretches the term beyond normal boundaries.

Thought Point

1. Do we become an individual with rights only at birth?
2. Is the foetus a separate individual like the violinist or is it part of the woman's body?
3. Would unplugging the violinist be the same as actively killing him?
4. The violinist was forced on the woman against her will; does this mean that this argument supports abortion only in cases of rape?
5. Is there a point at which a foetus is not a human being?
6. Does a person's right to life outweigh your right to decide what happens in and to your body?

RELIGIOUS APPROACHES FOR AND AGAINST ABORTION

The religious approaches to abortion all hinge on the idea of the sanctity of life, and the idea of ensoulment. Definitions of when the soul enters the body have changed over time. Thomas Aquinas, following Aristotle, believed that male foetuses became 'animated' or acquired a soul only 40 days after conception, whereas females were believed to take longer to develop, with ensoulment taking place after 90 days. The Catholic Church now says that human life begins when the woman's egg is fertilised by the male sperm – or rather it says that, as it is not certain when life begins, it is safer to say it is at fertilisation. However, conception or fertilisation, the process by which the male sperm fertilises the female egg, is now known not to be a single moment, but rather a continuous process, taking two to twelve hours. Also to be considered is the recognition that, as late as fourteen days after conception, the embryo may divide into twins or triplets – this argument says that life cannot possibly begin at fertilisation because the soul cannot split, so the soul cannot enter the zygote (the pre-embryo) until the point when it can no longer split into more than one individual. Human life could continue to be sacred even if the point of its inception were advanced by a matter of days.

However, the Catechism of the Catholic Church says:

Human life is sacred because from its beginning it involves the creative action of God and it remains for ever in a special relationship with the Creator, who is its sole end. God alone is the Lord of life from its beginning until its end: no one can under any circumstance claim for himself the right directly to destroy an innocent human being.

(§2258)

The Catholic Church has consistently held the view that abortion is murder. In 1995 Pope John Paul II wrote specifically on abortion:

I declare that direct abortion, that is abortion willed as an end or as a means, always constitutes a grave moral disorder, since it is the deliberate killing of an innocent human being.

(*Evangelium Vitae* 62)

For many Catholics the stance against abortion is part of the Church's social teaching that the old, the young, the homeless, the immigrant, the unemployed, etc. must be helped to achieve a good quality of life. The Church argues that, if life is to be protected for the unborn, then it must be protected compassionately throughout life in practical ways.

The Church of England shares the Catholic view that abortion is against the moral law, but at the same time recognises that there can be situations where it may be morally preferable – such as when the pregnancy threatens the life of the mother, or there is very serious foetal disability.

Both the Catholic Church and the Church of England recognise the importance of the individual conscience in making important moral decisions such as abortion. Most Christians also consider saving the mother's life rather than that of the unborn – Catholics using the doctrine of double effect where the idea of proportionate need (saving life) is used even though the effect may be wrong (terminating the foetus). In a case such as an ectopic pregnancy, the bad side-effect (the death of the foetus) can be foreseen. However, there is a problem with this as it is sometimes possible to prevent a woman from having surgery by giving her an intramuscular injection of methotrexate, but the doctrine does not allow this as it kills the foetus. One of the problems with this doctrine is that it all depends on the intention of the doctor. Whether the death of the foetus is intentional or whether it is a side-effect, the result is the same.

ETHICAL ISSUES IN LEGISLATION ABOUT ABORTION

The issues of whether the embryo or foetus is alive, whether it is human, whether it is a person and whether it has human rights are some of the obvious ethical issues that arise from the legislation of abortion. These are dealt with in this chapter.

However, many also argue for women's right to choose what to do with their own bodies and that the right to abortion is vital for women to achieve their potential as far as employment, education prospects, incomes and opportunities are concerned. Some would argue that denying abortion is a barrier to full social, economic and political equality for women. This approach points out that women are also people, not just a container for the foetus. Pregnancy has a major effect on the woman involved as was pointed out in the famous Roe v. Wade case in the USA in 1973:

> A pregnancy to a woman is perhaps one of the most determinative aspects of her life. It disrupts her body. It disrupts her education. It disrupts her employment. And it often disrupts her entire family . . . this . . . is a matter which is of such fundamental and basic concern to the woman involved that she should be allowed to make the choice as to whether to continue or terminate her pregnancy.
>
> (C.M. Condit, *Decoding Abortion Rhetoric* pp. 99f.)

This, simply put, says that it is a woman's right to terminate her pregnancy. Feminists also see the right to abortion as necessary for any hope of equality between males and females. The feminist position is often seen as putting the rights of the woman above those of the foetus or the father – the mother's rights come first and so there is actually no room in the feminist position for the distinction that the current law makes between early and late abortions and therefore there should be no reason why a pregnancy should not be terminated at any time, not just on grounds of serious abnormality.

This leads us to consider another ethical issue arising from the current abortion legislation: that it can lead to discrimination against disabled people, and shows that society give little value to those who are disabled. However, the law does not force women who may be carrying a foetus with abnormalities to abort that foetus; rather the doctors seek to meet the woman's request if she feels she wants to end the pregnancy. In reality doctors often encourage women to abort if the foetus is abnormal in some way – assuming that it is in the public's interest if there are fewer children born with conditions such as Down's syndrome or spina bifida. A woman who is told that the foetus has Down's syndrome will often decide to abort it because she thinks that she will not be supported by society or by the health and education services if she goes ahead with the pregnancy.

The ethical issue that needs considering here is whether the woman should be allowed to make decisions on the basis of her own conscience, not on cultural or economic factors. However, often a woman is not supported in the consequences of her choices; she is expected to take responsibility for the disabled child if she continues with the pregnancy on the grounds that she had the opportunity to abort and chose not to. Newspapers often have articles about the lack of support for both parents and disabled children. All of this reinforces the idea that our free choices are made within our social, cultural, political, economic and religious society, so that sometimes the law just demonstrates the idea that there is no free choice.

On the other hand, we also need to consider what society would be like if there were no abortion law, with the dangers of 'back street' abortions, and a woman being forced to continue the pregnancy even at the risk to her own life.

ISSUES ARISING FROM ABORTION

Does the definition of human life stop abortion being murder?

Murder implies the killing of human beings, so in order to answer this question it is necessary to think what is meant by a human being.

Thought Point

Make a list of all the qualities you think a human being has – compare your list to that of Mary Ann Warren.

- Explain the difference between a person and a potential person.
- Does it matter that the foetus is just a potential person?
- Is a new-born baby still a potential person? Does that matter?

The foetus is physically dependent on the mother as without the mother's life-giving nutrients and oxygen it would die. Everything the mother does, from smoking to drinking alcohol, affects the foetus, and when things go wrong with the foetus it affects the mother. The foetus depends solely on the mother for its existence. This is different from the new-born baby who depends on society – on other people – to feed it, clothe it and love it. The foetus then is not an independent person so killing it is not murder. However, one could argue that killing a child before it reaches consciousness is not murder – a new-born baby, even one that is premature and in an incubator, still survives independently of the mother's body. Even if you consider that the foetus is not a human and so it is not murder to have an abortion it is still eliminating a potential life.

Can abortion ever be said to be good?

It is difficult to justify the elimination of a potential human life as good, though in some situations such as pregnancy as a result of incest or rape, it might be seen as the lesser of two evils. Killing is seen as evil, but allowed in certain situations such as self-defence, and according to Judith Jarvis Thomson abortion could be seen in the same way.

There are two ways of looking at this question. Deontological ethics would say that an action is always right or wrong. Natural Law would say that the abortion is never good as it goes against the primary precept to preserve the innocent and stops procreation. Kantian ethics also has difficulties when answering the question of whether abortion can ever be considered good; when the categorical imperative is applied to abortion there are immediate difficulties. Abortion would be hard to universalise, as there are so many different situations and motivations for obtaining an abortion – all consideration of emotions is to be disregarded and yet abortion is an emotional decision, especially in situations where the mother has been raped, is very young or is carrying a severely disabled foetus. Kant would also take no account of the stage of pregnancy at which the abortion is to take place.

There is also the emphasis on treating people as ends in themselves and not as a means to an end – abortion would go against this if the foetus is considered to be a person. Kant's stress on acting out of duty alone, with no account taken of compassion or love, means that all consequences are ignored whatever they may be. However, one could say that Kant does consider the human rights of the foetus.

More teleological ethical theories may consider abortion to be good in some situations. Utilitarianism does not accept the principle that human life has absolute value and that this should be upheld whatever the consequences, but attempts to assess each individual situation on its own merits to promote the greatest happiness for those concerned. However, Utilitarianism works only if it is actually possible to assess the results of an abortion and decide whether they favour all concerned. In practice this is difficult as we cannot predict all consequences – the mother may react badly to the operation, which may go wrong, leaving her unable to have further children and so on. Preference Utilitarianism might be a better approach to abortion, as it considers the preferences of the mother, the harm to other family members and so on.

Utilitarianism does not have one blanket answer to the question of whether abortion is good, but looks at the merits of each individual situation – it is easy here to make a judgement that depends primarily on an emotional response to a difficult situation. Ultimately who is to decide whether any particular woman's reason is good enough? The real question is perhaps how much value we place on human autonomy.

Do humans have a right to life?

The question of the rights of the foetus and the rights of the mother is seen by many ethicists as central to the debate about abortion. It is difficult to answer this question with a straight yes or no. A potential person must always be given full human rights unless its existence interferes with the right to life, freedom and the pursuit of happiness of an existing and conscious human being. In some ways then a foetus does not have rights before birth but as soon as it is born it has full human rights – the location seems to make all the difference. Logically it is not possible to have two entities with equal rights occupying the same body – one will always have a greater right to life. If that right is given to the foetus, it automatically cancels out the mother's right to life. After birth the baby is still in many ways a potential person, but it no longer occupies the same body as the mother and has the full support of the law in defending its right to life.

On the other hand many people will consider viability as the moment from which a foetus has the right to life, and this seems to be a gradual process depending on your viewpoint and beliefs about personhood. For religious believers the foetus has moral status and therefore the right to life simply because it is a creation 'in the image of God' – this sees the foetus as a person in the process of becoming, not a thing in the process of becoming a person: if the foetus is a person, it is sacred and, therefore, has the right to life.

Ultimately what determines our attitude to abortion is the value we place on the foetus and whether we consider it to be a human being from conception – so all these issues arising from abortion feed into each other and one cannot be considered without considering the others.

RELIGIOUS AND PHILOSOPHICAL TEACHINGS ON ABORTION

Buddhist perspectives

In traditional Buddhism, abortion is viewed as breaking the first of the four precepts: this forbids killing or injuring living beings. Buddhist teachings are that life begins at conception.

Also the Buddhist belief in rebirth means that the foetus is regarded as the carrier of the kammic identity of someone who has recently died and must therefore be given the same respect as an adult human. Human consciousness is viewed as something which is received at conception, not acquired later. Bad kamma grows the later a foetus is aborted and a Buddhist monk who assisted with an abortion could be thrown out of the monastic sangha. Even if an abortion is viewed as the result of an individual's past bad kamma this is still not an excuse.

Buddhism views suffering as part of life and therefore is unwilling to accept abortion even in cases of rape or if the child will be born with a severe disability. The Dalai Lama has suggested a milder approach, particularly if the baby will be disabled or its birth will cause suffering for the parents.

Some Buddhists will consider an abortion and, in this case, the stigma of the act increases the later it is performed.

Within Buddhism there are different approaches to ethics. Absolutism suggests that any act of murder will bring bad kamma. A Utilitarian approach considers that, if the abortion is carried out on compassionate grounds, it may create good kamma. Other, Virtue-based Buddhists believe that the ethics are determined by the motives of the mother and doctors. The Mahayana Buddhists of Japan see abortion as a 'sorrowful necessity' and the parents apologise to the unborn child while praying for a better rebirth.

Hindu perspectives

Hindu teaching about killing is based on the principle of ahimsa (non-violence). The foetus is considered to be a full human being from shortly after the implanting of the atman at conception. An abortion would deprive the foetus of its future life and the possibility of good karma. However, the atman will be reborn.

Hindu society often sees reproduction as a public duty. However, abortion may be accepted if the mother's life is at risk. Also, ahimsa may be seen as applying to an act which does the least harm to everyone involved and therefore there may be other conditions in which an abortion would be accepted.

The traditional practice of the sex selection of boys over girls is based on history and economics. Male children are seen as contributing more to the family and not requiring a dowry. However, Hindu teaching is clear that such considerations are not grounds for abortion.

Jewish perspectives

Jewish law argues that the foetus is not a full human being. The teaching about miscarriage in Exodus 21 suggests that an action which causes this requires financial compensation to the husband. Killing the mother is seen as murder because she is a human being. Killing the foetus is not murder because it is not a human being. The Mishnah permits abortion if the life of the mother is threatened by the pregnancy. During birth the degree to which the foetus is considered a human being depends on how far from the mother's body the foetus has emerged.

Orthodox Judaism permits abortion when the life of the mother is in danger. However, Reform Judaism will permit abortion where the pregnancy was due to rape, the child is likely to be severely disabled or the parents will suffer from the birth of a child. The decision must be taken by the mother, supported by others and abortion must not be considered as a form of birth control.

Muslim perspectives

Respect for all life as being the creation of Allah means that abortion is generally viewed as a crime in Islam.

Some Muslim scholars hold that the foetus becomes fully human at 120 days (seventeen weeks). This is seen as the time of 'quickening' (when the mother first feels the baby move) and also when the baby receives the human spirit (Surah 32:9). Muslim scholars agree that after this time an abortion may be performed only to save the mother's life. However, prior to this time there are differences of opinion, with Shi'ite scholars maintaining that abortion is forbidden from conception and Sunnis holding various different opinions. Some maintain that the role of the woman as a source of life may mean that abortion is the lesser of two evils.

In general the argument is that Allah is compassionate and that people may not be required to keep strict laws if circumstances such as poverty mean that a child may cause further suffering.

There is disagreement among Muslim scholars and authorities, with some suggesting that, in cases such as rape and incest, the period during which an abortion is allowed may be extended.

The strong, historic link between Islam and science means that new developments may influence opinion.

Sikh perspectives

Sikhism maintains that life starts at conception. Therefore any abortion acts against God's wishes and is a sin. However, abortion is often permitted in cases of rape or to save the life of the mother.

The traditional desire to produce sons rather than daughters and the use of abortion to facilitate this is condemned by the Sikh authorities.

REVIEW QUESTIONS

Look back over the chapter and check that you can answer the following questions:

1. Explain the link between abortion and the sanctity of life.
2. What is the Doctrine of Double Effect?
3. How might it be argued that abortion is not murder?
4. How might a consideration of rights affect the arguments in relation to abortion?

Terminology

Do you know your terminology?

Try to explain the following key ideas without looking at your books and notes:

- Abortion
- Consciousness
- Doctrine of double effect
- Embryo
- Ensoulment
- Foetus
- Hippocratic Oath

- Ordinary and extraordinary means
- Personhood
- Primitive streak
- Quality of life
- Sanctity of life
- Viability

SAMPLE EXAMINATION QUESTIONS

(a) Explain the ethical issues involved when a country legislates about abortion. (30 marks)

In your answer you should cover some of the following: the legality of abortion (e.g. in Catholic or Muslim countries); any time limits imposed; the rationale behind these time limits; conditions necessary to procure an abortion, and human rights issues.

(b) Assess which has more value: the life of a would-be mother or the life of her unborn child. (15 marks)

- You may debate: the issue of rights such as who has rights and the strength of those rights; potentiality v. actuality (Singer); effect on the future (Utilitarianism); Universal Law (Kant), and religious views.
- You may answer solely from a religious perspective or from an ethical perspective or from both.

Further information on world faiths can be found at: http://subknow.reonline.org.uk/.

6 Euthanasia and the Right to Life

Essential terminology

Active euthanasia
Assisted dying/suicide
Autonomy
Involuntary euthanasia
Passive euthanasia
PVS (permanent vegetative state)
Slippery slope
Voluntary euthanasia

WHAT YOU WILL LEARN ABOUT IN THIS CHAPTER

- Definitions of the different types of euthanasia.
- The idea of the sanctity of life and how it applies to euthanasia.
- Ideas of autonomy.
- The difference between killing and letting die, and acts and omissions.
- The approaches of different ethical theories to euthanasia.

Study hint

Many of the issues of medical ethics are progressing all the time as science and technology move forward. To stay abreast of these issues it is a good idea to keep a folder of relevant newspaper cuttings and annotate them with how you think the different ethical theories would react to the issue.

THE AQA CHECKLIST ✔

- Euthanasia: active or passive
- Ethical issues involved in legislation about euthanasia; voluntary and involuntary; hospices and palliative care
- The right of humans to determine when to die
- Arguments for and against abortion and euthanasia with reference to religious and ethical teachings

ISSUES ARISING

- Can euthanasia ever be said to be 'good'?
- Do humans have a right to life?

WHAT IS EUTHANASIA?

'Euthanasia' comes from the Greek *eu* meaning 'well' and 'easy', and *thanatos* meaning 'death'. Euthanasia is the intentional premature ending of another person's life either by direct means (active euthanasia) or by withholding medical treatment, food and hydration (passive euthanasia), because the patient asks for it (voluntary euthanasia) or without their express request (involuntary euthanasia).

Active euthanasia involves an actual act of mercy killing. For example, if a doctor decides that it is in the patient's best interest that they die and so kills them for that reason this is active euthanasia. This may be done by lethal injection by another person, but the patient would not die as quickly on their own. It is illegal in the UK and many other countries.

Passive euthanasia involves helping someone die because it is judged that it is better for the person to be dead. This may be when a doctor with-holds life-saving treatment with the intention that the patient dies – but it has to be done for concern for the patient, not to free up hospital beds, etc. It is practised in the UK, and many of those who oppose active euthanasia see no problem with it.

The ethical question that these two forms of euthanasia raises is whether it is the same thing to kill someone as it is to let them die.

Voluntary euthanasia is carried out at the request of the person. This is illegal in the UK, but it is legal in the Netherlands under medical super-vision. There is campaigning in the UK for the same law here. In the UK there are Do Not Resuscitate orders or DNRs which can be seen as a chosen form of passive euthanasia. However, they are controversial as there have been cases of DNRs written into patients' notes without their consent. Guidelines issued by the British Medical Association say that DNR orders should be issued only after discussion with the patient and/or their family.

Non-voluntary euthanasia occurs when it is impossible to get the patient's consent – perhaps they have lost the ability to make a decision or are still an infant.

Involuntary euthanasia is carried out against the wishes of the patient, and few people would defend this approach. However, it is possible for someone to be the victim of involuntary euthanasia – such as having a DNR order applied regardless of the patient's wishes.

The ending of a life by euthanasia may thus be either through acts of omission or through intentional acts. Note – the active/passive distinction cuts across the voluntary/non-voluntary, involuntary distinctions. There can be passive and active versions of each.

The debate about euthanasia includes the following issues:

- the sanctity of life and the idea that it is God-given
- the maintenance of life as an absolute
- whether the act is in itself wrong, or is made wrong by the consequences
- the question of personal autonomy
- the motives that lead to euthanasia
- the difference between killing and letting die.

ETHICAL ISSUES INVOLVED IN LEGISLATION ABOUT EUTHANASIA

Voluntary euthanasia is still illegal in the UK, but is legal in the Netherlands – so what do we have to learn from their approach? It is true that advancing medical technology, greater life expectancy and the problems associated with unbearable suffering have changed attitudes towards euthanasia, and some countries look to the Netherlands as an example. However, the culture in that country is very different and cannot just simply be imported into the UK. In the Netherlands medical care is among the best in the world and palliative care is well advanced, with palliative care centres attached to all hospitals, whereas in the UK people rely on relatively few hospices – and these are only partially funded through the NHS. Also in the Netherlands, since the time of the German occupation in the Second World War, there has been an excellent relationship of trust between doctor and patient, with most patients knowing their doctor well and for a long time. In the Netherlands the request for euthanasia is carefully regulated by law and it must be voluntary and carefully considered. Generally it is carried out in the patient's home.

The situation in Switzerland is slightly different and their law has allowed the charity Dignitas (founded in 1998 to allow those with terminal illnesses to die with dignity) to flourish. Under a Swiss law dating back to 1937, assisted suicide is a crime only if those providing assistance can be shown to have acted out of self-interest. Two-thirds of those who have died at Dignitas are foreigners – whereas in the Netherlands there is no provision for foreigners. There have been many concerns about this charity in the UK, especially since some of those who ended their lives there were not terminally ill; for example, Robert and Jennifer Stokes in 2003. One of the most controversial cases since then has been that of Daniel James, the Loughborough University student who was diagnosed as tetraplegic after a rugby scrum collapsed on him during a training session in March 2007. His parents were not prosecuted on their return to the UK as the Criminal Prosecution Service (CPS) said that it would not be in the public interest because the case was so tragic. However, according to the Director of Public Prosecutions this did not mean that there would be a change in the law, in spite of the efforts of organisations such as Dignity in Dying (formerly the Voluntary Euthanasia Society). He said: 'The law is there to protect the vulnerable. In this time of economic recession and cuts in care services, unbearable pressure could be placed upon the elderly and vulnerable to contemplate assisted suicide.'

In 2006 the House of Lords blocked an Assisted Dying Bill in the UK which would have allowed people with less than six months to live, who were suffering unbearably, of sound mind and not depressed, to end their lives. The bill was delayed but the government has said that it would not block a further hearing. However, the debate highlighted the divisions between those who support the right to die and those who want better palliative care. The religious leaders united to say in an open letter to both Houses of Parliament (7 October 2005):

> Assisted suicide and euthanasia will radically change the social air we all breathe by severely undermining respect for life . . .
>
> We, the undersigned, hold all human life to be sacred and worthy of the utmost respect and note with concern that repeated attempts are being made to persuade Parliament to change the law on intentional killing so as to allow assisted suicide and voluntary euthanasia for those who are terminally ill.

HOSPICES AND PALLIATIVE CARE

Research has shown that most seriously ill people want to die at home, in their own bed, surrounded by family and friends. However, the reality is that most die in hospital. Hospices are a vital alternative. However, they are not only for those with terminal illnesses in the last weeks of life. There are three main aims of hospice care:

- To relieve pain. Hospices specialise in pain control and have led research in this area. They aim to bring all pain under control with minimum side-effects such as hallucinations.
- To help the patients and their relatives face up to death. Many hospices are Christian in origin, but do not try to convert patients; instead they aim to allow people to discuss death, something that does not often happen in today's society.
- To care for the emotional needs of all concerned and give help with bereavement.

Hospices focus on the patient who is still alive and still has a life, albeit short, to live. So a hospice would give a more personal care than a hospital –

patients are encouraged to get dressed, to socialise and even to have their hair done. If the patient wants to be at home to die then nurses attached to the hospices or Macmillan nurses, who work specifically in the field of cancer care, will support them in their home.

Many Christians support hospices and believe that, if there were enough of them and they were well funded with enough spaces, then euthanasia would not be required. However, it is not certain in which way their work would continue were an Assisted Dying Bill to be passed.

Dame Cicely Saunders, who founded St Christopher's Hospice in 1967, said:

> Anything which says to the ill that they are a burden to their family and that they are better off dead is unacceptable. What sort of society could let its old folk die because they are in the way?

She believed that hospices make euthanasia unnecessary.

So the hospice movement is more than just about providing palliative care, but also about promoting quality of life, controlling pain and other symptoms. They also provide emotional and social support for the patient and the family. Hospices take a holistic approach and treat each patient as an individual; this is slightly different from the palliative care offered in hospitals in the Netherlands. Most hospices also provide a home care service so that people can be helped in the community, and also run day-care centres and take patients for respite care to allow their family or carers some time off. For many of those working in hospices their approach is more of a philosophy than a type of palliative care that just considers pain treatment. Hospice staff try to help with psychological, emotional and spiritual issues as well as pain management. Hospices also care for children and there are a growing number of specialist children's hospices in the UK. They not only care for children with terminal illnesses who are expected to die in childhood but also offer respite care for severely disabled children.

A syringe

RELIGIOUS APPROACHES FOR AND AGAINST EUTHANASIA

There is an explanation of the sanctity of life and personhood in Chapter 5 on abortion, but we also need to consider its particular application to the question of euthanasia. Human life is recognised by most people as 'something sacred', and believers also see it as a 'gift from God'. There are, however, different views on what it is that makes us human: many believers would say that we are human from conception or at the latest from birth, whereas others might say that we can only be considered human when we think and act as conscious human beings. According to the first viewpoint, we are fully human whether we are embryos or comatose patients – immature or damaged we are still persons – whereas others may argue that a patient who is in a persistent vegetative state (PVS) may be a human but is not really a person because he or she is unable to be so; thus in all important aspects they are already dead. If this view of personhood is taken to its logical conclusion, all sorts of people, including the mentally disabled and the paralysed, could also be considered as incomplete persons and so already dead.

The Sanctity of Life is central to the Catholic position, set out in the *Declaration on Euthanasia* (1980), which defines euthanasia as 'an act or an omission which of itself or by intention causes death, in order that all suffering may in this way be eliminated'. To do this to another or to ask it for oneself is not allowed – in accordance with Natural Law; the first primary precept is self-preservation and so death should not be hastened by euthanasia. The document does, however, recognise that, while a time to prepare for death is useful, suffering can be so great both physically and psychologically that it can make a person wish to remove it whatever the cost. It accepts that very few can follow the path of Blessed Mother Teresa of Calcutta and limit the dose of painkillers so as to unite themselves with the sufferings of Christ, but it also says that 'suffering has a special place in God's plan of salvation'.

The doctrine of double effect plays an important part in Catholic thinking about euthanasia according to the teaching of Pope Pius XII, which distinguishes between painkillers that have a secondary effect of shortening life and drugs used to hasten death with a secondary effect of killing pain. It is the intention which is all-important. The document says that it is 'important to protect, at the moment of death, both the dignity of the human person and the Christian concept of life against a technological attitude that threatens to become an abuse'. The document refers to 'ordinary' and 'extraordinary' means – ways of attempting to save life which are disproportionate to the pain suffered. A major problem here is how 'extraordinary' means are to be measured – there is a lack of clarity here, as 50 years ago a patient kept alive today on a life-support machine would have died. Issues of quality of life are now being seen as important, and when death is imminent a patient may

Active euthanasia
The intentional premature termination of another person's life.

Passive euthanasia
Treatment is either withdrawn or not given to the patient in order to hasten death. This could include turning off a life-support machine.

Voluntary euthanasia
The intentional premature termination of another person's life at their request.

Involuntary euthanasia
This term is used when someone's life is ended to prevent their suffering, without their consent, even though they are capable of consenting.

PVS (persistent vegetative state)
When a patient is in this condition, doctors may seek to end their life. The relatives have to agree and usually the patient must be brain-stem dead.

refuse unnecessary treatment so long as 'the normal care due the sick person is not interrupted'. The introduction of Proportionalism is significant, but not all Catholic scholars would agree with this.

Germain Grisez and Joseph Boyle stress the importance of personhood and reject the view that one can cease to be a person and yet be bodily alive – they do not accept that a patient in a persistent vegetative state has lost that which makes them distinctively human: a human being is one, and bodily life is seen as a good in itself. Grisez and Boyle say that there are certain basic goods necessary for human well-being, including play and recreation, knowledge of the truth, appreciation of beauty, life and health, friendship and integration. They do not require this list to be in any particular order but they would absolutely reject euthanasia, as it attempts to achieve one good, such as freedom and dignity, by putting it in direct conflict with another: life and health. These basic goods cannot be compared or balanced off each other, and the key issue for them where euthanasia is concerned is that it is against the basic good of life.

The question of personhood, however, lies at the heart of the Proportionalist position held by Daniel Maguire. This view states that life is a basic but not an absolute good and, while it is important to respect and value life, nobody should always be obliged to prolong it in every situation. Maguire rejects the idea that God alone has the power over life and death and that God alone should decide the time of death for each person; this seems to imply that we belong to God and are his property. He points out that we do, in fact, intervene to save life and to preserve it, and that there is no real difference between ending life and preserving it so long as the principle of achieving a good death is adhered to. Maguire uses the ideas of weighing up the proportional values of living in any condition and choosing a good death in certain specific circumstances. He recognises that this is a departure from the traditional Christian ethic of 'not destroying innocent life', and that making judgements between conflicting values is difficult and can lead to mistakes, but ethical reflection can lead to euthanasia being on some occasions a legitimate moral choice.

Euthanasia may also be seen as legitimate once the dying process has begun – this view still maintains the Sanctity of Life position and respects life, but the dying process shows that life has reached its limit. The use of euthanasia to shorten the time taken to die by not prolonging life is considered legitimate, as humans can still have power over this without denying the sanctity of life. Consideration of the quality of life looks at whether the use of extraordinary means would usefully improve the quality of life of the patient. This idea is basically Utilitarian, as doctors consider the possible length of life of the patient, their state of mind, how the procedure would enhance their life, the resources needed and even the resources available – essentially the QUALYS (quality adjusted life year schedules) used in the

> **Germain Gabriel Grisez (1929–)**
>
> Germain Grisez is an important and influential Catholic moral theologian. His best-known work is *Way of the Lord Jesus*. He is opposed to Utilitarianism and also to those who oppose the teaching of the magisterium of the Catholic Church. Grisez has developed a version of Natural Law theory, known as 'New Natural Law'.

USA. This is very different from the Catholic view which allows the patient to refuse treatment if there is 'an acceptance of the human condition, or a wish to avoid the application of a medical procedure disproportionate to the results that can be expected, or a desire not to impose excessive expense on the family or the community'. No one is obliged to have a medical procedure which is risky or burdensome.

This view is also supported by Joseph Fletcher and the Situation Ethics approach to euthanasia. Fletcher supported the view that a person had the right to die because, for a Christian, death is not the end and ending a life of great pain may be the most loving thing to do. According to this view the quality of life is considered more important than the sanctity of life, and any 'extraordinary means' of keeping the person alive is to be avoided. Fletcher argued that suffering and pain are purposeless, demoralising and degrading – we do not allow animals to suffer in the way we expect humans to. He considers that human personality and dignity are of greater value than life itself. Jesus teaching 'Blessed are the merciful' is just as important as any command against killing.

ETHICAL ISSUES INVOLVED IN VOLUNTARY AND INVOLUNTARY EUTHANASIA

A person's right to life corresponds to the duty of others not to kill that person. The idea of a duty not to kill seems to rule out any form of euthanasia – but we do not see the duty not to kill as absolute, as we think some wars can be justified, or killing in self-defence or in the defence of others as justified; even capital punishment is justified by some people. It is, in fact, easier to justify killing in voluntary euthanasia, where the person chooses death, than in these other cases, where the person who dies does not choose to do so.

Life is a person's most valued and precious possession; can this then be just overturned if the person no longer wishes to live? Can the right to life, like any other right, be overturned or renounced? If that happens, can others say that they have a duty to kill them? If the person asks for voluntary euthanasia, are they then actually asserting their right to be killed in a particular way? However, who then has the duty to kill them? Many doctors who are happy to let people die, withdraw treatment or even assist suicide may not be so happy about having a positive duty to kill at a patient's request. Many doctors will argue that euthanasia goes on already, as they will give patients painkillers in such doses that death will be hastened, and in the case of the brain-dead or those in persistent vegetative states they will withdraw or withhold treatment to bring about death. However, we do see a difference between killing (taking life) and letting die (not saving life). There is a right not to be killed, but no right to have one's life saved.

James Rachels saw no distinction between active euthanasia (killing) and passive euthanasia (letting die). If anything he believed that passive euthanasia is worse, as it is cruel and inconsistent and the process of dying may be long and drawn out, bringing about more suffering than is necessary. The result is the same – the patient is dead.

Many arguments concerning euthanasia, whether active or passive, are influenced by the fear that allowing one kind of euthanasia will be the first step on a slippery slope, and the value of human life will be depreciated and made subordinate to economics and personal convenience. Helga Kuhse challenges this 'slippery slope' view and concludes that the situation in the Netherlands is not following the example of Nazi Germany in making some lives valueless for reasons other than mercy or respect for autonomy.

Peter Singer believes that the traditional Sanctity of Life ethic must collapse and we need to develop a new ethic, as people now believe that the low quality of a person's life, as judged by the person, can justify them taking their life or justify someone else doing it for them. In cases where a person cannot make a judgement or express a view about the quality of their own life, someone else should do it for them. However, there is so much more that contributes to the quality of a person's life than that which can be measured medically, and Singer also fails to consider that a person's life has a value to the wider community as well as to the individual.

> **James Rachels (1941–2003)**
>
> James Rachels taught at the University of Richmond, New York University, the University of Miami, Duke University, and the University of Alabama at Birmingham. Rachels argued for moral vegetarianism and animal rights, preferential quotas, and the humanitarian use of euthanasia.

THE RIGHT OF HUMANS TO DETERMINE WHEN TO DIE

Suicide is the deliberate termination of one's own life, and many people, not only those who are religious, are appalled that people could even think of choosing death over life. They feel it demeans life and denies its meaning. All sorts of things give our life meaning – it may be 'God's plan' or it may be family or career – and suicide makes all this meaningless and trivial, as the act is not natural and breaks the timeless cycle of birth and death.

Henry Sidgwick said that only conscious beings can appreciate values and meanings, and so they see life as significant and part of some eternal plan, process or design. Suicide, therefore, is a statement by an intelligent, conscious being about the meaninglessness of life, but it is a statement which society rejects and in the past suicide was seen as a criminal act.

Suicide, then, breaks the social contract, but it also breaks the bond between God and humanity – Thomas Aquinas also saw suicide as an unnatural act and a rejection of God's gift of an immortal soul. This view lay at the heart of the old legislation about suicide, which the state had a right to prevent and punish.

Assisted dying or suicide
When a person takes their own life with the assistance of another person. When the other person is a doctor, it is called physician-assisted suicide.

Thought Point

1. Is the Sanctity of Life ethic out of date? What could replace it?
2. What problems do you see in the doctrine of double effect?
3. Is there any point to suffering and can it help a person to become nearer to God?
4. What problems do you foresee in stressing the quality of life?
5. Is it wrong to help humans to die when they are actually dying? How do we decide when the dying process has begun?

Today suicide is no longer illegal but the state still attempts to treat people as possessions and not allow them full autonomy and freedom – so the 'nanny state' protects drug addicts, alcoholics, smokers and the obese from themselves.

However, suicide is subject to a double moral standard: self-sacrifice in the form of martyrdom for either religious or political beliefs is admired, and for a believer such a death is seen as part of a journey leading to life with God; to die on the battlefield is courageous, and many people are involved in life-threatening occupations such as the fire and rescue service, the armed forces and the police; certain industries such as the manufacture of cigarettes, alcohol and armaments increase the mortality rate. Death here is controlled by religion, the state and political parties, whereas suicide is a free act and does not serve any social ends or uphold group values and structures.

- Is it morally justified to commit suicide to avoid forthcoming pain, loss of self-control or coma?
- Is it morally justified to ask others to help you commit suicide if you are incapable of doing it yourself?

John Stuart Mill (*On Liberty*, 1859) writes that in matters that do not concern others individuals should have full autonomy. Those who support voluntary euthanasia believe that personal autonomy and self-determination are paramount and any competent adult should be able to decide on the time and manner of their death.

The right to have one's life ended by euthanasia is the subject of ethical, social and legal limitations. In some countries such as the Netherlands and Belgium it is allowed and socially acceptable to have a doctor end one's life if death is imminent and the quality of life is very poor. However, the patient has to be of sound mind and to request death repeatedly.

However, what if the patient's wishes are based on faulty information about their illness or depression clouds their judgement? What if a cure is found just after the patient's death? What if the request for euthanasia is easier to respond to than providing good palliative care? Personal autonomy is an important value but it is often in conflict with other equally important ones – how do we work out which value overrides another and which are the true basic goods? Kant would value personal autonomy, but for Kant the outcome of an action is not relevant to whether it is right or not. He also disagreed with making moral choices out of compassion, kindness or any other emotion – only reason leads to right actions. However, applying the categorical imperative to euthanasia does not give a clear response. One could say that euthanasia on a universal scale would not be right as can be seen from his writings on suicide in the *Fundamental Principles of the Metaphysic of Morals*:

> Firstly, under the head of necessary duty to oneself: he who contemplates suicide should ask himself whether his action can be consistent with the idea of humanity as an end in itself. If he destroys himself in order to escape painful circumstances, he uses a person merely as a means to maintain a tolerable condition up to the end of life. But a man is not a thing, that is to say, something which can be used merely as means, but must in all his actions be always considered as an end in himself. I cannot, therefore, dispose in any way of a man in my own person so as to mutilate him, to damage or kill him.

Kant believed that human life should be treated only as an end in itself and never as a means to an end – suicide for Kant cannot be morally justified, and logically one could say the same about euthanasia. However, we are merely interpreting what we believe Kant said, and some modern followers of Kant could argue that a person's ends are best served by ending their suffering.

Autonomy
In ethics this means freely taken moral decisions by an individual.

Slippery slope
A concept used to suggest that when one moral law is broken others will also be gradually broken and there will be no moral absolutes.

Thought Point

In pairs or groups research one of the following and apply religious and ethical teaching to it:

1. Tony Bland and his doctor, Jim Howe
2. Diane Pretty
3. Annie Lindsell
4. Baby Charlotte Wyatt

5. Mary Ormerod
6. Terri Schiavo
7. Dr Anne Turner and *Dignitas*.

Further research

Dr Andrew Fergusson – chairman of Healthcare Opposed to Euthanasia (HOPE)
Dame Cicely Saunders – founder of the modern hospice movement
Baroness Warnock
Euthanasia in the news

RELIGIOUS AND PHILOSOPHICAL TEACHINGS ON EUTHANASIA

Buddhist perspectives

Essentially, Buddhism is opposed to euthanasia. Death is a very important event which links one life to the next. Buddhist teaching is that the state of mind of the dying person can impact on the next life and therefore people should have a 'good' death free of anxiety. The first precept, not to kill or injure a living being, means that it is difficult to approve of voluntary euthanasia where someone is required to end a person's life.

Buddhist monks in particular are forbidden from taking a life even if the quality of that life is very poor. Good or bad kamma is produced according to the intention of an act and therefore there is no distinction to be made between active or passive euthanasia. While personal freedom is an important aspect of Buddhist teaching, it does not extend to the right to take one's own life. Also, there is no guarantee that the ending of suffering in this life will mean that the next life will be better.

Compassion is not sufficient grounds for taking a life as the intent is still to kill. However, someone who is terminally ill and has accepted their death need not have their life preserved at all costs.

It is accepted that sometimes the amount of drugs necessary to relieve a person's pain and suffering may also hasten their death but the drugs are permitted as the intent is not to kill.

A person in a coma may appear to be unable to prepare themselves for a good death and create good kamma. However, because Buddhists value all living creatures, consciousness is not necessarily a relevant consideration, and it might be possible that some spiritual or mental activity is continuing. In these circumstances involuntary euthanasia is not therefore permissible.

The case is different when dealing with patients who are brain-dead. In these circumstances turning off a life support machine would not be considered as killing.

Hindu perspectives

Within Hinduism life has a very special place but not in the same way as the 'Sanctity of Life' ideas of Western traditions. There is great respect for long life but also a belief that, while life can work towards enlightenment, it can also hold it back. Liberation from samsara (the cycle of birth and death) is the goal of human life.

Hindu teaching on voluntary euthanasia is therefore based on four values:

- a general respect for life
- a belief that human life is necessary to reach enlightenment but that it can prevent it
- an idea of accepting death when it comes and rejoicing in it
- the heroism of honourably accepting defeat and heroic death in battle.

Hinduism may accept that someone in acute suffering or extreme old age might wish to free themselves from this. If someone in these circumstances asks for assistance this is acceptable but they must make their own decision. The lawgivers viewed self-willed death chosen by the individual on religious grounds as a legitimate way of dealing with suffering and old age and it was not considered suicide. In these circumstances voluntary euthanasia can be seen as a religious act following dharma.

There are different views, and some teachers maintain that it is essential for people to live through the four samskaras of life.

There is a conflict between Western opposition to self-willed death from, for example, voluntary starvation or medical assistance and there is an opinion that the concept of the freedom to die could be exploited and extended beyond religious belief. This might then introduce the concept of involuntary euthanasia which is unacceptable because Hinduism requires the individual to make the determination themselves. However, the releasing of the atman from the body might suggest that involuntary euthanasia be justified if, for example, the person was in a coma.

Jewish perspectives

In Judaism the approach to death is based on the approach to life. Therefore every moment of life should be celebrated with thanks to G-d. The idea that life is a gift from G-d means that death should not be hastened even when it is inevitable. Judaism is ultimately concerned with life rather than death.

Jewish law forbids taking a life unless in self-defence, in justified war or to save someone else. However, martyrdom is acceptable as a gift to G-d. Passive voluntary euthanasia is permitted if life is otherwise being prolonged artificially, and in certain circumstances passive involuntary euthanasia may be acceptable. Active euthanasia is always viewed as murder. This is based on the teaching that only G-d has the right to end a life and the quality of that life is not a relevant consideration. Life should not be prolonged artificially, however, if this prevents the natural end in death.

Muslim perspectives

In general, Islam condemns any form of 'mercy-killing'. Both the patient and the doctor are required to leave the decision of the time of death to God. However, in the case of brain death, for example, turning off life support could be seen as carrying out God's will. The Qur'an teaches that only God can take away life and that people should accept his will in relation to death. In cases of martyrdom, it is acceptable if someone kills themselves accidentally but not if they do so deliberately.

Disagreements between Muslim scholars over when life ends and whether there is simply a transition between this life and the next means that it is unclear as to whether it would always be acceptable to switch off life support when there appears to be no prospect of the person recovering.

Sikh perspectives

Sikhism views life as a gift from God. Therefore the human gurus opposed suicide. Suffering is part of life and creates karma. However, the unnecessary prolonging of life is not accepted, as caring for others is a central tenet of the faith.

REVIEW QUESTIONS

Look back over the chapter and check that you can answer the following questions:

1. (a) Explain the link between euthanasia and the sanctity of life.
    (b) Explain the link between euthanasia and the quality of life.
2. What is the difference between killing and letting die? Does it matter?
3. What are QUALYS?
4. Explain the methods and importance of the modern hospice movement.

Terminology

Do you know your terminology?

Try to explain the following ideas without looking at your books and notes:

*   Autonomy
*   Active euthanasia
*   Involuntary euthanasia
*   Voluntary euthanasia
*   Passive euthanasia
*   Slippery slope

❓ Examination Questions Practice

Read the question carefully – if it asks you to write about voluntary euthanasia, do not write about other sorts just because you know about them. Do not just reproduce 'My euthanasia essay'.

SAMPLE EXAMINATION QUESTIONS

(a) Examine the role and purpose of the hospice movement today. (30 marks)

In your answer you should show:

- awareness of the structure of the hospice movement as established by Cicely Saunders
- its links with religious faith
- the fact that people go to hospices to prepare for death but not necessarily to die
- support given to the family and patient both at home and at the hospice
- palliative care
- an awareness of the difference between the sanctity and quality of life.

(b) Assess the claim that humans have a right to life. (15 marks)

In your answer you need to consider the debate between the concepts of 'right' and 'life'. You may argue these from a religious perspective or an ethical one or both.

Arguments for a right to life include:

- The idea that we own our bodies, we can do with them what we like, even how and when we die (with examples).
- The idea of achieving our potential.
- The Universal Declaration of Human Rights.
- The quality of life debate.
- Utilitarian and Kantian concepts.

Arguments against a right to life include:

- God decides when we are born and when we die.
- We do not choose when we are born so why choose when we die?
- Hospitals may take parents or other family members to court for permission to terminate a life.
- Euthanasia is legal in some countries and some American states.
- It is often seen as a kindness to 'put someone out of their misery'.

Further information on world faiths can be found at: http://subknow.reonline.org.uk/.

AS UNIT B
RELIGION AND
ETHICS 2

7 Kant

Essential terminology

A posteriori
A priori
Absolute
Absolutism
Autonomy
Categorical imperative
Copernican Revolution
Duty
Good will
Hypothetical imperative
Kingdom of Ends
Law
Maxim
Summum bonum
Universalisability

WHAT YOU WILL LEARN ABOUT IN THIS CHAPTER

- Kant's understanding of pure reason, a priori knowledge and objectivity.
- Practical moral reason – the hypothetical and categorical imperatives.
- Kant's ideas of the moral law, good will, duty and the *summum bonum*.
- The strengths and weaknesses of Kant's theory of ethics.
- How to apply Kantian ethics to ethical dilemmas.

THE AQA CHECKLIST ✔

- The deontological approach; reason and morality; contrast with teleological approaches
- The theory of duty
- The categorical imperative
- *Summum bonum*
- The application of Kant's approach to **one** ethical issue of the candidate's choice **apart from environmental issues**.

ISSUES ARISING

- Can reason be the basis of a successful ethical system?
- What are the strengths and weaknesses of Kant's ideas as an ethical system?
- How important is duty in Kant's ethics?

**Immanuel Kant
(1724–1804)**

Portrait of Emmanuel Kant (oil
on canvas) by German School
(eighteenth century)

© Private Collection/The
Bridgeman Art Library

Immanuel Kant was born
in Königsberg, Prussia,
on 22 April 1724. He was
educated at the Collegium
Fredericianum and the
University of Königsberg.
He studied Classics and,
at university, physics and
mathematics. He had to
leave university to earn a
living as a teacher when his
father died. Later, he
returned to university and
studied for his doctorate.
He taught at the university
for 15 years, moving from
science and mathematics
to philosophy. He became
Professor of Logic and
Metaphysics in 1770. He
held unorthodox religious
beliefs based on
rationalism rather than
revelation, and in 1792 he

- Are Kant's ideas about human beings realistic?
- How compatible are these aspects of Kant's ethics with a religious approach to ethics?

WHAT IS KANT'S THEORY OF ETHICS?

Immanuel Kant believed in an objective right and wrong based on reason. We should do the right thing just because it is right and not because it fulfils our desires or is based on our feelings. We know what is right not by relying on our intuitions or facts about the world but by using our reason. To test a moral maxim, we need to ask whether we can always say that everyone should follow it and we must reject it if we cannot.

Kant opposed the view that all moral judgements are culturally relative or subjective so that there are no such things as moral absolutes. Kant's approach to ethics was deontological, where the right takes precedence over the good, and basic rights and principles guide us to know which goods to follow. Modern deontology avoids too close a link with Kant and rejects his absolutism and complete disregard for consequences; however, his moral theory has been and continues to be influential.

KANT'S COPERNICAN REVOLUTION

In order to understand Kantian ethics it is important to understand the philosophical background and the time in which he lived. Kant's ethical theory was a product of its time and of Kant's reaction to that time, in which great philosophical upheavals were taking place. Kant, like Descartes, started off as a rationalist, believing that we know truth through the mind. Opposed to this view were the empiricists such as Locke, Berkeley and Hume who argued that human knowledge comes from our experiences. This leads to Utilitarian ethics of some sort. Kant eventually moved to a midway position between rationalism and empiricism.

Kant's main area of study was to investigate the formal structures of pure reasoning, causality, a priori knowledge (knowledge not based on experience) and the question of objectivity. He wrote these ideas in the *Critique of Pure Reason* (1781; 2nd edn 1787). He then went on to demonstrate the formal structure of practical-moral reasoning in the *Critique of Practical Reason* (1788) and to study the conditions of the possibility of aesthetics and religion in the *Critique of Judgement* (1790).

Kant's work was a reaction against the rationalists and empiricists, and he was concerned with the problem of objective knowledge: can I have any knowledge of the world that is not just 'knowledge of the world as it seems to me'? He is asking: 'How do we know what we know and what does it mean to know?'

The views of other philosophers about knowledge include the following:

- Descartes (1596–1650) – believed that the foundation of knowledge is the knowledge of one's own existence: 'I think therefore I am.' Kant criticised this, as he said it did not tell us what 'I' is, or even that it is.
- Leibniz (1646–1716) – thought that we can have knowledge untouched by the point of view of any observer.
- Hume (1711–1776) – argued that we cannot have any objective knowledge at all.

Kant is closer to the rationalist views of Descartes and Leibniz and opposed to the empiricist views of Hume, which spurred him to explain his own view. Kant considers that our knowledge is not of the world as it is in itself, but of the world as it *appears* to us. If our sense organs were different, our languages and thought patterns different, then our view of the world would be different. Kant is saying that humans can never know the world as it really is (the thing in itself) because as it is experienced it is changed by our minds – the world we now see is a *phenomenon* (like a reflection in a mirror). Kant argued that various structures or categories of thought (space, time and causality) were built into the structure of our minds – we have been pre-programmed. This means that all we can really know about scientifically are our own experiences and perceptions, which may or may not correspond to ultimate reality.

Kant called this analysis the Copernican Revolution, as its implications for us are just as vital as the implications of believing that the solar system revolves around the sun. Science then can never give us any knowledge of objective reality, as it can never move beyond the view of the world given to us by the categories of our mind. However, Kant did think that these categories could be described as objective, as they are the objective laws of our mind – this is *pure reason* and tells you what is the case.

Kant argued that the mind determines the way in which we experience things, not the external things themselves – so his starting point for ethics is obligation in the mind that says 'I ought . . .'

KANT'S MORAL THEORY

Practical reason looks at evidence and argument and tells you what ought to be done. This sense of the moral 'ought' is something which cannot simply depend on external facts of what the world is like, or the expected consequences of our actions. Kant saw that people are aware of the moral law at

was forbidden by the king from teaching or writing on religious subjects. When the king died in 1797, Kant resumed this teaching and in 1798, the year after he retired, he published a summary of his religious views. He died on 12 February 1804.

René Descartes (1596–1650)

René Descartes is often called the founder of modern philosophy. He was born in Touraine and was educated at a Jesuit school – La Flèche in Anjou. Here he studied mathematics and scholasticism. He then studied law at Poitiers and later took up a military career.

He went to Italy on pilgrimage in 1623–1624 and then, until 1628, he studied philosophy in France. He moved to the Netherlands in 1628 and, in 1637, published his first major work: *Essais Philosophiques* (Philosophical Essays). This book covered geometry, optics, meteors and philosophical method.

He died from pneumonia in 1650.

Gottfried Wilhelm Leibniz (1646–1716)

Gottfried Wilhelm Leibniz was a German philosopher, mathematician and statesman. He was born in Leipzig and studied at the universities of Leipzig, Jena and Altdorf.

In 1666 he began work for Johann Philipp von Schönborn, who was archbishop elector of Mainz. In 1673 Leibniz went to Paris. From 1676 until 1716 he was librarian and privy counsellor at the court of Hanover. His work comprised diplomacy, history, law, mathematics, philology, philosophy, physics, politics and theology.

Copernican Revolution
The discovery by Copernicus that the solar system revolves around the sun. Kant's analysis is often referred to thus metaphorically, as its implications for us are just as vital.

work within them – not as a vague feeling but a direct and powerful experience.

> Two things fill the mind with ever new and increasing admiration and awe the oftener and more steadily we reflect on them: the starry heavens above me and the moral law within me.
>
> (*Critique of Practical Reason*)

Kant's moral theory is explained in the *Groundwork of a Metaphysics of Morals* (1785): it tries to show the objectivity of moral judgement and the universal character of moral laws and attempts to base morality on reason as opposed to feelings, inclinations, consequences or religion. He roots his view of morality in reason to the exclusion of everything else, and rejects especially Hume's idea that morality is rooted in desires or feelings. Kant saw emotions as a threat to the autonomy of the moral agent, as we can be so easily swayed by them, so we cannot choose freely. He does not reject desires and feelings, but says that they have nothing to do with morality. Only reason is universal. It may be human nature to feel emotions, but for Kant the moral agent uses reason and will; there is no room for emotions. Emotions can lead to individual variations which are not possible to universalise – so we might give money to beggars one day because we feel sorry for them, but ignore them on another day as we are preoccupied and upset by a row we had that morning. Kant does not condemn compassionate acts but says that they are not moral but amoral. We cannot praise someone for having compassionate and sympathetic inclinations. If we are to choose freely to do the right thing, emotions cannot get in the way.

Kant approached morality in the same way as he approached knowledge (looking at the a priori categories through which we make sense of the world) – he looked for the categories we use: what makes a moral precept moral? Kant declared that these were rooted in rationality, were unconditional or categorical, completely unchanging and presupposed freedom.

Freedom

For Kant, if I am to act morally then I must be capable of exercising *freedom* or autonomy of the will. The opposite of this is *heteronomy* – that something is right because it satisfies some desire, emotion, goal or obligation. Kant sees two sorts of freedom: free actions which follow the correct process of reasoning – actions done by duty not hindered by emotions, desires or goals; and actions which are free from external forces: for example, a bank clerk who gives the money to a robber because they have a gun held to their head is not performing a free action, any more than the bank clerk who refuses to hand over the money because they want to be seen as a hero is performing a free action.

Reason must not be subservient to anything else even if this is the happiness of the majority.

Good will

The idea of a 'good will' is Kant's starting point for his morality. For Kant the sense of moral obligation is to be found in the mind, not by considering experiences.

> It is impossible to conceive of anything at all in the world, or even out of it, which can be taken as good without qualification, except a good will. Intelligence, wit, judgement and any other talents of the mind we care to name, or courage, resolution, and constancy of purpose, as qualities of temperament, are without doubt good and desirable in many respects; but they can also be extremely bad and hurtful when the will is not good which has to make use of these gifts. . . . Good will, then, like a jewel, it would still shine by its own light, as a thing which has its whole value in itself. Its usefulness or fruitfulness can neither add to nor take away anything from this value.
>
> (*Groundwork for the Metaphysics of Morals*, 1785)

It is only the 'good will' which counts and which is the starting point for ethics. Abilities, talents and even virtues count for nothing, as do consequences. Only the will is within our control and so only the will can be unconditionally good and can exercise pure practical reason. This will means the total effort involved in making a conscious moral choice. Thus the morality of an action must be judged by the motivation behind it – so if two people (Jack and Jill) perform the same act for the same reason, but events beyond Jill's control prevent her from achieving it, she is still praiseworthy even if she did not succeed. Both Jack and Jill can be judged equal on moral grounds in terms of the will behind their actions.

This is the opposite of Hume's argument that morality is based only on making people happy and fulfilling their desires – it is just a servant of the passions, and morality is founded on our feelings of sympathy for others and depends on our human nature.

A posteriori
Used of a statement which is knowable after experience.

A priori
Used of a statement which is knowable without reference to any experience.

David Hume (1711–1776)

David Hume was born in Edinburgh on 7 May 1711. He was a historian and philosopher. He influenced the development of scepticism and empiricism. He worked in an office in Bristol for a short time and then moved to France.

A Treatise of Human Nature was published in three volumes between 1739 and 1740. Hume went back to his family home in Berwickshire and worked on *Essays Moral and Political*, published in 1741 to 1742.

Hume moved to Edinburgh in 1751 and became librarian of the Advocates' Library. He was a friend of Jean-Jacques Rousseau and brought him to Britain, but the friendship collapsed owing to Rousseau's mental condition. Hume died on 25 August 1776.

Autonomy
Self-directed freedom, arriving at moral judgement through reason.

Absolute
A principle that is universally binding.

Hume

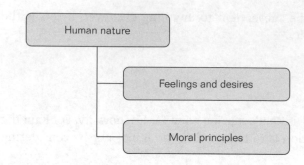

Duty is what makes the good will good. It is important that duty should be done for its own sake and it does not matter whether you or others benefit from your action – our motives need to be pure. Doing duty for any other reason – inclination, self-interest, affection – does not count. The good will chooses duty for duty's sake.

Kant does not rule out pleasure in doing one's duty, but pleasure will not help us to know what duty is or the morality of our actions. According to Kant, there is no moral worth in the feeling of satisfaction we get from doing our duty – if giving to charity out of love for others gives you that warm glow of having helped others, it is not necessarily moral. If I give to charity because duty commands it, then I am moral. So, even though the act of giving to charity has the same result, according to Kant one way is moral and the other is not. *We are not moral for the sake of love but for duty's sake only.* He is arguing against Hume that duty and reason can help us guide our emotions so that we are not dominated and ruled by them.

Duty: a charity collection box

Kant

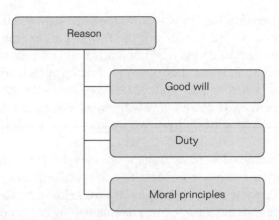

Reason
- Good will
- Duty
- Moral principles

Kant was looking for some sort of objective basis for morality – a way of knowing our duty. Practical reason, therefore, must give the will commands or imperatives. He makes the distinction between two kinds of imperatives – non-moral (hypothetical) and moral (categorical).

THE HYPOTHETICAL IMPERATIVE

Hypothetical imperatives are not moral commands to the will, as they do not apply to everyone. You need to obey them only if you want to achieve a certain 'goal' – that is why a hypothetical imperative always begins with the word 'if'.

For example: *if* I want to lose weight I ought to go on a diet and exercise more. A hypothetical imperative depends on the results and aims at personal well-being.

THE CATEGORICAL IMPERATIVE

Categorical imperatives, on the other hand, are *moral commands* and do not begin with an 'if', as they tell everyone what to do and do not depend on anything, especially desires or goals. According to Kant these categorical imperatives apply to everyone (like the categories of pure reason which apply to everyone) because they are based on an *objective a priori law of reason* which Kant calls the categorical imperative. This is a test to judge whether an action is in accordance with pure practical reason. There are a number of different forms of this, but they are variations on three basic ones:

Absolutism
An objective moral rule or value that is always true in all situations and for everyone, without exception.

Good will
Making a moral choice expresses good will.

Duty
A motive for acting in a certain way which shows moral quality.

Hypothetical imperative
An action that achieves some goal or end.

Categorical imperative
A command to perform actions that are absolute moral obligations without reference to other ends.

Law
Objective principle, a maxim that can be universalised.

Maxim
A general rule in accordance with which we intend to act.

First formulation

Act only according to that maxim whereby you can at the same time will that it should become a universal law. Kant calls this the *Formula of the Law of Nature*. This first formulation of the categorical imperative asks everyone to universalise their principles or maxims without contradiction. In other words, before you act ask yourself whether you would like everyone in the same situation to act in the same way. If not, then you are involved in a *contradiction* and what you are thinking of doing is wrong because it is against reason.

Kant always wants to universalise rules, as he wants everyone to be free and rational, and if rules are not universalisable then others will not have the same freedom to act on the same moral principles as I use. However, Kant does not claim that everyone should be able to do the same thing as I choose to do in order for it to be moral – but rather everyone should be prepared to act on the same maxim.

Kant uses promise-keeping as an example. I cannot consistently will that promise-breaking for my own self-interest should be a universal law. If I try to make a universal law of the maxim 'I may always break my promises when it is for my benefit', the result will be that there is no point in anyone making promises – this is inconsistent and so cannot be a moral imperative.

To make his argument as clear as possible Kant uses four examples, including the one of promise-keeping, in *Groundwork of the Metaphysics of Morals,* 1785:

- A man feels sick of life as a result of a series of misfortunes that have mounted to the point of despair, but he is still so far in possession of his reason as to ask himself whether taking his own life may be contrary to his duty to himself. He now applies the test 'Can the maxim of my action really become a universal law of nature?' His maxim is 'From self-love I make it my principle to shorten my life if its continuance threatens more evil than it promises pleasure'. The only further question to ask is whether this principle of self-love can become a universal law of nature. It is then seen at once that a system of nature by whose law the very same feeling whose function is to stimulate the furtherance of life should actually destroy life would contradict itself, and consequently could not subsist as a system of nature and is therefore entirely opposed to the supreme principle of all duty.
- Another finds himself driven to borrowing money because of need. He well knows that he will not be able to pay it back; but he sees too that he will get no loan unless he gives a firm promise to pay it back within a fixed time. He is inclined to make such a promise; but he still has enough conscience to ask: 'Is it not unlawful and contrary to duty to get

out of difficulties in this way?' Supposing, however, he did resolve to do so; the maxim of his action would be: 'Whenever I believe myself short of money, I will borrow and promise to pay it back, though I know that this will never be done.' Now this principle of self-love or personal advantage is perhaps quite compatible with my own entire future welfare; only there remains the question 'Is it right?' I therefore transform the demand of self-love into a universal law and frame my question thus: 'How would things stand if my maxim became a universal law?' I then see straight away that this maxim can never rank as a universal law of nature and be self-consistent, but must necessarily contradict itself. For the universality of the intention not to keep it would make promising, and the very purpose of promising, itself impossible, since no one would believe they were being promised anything, but would laugh at utterances of this kind as empty shams.

- A third finds in himself a talent whose cultivation would make him a useful man for all sorts of purposes. However, he sees himself in comfortable circumstances, and he prefers to give himself up to pleasure rather than bother about increasing and improving his fortunate natural aptitudes. Yet he asks himself further: 'Does my maxim of neglecting my natural gifts, besides agreeing in itself with my tendency to indulgence, agree also with what is called duty?' He then sees that a system of nature could indeed always subsist under such a universal law, although (like the South Sea Islanders) every man should let his talents rust and should be bent on devoting his life solely to idleness, indulgence, procreation and, in a word, to enjoyment. Only he cannot possibly will that this become a universal law of nature or should be implanted in us as such a law by a natural instinct. For as a rational being he necessarily wills that all his powers should be developed, since they serve him, and are given to him, for all sorts of possible ends.

- Yet a fourth is himself flourishing, but he sees others who have to struggle with great hardships (and whom he could easily help); and he thinks: 'What does it matter to me? Let everyone be as happy as heaven wills or as he can make himself; I won't deprive him of anything; I won't envy him; only I have no wish to contribute to his well-being or to support in distress!' Now admittedly, if such an attitude were a universal law of nature, humankind could get on perfectly well – better no doubt than if everyone prates about sympathy and good will and even takes pains on occasion to practise them, but on the other hand cheats where he can, traffics in human rights, or violates them in other ways. But although it is possible that a universal law of nature could subsist in harmony with this maxim, yet it is impossible to will that such a principle should hold everywhere as a law of nature. For a will which decided in this way would be in conflict with itself, since many a situation might arise in which the man needed love and sympathy from others, and in which by such a law of nature sprung from his own will he would rob himself of all hope of the help he wants for himself.

Kant's followers disagree about how to apply this universal law test. Hare suggests an alternative approach to test a proposed moral maxim:

- Try to understand the consequences of following it on affected individuals.
- Try to imagine yourself in the place of these individuals.
- Ask yourself whether you want the maxim to be followed regardless of where you imagine yourself in the situation.

The challenge then is to distinguish right maxims from wrong ones. This is the role of reason in choosing only maxims that can be universalised.

Second formulation

So act as to treat humanity, whether in your own person or in that of any other, never solely as a means but always as an end. Kant calls this the *Formula of End in Itself*. He means that we should not exploit others or treat them as things to achieve an end, as they are as rational as we are. To treat another person as a means is to deny that person the right to be a rational and independent judge of his or her own actions. It is to make oneself in some way superior and different. To be consistent we need to value everyone equally.

Kant saw the first two formulations as two expressions of the same idea. He summed this up as follows: 'Principles of action are prohibited morally if they could not be universalised without contradiction, or they could not be willed as universal laws' (*Groundwork of the Metaphysics of Morals*).

The third formulation follows from the other two.

Third formulation

Act as if a legislating member in the universal Kingdom of Ends. This Kant calls the *Formula of a Kingdom of Ends*. Everyone should act as if every other person was an 'end' – a free, autonomous agent. Kant believed that each person is autonomous and moral judgements should not be based on any empirical consideration about human nature, human flourishing or human destiny. However, this idea of the autonomy of the individual does not mean that everyone can just decide their own morality, but rather that each

Kingdom of Ends

A world in which people do not treat others as means but only as ends.

individual has the ability to understand the principles of pure practical reason and follow them. Pure practical reason must be impartial and so its principles must apply equally to everyone.

Any law which persons make for themselves must also be seen as binding upon others. So you have to imagine yourself as a person writing a law for a new kingdom, in which everybody must treat everybody else as ends in themselves. Any action that ignores the individual dignity of a human being in order to achieve its ends is wrong.

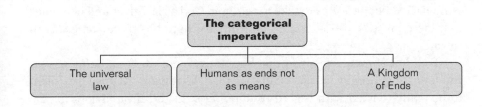

Thought Point

1. Why does Kant believe that the 'good will' is the only thing that is good without qualification? Can you think of anything else that is good without qualification? What are Kant's supporting reasons? Do you agree with him?

2. How would Kant suggest that, where there is a clash of duties, we know what takes precedence by following the categorical imperative? Does this work? Discuss the following:

   • It is your turn to make a presentation in class and you are running late. On the way you witness a car crash and are asked to wait to make a statement to the police.

   • If only actual persons are ends in themselves, how would a Kantian approach a student who accidentally becomes pregnant and decides to have an abortion so as to continue her studies?

   • 'If I had to choose between betraying my country and betraying my friend I hope I should have the guts to betray my country' (E.M. Forster). Do you agree?

THE THREE POSTULATES OF PRACTICAL REASON

Apart from making the individual the sole authority for moral judgement, Kant's theory of ethics seems to grant freedom to do anything that can be consistently universalised. This morality sets limits but does not give direct guidance; therefore, in order for it to make sense Kant has to postulate the existence of *God*, *freedom* and *immortality*.

Kant's ethical theory could, in fact, be said to be a religious morality without God but he seems to take for granted God as lawgiver and he argues that there must be a God and an afterlife, as there has to be some sort of reward.

Kant has already explained that happiness is not the foundation or reason for acting morally, but he claims that it is its reward. Kant's ideas seem to be really twisted with regard to happiness. In the *Groundwork for the Metaphysics of Morals* (1785) he writes:

> The principle of personal happiness is the most objectionable not merely because it is false and because its pretence that well-being always adjusts itself to well-doing is contradicted by experience; not merely because it contributes nothing to morality (since making a man happy is quite different from making him good) but because it bases morality on sensuous motives.

However, he also says that we have a duty to make ourselves happy, not because we want to be happy but because it is necessary for us to do our other duties. Kant seems to put duty in a sort of vacuum, totally separate from our everyday lives.

To solve this dilemma Kant looks at the postulates of *God* and *immortality*: after death, in the next world, there is no conflict between 'duty' and 'happiness', as 'duty' is part of the natural harmony of purposes created by God. Kant thought that our aim in acting morally is not to be happy but to be worthy of being happy. The *summum bonum* or highest good is a state where happiness and virtue are united – but for Kant it is the virtuous person who has a 'good will' which is vital for morality; happiness is not guaranteed. The summum bonum, however, cannot be achieved in this life and so there must be life after death where we can achieve it – thus for Kant, morality leads to God.

Kant stresses that the summum bonum also means the *bonum consummatum* – achieving the good. This achievement of the good is a state of happiness and fulfilment. Doing your duty then results in this state of happiness and fulfilment – the highest good – which must be achievable.

Summum bonum
The supreme good that we pursue through moral acts.

STRENGTHS OF KANT'S THEORY OF ETHICS

- Kant's morality is very straightforward and based on reason.
- There are clear criteria to assess what is moral.
- The moral value of an action comes from the action itself.
- Kant's categorical imperative gives us rules that apply to everyone and command us to respect human life.
- It makes clear that morality is about doing one's duty and not just following feelings or inclinations. This means that we cannot assume that what is good for us is morally good and so good for everyone else. This is Kant's equivalent of the Golden Rule of Christian ethics.
- It aims to treat everyone fairly and justly and so corrects the Utilitarian assumption that the minority can suffer so long as the majority are happy.
- Kant sees humans as being of intrinsic worth and dignity as they are rational creatures. Humans cannot be enslaved or exploited. This is the basis of the Universal Declaration of Human Rights.

WEAKNESSES OF KANT'S THEORY OF ETHICS

- Kant's theory is abstract and not always easily applied to moral situations – it tells you what *types* of actions are good, but it does not tell you what is the right thing to do in particular situations. As Alasdair MacIntyre points out, you can use the universalisability principle to justify practically anything:

> all I need to do is to characterise the proposed action in such a way that the maxim will permit me to do what I want while prohibiting others from doing what would nullify the action if universalised.
> (Alasdair MacIntyre, *A Short History of Ethics*)

Universalisability

If an act is right or wrong for one person in a situation, then it is right or wrong for anyone in that situation.

- Kant's emphasis on duty seems to imply that an action is made moral by an underlying intention to do one's duty. However, it is not always possible to separate 'intentions' from 'ends', as intentions are closely linked with what we do (e.g. intending to come to the help of a friend who is being beaten up is not the same as actually doing so). In addition, our motives are not always pure and people seldom act from pure practical reason; we more often help others because we like them or we feel sorry for them. Some philosophers think that putting duty above feeling is cold and inhuman. Kant's theory severs morality from everyday life and everyday feelings and emotions.

- Many people would consider that thinking about the result of an action is an important part of ethical decision making, and, if the outcome hurts another person, most people would feel guilty.
- Kant's system seems to work only if everyone has the same view of the final purpose and end of humans. It depends on some notion of God to justify this rationally ordered world. We do not all even have the same views on life and obeying the moral law could put one at a real disadvantage when dealing with people who are wicked, amoral or simply less rational.
- Kant is clear when explaining the conflict between duty and inclination but he does not help us understand the conflict between different duties, each of which could be justified.
- In addition, though Kant tells us in general terms to respect others and not treat them as ends, this does not tell us what to do in individual cases. What about the terminally ill patient who wants help to die? What about protecting the innocent victim from murderers? What about stealing a drug to help a loved one to live? What about conscription in time of war? Kant's theory here seems to lead either to a position where no decision can be made or to a situation where I may consider doing my duty as just plain wrong.

THE THEORY OF W.D. ROSS

These problems with Kant's theory of ethics led W.D. Ross to make certain changes. He argued that exceptions should be allowed to Kant's duties – Ross called these *prima facie duties* (first sight duties). These duties are conditional and can be outweighed by a more compelling duty (e.g. 'Never take a life' could be outweighed by 'Never take a life except in self-defence').

Ross lists seven prima facie duties:

1. fidelity or promise-keeping
2. reparation for harm done
3. gratitude
4. justice
5. beneficence
6. self-improvement
7. non-maleficence.

These stress the personal character of duty. The first three duties look to the past and the last four to the future, but they do not need to be considered in any particular order, but rather as to how they fit the particular situation. For example, whom should I save from drowning: my father or a famous doctor?

A Utilitarian would save the doctor because he or she could help more people. Ross says we have a special duty of gratitude to our parents which outweighs any duty to a stranger. Ross shows that there are possible exceptions to any rule and these exceptions depend on the situation in which I do my duty, the possible consequences of doing my duty and the personal relationships involved.

Problems with Ross's theory:

* How do we know what a prima facie duty is?
* How do we know which one is right where there is a conflict between them?

Ross says that we simply know which acts are right by consulting our deepest moral convictions, but is this an adequate response? Can we be sure that Ross's list of duties is correct?

RELIGIOUS ETHICS AND KANTIAN ETHICS

Kantian ethics would seem, at first glance, to fit well with Christian ethics, especially the second formulation of the categorical imperative which gives humans intrinsic value and says that they should not be treated as 'means to an end but as ends in themselves'. This intrinsic value is clearly seen in biblical ethics: 'So God created man in his own image' (Genesis 1:27a). For Kant, as for Christian ethics, the end can never justify the means. Kant's idea of universalisability is: if you can will your action to be universalised, then it would be an action that would be considered good in all situations, including your own. Again this is the same as Jesus' Golden Rule (Matthew 7:12).

However, Jesus teaches that rules are not paramount and that law is given to humans to help them live a good life. Jesus cured people on the Sabbath and, when questioned about this, replied that the Sabbath was made for man, not man for the Sabbath (i.e. people are not subordinate to the law), but Kant enforces rigid rules with no exceptions under his principle of universalisability. Kant also argues that right moral action can be deduced using reason alone, leaving no room for authority, tradition or even biblical revelation. Kantian ethics are a priori (morality is innate and knowable through reason), unlike Natural Law which is a posteriori and discovers what is right through experience.

Some approaches to religious ethics expect people to accept the moral teaching of the religion or of God, whereas others expect moral decisions to be made freely – but, whichever approach is followed, religious ethics are God-centred. Both Kantian and religious ethics have resemblances in that moral law cannot exist without God, but with Kant the slight difference is that he thinks that, although humans can never prove the existence of God, we must act as if he existed. For Kant it is essential that people should not just accept the moral law blindly, but understand it, use reason and justify all ethical actions.

APPLICATION OF KANTIAN ETHICS TO AN ETHICAL DILEMMA – GENETIC ENGINEERING

Genetic engineering includes cloning, research on embryonic stem cells, so-called designer babies and genetically modified organisms (GMOs).

Kant says that humans should never be thought of as a means but always as an end. This second formulation of the categorical imperative is often used to protect human dignity. Creating a human life (embryo) for the purpose of obtaining cells which could be used as therapeutic material would not be protecting the dignity of that particular human life. The idea of using individuals to help others in this way is sometimes referred to as 'instrumentalisation', and, if Kant is applied too rigidly, his ethical theory could also prohibit blood transfusions – as the patient needing the transfusion knows nothing of the anonymous donor and is using the person's blood simply as a means to an end. It is standard practice in IVF treatment to create spare embryos – are these created instrumentally?

However, Kant's principle states: '*Act in such a way that you always treat humanity, whether in your own person or in the person of any other, never simply as a means but always at the same time as an end*' (*Grounding for the Metaphysics of Morals*, 2005). This is rather vague and may be interpreted selectively according to one's point of view.

We also need to consider what the moral status of a human embryo is – is it the same as a born human and does Kant's principle, or indeed any other principle about persons and personhood, apply to embryos? Some people will think that an embryo is a full member of the moral community with all the rights that humans possess and cite the sanctity of life to support their position.

On the other hand, is it possible to apply Kantian ethics to the idea of attempting to conceive a child to get a 'son and heir'? Is this any different from the idea of selecting an embryo as a genetic match for curing a sibling? Others will consider that it is too simplistic to apply Kant's categorical imperative to any form of genetic engineering and that it is better to do some good than to do no good, and from an ethical point of view it cannot be good to waste spare embryos produced from IVF when they could be used for therapeutic purposes – after all, they were not produced simply as a means.

When applying Kant's categorical imperative to difficult modern ethical dilemmas such as genetic engineering, it is important not to be too dogmatic but to look at the question from different angles.

One must also consider the question of genetically modified organisms – is it better to view this as a means to feed the hungry, or do we again treat people (small farmers) as a means to an end by putting them in thrall to the multinationals? These are some of the questions that need to be considered and discussed when applying Kantian ethics to genetic engineering in its many forms.

REVIEW QUESTIONS

Look back over the chapter and check that you can answer the following questions:

1. What did Kant mean by 'good will'?
2. Why is duty important to Kant?
3. Make a spider diagram or or mind map of the categorical imperative, with examples.
4. Make a chart of the strengths and weaknesses of Kantian ethics.

Terminology

Do you know your terminology?

Try to explain the following terms without looking at your books and notes:

- the categorical imperative
- the hypothetical imperative
- duty
- good will
- the Kingdom of Ends
- maxim
- The summum bonum
- Universalisability

SAMPLE EXAMINATION QUESTIONS

(a) Explain the importance Kant placed upon one doing one's duty. (30 marks)

This question is about duty.

*   In your answer you should define 'duty' and explain the concept of good will, the *summum bonum*. Duty is what makes the good will good. Kant said doing one's duty was to perform actions that were morally required, and to avoid actions that were morally forbidden.
*   You should show that duty is not about doing something in order to gain good results or consequences as this is to act out of self-interest. Duty is unconditional, and an action should be carried out without emotion or regard for personal feelings or of consequences. Doing one's duty is connected to the existence of universal moral laws that all should keep.
*   You should give relevant examples to show your understanding of the concepts.

(b) Assess the claim that doing one's duty is the most important aspect of Kantian ethics. (15 marks)

You might include some of the following in your answer.

Arguments for importance of duty:

*   Duty is doing the good will, which is the highest form of good.
*   Duty is doing the right thing.
*   Duty is a rational response and is not weakened by acting emotionally.
*   Duty is unconditional.
*   Duty involves the creation of moral universal laws, which serve in the best interests of everyone.

Arguments against importance of duty:

*   Being happy is also good.
*   Sometimes we need to act out of emotion or compassion.
*   Duties can conflict (e.g. it might be our duty to conceal the truth).
*   It could be argued that the three formulations of the categorical imperative are more encompassing than doing one's duty.

8 Natural Law

Essential terminology

Absolutism
Apparent good
Divine Law
Deontological ethics
Eternal Law
Intrinsically good
Natural Law
Primary precepts
Purpose
Real good
Secondary precepts

WHAT YOU WILL LEARN ABOUT IN THIS CHAPTER

- The origins of Natural Law.
- Aquinas' theory of Natural Law.
- The strengths and weaknesses of Natural Law.
- How to apply Natural Moral Law to ethical dilemmas.

THE AQA CHECKLIST ✔

Natural Law and ethics

- Aristotle's four causes: material cause, efficient cause, formal cause, final cause
- Aquinas' development of the idea of natural good, Natural Law, law of double effect
- Casuistry; Natural Law in action
- A modern development: Finnis and practical reason
- The application of Natural Law to **one** ethical issue of the candidate's choice **apart from environmental issues**.

ISSUES ARISING

- What is the place of cause at the centre of life?
- What are the strengths and weaknesses of Natural Law as an ethical system?
- Is there such a thing as natural good?
- How compatible is Natural Law with a religious approach to ethics?

WHAT IS NATURAL MORAL LAW?

Deontological ethics
Ethical systems which consider that the moral act itself has moral value (e.g. telling the truth is always right, even when it may cause pain or harm).

Purpose
The idea that the rightness or wrongness of an action can be discovered by looking at whether or not the action agrees with human purpose.

Natural Law includes those ethical theories which state that there is a natural order to our world that should be followed. This natural order is determined by some supernatural power. Natural Law as we understand it originated in the philosophy of the ancient Greeks, especially that of Aristotle, and was developed by Thomas Aquinas. It is an absolute theory of ethics but it is rooted not in duty, or in an externally imposed law, but in our *human nature* and our search for genuine *happiness* and *fulfilment*. Aquinas considered that by using our reason to reflect on our human nature, we could discover our specific end (telos) or purpose and, having discovered this, we could then work out how to achieve it. This understanding of God's plan for us, built into our nature at creation, Aquinas called Natural Law.

- Natural Law is *not* just about 'doing what comes naturally' – it is not about what nature does in the sense of being observed in nature. Natural Law is based on nature interpreted by people – *reason*.
- Natural Law is not exactly a law in that it does not give you a fixed law – it is not always straightforward and there is some flexibility in its application.

THE ORIGINS OF NATURAL LAW

The Stoics
Stoicism was a Greek school of philosophy founded by Zeno of Citium in the third century BCE. Stoics saw damaging emotions as errors of judgement. They maintained that it was virtuous for a person's will to be in agreement with nature.

The earliest theory of Natural Law first appeared among the Stoics, who believed that God is everywhere and in everyone. Humans have within them a divine spark which helps them find out how to live according to the will of God, or in other words to live according to nature. Humans have a choice whether to obey the laws that govern the universe but they need to use their reason to understand and decide whether to obey these cosmic laws.

Thomas Aquinas linked this idea of a cosmic Natural Law with Aristotle's view that people, like every other natural object, have a specific nature, purpose and function. Aristotle considered that, not only does everything have a purpose (e.g. the purpose of a knife is to cut), but that its *supreme good* is found when it fulfils that purpose (e.g. the knife cuts sharply). His idea of purpose leads to his idea of what is good. In the beginning of *Nicomachean Ethics* he writes: 'Every craft and every investigation, and likewise every action and decision seems to aim at some good; hence the good has been well described as that at which everything aims.'

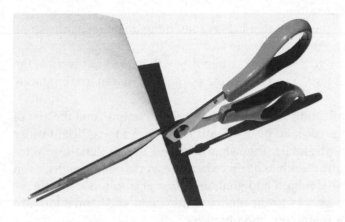

Purpose

The supreme good for humans is eudaimonia, which is usually translated as happiness but includes the idea of living well, thriving and flourishing with others in society. Aristotle saw this as the final goal for humans, but this is to be achieved by living a life of reason. Aristotle saw reason as the highest of all human activities: 'Reason is the true self of every man, since it is the supreme and better part. . . . Reason is, in the highest sense, a man's self' (*Nicomachean Ethics*).

Reason

Aristotle and Plato: detail from the *School of Athens* in the Stanza della Segnatura, 1510–11 (fresco) (detail of 472) by Raphael (Raffaello Sanzio of Urbino) (1483–1520)

Vatican Museums and Galleries, Vatican City, Italy/The Bridgeman Art Library

Nationality/copyright status: Italian/out of copyright

Understanding Aristotle's theory of causality is vital for understanding his approach to ethics: there are four causes that lead to a thing being the way it is:

- *Material cause* – the matter or stuff a thing is made from – e.g. a statue may be made from stone
- *Formal cause* – the kind of thing that it is (the form, idea or plan) – e.g. the model for the statue
- *Efficient cause* – the agent that brings something about – e.g. the stone carving tools and the sculptor
- *Final cause* – the goal, purpose or aim that a thing moves towards, the reason why it is the way it is – e.g. the purpose or reason for the statue.

According to Aristotle things have an essence or real nature, and the aim of life is to fulfil this essence. So he distinguishes between the efficient cause and the final cause – the final cause, when achieved, means that the essence is fulfilled. So for Aristotle ethics begins when one works out through reason what is one's essential nature and goal, and then acts in order to achieve this. Reason is seen as not just the ability to think and understand but also how to act: ethics is reason put into practice.

THE NATURAL LAW OF THOMAS AQUINAS

Thomas Aquinas (1225–1274) was very influenced by Aristotle's writings, which had been lost as far as European philosophy was concerned but preserved by Islamic scholars. Aristotle's philosophy had been 'rediscovered' just before Aquinas took up his position at the University of Paris.

Aquinas used the ideas of Aristotle and the Stoics as an underpinning for Natural Law:

1. Human beings have an essential rational nature given by God in order for us to live and flourish – from Aristotle and the Stoics.
2. Even without knowledge of God, reason can discover the laws that lead to human flourishing – from Aristotle.
3. The Natural Laws are universal and unchangeable and should be used to judge the laws of particular societies – from the Stoics.

THE PURPOSE OF HUMAN BEINGS

Like Aristotle, Aquinas concludes that humans aim for some goal or purpose – but he does not see this as eudaimonia. Humans, for Aquinas, are above all made '*in the image of God*' and so the supreme good must be the development of this image – *perfection*. However, unlike Aristotle, Aquinas did not think that this perfection, or perfect happiness, was possible in this life. Aquinas sees happiness as beginning now and continuing in the next life. The purpose of morality is to enable us to arrive at the fulfilment of our natures and the completion of all our desires.

In his book *Summa Theologiae*, Aquinas attempts to work out what this perfection actually is by examining the 'reflections' of Natural Moral Law as revealed by:

- *Eternal Law* – the principles by which God made and controls the universe and which only God knows completely. We only know these as 'reflections'; in other words, we have only a partial and approximate understanding of the laws which govern the universe.
- *Divine Law* – this is the Bible, which Aquinas believed 'reflects' the Eternal Law of God. However, this 'reflection' can be seen only by those who believe in God and only if God chooses to reveal it.
- *Natural Law* – this refers to the Moral Law of God which has been built into human nature; it is also a 'reflection' of the Eternal Law of God. However, it can be seen by everyone as it does not depend on belief in God or God choosing to reveal it – we simply need to use our reason to understand human nature.

Eternal Law

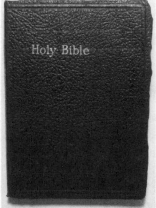

Divine Law

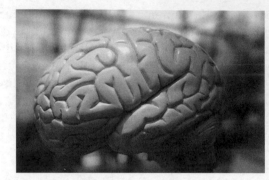

Natural Law

Human laws

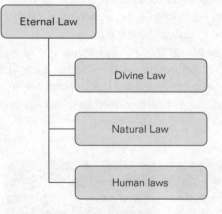

Eternal Law

The principles by which
God made and controls the
universe, which are fully known
only by God.

Divine Law

The Bible – this reflects the
Eternal Law.

Natural Law

The theory that an eternal,
absolute moral law can be
discovered by reason.

Apparent good

Something which seems to be
good or the right thing to do but
which does not fit the perfect
human ideal.

Real good

The right thing to do – it fits the
human ideal.

NATURAL INCLINATIONS

Aquinas thought that God had instilled in all humans inclinations to behave
in certain ways which lead us to the highest good and, by using our reason,
we can discover the precepts (laws) which express God's Natural Law built
into us.

The most fundamental inclination, according to Aquinas, is to act in such
a way as to achieve good and avoid evil. He thought this because we are
designed for one purpose – perfection – and so we would not knowingly
pursue evil. Aquinas saw that in fact humans do not always behave like this
and explained this by saying that we got things wrong and followed apparent
good – something we think is good but in reality does not fit the perfect
human ideal. For example, if someone has an affair they do not do so with
the express purpose of hurting their partner but because they think they are
'in love' and this is a good thing to do. In order to work out what is a real (or

actual) good and what is an apparent good we need to use our reason correctly and choose the right thing to do. There is an 'ideal' human nature that we can all live up to or fall away from and our moral actions determine whether we achieve this or not.

When humans act in accordance with their true nature, they act in accordance with their final purpose, so both the intention (interior act) and the act (exterior act) are important and need to be correct. However, Aquinas did believe that acts were good or bad in themselves and we need to use our reason correctly ('right use of reason' as Aquinas called it) to work out what to do.

So, looked at in this way, Natural Law is not so much a theory or a way of making moral decisions, but rather a way of stressing that our nature is knowable and we need to use our reason to know it and understand it. This becomes clearer as Aquinas explains the fundamental primary principles of Natural Law, which he believes are fixed.

Thought Point

1. How does Aquinas use and change Aristotle's ideas?
2. Explain how Natural Law, according to Aquinas, can lead us to the supreme good.
3. Explain where Natural Law may be found and how it can show us how we ought to behave.

Primary and secondary precepts

Aquinas saw the primary precepts of Natural Law as always true and applying to everybody without exception, as they are a direct 'reflection' of God's Eternal Law. The primary precepts are as follows:

- the preservation of life
- reproduction
- the nurture and education of the young (to learn)
- living peacefully in society
- to worship God.

These primary precepts are always true in that they point us in the right direction and are necessary for human flourishing.

The secondary precepts, on the other hand, are dependent on our own judgements of what actually to do in a given situation and are open to faulty

> **Study hint**
>
> Aquinas thought that all humans share a single nature and so there should be a single aim or purpose for all humans. If we do not believe that there is a final purpose for all humans, then Natural Law makes no sense.

reasoning and may lead to completely wrong choices; this makes them more teleological than deontological. The secondary precepts require experience, the use of reason and the exercise of wisdom.

Using excellent reason is vital and its role is to guide us towards those 'goods' that will enable us to thrive and flourish as people. You cannot simply read the secondary precepts from the primary precepts like a list of instructions; so, for example, the primary precept of reproduction might need secondary precepts that explain what is acceptable sex and what is an acceptable way to have children (e.g. IVF). You need to apply practical wisdom, which is an ability to work out what is good and what will lead humans to perfection – this needs imagination and creativity, not blanket rules.

The secondary precepts make Aquinas' understanding of Natural Law realistic and quite flexible. It does not imply a body of principles from which we simply work out our moral decisions, but takes account of our human limitations and weaknesses. Natural Law may seem rigid, but the secondary precepts have to be interpreted in the context of the situation and, according to Aquinas, the more detailed you try to make it, the more the general rule allows exceptions.

What is good for us depends on our natures, not on our decisions – this allows for right and wrong decisions as we have to decide what really leads to human fulfilment, and here lies the problem. Hughes (*Natural Law*, 1998) says that we tend to see human fulfilment through our own life experiences and from what we have learned is human fulfilment, and forget to apply reason – both reason and practical wisdom are necessary.

THE DOCTRINE OF DOUBLE EFFECT

Aquinas saw the primary precepts as objectively true for everyone, and he believes that by using our reason we can discover the right action in every situation by following this principle. In this he is absolutist. There are times when we have moral dilemmas in which we cannot do good without a bad consequence. To solve this dilemma the doctrine of double effect was devised, roughly saying that it is always wrong to do a bad act intentionally in order to bring about good consequences, but that it is sometimes all right to do a good act despite knowing that it will bring about bad consequences. However, these bad consequences must only be unintended side-effects – the bad consequences may be foreseen but not intended. So, if a pregnant woman has cancer she could have a hysterectomy, even though this would result in the death of the foetus. The same would apply to an ectopic pregnancy (where the embryo is developing in the fallopian tubes): it is acceptable to remove the embryo, as the intention is to save the life of the mother rather than to kill the foetus.

SUMMARY OF NATURAL LAW

Natural Law underpins the ethics of the Catholic Church, but in reality it attempts to establish a standard for morality which is independent of God's will (see the Euthyphro Dilemma, p. 288) and does this by claiming:

The universe is controlled by laws of nature (Eternal Laws).

These laws work in harmony in a rational structure.

The laws of nature also express purpose (e.g. eyes fulfil the purpose of seeing).

The laws of nature also express values (e.g. eyes which can see are 'good' and those which cannot are 'bad'). To be good is to follow our in-built purpose – do what is natural (of nature) as it is good and avoid what is unnatural (not of nature) as it is bad.

The laws of nature are rational so we can understand them by using our reason.

Morality then is independent of religion and both the believer and the non-believer have to find out how to live a moral life by listening to reason.

Intrinsically good
Used of something which is good in itself, without reference to the consequences.

Thought Point

1. The Catholic Church has a number of secondary precepts on issues such as abortion. Would the prohibition of the abortion of a foetus growing in the fallopian tubes represent incorrect reasoning?
2. The biological purpose of sex is procreation, but it may have a secondary purpose of giving pleasure and showing love. Does sex always need to be open to the possibility of procreation? How far should the secondary purpose be considered?
3. The doctrine of double effect is often used in war. Is it acceptable to bomb a military command base in the centre of a civilian population and next to a hospital if the deaths of the civilians are not intended but simply foreseen?
4. 'All human beings have a common human nature, and homosexuality is against human nature.' Consider arguments for and against this statement.

STRENGTHS OF NATURAL LAW

- It allows for a clear-cut approach to morality and establishes common rules.
- The basic principles of preserving human life, reproduction, learning and living in society are common in all cultures and so Natural Law is reasonable.
- Natural Law does not simply dictate what should be done in individual cases from general moral principles.
- Natural Law concentrates on human character and its potential for goodness and flourishing rather than on the rightness or wrongness of particular acts, and so it allows for some measure of flexibility.
- Moral decision making is not done by reason alone. Aquinas also involves the imagination – the body, the emotions and passions – and practical wisdom.
- All those things that we require for happiness – health, friends – are morally good. The purpose of morality is the fulfilment of our natures.

WEAKNESSES OF NATURAL LAW

- Natural Law finds it difficult to relate complex decisions to basic principles in practice (e.g. should more money be spent on schools than on hospitals?).
- Natural Law depends on defining what is good, but according to G.E. Moore this commits the *naturalistic fallacy*. Moore argues that goodness is unanalysable and unnatural, and so cannot be defined by any reference to nature. Aquinas argues that humans are social animals and it is part of our nature to want to live peacefully in the company of others and to care for them. He then goes on to argue that, as this 'property' of caring for others is part of our human nature, it must be *good*. Moore criticises this by saying, '*You cannot derive an ought (value) from an is (fact)*' – so it may be a fact that I have within me the natural inclination to care for others, but that does not mean that I *ought* to care for them. In reality we do not make divisions between facts and values in the way we experience the world – because we are moral beings we unite these together.
- Others argue that Natural Law is based on assumptions about the world and the in-built purpose of things that are questioned by modern science.
- Darwin shows that nature has particular characteristics due to natural selection. The world has no rational system of laws governing it but the laws of nature are impersonal and blind with no intention of moving towards particular purposes. There is no divine purpose – it is simply the way things are.

- Kai Neilsen argues against Aquinas' belief in a single human nature common to all societies. Differing moral standards and cultural relativism challenge the idea of a common Natural Law. Maybe people have changeable natures (e.g. some are heterosexual and some are homosexual), and Natural Law is more complex than Aquinas thought.
- Karl Barth thought that Natural Law relies too much on reason, as human nature is too corrupt to be trusted, and not enough on the grace of God and revelation in the Bible.
- Some Catholic scholars also distrust philosophical theories such as Natural Law, and insist it must be supplemented by revelation or by Church teaching – this has led to some rigid interpretations of Natural Law.
- Vardy and Grosch criticise the way Aquinas works from general principles to lesser purposes and see his view of human nature as unholistic and too simplistic.

MODERN APPRAOCHES TO NATURAL LAW – JOHN FINNIS

John Finnis published *Natural Law and Natural Rights* in 1979 and revived the discussion on Natural Law with what is now called a *New Natural Law* theory. Although he is a professor of jurisprudence at Oxford, Finnis approaches Natural Law in the same way as Aquinas – as a type of moral theory not a type of legal theory, but with one difference: without the need for God. He, therefore, continues the emphasis that *all* people have the ability to understand basic moral obligations and that these moral obligations apply to all people regardless of their nationality, beliefs or culture.

Finnis defines Natural Law as requiring 'a set of basic practical principles which indicate the basic forms of human flourishing as goods to be pursued and realised, and which are in one way or another used by everyone who considers what to do, however unsound his conclusions' (*Natural Law and Natural Rights* p. 23). He focuses on goods and says that these are in fact good, so that people will understand what they morally ought and ought not to do. However, he does allow for flexibility in the ways people pursue these basic goods, and like Aquinas he recognises that people do not always use their reason well. Finnis, therefore, expects there to be some level of disagreement about some of the difficult moral questions, as Natural Law is not some kind of computer program but a way of making decisions about moral issues and how to live life, given certain assumptions about what people need to live their lives well and to flourish.

Finnis has a list of *seven basic goods* that are aspects of basic human flourishing:

> **John Finnis (1940–)**
>
> **John Finnis** is an Australian philosopher who specialises in the philosophy of law. Finnis is Professor of Law at University College, Oxford, and at the University of Notre Dame, Paris.
>
> *Natural Law and Natural Rights* (1979) is considered as a definitive work on Natural Law philosophy. Finnis draws on traditions from Oxford and Catholic Thomism (that is, the thought of Thomas Aquinas) and challenges the Anglo-positivist approach to legal philosophy.

1. *Life* – the basic universal drive for self-preservation.
2. *Knowledge* – this is important for its own sake. It is good to find out the truth and muddle and ignorance are bad.
3. *Play* – this means engaging in performances 'which have no point beyond the performance itself, enjoyed for its own sake' (p. 87). Play is vital to human culture.
4. *Aesthetic experience* – the realisation and appreciation of beauty in many different things: play, music, art, nature, the pursuit of knowledge.
5. *Sociability (friendship)* – good friendship, he says, requires that one acts for the sake of one's friend's well-being. It is the unifying force in community and society so that all members find fulfilment.
6. *Practical reasonableness* – this is both a basic good and the way in which people ought to pursue the basic goods. It means the way in which one is able to use one's own intelligence to choose one's actions and lifestyle and to shape one's character. Finnis considers this so important that he develops it further in a section of his book.
7. *Religion* – this does not mean any particular religion, but more a concern for the order of the cosmos.

Finnis considers that these basic goods apply to all people regardless of their culture, and refers to anthropology to back up this view. He sees all of these goods as self-evident, but the goods in themselves do not give any moral rules; these come from the application of *Practical Reasonableness* to the basic goods.

Practical Reasonableness

Practical Reasonableness has a dual role in Finnis's theory; it is one of the basic human goods, but it is also the method for working out what ought or ought not to be done in the pursuit of the other basic goods.

Practical Reasonableness means that a person has to have a rational plan for life and look at life holistically so as not to consider one basic good more important than the others – in other words, to be open to the value of all the basic goods, and not give too much value to instrumental goods such as wealth, fame or pleasure. It also follows the Golden Rule: 'Do to others what you would have them do to you.' The person must also have a certain detachment so that he or she is open to all the basic forms of good, not following the impulses of the moment. One should also bring about good in the world and respect all human life. All the basic values must be considered when making a moral decision – so Finnis says that Utilitarianism and consequentialism are irrational. Finally, Finnis says that people need to favour the common good of their communities and act in accordance with their consciences. If each of these requirements of Practical Reasonableness is followed then the result will be morality.

Some scholars have criticised Finnis's approach to Natural Law as it presumes that the basic goods are self-evident and ignores any idea of a common human nature. Joseph Koterski S.J. in particular says that there is no philosophy of human nature and therefore Finnis is not true to Aquinas and so his theory is rather a sort of 'Christian Kantianism'. However, Finnis's approach does avoid charges of the naturalistic fallacy.

However, Finnis's list of basic human goods, which he admits is simply his version, is a strong list because of its anthropological support. His list does have a sense of universality, such as when he writes: '*All* human societies show a concern for the value of human life . . . and in none is the killing of other human beings permitted without some fairly definite justifications' (p. 83). Finnis clearly states that Natural Law theory lays the groundwork for general moral rules to be formulated – this cannot, in fact, be restrictive. Finnis's ideas, along with those of Germain Grisez in the USA, have been influential in reviving the discussion of Natural Moral Law.

APPLICATION OF NATURAL LAW TO AN ETHICAL DILEMMA – VOLUNTARY EUTHANASIA

Natural Law is nature interpreted by human reason – by observing nature it deduces the final purpose of everything. Acting in keeping with essential nature is right, and going against it is wrong. To achieve the final purpose Natural Law sets out primary precepts as always true and applying to everybody – the first of these is the preservation of innocent life. Natural Law recognises human life as having unique value and sees that each person has a duty to live their life in accordance with God's plan that human life should be fruitful and find its full perfection in eternal life. As a secondary precept, therefore, Natural Law prohibits suicide (and voluntary euthanasia) as this rejects God's final purpose and denies the natural instinct to live. The preservation of life could mean that more resources are put into palliative care, effective pain relief and hospice treatment, and so people's dignity is affirmed and they can die in peace.

Another angle would be to consider the effect on the primary principle of living harmoniously in society. There could be pressure put upon the elderly and terminally ill, and their contribution to society could be devalued as today's right to die becomes tomorrow's duty to die. However, Maguire argues that, though the principle of 'no direct killing of innocent life' is true most of the time, in certain circumstances the principle would have to give way to the principle of achieving a good death. He does agree, however, that making a judgement between conflicting values is not easy and may be mistaken, but he maintains that the whole purpose of ethical reflection and using reason to reach moral decisions is to achieve a finer sensitivity to the conflicting values and make the possible options less arbitrary – thus voluntary euthanasia may sometimes be a good moral choice.

It is also worth looking at the doctrine of double effect and how, though Natural Law forbids any act whose direct effect is death, it is possible to allow actions (such as relief from pain) whose indirect effect may be death. There is no moral problem for Natural Law when death is merely a side-effect.

The main case for voluntary euthanasia rests on the claim that the quality of life does not justify life being allowed to continue and that it is merciful, in the patient's best interests and according to the patient's own wishes that death be assisted. Natural Law, on the other hand, maintains life as an absolute value which no other 'good' can outweigh.

REVIEW QUESTIONS

Look back over the chapter and check that you can answer the following questions:

1.   Where did Natural Law come from?
2.   What did Aquinas see as the purpose of human beings?
3.   How do we discover the primary and secondary precepts and what are they?
4.   Make a chart of the strengths and weaknesses of Natural Law.

Terminology

Do you know your terminology?

Try to explain the meaning of the following ideas without looking at your books and notes:

*   Apparent good
*   Deontological ethics
*   Intrinsically good/bad
*   Primary precepts
*   Secondary precepts

Examination Questions Practice

Read the question carefully – many candidates know all about the weaknesses of Natural Law, but not so much about its strengths. Answer the question set, not the one you would like to have been set.

SAMPLE EXAMINATION QUESTIONS

(a) Explain, with reference to an ethical issue apart from environmental issues, how Natural Law works. (30 marks)

It is for you to decide which ethical issue to address.

- Depending on your choice of issue, you should show understanding of the part human life plays (if relevant) and God (if relevant).
- You should show some awareness of the impact of the issue on the rest of society.
- You should make reference to the 'goods' involved, and the reason for this.
- Remember that you cannot gain the highest levels if you explain Natural Law without reference to an ethical issue.

(b) Assess the strengths and weaknesses of Natural Law as an ethical system. (15 marks)

In your answer you need to debate and weigh up some of the strengths and weaknesses of Natural Law.

Strengths might include:

- clear-cut approach
- use of reason
- morality
- its flexibility.

Weaknesses might include:

- inability to cope with complex situations
- Moore's naturalistic fallacy
- too simplistic (Vardy and Grosch)
- an over-reliance on reason.

9 Religious Views of the Created World

WHAT YOU WILL LEARN ABOUT IN THIS CHAPTER

- The idea that the universe is created by a supreme being who sustains the world.
- The status of humans in creation and their duties to creation.
- The morality expected by God as creator.

THE AQA CHECKLIST ✔

Candidates will be expected to have studied the views of **one** religion, but, where appropriate, may refer to more than one religion in their answers.

- The creation of the world by God, the best of all possible worlds.
- The world created according to God's intentions.
- God sustains the created world.
- The status and duty of humankind in the created world.
- Status of the non-human world.

ISSUES ARISING

- Is God's world perfect and must it be so?
- What are the ethical implications of the idea that God sustains creation?
- What are the strengths and weaknesses of religious views about:

- the status and duty of humans in the created world?
- the status of the non-human world?

THE CREATION OF THE WORLD BY GOD – THE BEST OF ALL POSSIBLE WORLDS

If God is seen as perfect then it seems reasonable to suppose that he would have created a perfect world, but if God is conceived of as total perfection then we have to ask how he is related to the universe as we understand it.

According to Plato the universe is shaped, not created, by the Demiurge, in such a way that it conforms to the Form of the Good, but it is never perfect. For Aristotle, Plato's pupil, all ideas of the world of the Forms are rejected and forms needed to be embodied in matter to be real. However, Aristotle saw the need for an eternal and unchanging substance – the best of all beings which is itself the cause of all change in the universe. This God, though, never actually does anything but simply changes things by being there. For both Plato and Aristotle God is not a creator and they do not try to explain how matter exists, it is just there, and this fact alone explains why the world is not as good as it might be.

In the Old Testament tradition God is the absolute creator of the universe and it is this idea of creation that came to define God in Christian thought. The creation stories in the Scriptures (Genesis 1 and 2) show that each aspect of creation is good and is created by God, and so belongs to him. Augustine understood God as the one perfect creator who created a universe which is good – God has to be good by definition and so any universe he creates must reflect his goodness and be full of happy, free, wise beings. God is rational and God creates what is good – this is a nice neat explanation, but it does not fit with what we ourselves see: the world is not perfect and it contains much evil and suffering.

God creates *ex nihilo* (from nothing) and God as the origin of everything is also used to explain the idea of God's absolute authority over all of creation. Paul writes:

> But who indeed are you, a human being, to argue with God? Will what is moulded say to the one who moulds it, 'Why have you made me like this?' Has the potter no right over the clay, to make out of the same lump one object for special use and another for ordinary use?
>
> (Romans 9:20–1)

Creation ex nihilo is not, however, the only way to understand God as creator. There is also the idea that creation was *ex Deo*, or out of God's very being, because everything that exists was created from God by God. This idea of creation ex Deo can be found in process theism which means that God is not totally separate from material reality; God shares our existence through our experiences of it. As we grow, as we develop, so does God; as we suffer, so does God. This does give an explanation for the pain and suffering in the created world as people are responsible for their action and no one, not even God, causes people to act as they do. God's sustaining role is persuasive rather than coercive.

Creation ex nihilo maintains the distinction between God and the created world and shows that all that exists depends on God, but God himself remains completely independent of our existence – God and the universe are completely different. On the other hand, creation ex Deo allows for a mutually interdependent relationship between God and the universe.

In Christian thought God is seen as not only the creator of the universe but also its sustainer – all that exists does so only because God wills it to exist. This idea is clearly seen in the Old Testament where God cares about what people do – he wants them to fulfil their purpose; to grow and flourish and live well as humans. Being moral then is about obeying God:

> Morality may exist without religion. . . . But the sort of religion the Hebrew prophets taught gives to morality an absoluteness, a compassion, a power and a hope which is simply not available to secular morality. Belief in God has one of its firmest roots in the sense of the absoluteness of morality, the need for forgiveness, and the hope for the triumph of good.
>
> (Ward 2003 p. 99)

Ward explains that the idea of God as sustainer of creation is one of an active and loving God which draws all things to itself.

There still remains, however, the problem of evil and suffering in the world. If there is an overall purpose and meaning in the world, and everything is under the absolute control of God, then the implication must be that God is responsible for all suffering and evil in the world. The problem of the existence of evil in the world is based upon some basic assumptions about how religious believers see the world:

- The world can be understood rationally.
- There is a meaning and purpose to everything that happens.
- God created the world and God is good and loving.
- God has absolute control over his creation.

Suffering and evil need to be explained as part of God's intention for the world, and God needs to be seen as right and just. There are two forms of evil in the world: moral evil, which results from the free choice of individuals to inflict suffering, and natural evil, such as disease, death, etc. which would still exist if everyone behaved perfectly, as disease, death, etc. are part of how the world is made. There are two traditional approaches to this problem: that of Augustine and that of Irenaeus.

Augustine argued that evil is a lack of goodness, a deprivation. He argued that evil came into the world with the 'fall' of the angels and then that of Adam and Eve, which meant that humans would be imperfect from the time of the Fall. The world then is good, but not as good as it was when created by God. One major criticism of this approach is to question why an omnipotent God did not make a world where there was no Fall from perfection. Unfortunately we do not know what perfection is like as we can only see things from our human perspective: if this is the only world that God could have created then he is limited as we are, but he could have created worlds without the imperfections of this one; consequently he is responsible for the imperfections of this world, or he is not good.

Irenaeus attempted to solve this dilemma in a different way – God allows evil and suffering to exist in order to bring about a greater good: human freedom and a relationship with God. This approach sees human life as imperfect, but, having been made in the image of God, humans need the existence of both good and evil in order to grow and develop. Hick develops this idea and sees evil as necessary in order for spiritual growth to take place – he describes the world as a 'vale of soul-making'.

The fact that God did not create a possible world in which there is no moral evil is defended by what is known as 'the free will defence'. This argument is presented by Swinburne, who points out that evil is necessary for there to be real moral choice, but then he makes an important distinction between the possibility of evil and the fact of evil. The implication of the 'free will defence' is that it is better to have a world in which people can choose freely between good and evil, rather than a world with no free choice at all. In order for us to be free and to develop as human beings we have to live in a world which includes genocide, murder, torture, terrorism, etc.

Brian Davies says that these arguments depend on the idea that God is a moral agent. However, this idea conflicts with the God of classical theism – if God is changeless it does not make sense to see God as making choices like any human moral agent, nor is there any alternative God creating alternative worlds against which our own can be compared. God, he claims, cannot be a moral agent, as a moral agent must be able to succeed or fail.

THE STATUS AND DUTY OF HUMANKIND IN THE CREATED WORLD

Humans are seen as being the pinnacle of creation, made in imago Dei (in God's image). This means that they are moral beings and as such have a duty to care for God's creation. In Christianity humans are said to have dominion over the created world. This dominion is not an easy concept to interpret as regards human duties to the created world. Dominion can be seen as power. This is often seen as the main Western interpretation: the natural world exists for the benefit of human beings. God does not care how we treat it. Human beings are the only morally important members of this world. The created world is not seen as having any intrinsic value, except as far as it benefits humans. This view is seen in the teaching of Aquinas, who held that animals act purely on instinct whereas humans have rational thought. However, animals are part of God's creation and as such should be treated well, though they may be used (eaten, etc.) by humans. There are further ideas about this interpretation of dominion in the chapter on the environment.

Dominion can also be seen as stewardship. Humans are put in Eden to protect and preserve it: 'The LORD God took the man and put him in the garden of Eden to till it and keep it' (Genesis 2:15).

Humans may be the peak of creation, but only because we have the role of stewardship – we are to care for and conserve creation because it belongs to God: humans are merely caretakers of this property. Humans are co-creators with God and need to use and transform the natural world with care. Creation is made by God and is good, and so must be preserved because it has intrinsic value. The Fall (Genesis 3) is seen by some as the reason for our poor treatment of the created world because from this point we became poor stewards of creation:

> The earth dries up and withers, the world languishes and withers; the heavens languish together with the earth. The earth lies polluted under its inhabitants; for they have transgressed laws, violated the statutes, broken the everlasting covenant.
>
> (Isaiah 24:4–5)

Christians teach that we need to use our increasing knowledge to rectify this and re-establish the bond between God and humanity, between God and the natural world. Both humans and the created world are in need of redemption.

Thought Point

Compare and find evidence for the different interpretations of Dominion (there is more information in the chapter on the environment). How do the different interpretations guide religious attitudes and behaviour to the created world?

For Christians, Christ is involved with God's creation from the beginning, and both John and Paul in the New Testament teach a vision of a cosmic Christ who gives meaning to the whole of the created world – it was created 'in him and for him':

> All things came into being through him, and without him not one thing came into being.
>
> (John 1:3a)

> for in him all things in heaven and on earth were created, things visible and invisible, whether thrones or dominions or rulers or powers – all things have been created through him and for him.
>
> (Colossians 1:16)

Christ is seen as pre-existent, participating in God's work of creation and supreme over all creation, so also the universe is sustained by him. In this way Paul in the letter to the Colossians explains that Christ is the only mediator between God and humanity, the unique agent of cosmic reconciliation. This doctrine of creation shows the life, death and resurrection of Jesus as constituting a restoration of creation, yet to be finalised. Or, as Karl Rahner sees it, Christ is the very grace of God which mediates between God and creation.

These ideas link God and creation in a special way for Christians as they believe that God became human, so God continues to be linked with creation in a unique way. One of the ways this is explained is by using the idea of God's immanence – he interacts with all nature and so humans must respect all of creation which is not completed but is an ongoing enterprise. This idea is best explained by the scientific idea of the fertility of the universe: the universe contains billions of stars which as they live and die release into the universe the chemical elements necessary for life – we are all literally made of stardust.

Science sees no clear threshold between the living and the non-living, but the combination of chance and necessity – or, to give it a more scientific term, chemical complexity or continuous evolution – in the universe gives it a direction. Christians believe that the universe depends on God, it is a gift from God and it cannot exist independently of God, but as early Christian writers such as Augustine saw it the universe participates in the creativity of God. It is difficult to explain these ideas other than by rather weak analogies such as God working with creation, with humans as a parent will with a child. God lets the universe, including humans, be what it will be in its continuous evolution, interacting with it but without continuously intervening.

A different perspective on the duties of humans towards the created world is the idea of humans being co-creators with God. This is found in Genesis 1:27 where humans are made in God's image and in Psalm 8 where humans are placed just below the creator in the heavenly order and almost Godlike qualities are attributed to people. As co-creators we have responsibility just as God does, but the second creation story reminds us of the dangers of 'playing God'.

THE STATUS OF THE NON-HUMAN WORLD

The status of the environment and the status of animals are dealt with in Chapter 10 on the environment.

Buddhist perspectives on the (un)created world

Belief in the cycle of rebirth is central to Buddhist understanding of life and the world. This cycle has no known beginning and has existed through multiple world systems. Unlike Western faiths, Buddhism sees no purpose in life. The only beings who are born into the world are those who are unenlightened. Therefore the only hope is to attempt to transcend this existence.

Buddhist views of the (un)created world are based on an understanding of the problem of evil. All life is full of suffering and is something to escape from. It is not believable that any powerful moral being would have created such a world with its suffering. Therefore there is no need for belief in a creator. Buddhism does not totally reject the idea of gods but these are also in the cycle of rebirth and are not capable of creation.

Buddhist teaching is that there are many worlds and only the very highest is beyond the cycle of rebirth. Below this are:

•   the realms of pure form – 16 heavens in which the gods live
•   sense desire levels including this world
•   animal levels – the hells which are full of suffering.

It is kamma which controls movement between the worlds. Kamma is created by past actions and dictates whether a person's rebirth is into a higher or lower world. All killing creates bad kamma but taking a human life is the worst because it is good fortune to have reached that level. Kamma is determined by previous lives but people still have free will in this world. In the lower levels it is harder to create good kamma and in the heavens there is little opportunity to do good or bad acts.

Hindu perspectives on the created world

Hinduism has various teachings about creation. Some of these see an instance of creation, such as Brahmanda – the cosmic age which gave birth to all life. Others see a continuous cycle of creation and destruction.

As there are different views of creation there are also differences about the place of humanity. The Samkhya and Tantric teachings are that humanity lives in accordance with the elements and the environment. On the other hand, the Advaita Vedanta tradition sees the role of humans as being to transcend the world and views it as *maya* (illusion).

However, the concept of dharma means that people need to act for the safekeeping of the world and this was reflected in the teachings of M.K. Gandhi.

Jewish perspectives on the created world

The two creation accounts in Genesis show the power of G-d and his acts to create a beautiful world for life to exist in. The world was created by the divine will from nothing and G-d still continues the creation from day to day.

In the account of creation in Genesis 1, humans are created last and can be seen as the pinnacle of the creative act. They are given dominion over the Earth. However, in Genesis 2 they are the first part of creation and are given the duty of stewardship. Whichever view is taken, the Earth is the property of G-d, not of living beings.

Judaism considers that all living things are essentially good as being created by G-d and all are created for themselves, not for others. The weekly rest of the Sabbath reminds people of the need to avoid overusing creation as does the instruction to leave land fallow once every seven years.

Muslim perspectives on the created world

Islam sees Allah as the creator with power over all things. The whole of creation was brought into existence by his word and, at the end, everything returns to him. God's power is seen in the huge diversity of creation. The Qur'an teaches that creation is full of signs for the faithful and that these must be protected as they demonstrate God's majesty and power.

Human beings are one part of creation and have the same purpose as every other aspect, which is to serve Allah. However, even before the first human was created, God announced that they were to be vice-regents and, so, stewards of the Earth with power and authority over it. This places humanity in a higher position than the angels. Humans are therefore watched and will be held to account over their stewardship. It is clear from the Qur'an that environmental ethics are important and a matter of great responsibility for humanity in submitting to Allah's will and serving him.

Sikh perspectives on the created world

Sikh teaching is that at one point in time God created the world by hukam (divine order – the will of God). Having created the universe, God now lives within it and within everything. God's creation continues and he is the sustainer of all life.

Human beings have a special place within creation and all other living things are in existence to help humanity fulfil its purpose. However, when people see God they will realise that everything else is false and unreal. Despite their special merit, humans are fallible and trust should therefore be placed in God.

The way to become liberated and reborn into a better state is for humans to work towards being God-centred rather than self-centred. The world is the place where humans have the opportunity to perform good acts and work towards liberation. The suffering of life in the world is caused by humans who are not focused on God.

REVIEW QUESTIONS

Look back over the chapter and check that you can answer the following questions:

1. Explain the relationship between the created and the uncreated world.
2. What is the significance of the teaching about *ex nihilo*?
3. Examine the relationship between the concepts of stewardship and dominion.

4. How is an understanding of teachings about the created and uncreated world important in discussions about the problem of evil?

Terminology

Do you know your terminology?

Try to explain the following key ideas without looking at your books and notes:

- Dominion
- *Ex nihilo*
- Stewardship

SAMPLE EXAMINATION QUESTIONS

(a) Explain what it means to say that God is the sustainer of the world. (30 marks)

Most candidates will answer this from the perspective of one religion; however, information from more than one religion is permissible in this answer as it is asking for a generic answer.

- 'Sustain' means to keep going; each new act of creation implies this.
- Religious people believe that God continues to create every day.
- Each new invention and development can be argued to have come from God.
- The world still exists, therefore it is being sustained.

(b) Assess what part humanity plays in sustaining the world. (15 marks)

This can be argued from a religious and/or a non-religious perspective.

For:

- conservation
- stewardship
- the responsibility, implied in most scriptures, that we have to sustain the world; to keep it as God intended
- interest in renewable energy.

Against:

- abuse of the world
- negligence and lack of responsibility
- the idea that the world will go on for ever.

Further information on world faiths can be found at: http://subknow.reonline.org.uk/.

Essential terminology

Anthropocentric
Biocentric
Biodiversity
Conservation ethics
Deep ecology
Dominion
Ecosophy
Gaia hypothesis
Geocentric
Holistic
Intrinsic value
Instrumental value
Sentience
Shallow ecology
Stewardship

10 Environment, both Local and Worldwide

WHAT YOU WILL LEARN ABOUT IN THIS CHAPTER

- The main threats to the environment.
- Different ethical approaches to the environment, both religious and secular.
- An understanding of the underlying principles and implications of these different approaches for making decisions about the environment.
- How to assess the different approaches and to evaluate their strengths and weaknesses.

THE AQA CHECKLIST ✔

- Environment, both local and worldwide
- Threats to the environment: pollution and its consequences, especially global warming; conservation of living environment, e.g. forests, animals, sea creatures
- Protection and preservation of the environment
- The developing Third World and attempts to restrict this development
- Religious teachings about human responsibility for the environment.

ISSUES ARISING

- Is protection of the environment an issue only for the rich?
- Is protection of the environment only for the good and benefit of humankind?
- How far should humans be forced to be environmentally responsible?

WHAT IS ENVIRONMENTAL ETHICS?

Environmental ethics considers the ethical relationship between people and the natural world and the kinds of decisions people have to make about the environment:

- Should we continue to cut down the rain forests for the sake of human consumption?
- Should we continue to manufacture petrol-driven cars when we have the technology to make cars which do not pollute the environment?
- Should we knowingly cause the extinction of other species?
- What are our environmental obligations to future generations?
- Should humans be forced to live a simpler lifestyle in order to protect and preserve the environment?

Most people recognise that our planet is in a bad way and we all seem to have an opinion on environmental issues, such as climate change or the use of four-wheel-drive cars in cities. The importance of environmental ethics is brought home daily by the news of global warming and its effect on our lives, both now and in the future.

There has been a rapid growth in knowledge and technology, so that humans now face choices we have never had to face before that affect the continuation of humanity and the world within which we live.

Environmental ethics has grown in importance in our times because to make no decisions about environmental issues is to decide in favour of the status quo, and that, we are told, is no longer an option.

However, there is no agreed ethics for environmental issues, and no international environmental code. Environmental ethics simply tries to answer the questions of how humans should relate to their environment, how we should use the Earth's resources and how we should treat other species, both plant and animal, but there are also those who are of the opinion that constant change is simply a fact of this planet and the planet will readjust to new conditions as it did in the past. There are differences among scientists as to the exact cause and nature of environmental problems and how to solve them, and so there are differences in the approaches to environmental ethics; some think the traditional forms of ethical thought are good guides and some that these traditional forms (at least in the West) are too human-centred.

There are also the views of Christians and other religious believers who have a particular take on their role and responsibility towards the natural world.

THREATS TO THE ENVIRONMENT

Climate change

There is agreement among most scientists that the greatest environmental challenge that the world faces is climate change. Over the last hundred years the average global surface temperature has risen by about 0.74°C. This seems a very small amount but 11 of the hottest years recorded have all taken place since 1995. Rising global temperatures are bringing about changes in weather patterns and will continue to do so. According to the Intergovernmental Panel on Climate Change (IPCC) this is caused by rising levels of carbon dioxide in the atmosphere, and the main source of this increase is human activity – mainly the burning of fossil fuels such as coal and oil.

According to the IPCC, If this continues, the twenty-first century will have a rise in temperatures, rise in sea levels, more heat waves, droughts, floods and cyclones. This will affect us in the UK, but internationally there may be severe problems for people in regions that are particularly vulnerable. We are aware of the bigger picture, but in reality the issue is more complex. For example, the shrinking of the ice in the Arctic and in Antarctica is often in the media; however, in Greenland ice is being lost around the coasts, but thickening in central regions, while in western Antarctica there is significant melting, but thickening in the east. Recently German scientists have published a new computer model of a natural cooling cycle, showing that we may be entering a natural cooling now which will last about ten years – but that does not prove climate change to be wrong – it will warm up again.

Another major cause of climate change is deforestation due to the spread of civilisation, resulting in rising 'greenhouse gases'. Some scientists think that our use of fossil fuels would have little impact upon the climate of the planet were it not for deforestation, industrialisation and logging without global reforestation. Our way of life and the ever increasing world population are making us use up the world's resources at an ever increasing rate. Many of these resources are non-renewable, and much of this environmental damage disproportionally affects the poorest people of the world who live in the areas that are affected to the greatest extent.

The issue of climate change brings up many ethical issues – whether the environment should be protected or whether humans should be considered first, whether we should conserve species or allow them to become extinct naturally.

PROTECTION AND PRESERVATION OF THE ENVIRONMENT

Animal rights

All humans are considered to have moral standing: whatever age or race they are, their continued welfare is considered to have intrinsic value. We are considered to have moral standing by virtue of being human; being moral agents, knowing right from wrong; having personhood and self-consciousness. However, can the same be said of the environment? Animals have sentience so can we, therefore, extend moral standing to them? In the past our attitude and treatment of animals was very different – extinction was the result of our deliberate hunting and killing. However, we still use animals in sport, we farm them, often intensively; we keep them in zoos and experiment on them for research. It is a mark of our change in attitude towards animals that there is now a centre in Oxford for Animal Ethics.

Andrew Linzey was the first Professor of Ethics, Theology and Animal Welfare at Oxford, and writes extensively against animal cruelty, hunting, fur farming and animal experimentation. Linzey considers that God's love for creation is inclusive of animals, and so he advocates vegetarianism as most meat is the product of intensive farming and that we should live more simply so that others may live. He writes:

> Since animals belong to God, have value to God and live for God, then their needless destruction is sinful. In short: animals have some right to their life, all circumstances being equal.
>
> Western society is so bound up with the use and abuse of animals in so many fields of human endeavour . . . that it is impossible for anyone to claim that they are not party, directly or indirectly, to this exploitation either through the products they buy, the food they eat, or the taxes they pay.
>
> (*Christianity and the Rights of Animals* 1987)

This view is endorsed also by Peter Singer, but for different reasons. He used a set of criteria for moral status based on sentience. This means that moral worth includes animals – if not, we are guilty of 'speciesism'. Our treatment of all humans and animals should be equal.

Instrumental value

The idea that something's value lies in its usefulness for others.

Conservation ethics

The ethics of the use, allocation, protection and exploitation of the natural world.

Biodiversity

The variety of living things on Earth.

Sentience

The ability to feel pleasure and pain.

Andrew Linzey

Andrew Linzey is an Anglican priest, theologian and writer. He is a member of the Faculty of Theology at Oxford and held the world's first academic post in Ethics, Theology and Animal Welfare. From 1987 to 1992 he was Director of Studies of the Centre for the Study of Theology at the University of Essex, and from 1992 to 1996 Special Professor in Theology at the University of Nottingham. In 1998 he was Visiting Professor at the Koret School of Veterinary Medicine at the Hebrew University of Jerusalem, and is currently Honorary Professor at the University of Birmingham,

Special Professor at the Saint Xavier University, Chicago, and an Honorary Research Fellow at St Stephen's House, Oxford.

Linzey is Director of the Oxford Centre for Animal Ethics, which aims to encourage academic research and public debate on issues surrounding animal-related ethics.

Singer is a Preference Utilitarian, and so believes that animals should receive equal preference. He argues that the principle of equality we apply to people of different races should also apply to animals. Both animals and humans should be treated equally. Singer has been called the philosopher of the animal liberation movement and also advocates vegetarianism and no animal experimentation.

Criticism of animal rights

On the other hand it can be argued that animals are not moral agents and so we do not have the same moral obligation to give them moral standing as we do to humans. So while there are many good reasons for treating animals humanely (out of compassion or out of respect for the wishes of other humans), it makes no sense to ascribe rights to them. Singer would counteract this, saying that many humans (infants and the severely mentally disabled) are not moral agents and still have moral rights. However, an alternative approach can be found in Kant's ethical theory, which is generally seen as anthropocentric, based on the idea that rational nature alone has absolute and conditional value. It may seem that a theory of this kind would allow the exploitation of the natural world; if only rational nature counts as an end in itself, then everything else may be used as a means to an end. However, Kant denies that domestic animals are to be treated only as tools and insists that there are moral limits on how we should use them. Animals should not be worn out and overworked, nor should they be cast aside once they are too old. Kant thinks it is all right to kill animals for food, but killing for sport he sees as morally wrong.

Kant also thinks that we have moral duties regarding the natural world and must not destroy it. This seems at odds with Kant's statements that we have duties only towards rational beings, but he explains that treating animals or the natural world badly makes us into cruel and callous people who will then treat other people badly. People who torment animals are likely to do the same to humans, according to Kant. So cruelty towards animals would not be condemned in its own right, but because of its consequences for humans it should be considered intrinsically wrong. According to Kant, a person cannot have good will unless he or she shows concern for the welfare of non-rational beings and values the natural world for its own sake.

Roger Scruton in *Animal Rights and Wrongs* (1996) used an argument based on Kant's approach which restricts animal rights to animals which are kept by humans, but says that we do not have a duty of care to wild animals. He considers that wild animals have no greater standing than wild plants, which we may respect because they are beautiful or interesting or a valuable

Roger Vernon Scruton (b. 27 February 1944)

Roger Scruton is an English conservative philosopher. From 1969 to 1971 he was Research Fellow at Peterhouse, Cambridge, and from 1971 to 1992 he was Lecturer and then Reader and Professor of Aesthetics at Birkbeck College, London. From 1992 to 1995 he was Professor of Philosophy at Boston University and is now Research Professor at the Institute for the Psychological Sciences in Arlington County, Virginia, and Visiting Professor at Princeton University.

part of the ecosystem, but that is all. Scruton would allow fox hunting but not factory farming.

The arguments against animal rights are based on the thesis that animals have no rights because rights can exist only between people who are moral agents and can make moral claims on each other. Singer's Preference Utilitarian view neatly sidesteps this argument by not claiming that animals have rights but claiming that we should give consideration to animal welfare. However, Utilitarianism is consequentialist, and what may seem the best consequence in the short term may not be so in the long term.

In his essay 'Why I Am only a Demi-Vegetarian' (in *Essays on Bioethics* 1993) R.M. Hare says that if we follow Singer and all become vegetarians the meat industry would collapse. Hare does not see this as the most preferable action as it would result in only the most efficient producers staying in the market – they will charge least for their product and are the least ethical in their treatment of animals. Hare suggests being a demi-vegetarian – eating mainly vegetables but eating a small amount of meat from ethical farmers.

Thought Point

1. Research different views on climate change and assess the strengths and weaknesses of each view.
2. Make a list of everything you think should have moral standing and justify your answer.
3. Give reasons for and against being vegetarian in order to conserve the environment.

CONSERVATION OF THE LIVING ENVIRONMENT

Should moral standing be extended to all living things including the plants and trees that are so essential for our survival? Singer argues that, because plants are non-sentient, there is a problem in trying to determine their interests in staying alive.

Or should moral standing be extended to the whole Earth? The rocks, mountains seas, rivers and the ecosystems – in short the entire natural world? Singer would not agree and admits that, although the argument for the preservation of the environment may be strong, it is difficult to argue for its intrinsic value. He proposes an alternative approach: in his book *Practical Ethics*, Singer advocated the preservation of 'world heritage sites', unspoilt parts of the world that acquire 'scarcity value' as they diminish over time. Their preservation ensures their survival for future generations to enjoy. It should be left to future generations to decide whether they prefer unspoilt countryside or urban landscape.

A tropical rain forest would be a good example of a world heritage site, as it is a very specialist ecosystem with vegetation that has taken years to evolve. Clearing the rain forest to develop farmland is often pointless owing to the soil conditions, and once destroyed the rain forest cannot be replaced. Conservation ecology or, as it is often known, shallow or light green ecology takes the view that the only value in animals and plants is their extrinsic, instrumental value for humans. They are a means to an end – conservation is important for our welfare and that of future generations. Conservation ethics looks at the worth of the environment in terms of its utility or usefulness to humans. Conservation is a means to an end and is purely concerned with humanity – so a person chooses to avoid pollution and to reduce, reuse and recycle because these actions seem beneficial to humans in one way or another.

This is the ethic which formed the underlying arguments for the three agreements reached in Rio in 1992 and for the Kyoto summit in 1997. Shallow ecology or light green environmentalism restricts independent moral status to humans – it is anthropocentric. Biodiversity should be preserved, as particular species of animals and plants provide us with medicines, food and raw materials. So shallow ecology will accept that environmental damage can continue if humans benefit from it. The clearing of rain forests can be justified if it can be shown to benefit humans – making space for people to live or for farming. The preservation of a rain forest may also be the right thing to do provided it can be shown to benefit humans. Neither animals nor plants have rights, and any respect shown to them depends on how humans benefit.

As may be seen from the different approaches to the environment examined already in this chapter, many are based to some extent on Utilitarianism. Since it is clear that destroying the environment will bring long-term harm to all species, including humans, Utilitarians will weigh up the long-term harm against the short-term gain made from exploiting natural resources.

Quantitative Utilitarianism looks at a situation and weighs up whether the moral course of action is the maximisation of higher pleasures for present and future generations. So, for example, when in the Lake District there was a proposal to impose a 10 mph speed limit on Windermere, a lake that lies within the National Park, a designated area of peace and tranquillity, but which is much used by power-boat enthusiasts and water-skiers, whose activities contribute substantially to the local economy, a Benthamite would have weighed up the amount of pleasure and pain of all those involved. However, the assumption that pleasure is a uniform feature of different types of experience, and simply varies according to how much there is, is questionable.

Modern Utilitarians would use a cost–benefit analysis, and this was the approach of David Pearce's NIB *Blueprint for a Green Economy* (1995). Applying this approach to Windermere, it is easy to assess the economic benefit of some of the elements in the situation: power boating brings money into the area. But how can this be weighed against the loss of tranquillity? Environmental economics would say that tranquillity is also of value and it is simply a case of determining the strength of preferences for it – but is money an appropriate measure of environmental goods? And do people's preferences accurately reflect what is good for them? Should the fate of the environment be dependent on human preferences? In addition, we never know the final result of our actions. What may seem to be to the advantage of the environment, now, may in the long term prove to be harmful.

It is worth noting the approach of qualitative Utilitarianism: Mill puts the enjoyment and study of nature at the top of his list of higher pleasures – and therefore environmental preservation is imperative. Preference Utilitarianism considers that the moral course of action is the maximisation of preference satisfaction for the current generation. Assuming that neglecting the environment has no major effect on the current generation, then the case for preserving the environment is weak. In *Practical Ethics* Peter Singer uses the example of building a hydroelectric dam across a gorge that would create employment, stimulate economic growth and provide a cost-effective energy supply but have associated costs. Such costs would include the loss of a beauty spot favoured by walkers and a good place for white-water rafting and the destruction of the habitat of some endangered species and wildlife.

For the Preference Utilitarian, the preference satisfaction of a cheap source of electricity would outweigh the preferences of the walkers and the white-water rafters, as well as those of the animals and plants. However, the qualitative Utilitarian would consider the long-term interests of future generations.

However, for many people contact with the natural world is a part of the good life – part of having a good quality of life – so swimming with dolphins, hill walking, seeing cherry trees in bloom are experiences that are valued for their own sake, not just as an instrumental good.

Looking at this from another angle, Michael LaBossiere argues in the *Philosopher's Magazine* (issue 15) that species should be allowed to die out, as this is just part of the natural process of evolution – humans, he says, are a natural species and so any species that becomes extinct as a result of human activity is simply becoming naturally extinct. Humans have no obligation to prevent natural extinction, but this does not mean that humans should have a free hand in eradicating species, even when it would benefit humanity.

THE DEVELOPING THIRD WORLD AND ATTEMPTS TO RESTRICT DEVELOPMENT

It is often thought that environmental concerns about the climate are the concern of the industrialised Western nations. However, a draft of the UN report on climate shows that fast-developing nations, such as India and China, have slowed their rising greenhouse gas emissions by more than the total cuts demanded of the rich nations by the Kyoto Protocol. Many developing countries argue that they should not be denied the right to develop their economies, which inevitably means an increase in energy consumption. They also say that the responsibility for climate change lies with the developed nations and their industrial activities. This does not mean that the developing countries are inactive; China believes that population growth is a key element in controlling emissions and that their one child per couple policy introduced in the early 1980s had the side-effect of slowing global warming by limiting the Chinese population.

The most important question here is whether developing countries should be restricted in their development if this development is environmentally damaging. Population growth in developing countries is unsustainable, but this is closely related to the extreme levels of poverty many of them endure, partly as a consequence of the international economic order which helps the economic interests of the industrial nations. Much of the environmental problems and destruction is related to international economic relationships. Developing countries are the exporters of increasing amounts of raw materials and natural resources to maintain the wealth of the industrial nations. Nearly three-quarters of the population of developing countries lives below the poverty line – millions of children die each year of malnutrition or easily curable diseases, and in the same period nearly 30 million hectares of natural tropical forests are destroyed.

Interestingly, one of the reasons for this destruction of trees and habitats is the issue of pollution and the demand for biofuels which have an important role in combating climate change. Biofuels use the energy contained in organic matter – crops like sugar cane, corn and palms – to produce ethanol, an alternative to fossil-based fuels like petrol. Many say that this is immoral as the heavily subsidised biofuel industry is diverting land which should be used for food production to feed people in the developing nations. However, again the principle of looking at the long term needs to be applied, as land is being switched from forest or agriculture to plant palm plantations. Biofuels could be important for the future and have a positive impact on the climate but there need to be guarantees in place that the crops will only be grown, harvested and distributed and owned in such a way that the climate, and the local societies and environment, benefit. Historically we do not have a very good record of this as our treatment of the whaling industry and the Russian fishing off Antarctica were hardly good models of sustainability.

THE RELIGIOUS APPROACH TO ENVIRONMENTAL ETHICS

For the purpose of this book a Christian approach will be followed.

Dominion

The foundation for a Christian approach to the environment is seen by many believers to be the Bible, but as with many ethical issues biblical teaching is not always clear, and the idea that we humans have 'dominion' over the natural world is seen by many as anthropocentric. Peter Singer, an atheist, criticises this tradition in his book *Practical Ethics*:

> According to the Dominant Western tradition, the natural world exists for the benefit of human beings. God does not care how we treat it. Human beings are the only morally important members of this world. Nature itself is of no intrinsic value. . . . Harsh as this tradition is, it does not rule out concern for the preservation of nature, as long as that concern can be related to human well-being.

Singer points out that the teachings of Aristotle influenced Aquinas, who continued to view humans as the only morally important beings – there being no intrinsic value in the natural world.

In the first creation story (Genesis 1), humanity is given a particular responsibility for the created world and this hinges on two words – 'subdue' and 'have dominion' – but what exactly do these two words mean? Like Singer, Lynn White considered these commands to be at the root of many of our environmental problems and he published a very influential article to this effect in the journal *Science* in 1967.

However, Celia Deane-Drummond criticised this view as it does not account for environmental destruction in times and places not affected by the Judaeo-Christian tradition, and also because it is based in a mistaken interpretation of the text. The command ' to subdue' the Earth is a translation of the Hebrew word *kabash* which is used elsewhere in the context of conquering the land – it is concerned with bringing order and well-being rather than with destruction. The word 'dominion' is a translation of the Hebrew *radah* and is used in a relationship connection – not being a despotic, tyrannical ruler, but like the kings of Israel called to reign with due regard

Anthropocentric
Used of an approach to the environment that places human interests above those of any other species.

Intrinsic value
The concept that something's value lies in itself.

for the well-being of their subjects and the land over which they ruled. The second creation story also reminds people of this responsibility – Adam is formed of the dust of the earth, and then commanded to till and care for the soil. People are part of the Earth, but with a particular responsibility for it.

However, the story of creation, upon which so much of this understanding is based, is itself open to interpretation. God seems to value the natural world: 'God saw that it was good' (Genesis 1:10a), and the blessing to 'Be fruitful and multiply' (Genesis 1:22a) is given to all creation. Creation is called to praise and glorify God (e.g. Psalm 148:3–10; Isaiah 55:12; Micah 6:1–2).

God is shown as having continuing concern about his creation – not even a sparrow falls without God's knowledge and permission:

> Are not two sparrows sold for a penny? Yet not one of them will fall to the ground apart from your Father. And even the hairs of your head are all counted. So do not be afraid; you are of more value than many sparrows.
>
> (Matthew 10:29)

If God values creation, and creation in return can respond to God, then it seems that the Bible says that all of creation has intrinsic value. This contrasts with the view that God has a special concern for humanity – we are made in God's image: 'So God created humankind in his image, in the image of God he created them; male and female he created them' (Genesis 1:27).

We are given dominion over all creatures:

> Then God said, 'Let us make humankind in our image, according to our likeness; and let them have dominion over the fish of the sea, and over the birds of the air, and over the cattle, and over all the wild animals of the earth, and over every creeping thing that creeps upon the earth.
>
> (Genesis 1:26)

This surely backs up Singer's view of anthropomorphism and anthropocentrism in the biblical texts. Or are humans, being made in the image of God, also supposed to delight in the intrinsic value of the natural world?

St Francis of Assisi understood that God communicates to us through the natural world – through animals, birds and trees – and that it is a sin to destroy them. In general, his attitude towards the environment was typical of his time: the natural world is inherently good and it is a sign of God's goodness, and so its purpose is to inspire our respect and love. However, he took this a stage further, as he believed that *all* creatures had the ability and the duty to worship God, all are part of the same creation with the same intrinsic value.

Stewardship

Dominion may be understood as considering that the natural world can be treated however we wish and be tamed for our use. According to Singer this is the root cause of our environmental problems, and it is true that the command to 'subdue' the Earth (Genesis 1:28) needs looking at. When the second creation account in Genesis 2 is compared to the first, we are told that man is put in Eden to protect and preserve it: 'The Lord God took the man and put him in the garden of Eden to till it and keep it' (Genesis 2:15).

Humans may be the peak of creation, but only because we have the role of stewardship – we are to care for and conserve creation because it belongs to God: humans are merely caretakers of this property. Humans are co-creators with God and need to use and transform the natural world with care. Creation is made by God and is good, and so must be preserved because it has intrinsic value.

The effect of human sin

The Fall (Genesis 3) is seen by some as the reason for our environmental problems because from this point we became poor stewards of creation:

> The earth dries up and withers, the world languishes and withers; the heavens languish together with the earth. The earth lies polluted under its inhabitants; for they have transgressed laws, violated the statutes, broken the everlasting covenant.
>
> (Isaiah 14:4–5)

Christians teach that we need to use our increasing knowledge to rectify this and re-establish the bond between God and humanity, between God and the natural world. Thus for Christians the environment must be protected, and past mistakes must be used as learning tools and rectified where possible – this will ensure that the Western style of life does not impinge unfairly on the lifestyles of those in poorer nations and on the natural world as a whole.

Christians believe that care for the environment and the avoidance of needless exploitation of the natural world for selfish gain will help bring about peace, harmony and justice. Ultimately, Christian ethics is rooted in the relationship with God, and a Christian's relationship with God depends on how he or she uses creation and contributes to bringing about the Kingdom of God (1 Corinthians 15:21–2; Romans 5:12–21). Love of God and love of one's neighbour are fundamental in Christian ethics and apply also to the environment.

Dominion
The Judaeo-Christian idea that humans have a special place in the natural world and have responsibility for it.

Stewardship
A way of interpreting the use of dominion, which sees humans as caretakers of the natural world.

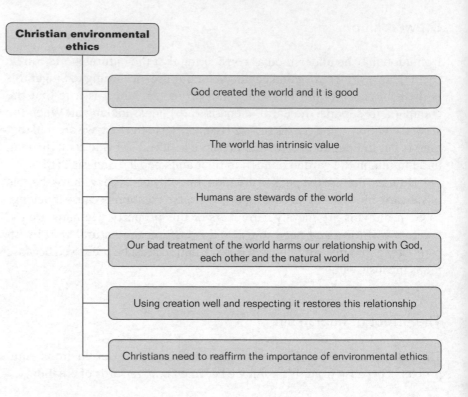

Christian environmental ethics

- God created the world and it is good
- The world has intrinsic value
- Humans are stewards of the world
- Our bad treatment of the world harms our relationship with God, each other and the natural world
- Using creation well and respecting it restores this relationship
- Christians need to reaffirm the importance of environmental ethics

Rapture and end-time theology

However, there are Christians, especially some influential right-wing fundamentalists in the USA, who would follow Singer's interpretation of biblical teaching. They do believe that humans have 'dominion' and that the Genesis creation story teaches that 'man' is superior to nature and can use its resources unchecked. Those who believe in the 'end-time' feel that concern for the Earth and the natural world is irrelevant because they have no future. Destruction of the environment is to be welcomed, and even helped along, as it is a sign of the coming of the Apocalypse and the Second Coming of Christ:

> When he opened the sixth seal, I looked, and there came a great earthquake; the sun became black as sackcloth, the full moon became like blood, and the stars of the sky fell to the earth as the fig tree drops its winter fruit when shaken by a gale. The sky vanished like a scroll rolling itself up, and every mountain and island was removed from its place.
>
> (Revelation 6:12–14)

John Hagee, senior pastor of Cornerstone Church in San Antonio, Texas, says that the environmental and social crises of today are portents of the

Rapture, when born-again Christians living and dead will be taken up into heaven: 'All over the earth, graves will explode as the occupants soar into the heavens', he preaches. Non-believers left behind will have seven years of suffering, culminating in the rise of the Antichrist and the final battle of Armageddon. Once the battle is won, Christ will send the non-believers to hell and re-green the Earth, where he will reign in peace with his followers.

All this may sound totally far-fetched, but this view is powerful in the world and held by many Americans in positions of power – why care about climate change or signing the Kyoto Agreement to limit greenhouse gases if you and those close to you will be rescued in the Rapture?

Thought Point

1. If all life is created by God, show how the teleological argument for the existence of God implies respect for his creative design.
2. Explain how the biblical sources could back up differing approaches to the environment.
3. Explain why it is important that the natural world should have intrinsic value.
4. 'Humans should care for their own kind first.' How far do you think religious ethics would agree with this?

> **Rachel Louise Carson (1907–1964)**
>
> Rachel Carson was born in Springdale, Pennsylvania, and studied at the Pennsylvania College for Women and Johns Hopkins University. From 1931 to 1936 she taught zoology at the University of Maryland. She held the post of aquatic biologist at the United States Bureau of Fisheries from 1936 to 1952.

PHILOSOPHICAL APPROACHES TO THE ENVIRONMENT

The modern study of environmental ethics was a response to the work of scientists such as Rachel Carson and her influential book *Silent Spring* (1962), which explored the idea of interconnectedness through a study of the use of pesticides and how their effect is felt through the food chain. The fate of one species is linked with that of all other species, including humans. In the 1960s the Australian writer Alan Marshall wrote that there have been three main ethical approaches to the environment:

1. libertarian extension or deep ecology
2. ecologic extension or eco-holism (including the Gaia hypothesis: see p. 161)
3. conservation ethics or shallow ecology.

These divisions within the environmental movement are separated by the terms shallow and deep and, when applied to thought, shallow is bad

Biocentric
Used of an approach to the environment that considers the biological nature and diversity of the Earth to be of supreme importance.

Deep ecology
An approach to environmental ethics that sees all life forms as of value and human life as just one part of the biosphere. It rejects anthropocentrism.

Shallow ecology
The concept that the Earth is cared for to make conditions better for humans.

and deep is good, so today they are often referred to as dark green and light green.

Libertarian extension – deep ecology

This really began in 1949 when Aldo Leopold's book *Sand County Almanac* was published shortly after his death. This inspired a new approach to the environment and an interest in ecology as a science. The book is a mixture of natural history and philosophy, and calls for a new approach to the environment: 'A thing is right when it tends to preserve the integrity, stability, and beauty of the bionic community. It is wrong when it tends otherwise.'

Leopold stated that we need to develop an ethics to deal with humans' relationship to land, animals and plants, and to extend our social conscience from people to land, and that it is not right to see the natural world simply in terms of its economic worth to humans.

In 1973 one of the founding fathers of environmental philosophy, Arne Naess, published a short paper called 'The Shallow and the Deep, Longrange Ecology Movement'. He basically stated that there are two ecology movements: the first is concerned mostly with pollution, the depletion of natural resources and the usefulness of the Earth for humans (anthropocentrism), and the second is concerned with the richness, diversity and intrinsic value of all the natural world – this is deep ecology.

He argued for the intrinsic value and inherent worth of the environment. According to Naess, every being, whether human, animal or vegetable, has an equal right to live and blossom. He called this ecosophy, which he defined as follows: 'By an ecosophy I mean a philosophy of ecological harmony or equilibrium' (in Drengson and Inoue, *The Deep Ecology Movement* p. 8).

Naess rejected any idea that humans are more important because they have a soul, use reason or have consciousness. So nature does not exist to serve humans; humans are simply a part of nature and all species have a right to exist for their own sake, regardless of their usefulness to humans. This view requires a complete change in how humans relate to the natural world, and Naess actually opposes the Christian view of stewardship as arrogant and depending on the idea of superiority which underlies the thought that humans exist to watch over nature like some sort of intermediary between God and his creation.

Naess and the American philosopher George Sessions listed an eightfold deep-ecology platform that may be summarised as follows:

1. All life has value in itself, independently of its usefulness to humans.
2. Richness and diversity contribute to life's well-being and have value in themselves.

Ecosophy

A word formed by contracting the phrase 'ecological philosophy'. It refers to philosophies which have an ecocentric or biocentric perspective such as deep ecology.

3. Humans have no right to reduce this richness and diversity except to satisfy vital needs in a responsible way.
4. The impact of humans in the world is excessive, and rapidly getting worse.
5. Human lifestyles and population are key elements of this impact.
6. The diversity of life, including cultures, can flourish only with reduced human impact.
7. Basic ideological, political, economic and technological structures must therefore change.
8. Those who accept the foregoing points have an obligation to participate in implementing the necessary changes and to do so peacefully and democratically.

Naess proposes therefore that humans should:

- radically reduce the Earth's population
- abandon all goals of economic growth
- conserve diversity of species
- live in small, self-reliant communities
- 'touch the Earth lightly'.

However, many consider that these ideas are simply not practical or realistic, especially as the human population is increasing rapidly and humans have just as much right to reproduce as any other species.

As a result of these problems, Richard Sylvan developed an alternative approach to deep ecology called *deep green theory*, which involves respect but not reverence for the environment.

Ecologic extension – eco-holism

This emphasises not the rights of humans but the interdependence of all ecosystems and sees the environment as a whole entity, valuable in itself. This is often known as *eco-holism* and its most popular form is James Lovelock's Gaia hypothesis.

The Gaia hypothesis challenges the view that humans are the most important species and sees humans as part of a living whole – Gaia. Gaia theory was put forward by James Lovelock in a number of books. The word 'Gaia' was first applied to ecology by the novelist William Golding and comes from the name of the Greek goddess of the Earth. All the life forms of the planet are a part of Gaia – looking at the Earth from space, Lovelock saw not so much a planet of diverse life forms as a planet transformed by a self-regulating living system; it was almost a living being.

James Ephraim Lovelock (1919–)

James Lovelock was born on 26 July 1919 in Letchworth. He read chemistry at the University of Manchester and then biophysics in London. He held posts at Harvard Medical School and Yale University.

In 1957 he invented the electron capture detector which has since been used to study the global atmosphere. His studies of the differences between the atmospheres of the Earth and other planets led to the development of the Gaia theory.

Holistic
Used of an approach to the environment that considers a range of factors, including the importance of balance within the ecosystem.

Gaia hypothesis
A theory of James Lovelock.

Geocentric
Used of an approach to the environment that considers the geological nature and diversity of the Earth to be most important.

Gaia – Earth from space

In his early work Lovelock argued that Gaia is regulated by the living organisms within it to maintain suitable conditions for growth and development – he later rejected this position and saw the regulation as conducted by the whole of Gaia, not just the living organisms. He examined the fossil evidence which showed that climatic change had, in fact, taken place within a very narrow range so that life was never destroyed. Conditions seem to have favoured life; they are not random but intelligently organised – this he claims was carried out not by God, as religious believers maintain, but by Gaia herself. However, God could be an explanation for the existence of Gaia and for maintaining her in existence. This theory opposes the Darwinian idea of the survival of the fittest, whereby species evolve to suit the conditions available, and says that the conditions on Earth are actually managed by Gaia herself. The world is a result not of chance but of self-engineering.

According to Lovelock, life cannot be destroyed. There are many types of algae that are resistant to ultraviolet radiation, so, even if the ozone layer were to be destroyed, life would continue and new life would evolve. On the Bikini atoll where nuclear bombs were tested in 1946–58, life has returned; the same may be said for the site of the Chernobyl nuclear reactor disaster in 1986. Human life may be wiped out, but humans are just a part of Gaia, and Gaia herself would survive without our presence. This theory challenges humans to change their perceptions and see themselves as part of a whole. If we abuse Gaia then we risk our own survival, as Gaia owes us nothing and we owe her our very existence.

The Earth, then, is a unified, holistic living entity with ethical worth, and in the long run the human race has no particular significance, but we are part of it and all the organisms on Earth are interdependent.

Lovelock's latest book, *The Revenge of Gaia*, is more pessimistic about climate change and our reluctance to confront it. He now considers that, as the global temperatures rise higher and higher and there are more climatic disasters, the planet may not be able to recover as he previously thought. With a three-degree temperature rise the rain forests will start to die, releasing vast new amounts of carbon dioxide; in the oceans the algae will fail and stop absorbing carbon; there will be floods, crop failures and massive human migrations.

Lovelock advocates the rapid expansion of nuclear power to cut fossil fuel emissions. He writes:

> Renewable energy sounds good, but so far it is inefficient and expensive. It has a future, but we have no time now to experiment with visionary energy sources: civilisation is in imminent danger and has to use nuclear energy now, or suffer the pain soon to be inflicted by our outraged planet.

Shallow ecology versus deep ecology

Shallow ecology	Deep ecology
Natural diversity is valuable as a resource.	Natural diversity has intrinsic value.
Species should be saved as a resource for humans.	Species should be saved for their intrinsic value.
Pollution should be decreased if it threatens economic growth.	Decrease in pollution has priority over economic growth.
Population growth threatens ecological equilibrium.	Human population is excessive today. Overdeveloped countries.
'Resource' means resource for humans.	'Resource' means resource for living things.
Decrease in standard of living is intolerable.	Decrease in quality of life is intolerable.

WHAT ARE THE ISSUES?

Is protection of the environment only an issue for the rich?

At first glance it would seem that this question is simply stating that the rich nations mainly caused the problems with the environment and so they must be the ones to solve it. However, it cannot be that simple – we are all affected by issues such as climate change as the Archbishop of Canterbury, Rowan Williams, said in his address at York Minster on 25 March 2009:

The ecological crisis challenges us to be reasonable. . . . I don't intend to discuss in detail the rhetoric of those who deny the reality of climate change, except to say that rhetoric (as King Canute demonstrated) does not turn back rising waters. If you live in Bangladesh or Tuvalu, scepticism about global warming is precisely the opposite of reasonable: 'negotiating' this environment means recognising the fact of rising sea levels; and understanding what is happening necessarily involves recognising how rising temperatures affect sea levels . . . it is not possible rationally to deny what the inhabitants of low-lying territories in the world routinely face as the most imminent threat to their lives and livelihoods.

He went on to say that climate change and the ecological problems we face are a matter of justice, both towards the poorer nations who bear the consequences of the actions of the richer nations and to those who will succeed us – our children and grandchildren.

The problems of dwindling natural resources, overpopulation and the environmental crisis affect us all, and so we will need to develop greater interdependence and a sense of global responsibility. This was the message of the Helsinki Declaration in 1990 when it argued for sustainable development, and was repeated by Gordon Brown, then Chancellor of the Exchequer, in 2005: 'If our economies are to flourish, if global poverty is to be banished, and the well-being of the world's people enhanced, we must make sure we take care of the natural environment and resources on which our economic activity depends.'

It is true that richer nations are able to provide environmental improvements that are beyond poorer nations, and so they have a responsibility to export this, not just the environmental problems. One excellent example of this is the so-called 'Millennium Village' of Sauri in Kenya, where half the funding for improvement came from local and national government and half from the international community. Continuous farming had exhausted the soil, and villagers were taught fallow farming techniques and how to use leguminous crops and fertiliser to improve the soil – harvests increased vastly. Villagers worked together, education and health care improved and they in turn exported their techniques to other surrounding villages. This idea has now spread to Ethiopia. The scheme is simple and local, working to improve the environmental problems and so the lives of the people. It gives a practical solution at a small level – we have seen it also in the UK with the growth of bioregionalism: local food grown and sold locally in farmers' markets.

Wealth is not the only factor involved in environmental destruction – the average Norwegian is better off than the average US citizen, but contributes about half as much to climate change.

Is protection of the environment only for the good and benefit of humankind?

As we have seen, there are a number of approaches to this question, depending on your religious or philosophical stance. Christianity and many other religions tend to say that humans are above other creatures – being in the image of God. Also animals do not possess rational thought or free will, nor are they moral agents.

As was seen in the ideas put forward by Peter Singer and others, this approach ignores our interdependence, and promotes a selfish view that has led us to exploit the natural world for our own benefit – leading, as Kant pointed out, to our own downfall.

The ideas of the dark green ecology movement come into force here. However, ultimately whether one takes a light green stance and conserves and protects the environment for the benefit of humans – a sort of lifestyle stance – or whether one takes a dark green stance and looks to the interconnectedness of the biosphere, both aim to protect the environment, though with different starting points, different ideologies and different motives.

More recently 'bright greens' have emerged as another group who believe that using new technologies and better designs are the way forward to protect the environment. The reasons for protecting the environment become less important than the fact that we actually use our knowledge and skills to do something about it.

How far should humans be forced to become environmentally responsible?

Should we be forced to lead a more environmentally friendly way of life and make sure that everyone takes responsibility? Whether we believe that climate change is caused by human activities or not, should the decision to act be ours, not the government's?

Recently (1 February 2009) Jonathon Porritt, who chairs the government's Sustainable Development Commission, caused a stir by claiming that curbing population growth through contraception and abortion must be at the heart of policies to fight global warming, and that any family that had more than two children was totally irresponsible.

Environmental policies are now part of every organisation, and already affect our lives from the type of lightbulb we buy to when our rubbish is collected and how it is disposed of. In many ways we in the UK are forced to be environmentally friendly by law, through constant media advertisements and through taxation – already environmental taxes count for over 7 per cent of our total tax and social contributions.

> **Jonathon Espie Porritt (b. 6 July 1950)**
>
> Jonathon Porritt, CBE, is an English environmentalist and writer. In the 1970s and 1980s, Porritt was a prominent member of the Ecology Party. He was Chair of the UK Ecology Party (now the Green Party) from 1978 to 1984. He was one of the founders of Friends of the Earth, England, Wales and Northern Ireland, and became Director in 1984.

It is not possible to know exactly whether people do take totally personal responsibility for the environment or whether the influence of governments and the media is a subtle way of forcing people into action. Perhaps the average person would lead an environmentally non-destructive lifestyle if given the chance, but governments and businesses must bear some of the responsibility for enabling people to do so by providing them with public transport, making it easy for them to recycle, selling products in biodegradable packaging, etc. Perhaps it is the time to introduce new policies that have governmental backing but rely on individual responsibility and action – a new look at the environment and economics along the lines of E.F. Schumacher's *Small Is Beautiful: Economics as if People Mattered* (1973).

Thought Point

Read the passage below assigned to your group. Summarise the main points. Identify the key ethical arguments in the passage.

Choose one environmental problem (e.g. destruction of the rain forest, saving an endangered species, pollution or global warming) and consider the implications of implementing the environmental ethic from the passage you have read. Look at both positives and negatives.

Give your own views on the environmental ethic put forward in your passage – as a group or as individuals if there is disagreement.

Reading 1

'The Land Ethic' from Aldo Leopold's *A Sand County Almanac* (1949) (pp. 201–4)

There is as yet no ethic dealing with man's relation to land and to the animals and plants that grow upon it. Land, like Odysseus' slave girls, is still property. The land relation is still strictly economic, entailing privileges, but not obligations.

The extension of ethics to this element in human environment is, if I read the evidence correctly, an evolutionary possibility and an ecological necessity. . . . The land ethic simply enlarges the boundaries of the community to include soils, waters, plants, and animals, or collectively: the land.

This sounds simple: do we not already sing our love for obligation to the land of the free and the home of the brave? Yes, but just what and whom do we love? Certainly not the soil, which we are sending helter-skelter downriver. Certainly not the waters, which we assume have no function except to turn turbines, float barges, and carry off sewage.

Certainly not the plants, of which we exterminate whole communities without batting an eye. Certainly not the animals, of which we have already exterminated many of the largest and most beautiful species. A land ethic of course cannot prevent the alteration, management, and use of these 'resources' but it does affirm their right to continued existence, and, at least in spots, their continued existence in a natural state.

In short, a land ethic changes the role of *Homo sapiens* from conqueror of the land-community to plain member and citizen of it. It implies respect for his fellow-members, and also respect for the community as such.

Reading 2

'Utilitarian Environmental Ethics' from Peter Singer's *Practical Ethics* (1979) (pp. 56–7)

The argument for extending the principle of equality beyond our own species is simple, so simple that it amounts to no more than a clear understanding of the principle of equal consideration of interests. We have seen that this principle implies that our concern for others ought not to depend on what they are like, or what abilities they possess (although precisely what this concern requires us to do may vary according to the characteristics of those affected by what we do). It is on this basis we are able to say that the fact that some people are not members of our race does not entitle us to exploit them, and similarly the fact that some people are less intelligent than others does not mean their interests may be disregarded.

But the principle also implies that the fact that beings are not members of our species does not entitle us to exploit them, and similarly the fact that other animals are less intelligent than we are does not mean that their interests may be disregarded. . . . A stone does not have interests because it cannot suffer. Nothing that we do can possibly make any difference to its welfare. A mouse, on the other hand, does have an interest in not being tormented, because mice will suffer if treated in this way.

Reading 3

'Instrumental Environmental Ethics' from David Pearce et al.'s *Blueprint for a Green Economy* (1995) (pp. 5–7)

One of the central themes of environmental economics, and central to sustainable development thinking also, is the need to place proper values on the services provided by natural environments. The central problem is that many of these services are provided 'free'. They have a zero price simply because no market-place exists in which their true values can be revealed through the acts of buying and selling. Examples might be a fine view, the water purifications and storm protection functions of coastal wetlands, or the biological diversity within a tropical rainforest. The elementary theory of supply and demand tells us that if something is provided at a zero price, more of it will be demanded than if there was a positive price. Very simply, the cheaper it is the more will be demanded. The danger is that this greater level of demand will be unrelated to the capacity of the relevant natural environments to meet the demand. For example, by treating the ozone layer as a resource with zero price there never was any incentive to protect it. Its value to human populations and to the global environment in general did not show up anywhere in a balance sheet of profit or loss, or of costs and benefits. The important principle is that resources and environments serve economic functions and have positive value. To treat them as if they had zero value is seriously to risk overusing the resource. . . . We have a sound *a priori* argument for supposing that the environment has been used to excess.

Reading 4

'Deep Ecology' from Devall and Sessions's *Deep Ecology* (2001) (p. 70)

Basic principles:

1. The well-being and flourishing of human and non-human life on Earth have value in themselves (synonyms: intrinsic value, inherent value). These values are independent of the usefulness of the non-human world for human purposes.
2. Richness and diversity of life forms contribute to the realisation of these values and are also values in themselves.
3. Humans have no right to reduce this richness and diversity except to satisfy *vital* needs.
4. The flourishing of human life and cultures is compatible with a substantial decrease of the human population. The flourishing of non-human life requires such a decrease.
5. Present human interference with the non-human world is excessive, and the situation is rapidly worsening.
6. Policies must therefore be changed. These policies affect basic economic, technological, and ideological structures. The resulting state of affairs will be deeply different from the present.
7. The ideological change is mainly that of appreciating *life quality* (dwelling in situations of inherent value) rather than adhering to an increasingly higher standard of living. There will be a profound awareness of the difference between big and great.
8. Those who subscribe to the foregoing points have an obligation directly or indirectly to try to implement the necessary changes.

Buddhist perspectives on the environment

Buddhism works towards integrating with the natural world, particularly because rebirth may be as an animal. Nevertheless humanity is the main focus of the religion because it is from this stage that enlightenment is possible.

Buddhism does not view humanity as stewards but as having a responsibility towards the less sentient beings who live with them in the world.

Ahimsa (non-violence) is central to Buddhist teaching and the requirement to avoid harm to all living beings impacts on attitudes towards exploitation of natural habitats.

The consumption of resources must also be monitored and carried out responsibly because of the ever-growing population of the world.

Plants are not necessarily recognised as sentient life forms but the conservation of forests, for example, is seen as important both for the other life there and as places for withdrawal and meditation.

There are now conservation movements within Buddhism which seek to promote sustainable development and prevent damage to ecosystems.

Hindu perspectives on the environment

Hinduism teaches that all life is of equal value and has the same right to exist. Therefore only God has sovereignty and dominion over life. Humans have no special privileges and indeed have special responsibility towards other life forms because they may be reborn as one of these. In addition, respect must also be shown towards trees and other plants. Rivers are seen as sacred, in particular the River Ganges.

Humans may use the natural resources of the Earth but not abuse or exploit it. Environmental ethics are therefore based on the entire world, not just the concerns of humanity.

Jewish perspectives on the environment

For Judaism, human life has privileges, and nature is something which can be used as well as protected. The needs of nature and humanity must be kept in balance. In particular animals must not be pushed to the point of extinction because of the possible need for them in the future. The need to protect species is seen in the story of Noah and the flood.

Although, at creation, humanity is afforded dominion and stewardship, this is seen as a duty to respect and conserve rather than exploit.

Jewish teaching about these issues is complex. The laws of *kashrut* state which foods can be eaten and which cannot. The slaughtering practice of *shechitah* is designed to keep the suffering of animals to the minimum. There are also laws about which trees can be felled for use in war and which cannot. The teaching of rest on the Sabbath is also seen as reminding humanity of the need not to exploit nature or other life forms.

Although human life has priority over other forms, Judaism teaches that all beings exist for themselves and not for others.

Although Judaism sees the importance of preserving and protecting nature, the preservation of human life is more important.

Natural resources must not be wasted because everything belongs to G-d.

Muslim perspectives on the environment

Muslim teaching on the environment is based on the teaching that the natural world was created by God with all the elements in balance.

The relationship between humanity and the environment is one based on justice. Humans are to enjoy and utilise the environment but are also, as vice-regents, to protect and promote all aspects of it.

The Prophet said that the world was a mosque in which to worship Allah.

Sikh perspectives on the environment

Sikhs respect the dignity of all life and believe that they should live in harmony with creation. Guru Nanak Dev Ji: 'The Earth is your mother.'

The relationship between humans and creation is seen as the wisdom of the universe. Sikhs see the present environmental problems as showing that humanity has tried to dominate creation and has exploited and enslaved it. It is through the wisdom of the universe that the ecological balance can be restored.

Further information on world faiths can be found at: http://subknow. reonline.org.uk/.

REVIEW QUESTIONS AND ACTIVITIES

Look back over the chapter and check that you can answer the following questions:

- Explain religious approaches to the environment and Singer's objections.
- Make bullet point notes on the Gaia hypothesis. List reasons for and against it.
- Make a chart comparing deep (dark green) and shallow (light green) ecology.

Terminology

Do you know your terminology?

Try to explain the following key ideas without looking at your books and notes:

- Anthropocentric
- Biocentric
- Biodiversity
- Conservation ethics
- Deep ecology
- Dominion
- Ecosophy
- Gaia hypothesis
- Geocentric
- Holistic
- Instrumental value/Intrinsic value
- Sentience
- Shallow ecology
- Stewardship

SAMPLE EXAMINATION QUESTIONS

(a) Examine religious teachings about humanity's responsibility towards the environment. (30 marks)

You may answer this question from the perspective of more than one religion.

- You should mention the concepts of dominion v. stewardship if relevant.
- Your responses should be based in religious teachings from sacred texts, leaders and tradition.
- You should focus on humanity's responsibility to the environment and not just environmental issues.

(b) Assess the strengths and weaknesses of these teachings. (15 marks)

In your answer you need to consider both sides of the discussion.

'Strong' arguments:

- Respect for all life.
- Doing what God wants.
- Encouraging people to think of other species and other (future) people, not just themselves.
- A more eco-friendly approach.
- Some religious teachings have been shown to 'work' (e.g. concept of a sabbatical year for fields (lying fallow)).

'Weak' arguments:

- Teachings are out-of-date, and in some cases wacky.
- Utilitarianism would advocate greatest pleasure now.
- Why force religious teachings on non-religious people?
- Teachings are sometimes contradictory, so which do we follow?
- Teachings are often seen as idealistic rather than realistic.

A2 UNIT 3A
RELIGION AND
ETHICS

11 Libertarianism

Essential terminology

Autonomous moral
   agent
Compatibilism
Determinism
Hard determinism
Incompatibilism
Libertarianism
'Ought implies can'
Predestination
Soft determination

WHAT YOU WILL LEARN ABOUT IN THIS CHAPTER

*   The link between free will and moral responsibility.
*   The ethical theories of hard determinism, libertarianism and soft determinism or compatibilism.
*   The influences of genetics, psychology and social environment on our moral choices.
*   Religious ideas of free will and predestination.
*   The strengths and weaknesses of determinism and free will.
*   The link between free will, determinism and moral responsibility.

THE AQA CHECKLIST ✔

Libertarianism, free will and determinism

*   Free will: question of genetics and environment; free will curtailed by volition; contracting into societies; conflict of free wills
*   Libertarianism: the personality and the moral self; the conscience; the causally undetermined choice
*   Determinism: the principle of causality; 'hard' determinism and 'soft' determinism; internal and external causation
*   A religious perspective on libertarianism and determinism.

Hard determinism
The belief that people do not have any free will and that all moral actions have prior causes. This means that nobody can be held morally responsible.

Libertarianism
The belief that determinism is false and people are free to make moral choices and so are responsible for their actions.

Soft determinism
The belief that determinism is true in many aspects, but we are still morally responsible for our actions.

Compatibilism
The belief that it is possible to be both free and determined, as some aspects of our nature are determined, but not our ability to make moral decisions.

Determinism
The view that every event has a cause and so, when applied to moral decisions, we do not have free will.

Predestination
The belief that God has decided who will be saved and who will not.

Free will
The ability to choose freely, and the ability to make choices that are not curtailed by any external agency.

ISSUES ARISING

- How free are human actions and choices?
- Is it the case that, unless you are in complete isolation, you can never have true libertarianism?
- Does libertarianism require no influences to be truly free?
- If we are not free, can we be held responsible for our actions?
- Strengths and weaknesses of libertarianism, free will and determinism for making ethical choices.

WHAT IS DETERMINISM?

Most people agree that people are morally responsible only for the actions they carry out freely and deliberately – actions that are freely chosen. Determinism, however, states that there are laws of nature which govern everything which happens and that all our actions are the result of these scientific laws and every choice we make was determined by the situation immediately before it, and that situation was determined by the situation before it and so on as far back as you want to go. Freedom of choice is just an illusion and so personal responsibility is a meaningless concept, as are blame and punishment. This makes it difficult to make any sense of the idea that people are to be held morally and legally responsible only for actions carried out freely and deliberately. However, we do feel a sense of responsibility for what we have done even if we did not choose that action; for example, a driver who kills a child who ran out in front of their car would blame themselves for the death, even if it was not their fault and they could not have prevented it.

Philosophers have traditionally responded to this problem in different ways.

- Hard determinists accept determinism and reject freedom and moral responsibility.
- Libertarians reject determinism and accept freedom and moral responsibility.
- Soft determinists or compatibilists reject the two previous views that free will and determinism are incompatible, and argue that freedom is not only compatible with determinism but actually requires it.

Genetics and environment

We perceive ourselves as having free will and so do not have constantly to think and question what influences us to think and behave as we do. We simply tend to do things and make moral decisions because they make sense to us, once we have weighed up our options and considered the consequences. However, this does not necessarily mean that our decisions are made independent of deterministic factors – our environment, memory, impulses, etc. are almost hard-wired into our consciousness – our free will uses these factors to make decisions. This does not mean that these factors determine the decision, they simply influence it.

Philosophers throughout the ages have disputed whether we do in fact have free will or whether our decisions are totally determined. Scientists have also become interested in this question. A long-term study of twins by Kay Phillips in the USA found much evidence that genes influence human behaviour. She is attempting to isolate certain genes that make people act in a certain way. However, she says that this does not mean that people are determined to exhibit these behaviours: 'Influence is a key word. Genes influence, not dictate behaviour. Behaviour is also influenced by environment and by free will. Genetics does not by any means take away free will.'

The influence of environment, upbringing and education upon our actions, and so our lack of responsibility for them, is illustrated by the Leopold and Loeb Case in 1924, when Clarence Darrow (1857–1938), an American lawyer and civil libertarian, defended two young men, Nathan Leopold and Richard Loeb, on a charge of murdering a young boy, Bobby Franks. The perfect crime the two men planned went wrong and in the subsequent court case Darrow, their defence lawyer, pleaded for the death penalty to be commuted to life imprisonment, as the two young murderers were the product of their upbringing, their ancestry and their wealthy environment. He also commented on their university education and their study of Nietzsche.

> What has this boy to do with it? He was not his own father; he was not his own mother; he was not his own grandparents. All of this was handed to him. He did not surround himself with governesses and wealth. He did not make himself. And yet he is to be compelled to pay.
>
> (Clarence Darrow)

Free will curtailed by volition

According to Thomas Hobbes, free will means that a person can act freely and could choose to act in a different way if the person decided to. If someone's free will is denied through some form of constraint or, for example,

Incompatibilism

The belief that determinism is logically incompatible with free will. Thus some incompatibilists will say that determinism is a fact and so we are not free, but most take the opposite view that free will is a fact and so determinism is false.

through rape, it is because someone else is overriding the victim's own preferences and choices. So you could also say that a person who is not in control of their actions through drink or drugs also has no freedom of choice in their decisions.

However, we do need to consider what sort of freedom our minds actually have – our choices are curtailed by our knowledge, our values and how we see both ourselves and our environment. Not only are our choices curtailed by external influences: they are curtailed also by our past thoughts and past decisions. Nor can our choices do the impossible – we cannot fly using our own bodies just because we freely will to do so.

The only way round this is by our self-awareness, our consciousness. Existentialists such as Jean-Paul Sartre would argue that our free will is central to us as humans. He said that the slave is as free as the master, as each is equally free to give meaning to their situation. Free will then is not the elimination of all influencing factors, but our ability to be autonomous and self-determining, to deal with ideas, to be imaginative, to plan the future, and our awareness and monitoring of our own thinking. Free will is the ability to make intelligent choices. We weigh up the pros and cons, because we are able to reason.

One thing that is seen to limit our choices though is the way nature, nurture and free will interact – our thoughts help select our environment and our environment affects our thoughts and choices. Free will does not mean that our choices are free from the hard-wiring of our brains, from our genes or from environmental influences and previous experiences, but it is the ability to make conscious choices with an awareness of the possible consequences and the fact that we are doing the choosing.

The conflict of free wills

If God knows everything and all our actions are predetermined, then we have no free choices, no free will. This also means that there can be no praise or blame for any of our actions – they were simply inevitable. God, with his foreknowledge, not only knows exactly what choices we will make but actually chooses what we would choose. He knows what will influence our choices, and he controls these factors.

Alternatively, this cause and effect applies only to our physical selves, meaning that our spiritual self is free to make moral choices. If we have this freedom we can act contrary to God's will and be as sinful as we like – God does not stop evil occurring, in fact he allows it as it strengthens us so we can achieve what is good. The fact that God knows both the good and the bad things that we do does not mean that we have no freedom – we still have the choice to act differently. According to St Augustine free will is

God's gift to us; the future is not predetermined but it is understood by God. God's knowledge is outside time and so leaves us free, though limited by our nature.

Alternatively God does not know the future because it has not yet happened, and so it is not knowable, but this places limitations on God's omniscience.

LIBERTARIANISM

The view of those who reject determinism and say we have complete moral responsibility is called libertarianism, as they believe determinism is false and we have free will. Libertarians say that the ideas of cause and effect cannot be applied to human behaviour and choices; we do have freedom to act and we are morally responsible for our actions.

Libertarians do not believe that we are compelled to act by outside forces but that moral actions are the result of the values and character of the individual. This view means that we have free choice and can choose different ways to act, whereas determinism means that we do the only thing we can do and so never really have a choice about anything. The most common argument for libertarianism is that it appeals to our intuitions – we see ourselves as free agents, able to make moral choices, not as puppets on a string or robots. Unlike puppets or robots we have a mind, and it seems reasonable to conclude that having a mind is necessary in order to have free will. Peter van Inwagen uses the analogy of choosing which branch to go down when travelling along a road, whereas determinism is like travelling along a road with no branches – we cannot choose a different way, or reach a different destination.

Libertarians also argue that, unlike Darrow's argument that we do not 'make ourselves', we do 'make our actions' and we could have chosen to do something else. This, they argue, is clear because when asked to defend our actions we blame ourselves, or wonder if we did the right thing – we evaluate our action by asking ourselves whether, at that time, we could have acted differently. We would only blame, criticise or regret if we believed we had alternative ways of acting. This is a commonsense view of ourselves as choosers and agents with the future open to us in the way the past is not. We know that unforeseen events can alter events in the future – for example, students may always achieve A grades in practice examination papers, but this does not mean that on the day of the final examination they will do so. Their experience may predict that they will do so, but on the day of the examination they may have a bad cold, their dog may have died or they may misread a question – from our observation of the world around us we know that things can always go wrong.

Werner Heisenberg (1901–1976)

Werner Heisenberg was born on 5 December 1901 in Würzburg, Germany, and studied at the University of Munich. As a physicist and Nobel Laureate he developed a system of quantum mechanics. His uncertainty principle had a profound influence on physics and philosophy.

Jean-Paul Sartre (1905–1980)

Jean-Paul Sartre was born in Paris on 21 June 1905. He studied at the École Normale Supérieure, the University of Fribourg, Switzerland, and the French Institute in Berlin.

Sartre was a leading existentialist. In his writings he related his philosophical theory to literature, psychology and political action.

Another answer to the claim of determinism is that it is not the case that all events have a cause: some events are uncaused, and human decisions and choices are an example of such uncaused events. Modern physics is often used to defend this view and especially Werner Heisenberg's uncertainty principle, which says that we cannot know both the location and the momentum of subatomic particles at the same time. He therefore thought it was better to refer to the statistical probabilities rather than formulate general laws. Using this principle as a basis, it seems that determinism is false.

Many scientists now agree that since the idea of cause does not apply to subatomic particles, not every event in the universe is caused – some are, in principle, unpredictable. Honderich rejects the claims of quantum physics, saying that they only apply at the subatomic level; it is certainly not true to think that quantum physics refutes Newtonian mechanics – it is more accurate to say that it qualifies Newton's view and puts his theories in a broader context.

However, using this argument to support libertarianism misses the point. The principle of causality is actually presupposed when considering freedom, as the opposite of causality is randomness. A universe in which there are random events is not one in which we have free will. Behaviour caused by a random event is no more freely chosen than behaviour completely determined by the laws of Newtonian physics. Nobody could be held morally responsible for an act that was caused by a random event occurring in their brain. Modern physics seems to maintain that the most basic laws of nature are not deterministic but probabilistic. Einstein said, 'God does not play dice' – but apparently Einstein was wrong.

For free choices to be real, a person must be able to cause the events he or she chooses. If all human actions take place independently of any cause at all, including the will of the individual, then there is no genuine freedom. I am only not free to act if I am forced or compelled.

This idea of freedom is also seen as a goal of moral action – even if our freedom is limited, we show our freedom in our aim to be free and act freely.

This is one of the great themes of existentialism. For Jean-Paul Sartre, freedom is both the goal and the measure of our lives – from nothing people make themselves what they choose. Freedom here is an end in itself, as it does not matter what a person chooses as long as they choose freely. People must fill their nothingness with freedom – everything depends on the individual and the meaning they give to their life. A person may try to avoid this freedom; then they are guilty of *mauvaise foi* and just conform to what is decided by others.

Sartre sees life as ultimately absurd, meaningless, and without any reason why an individual exists or chooses to do one thing rather than another. 'To be free is to be condemned to be free.' So freedom is both the underpinning of any morality and it is a goal – to be free is to have a humanly fulfilling life.

THE PERSONALITY AND THE MORAL SELF

Freud

Sigmund Freud was a psychoanalyst who formed a very influential theory of personality. He studied the human mind, and its effects on and reactions with the body. Freud believed there was no such thing as a soul, and in his view conscience of the mind was essentially mechanistic. From his work, Freud concluded that the human personality consisted of three areas:

1. *The super-ego* – the set of moral controls given to us by outside influences. It is our moral code or conscience and is often in conflict with the id.
2. *The ego* – the conscious self, the part seen by the outside world.
3. *The id* – the unconscious self, the part of the mind containing basic drives and repressed memories. It is amoral, has no concerns about right and wrong and is concerned only with itself.

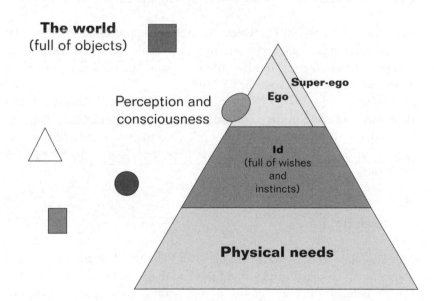

For Freud, the conscience is most clearly connected with the sense of guilt we feel when we go against our conscience. Conscience then is simply a construct of the mind – in religious people this would be in response to perceptions of God and in non-religious people it would be their responses to externally imposed authority. Freud did not believe in any absolute moral law and held that all our moral codes, and thus the content of our consciences, are shaped by our experiences – they are culturally dependent, and this explains the varieties of moral codes that are to be found in different societies.

Sigmund Freud (1856–1939)

Sigmund Freud was born in Freiberg, Moravia, on 6 May 1856. His family were driven out by anti-Semitic riots and moved, via Leipzig, to Vienna. He was inspired by the scientific work of Johann Wolfgang von Goethe and began his medical education in 1873. He studied the central nervous system under Ernst Wilhelm von Brücke.

He then worked at the General Hospital in Vienna to gain experience of psychiatry, dermatology and nervous diseases.

Super-ego
Freud's idea is that the super-ego reinforces ideas of correct behaviour implanted in us when we are young.

So if children learn their moral behaviour from their parents, teachers and other authority figures, is any moral choice they may make free? If the super-ego internalises the disapproval of others and creates the guilty conscience which grows into an internal force regardless of any individual rational thought or reflection, is it not just a form of moral control which traps us in its grasp?

Piaget and Kohlberg

Psychologists since Freud have expanded his ideas to include that of immature and mature consciences which develop as we grow up. This will not necessarily be a continuous development and some people will never reach the stage of having a mature conscience. According to Jean Piaget a child's moral development grows, and the ability to reason morally depends on cognitive development.

Piaget suggested two stages of moral development:

1. *Heteronomous morality* (between the ages of approximately 5 and 10 years) when the conscience is still immature, rules are not to be broken and punishment is expected if a rule is broken. The consequences of an action will show if it is right or wrong.
2. *Autonomous morality* (approximately ages 10+) when children develop their own rules and understand how rules operate in and help society. The move towards autonomous morality occurs when the child is less dependent on others for moral authority, and is able to make free decisions.

Child development

Lawrence Kohlberg followed Piaget's ideas and identified six stages of moral development which he believed individuals had to follow in sequence. People move from behaving in socially acceptable ways because they are told to do so by authority figures and want to gain approval, to keeping the law, to caring for others and finally to respect for universal principles and the demands of an individual conscience. Kohlberg felt that most adults never got beyond keeping the law.

Both Piaget and Kohlberg believed that most moral development and the development of an ability to make free decisions occur through social interaction.

Jean Piaget (1896–1980)

Piaget was born on 9 August 1896 in Neuchâtel, Switzerland. He studied biology at the University of Neuchâtel and then became interested in psychology. He worked in Zurich and at the Sorbonne. He became Director of the International Centre for Epistemology at the University of Geneva in 1955, and then co-director of the International Bureau of Education. He is best known for his work on the development of the intelligence of children.

Child development

Augusto Blasi

Augusto Blasi's writings and research on moral cognition, the development of the moral personality and self-identity are an important modern development. Blasi sees the self-as-agent, imbued with a sense of personal responsibility and obligation at the centre of moral identity. According to Blasi, one has moral identity to the extent that the self is organised around moral commitments which are central to one's self-understanding. He suggests that the centrality of a person's morality to their self-identity might be a major factor influencing the strength of the link between moral judgement and moral action, and so a major influence on one's moral behaviour. A good example of this is Nelson Mandela. The death of his father meant leaving the countryside to live with his influential uncle. His time at school was a preparation for moral judgements and action, which he built on in early adulthood. No single moment created his moral identity – it built up over time through the influence of family, education, his faith values and goals and through moral exemplars. This enabled him to endure many hardships, including 27 years' imprisonment in his fight against apartheid. To have moral identity is to have good moral reasons for the free decisions that one makes.

Conscience

Our sense of moral right and
wrong.

The conscience

Most people probably understand conscience as something which tells us
right from wrong, but when the issues are considered in more depth the
actual nature and function of conscience are harder to establish.

When considering the nature and function of conscience there are four
questions to keep in mind:

- What is conscience?
- Where does conscience come from?
- Is conscience innate or acquired?
- What is its function in ethical decision making?

Conscience is generally seen as a moral faculty, sense or feeling which compels individuals to believe that particular activities are morally right or wrong.
Conscience may also be seen to prompt different people in quite different
directions – one person may feel a moral duty to go to war, while another
may feel a moral duty to avoid war in all circumstances.

Most of us could make lists of behaviours we could not indulge in and
actions we could not perform following the dictates of our consciences. We
consider conscience to be a reliable guide. We could perhaps even agree with
Mark Twain, who wrote: 'I have noticed my conscience for many years, and
I know it is more trouble and bother to me than anything else I started with'
(*A Connecticut Yankee in King Arthur's Court*, 1889).

The last phrase is important, as it implies that conscience is something
we inherit at birth and remains a fellow traveller with us throughout our
lives. Experience seems to tell us, however, that this cannot be so – conscience
lacks consistency, whether between people in general or in any particular
person. Just think what appalling acts are performed with a clear conscience
(just obeying commands) or even in the name of conscience. Even individuals
are inconsistent, and matters about which we once had conscientious feelings
no longer affect us. If conscience is so changeable, how can it be a reliable
guide? Does it represent our views on moral issues only as we see them at
any given moment?

Views about conscience vary, and different writers will see it in different
ways and have different opinions about its role in ethical decision making.

BIBLICAL TEACHING

It is assumed by some biblical writers and early Christian teachers that our
conscience is God-given. This view is put clearly in Paul's letter to the
Romans:

When Gentiles, who do not possess the law, do instinctively what the law requires, these, though not having the law, are a law to themselves. They show that what the law requires is written on their hearts.

(Romans 2:14–15a)

Traditional Christian teaching is based on this – everyone knows what is right and wrong, as God has given us this ability. It is also implied that, by following their conscience, everyone can follow the divine law.

AQUINAS' APPROACH – REASON SEEKING UNDERSTANDING

Thomas Aquinas (1225–1274) saw conscience as the natural ability of people to understand the difference between right and wrong. He believed that all people aim for what is good and try to avoid the bad. He called this the synderesis rule and reckoned it was innate to seek the good – sin is a falling short of God's ideals, seeking what people think is good and is actually bad because they are not using their powers of reason properly. Aquinas understood that different societies have different views on what is right and what is wrong and, though he says people should always follow their conscience, he does see that people will sometimes get things wrong and make the wrong choices. He argued that conscience 'was the mind of man making moral judgments' and described it as containing two essential parts – synderesis and conscientia.

Synderesis means the repeated use of what Aquinas termed 'right' reason, by which a person acquires knowledge of basic moral principles and understands that it is important to do good and avoid evil. Conscientia is the actual ethical judgement or decision a person makes which leads to a particular course of action based upon these principles. Conscience, therefore, for Aquinas, is being able both to distinguish right from wrong and to make decisions when a person is confronted with difficult moral situations.

When Aquinas says it is always right to follow your conscience, he means that it is always right to apply your moral principles to each situation as best you can. He does not mean that if you follow your conscience you are always right – as, if your principles are wrong, your conscience will be wrong too.

Aquinas' idea of what he termed 'right' reason, by which a person acquires knowledge of basic moral principles and understands that it is important to do good and avoid evil, is what he called the actual ethical judgement or decision a person makes.

Aquinas says conscience is reasoning used correctly to find out what God sees is good. It is not just a voice inside us. Do we always use reason

Synderesis

Aquinas' idea of what he termed 'right' reason by which a person acquires knowledge of basic moral principles and understands that it is important to do good and avoid evil.

Conscientia

Aquinas called this the actual ethical judgement or decision a person makes.

in this way? Is reason, always guided by conscience, going to determine what we do, or do we rather use our emotions when making moral choices?

Some Christians would say that Aquinas' rationalistic approach does not consider revelation that comes directly from God.

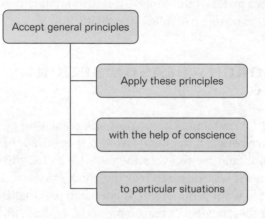

Accept general principles

Apply these principles

with the help of conscience

to particular situations

**Joseph Butler
(1692–1752)**

Joseph Butler became Dean of St Paul's Cathedral, London, in 1740, and Bishop of Durham in 1750. He is best known for his work *Analogy of Religion* (1736). He argued that belief in natural religion was no more rational than belief in revealed religion. He saw the two as complementary.

Self-love

Butler thought of this as wanting the well-being of self or enlightened self-interest, not selfishness.

Benevolence

Butler saw this as wanting the well-being of others.

BUTLER'S APPROACH – CONSCIENCE COMES FROM GOD

The eighteenth-century Anglican priest and philosopher Joseph Butler wrote that the most crucial thing which distinguished women and men from the animal world was the possession of the faculty of reflection or conscience. So being human involves being moral. He stated in one of his Sermons: 'There is a principle of reflection in men by which they distinguish between approval and disapproval of their own actions . . . this principle in man . . . is conscience' (*Fifteen Sermons*, 1726). Like Aquinas, Butler believed conscience could determine and judge the rightness or wrongness of different actions and thoughts. Conscience, for Butler, also held a powerful position within human decision making because, as he wrote, it 'magisterially exerts itself' spontaneously 'without being consulted'.

Therefore, there is something authoritative and automatic for Butler about the way conscience works when moral decisions have to be made. He gave to conscience the final say in moral decision making. Conscience, he said, governed and ordered such aspects and was the final moral authority: 'Had it strength, as it has right; had it power as it has manifest authority, it would absolutely govern the world.'

Butler saw human nature as hierarchical, and at the top is conscience. At its base are drives such as the drive for food which influence us without

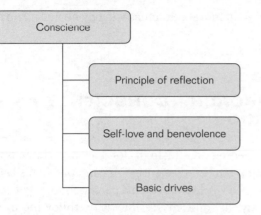

any thought for the consequences, and above these drives are two general impulses: self-love (wanting the well-being of self or enlightened self-interest, not selfishness) and benevolence (wanting the well-being of others). Higher than these and linked closely to the conscience is the 'principle of reflection' which makes us approve or disapprove of our actions. This is given to us by God and we have to use it to lead a proper, happy life. Conscience has supreme authority, and all moral decisions are decided under the guidance and authority of conscience.

An important point made by Butler was that conscience came from God. He believed conscience was a person's God-given guide to right conduct and its demands must therefore always be followed. He does not try to analyse whether conscience is based on reason or feeling or both: he just says that it obviously exists; it comes from God and must be obeyed if a person is to be truly happy.

Butler did not see mistakes made by conscience as a serious problem, as he believed that in any moral dilemma most people will see intuitively what is the right thing to do. However, he considers it wicked to 'blind' one's conscience to clear the way for a wrong action. People can easily convince themselves that all sorts of wrong actions are right and, for Butler, this corruption of conscience by self-deception is worse than the evil action which results from it.

Butler thinks that your conscience will tell you to watch out for the interests of others as far as possible. He has some important ideas which may be applied further:

- The consequence of an action is not what makes it right or wrong, as that has already happened.
- The purpose of conscience is to guide a person into a way of life that will make him or her happy.
- Conscience will harmonise self-love and benevolence – this may take

some sorting out, and so in moral dilemmas we may be uncertain about what to do.

- Conscience controls human nature.

NEWMAN'S APPROACH – CONSCIENCE AS THE VOICE OF GOD

The nineteenth-century theologian Cardinal John Henry Newman also adopted an intuitionist approach to conscience. For example, in his *Letter to the Duke of Norfolk* in 1874, he wrote that when a person follows conscience he or she is simultaneously, in some mysterious way, following a divine law.

Conscience is 'a messenger' of God and it is God speaking to us when we feel this intuitive moral knowledge and make decisions. Newman argued that, for Christians, conscience is more than simply 'a law of the mind', since it comes from God. Conscience does not invent the truth, but at its best it detects the truth. Elsewhere in his writings (*The Grammar of Assent,* 1870, chapter 5) Newman says:

> If, as is the case, we feel responsibility, are ashamed, are frightened, at transgressing the voice of conscience, this implies there is One to whom we are responsible, before whom we are ashamed, whose claims upon us we fear.

The fourth-century theologian Augustine of Hippo (354–430) had said the same thing, and he also believed that conscience was to be identified with the voice of God speaking to us. When we listen to it, we are really hearing the word of God whispering to us about what is right and what is wrong. Augustine urged all Christians to be concerned about conscience and to consider it most seriously. 'Return to your conscience, question it. . . . Turn inward, brethren, and in everything you do, see God as your witness', he wrote (*Ep Jo.* 8, 9: *Pl* 35, 2041).

Butler's, Newman's and Augustine's ideas on conscience are much less rationalist than Aquinas' and rely on a more intuitionist approach, whereby people are able to sense or intuit what is right and wrong, because God reveals this to them personally. So do these approaches on conscience mean that our ethical decisions are really free?

John Henry Newman (1801–1890)

John Henry Newman was born on 21 February 1801. He studied at Trinity College, Oxford, and, in 1822, became a Fellow of Oriel College. In 1828 he became vicar of St Mary's, the university church. Newman joined the movement founded by John Keble which called for the Church of England to react against theological liberalism, and to return to the theology and ritual of the time immediately after the Reformation. This became known as the 'Oxford Movement'. He wrote 29 papers for the *Tracts for the Times* (1833–41), which explained the need for this reaction.

In 1842 he retired from Oxford to the village of Littlemore, and, three years later, he resigned from the Anglican Church and became a Roman Catholic. In 1846 he became a Catholic priest and entered the Congregation of the Oratory. He published his best-known work, *Apologia pro Vita Sua* (Apology for His Life), in 1864. He was made a cardinal in 1879 and died on 11 August 1890.

MODERN UNDERSTANDINGS OF CONSCIENCE

The Roman Catholic Church at its Second Vatican Council (1962–1965) discussed the issue of conscience and agreed that there was a law inside each person which speaks to the individual heart. The emphasis given here was on an understanding of conscience as a personal and inner sense of right and wrong, but which worked like any law, and which held the person to obedience. One Council document, *The Pastoral Constitution of the Church in the Modern World*, stated that this law of the heart is, in fact, 'a law written by God. To obey it is the very dignity of man; according to it he will be judged.'

Modern scholars have attempted to define what conscience is in different ways from earlier thinkers. Vincent MacNamara, for example, argues that it is misleading to describe conscience as 'a voice', since this makes it sound like a special faculty or a piece of equipment which human beings possess, a separate thing inside the individual. He says it is much better to see conscience in terms of an attitude or an awareness people have that there is a moral path to be followed through life and that true human living does not revolve around profit and pleasure. MacNamara argues that the fact that people see that goodness and truth are important is another way of describing conscience; he puts it like this: 'it is not so much that I have a conscience – a special piece of equipment – as that I am a conscience. That is how I am, that is how I find myself. That is a basic truth about life.' This way of describing conscience is based in ideas about the kind of people we are and how we 'see' the world. You could say in a sense that it is linked to Virtue Ethics.

There are similarities in the work of Richard Gula, who argues that to consider conscience in terms of a series of laws, even a series of internal laws, is also misleading. He highlights two key terms in respect of the conscience: vision and choice. This is the ability to act, within a learned framework, through the needs of a Christian community and developed within a Christian understanding. The various communities which form our way of 'seeing' the world also determine the way our conscience works. Therefore, conscience is a way of 'seeing' and then responding, through the choices we make, to the world in which we live. Both MacNamara and Gula focus on a holistic approach to conscience.

Vernon Ruland tries to find a *via media* between rationalism and uncritical Divine Command theory and sees a moral decision as reflecting an 'ethics of loyal scrutiny' enriched by many sources of moral and religious wisdom. He explains that the God invoked in our conscience is not the exclusive property of Christians and points out that there are many interlinked sources of what he calls the ways of religious wisdom. Conscience seems to be less the 'voice of God' than our interpretation of that 'voice'.

St Augustine of Hippo (354–430)

St Augustine was born on 13 November 354, in Tagaste, Numidia. His father was a pagan but his mother Monica worked for Augustine's conversion. From the age of 15 to 30 Augustine lived with a woman from Carthage and in 372 had a son named Adeodatus, 'the gift of God'. Augustine was ordained in 391. He became Bishop of Hippo in 395.

Timothy O'Connell sees conscience as having three aspects or levels: first, it is our general sense of personal responsibility for who we are and what we become; second, it is our sense of obligation to search out the good, using all the resources of moral reasoning available to us, including the assistance of a moral community such as the Church; and finally it is the concrete judgement a person makes so that good as he or she sees it must be done. On this final level conscience is infallible and must be followed, but on the second level people can disagree in their conscientious judgements and wrong judgements can be made. Moral values are discovered by moral reasoning and are imposed by neither external nor internal laws but are discovered by historical human experience of the consequences of action for human fulfilment.

Daniel Maguire (*Death by Choice*, 1984) agrees with O'Connell, but adds that in discerning what is the correct moral choice we also need to consider the place of creative imagination, humour and the tragic experiences of life, especially great loss, as these open us up to new perceptions of value. Both O'Connell and Maguire see conscience as based on more than human reason; it is also based on the shared experience of the past, the shared experience of a culture and personal experience and affectivity.

CONSCIENCE AS A MORAL GUIDE

Crucial questions we need to address when considering conscience are: how important is it as a moral guide, and can it be relied upon? This brings us into discussion of two important areas. First, what authority or status should be given to individual conscience in moral decision making, and, second, how is a person's conscience formed so that it might be a good basis for making moral choices?

Within the Christian tradition, conscience is given overriding importance in moral decision making. Conscience must always be followed; a person is obliged to act in accordance with the dictates of conscience.

Aquinas gave considerable weight to the role of conscience. He believed that not following the dictates of conscience was always wrong, because by not following it a person was ignoring what he or she believed to be true. He believed conscience was a deep sense of right and wrong which came from God. Following one's conscience was like following the law of God and, even when conscience was mistaken, Aquinas believed that a person had a duty to follow it.

However, following one's conscience is no guarantee that one is always doing the right thing. It is sometimes possible to be mistaken about what is the right thing to do. This brings us to the second question about the reliability of conscience. For example, many people believe a particular course of action to be right at one time in their lives and then change their minds about that action at a later stage. Aquinas is again helpful in addressing this problem. He argued that it is the duty of everyone to inform and educate one's conscience. However, acting according to conscience, for Aquinas, is not a guarantee that a person is doing what is right; it ensures only that they will be morally blameless.

THE FORMATION OF CONSCIENCE

There are many external guides and pointers which help the individual conscience to make the right decision. To acquire an informed conscience is the responsibility of every person. Most of the approaches to conscience we have considered here think that conscience needs educating and forming.

In using conscience to make moral choices, individuals must ultimately make their own individual decision. No matter how influential external agencies are, following one's conscience always involves a personal evaluation. This is what separates the role of conscience in decision making from other methods. Following the dictates of conscience demands following what springs from the unique perception and grasp of the situation as perceived by the individual. No one can really be said to be following their conscience if they do not possess the courage and the freedom to work things out and decide for themselves.

PROBLEMS WITH CONSCIENCE

We have stated that for Christians conscience is often regarded as the voice of God. However, this raises some serious questions. If we were always certain that what our conscience told us to do in any moral situation was in fact God's command, it could be argued that we would never err or make mistakes, as God would not tell us things which are wrong. Clearly people do make errors of moral judgement which they regret later. In answer to this, some might reply that God does speak to us, but that we have not built up a sufficiently sensitive conscience to hear God's voice clearly – it is our fault, not God's.

If conscience is defined as being God's voice speaking to us, this implies that we know for certain what God commands of us. In addition, people often have doubts about what is the right thing to do and have difficulty deciding. Besides, even Christian denominations disagree on moral matters such as abortion – deciding what is the right thing to do is not always as clear-cut as 'the voice of God' definition suggests.

Furthermore, many atheists claim that conscience is important to them. Such claims do not rely upon God who, in some sense, regulates the moral order of the universe. For atheists, agnostics and humanists, conscience is part of being human and there is no need to involve God when moral decisions have to be made. Conscience appears to be a universal part of human moral living. Most people also seem to agree that both reason and the emotions are involved in the workings of conscience and that it is a most natural part of our human make-up, whether we are religious or not. When reason or the heart or both decide what ought to be done, we often feel emotionally drawn towards it, or even emotionally divided, if we partly shrink from doing it.

Following one's conscience, therefore, often implies that the whole being, body, mind and heart, is involved, in some way, when making the decision. We may often feel 'pangs of conscience' after doing what we consider to be the wrong thing or experience feelings of approval if we believe we have done the right thing. Enda McDonagh says: 'Conscience enables us to judge good and evil, reproaches us when we have done wrong, gives us peace when we have done well.' In this sense, conscience, although a deep part of us, appears to exist simultaneously as a separate entity, often standing over and against us as a judge or a supporter.

Finally, conscience implies personal responsibility, as Jack Mahoney wrote:

> And perhaps a little demythologising may be in order, for conscience is not a still small voice, not bells, nor a blind stab in the dark; it is simply me coming to a decision. When I say 'my conscience tells me' all I am really saying is 'I think'.
>
> (*Seeking the Spirit*, 1981, p. 18)

Thought Point

1. What philosophical problems occur when someone suggests 'Conscience is the voice of God'?
2. Is conscience learnt or innate?
3. 'It is not so much that I have a conscience – a special piece of equipment – as that I am a conscience.' What do you think MacNamara means by this?
4. What is the relationship between conscience and external authority in moral decision making?

ACTIVITIES

Form groups of two or three and agree on your own group definition of conscience, giving reasons for your choice.

Choose one recent event reported in the media which in your opinion demonstrates a courageous, free decision of conscience. Give reasons for your choice.

A religious perspective on libertarianism

The idea of libertarianism is that people are free to make autonomous decisions, free from constraint and coercion. Initially this idea seems to fit well with Christianity, which talks of Jesus setting people free. However, the New Testament writers do not mean that people are free to do as they like. The epistle of James refers twice to 'the law of liberty' (James 1:25, 2:25) and at first this seems a bit odd, as laws usually prevent us from doing things. Freedom is also a theme in John's Gospel; for example, when Jesus says: 'Jesus answered them, "Very truly, I tell you, everyone who commits sin is a slave to sin. The slave does not have a permanent place in the household; the son has a place there forever. So if the Son makes you free, you will be free indeed"' (John 8:34–6). Freedom in the New Testament refers to release from thoughts and behaviour which run counter to God's ideal plan for people – people are shown to have choices: they can satisfy their own idea or choose to serve God and other people. Freedom to make decisions is tempered with responsibility to the community. We cannot act in isolation, all our decisions affect other people.

The Free Will Defence theory explains our freedom in relation to God's goodness. Humans have to be free to choose God, as he does not want autonomous, robotic people who are determined to choose him, he wants them to choose good but if that is the case there must also be the possibility for people to choose evil. The Free Will Defence explains why God created us free and justifies evil.

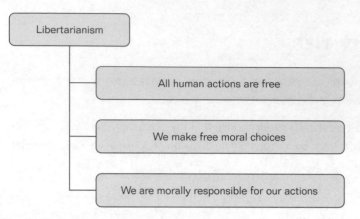

Evaluating libertarianism

* Libertarianism recognises that people have a sense of decision making, a sense of freedom, a sense of deliberating over their choices in life.
* Personal responsibility underpins our whole system of ethics and law.
* David Hume pointed out that, even if in nature event B consistently follows event A on every observed occasion, to say that event A causes event B is to go beyond observation. It is our way of interpreting the events, not a feature of the events in themselves.
* Libertarians insist that free will is the uncoerced power to choose – but how does a person decide what to do? What criteria do they use to make a decision? What about their past experiences, emotions, beliefs and values?

DETERMINISM

The fall of dominoes

The principle of causality

Determinism states that everything in the universe has a prior cause, including all human actions and choices. This means that all our decisions, viewpoints and opinions can be best understood when translated into the neutral language of natural science. This view has a long history and may be seen in the fatalism of Greek tragedy, in which people are the helpless victims of circumstances, necessity and the Fates.

> In the mind there is no absolute or free will; but the mind is determined to wish this or that by a cause, which has also been determined by another cause, and this last by another cause, and so on to infinity.
>
> (Baruch Spinoza, Part Two of the *Ethics*, 1677)

All theories of determinism are influenced by Isaac Newton's physics, according to which the universe is governed by immutable laws of nature such as motion and gravitation. The world is seen as a mechanism dominated by the law of predictable cause and effect. Followers of Newton, such as Pierre Laplace, placed such confidence in the all-pervasive power of causality that they thought that the minutest prediction could be made if only we knew the various causal factors involved. This included the actions of people – there is room for neither chance nor choice.

So freedom of choice is just an illusion – we may appear to have moral choices, but we think we choose freely only because we do not know the causes that lie behind our choices. This is illustrated by the philosopher John Locke, who describes a sleeping man in a locked room; on awakening he decides to stay where he is, not realising that the door to the room is locked. The man thinks that he has made a free decision, but in reality he has no choice. So it is with our moral choices – we think we make free decisions simply because we do not know the causes. This view was also taken by Paul-Henri Thiry (Baron) d'Holbach, who said that humans and human society and actions can all be understood in terms of cause and effect – freedom is again an illusion:

> You will say that I feel free. This is an illusion, which may be compared to that of the fly in the fable, who, upon the pole of a heavy carriage, applauded himself for directing its course. Man, who thinks himself free, is a fly who imagines he has power to move the universe, while is himself unknowingly carried along by it.

Ted Honderich also drew the conclusion that, since everything is physically determined, there is no choice and so no personal responsibility; there is not even any 'self' within us that is the origin of our actions – the mind is a by-product of brain activity, and actions are caused by 'psychoneural' events

Paul-Henri Thiry (Baron) d'Holbach (1723–1789)

Baron d'Holbach was born in December 1723 at Edesheim in the Rhenish Palatinate.

He was a French encyclopaedist and philosopher, a celebrated exponent of atheism and materialism. His most famous book was *Système de la nature* (1770), which he wrote under the pseudonym of J.B. Mirabaud. He denounced religion and put forward an atheistic materialism. He died on 21 June 1789 in Paris.

Ted Honderich (1933–)

Honderich is a Canadian from a Mennonite family. He was Grote Professor at the University of London from 1988 until 1998. His book *After the Terror* (2002) caused controversy over the questions he raised about the events of 11 September 2001.

Clarence Seward Darrow (1857–1938)

Darrow was an American lawyer. In 1924 he

involving both mind and brain. According to Honderich, there is no room for moral blame and no point in punishment for the sake of punishment. For Honderich each action is an effect, and there is no room for free will.

Hard determinism

Hard determinists are called 'hard' because their position is very strict: according to hard determinism all our actions had prior causes – we are neither free nor responsible. Hard determinism is incompatible with free will and moral responsibility, and as all our actions are caused by prior causes we are not free to act in any other way. A person is like a machine, and if a machine is faulty it just needs fixing. The same applies to a person. A person cannot be blamed for their violence; violence either needs 'fixing' or, if this fails, the person needs imprisoning to stop their violence impinging on others.

John Hospers was a modern hard determinist who advocated this approach; he says that there is always something which compels us both externally and internally to perform an action that we would think was the result of our own free will. He uses several psychoanalytical examples to make his point and concludes: 'It is all a matter of luck.' This is seen most clearly in the film *A Clockwork Orange* (1971).

The same position was taken up by Clarence Darrow, whose success, as we saw earlier, in his plea for Loeb and Leopold makes us question whether criminals are morally responsible for what they do: 'Punishment as punishment is not admissible unless the offender has the free will to select his course' (Clarence Darrow). In his closing speech for the defence Darrow said:

> Is Dicky Loeb to blame because out of the infinite forces that conspired to form him, the infinite forces that were at work producing him ages before he was born, that because out of these infinite combinations he was born without it? If he is, then there should be a new definition for justice. Is he to blame for what he did not have and never had? Is he to blame that his machine is imperfect? Who is to blame? I do not know. I have never in my life been interested so much in fixing blame as I have been in relieving people from blame. I am not wise enough to fix it. I know that somewhere in the past that entered into him something missed. It may be defective nerves. It may be a defective heart or liver. It may be defective endocrine glands. I know it is something. I know that nothing happens in this world without a cause.

More modern versions of hard determinism point to our genetic heritage, social conditioning or subconscious influences as prior causes. The most extreme modern version of hard determinism is behaviourism.

Behaviourism

White laboratory rats (*Rattus* sp.) in laboratory, close-up

Stone (Jonathan Selig) Getty Images

Psychological behaviourism was first discussed by John B. Watson, who suggested that behaviour can be predicted and controlled, as people live and act in a determined universe so that all human behaviour, including ethical decisions, is controlled by prior causes which are, in principle, knowable. Behaviour is influenced, according to Watson, by heredity and environment – nature and nurture. By manipulating the environment people's behaviour can be altered.

This idea is called 'conditioning' and was influenced by the work of Ivan Pavlov, who conditioned dogs to salivate (as if they were about to be fed) when they heard the sound of a bell. We are all familiar with this, as in schools we are conditioned to act in certain ways when we hear the school bell ring for a lesson change.

However, we are not always conditioned by our environment but will often use it to get what we want – even dogs will eventually go in search of food if no food appears. This sort of behaviour is known as operant conditioning and is most often linked to the work of B.F. Skinner, who investigated behaviour modification through reward and punishment. He claimed that behavioural science develops and psychologists learn to determine and control human behaviour; it is highly probable that human behaviour is not free but most likely determined. Moral behaviour is about what people ought and ought not to do, but if they could not have done

defended Richard Loeb and Nathan Leopold on the charge of murdering 14-year-old Robert Franks in Chicago. They were imprisoned, but were saved from the death penalty because of Darrow's defence.

In the Scopes (Monkey) Trial heard in Dayton, Tennessee (10–21 July 1925), Darrow defended a teacher who had broken state law by teaching Darwin's theory of evolution. In the Sweet case in Detroit (1925–1926), he successfully defended a black family who had fought against a mob which was trying to expel the family from their home in a white neighbourhood.

John Broadus Watson (1878–1958)

John B. Watson was born in Greenville, South Carolina, and studied at the Furman University and the University of Chicago. He is the founder of the school of psychology known as behaviourism.

Ivan Petrovich Pavlov (1849–1936)

Ivan Petrovich Pavlov was born in Ryazan in Russia. He studied theology and then medicine. He was the first Russian winner of the Nobel Prize for Physiology of Medicine (1904). At the presentation ceremony, Pavlov explained his ideas of 'unconditioned reflexes', 'conditioned reflexes' and reaction to an unrelated external stimulus. His research was published in *Conditioned Reflexes* (1926).

Burrhus Frederic Skinner (1904–1990)

B.F. Skinner was born in Susquehanna, Pennsylvania. He studied at Harvard University. Skinner became the leading exponent of the behaviourist school of psychology, explaining human behaviour in terms of physiological responses to external stimuli.

anything else then they had no freedom of choice and cannot be blamed for their actions.

Steven Pinker approached determinism from another angle and looked at the ideas of Darwin, developed recently by Richard Dawkins, that emotions such as guilt, anger, sympathy and love all have a biological basis. He developed the theory that our moral reasoning is a result of natural selection but he claims that this does not mean the end of moral responsibility. Evolution might, for example, predispose men to violence or to sleeping around, but this does not necessitate or excuse such behaviour – a moral sense is innate in us and so is 'as real for us as if it were decreed by the Almighty or written into the cosmos'.

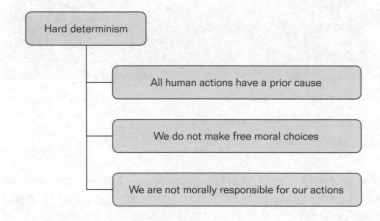

Evaluating hard determinism

- Hard determinism means we cannot blame or praise people for their actions.
- If hard determinism were true then people would not be morally responsible, and so would not deserve blame for even the most cold-blooded and calmly performed evil actions.
- All choices we make are just illusions – they are determined.
- Hard determinism, therefore, rejects the idea of punishment as retribution, but it does not reject any other views about the justification of punishment; for example, deterrence, self-defence or moral education.
- Classical physics is indeed deterministic, but modern quantum physics is not deterministic and so it makes no sense to worry about determinism in the twenty-first century. Modern physics maintains that the most basic laws of nature are not deterministic but probabilistic.
- If determinism is true then all the horrible things that happen in the world had to happen – this is a very pessimistic view of the world.

Soft determinism

Soft determinism says that some of our actions are determined but that we are morally responsible for our actions. Soft determinists argue that there is confusion between determinism and fatalism about what we mean by freedom of choice. Freedom of choice is not compatible with fatalism, 'what ever will be will be', which says that nobody can change the course of events, but it is compatible with determinism, a theory of universal causation, if we include our own values, choices and desires among the choices that determine our actions. Soft determinists agree that all human actions are caused, since if they were not they would be unpredictable and random. They mean that, when an individual's actions are free, they are not forced or compelled by any external pressure.

Soft determinism may be seen as the view that determinism is compatible with whatever sort of freedom is necessary for moral responsibility. Linking this to the developments in physics, perhaps we live in an indeterministic universe that is not completely described by modern physics because there are some events (e.g. some human behaviours) which are not determined and not random either. After all, who knows what physics will be like in 25 or 50 years' time?

A clue to solving this argument is given by Immanuel Kant, who believed that determinism applied to everything which was the object of knowledge, but not to acts of the will. He said that people work from two different and seemingly incompatible standpoints: the theoretical (pure reason) and the practical (practical reason). Pure reason concerns knowledge, the mind and the way we see the scientifically explicable world; practical reason concerns actions, the will and the way we see ourselves. We cannot look rationally for causes of our actions beyond a genuine act of our will. When we act we always think of ourselves as free. Kant says freedom is a postulate of practical reason. Kant's argument is that our own self-awareness, without which the world would not make sense to us, forces on us the idea that we are free, so we cannot get rid of the idea that we are free without ceasing to see ourselves as the originator of our actions.

Soft determinism, then, is not a position that combines the determinist and libertarian positions; it is not a compromise, it does not limit free will, but is a position taken as a result of the need to have some accountability and responsibility for human behaviour. Soft determinists clarify what they mean by free: we are not free to fly just using our own bodies to propel us through the air – this is to misuse the word 'free' and change it from meaning 'being able to choose' to 'being physically able to do'. According to soft determinists, we are morally responsible, and can reasonably be punished and praised, for those actions which are caused by our own desires and decisions.

Autonomous moral agent
Someone who can make a moral decision freely; someone who is totally responsible for their actions.

'Ought implies can'
The idea that someone cannot be blamed for what they could not do, but only for what they were capable of doing but did not do.

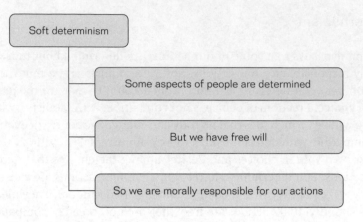

Evaluating soft determinism

- Soft determinism agrees that moral responsibility is important in our society, but that it is not reasonable to hold a person responsible for actions caused by their emotions, beliefs, desires and decisions if they have no choice about having them.
- It is, however, hard for the soft determinist to decide what exactly is determined and what can be freely chosen. The complex nature of people and the roles of physics, genetics and psychology make deciding what exactly is, or is not, a determining factor very hard.
- Soft determinism also allows for creativity in our choices – so not all our choices are the result of existing desires and habits.

Predestination – a religious perspective on determinism

Within the Judaeo-Christian tradition humans are in general considered to be autonomous and morally responsible to God. The myth of the Fall in Genesis 2 shows that humans are given responsibility for caring for the world, but their free will is restricted as Adam and Eve are forbidden to eat from the tree in the centre of the garden. However, they must have had free will as they are punished when they disobey God – this shows that they are responsible for their decisions and must face the consequences of the choices they made. However, the more God's omniscience and omnipotence are stressed, the greater a problem our free will becomes. If God is omniscient then he knows every decision we make – does this then mean that our future is already decided by God? Many philosophers and theologians have tried to address this problem. St Paul seems to say that God chooses who will be saved, and we should not question this as no one deserves salvation. We may seek salvation, which is available to all, but only God will give it.

We know that all things work together for good for those who love God, who are called according to his purpose. For those whom he foreknew he also predestined to be conformed to the image of his Son, in order that he might be the firstborn within a large family. And those whom he predestined he also called; and those whom he called he also justified; and those whom he justified he also glorified.

(Romans 8:28–30)

Here it is important to consider what Paul actually meant by 'predestined'. The Greek word used here means 'set before' or 'resolve'. Rather than the traditional understanding of predestination, this seems to imply that God knew beforehand that there would be people open to the gospel and willing to answer God's call. However, God does not determine how each person will respond – that is up to us.

For St Paul freedom is being bound not by the rules of the past but by overcoming sin, death and darkness through the resurrection of Christ. Humans are free how to choose to live their lives, but only God can decide their final destination. There are some parallels between St Paul's view of freedom and that of the soft determinist, but his ideas have not always been understood, and later theologians, not using the Greek New Testament, have interpreted the idea of predestination differently.

Determinism can also be seen in some versions of Christian predestination: the total irrelevance of our actions in this life as God has already decided whether we are saved or not saved. The doctrine of predestination was formulated by such theologians as Augustine of Hippo and John Calvin, and is based on the idea that God determines whatever happens in history and that humans have only a very limited understanding of God's purposes and plans. This idea is based not on words or on particular passages in the Bible but on ideas about revelation, and has to sit side by side with teachings about individual freedom and responsibility. According to Augustine, people need the help of God's grace to do good, and this is a free gift from God, regardless of individual merit. Consequently, God alone determines who will receive the grace that assures salvation.

However, the further idea that, while some were predestined to salvation, others were predestined to damnation was rejected. Many Christians, such as Pelagius, rejected any deterministic ideas, but determinism was formulated more precisely by John Calvin during the sixteenth century and is still followed by Presbyterian churches today. This belief says that, as humans are complete sinners who are incapable of coming to God, and have a sinful free will that is only capable of rejecting God, then predestination must occur or nobody could be saved. God is in total control and people cannot do anything to achieve salvation. According to Calvin, people are not all created with a similar destiny: eternal life is fore-ordained for some, and

John Calvin (1509–1564)

John Calvin was born in Noyon on 10 July 1509. He studied for the priesthood at the Collège de la Marche and the Collège de Montaigue, in Paris. He then studied law at Orlèans and Bourges.

In 1536 the first edition of his *Christianae Religionis Institutio* (Institutes of the Christian Religion) was published and this work led him to the forefront of Protestantism.

He married Idelette de Bure in Strasbourg but their only child died. In 1541 Calvin moved to Geneva, where he had been invited to modify the constitution in both sacred and secular matters. He wrote a catechism and commentaries on almost all the books of the Bible. He caught quartan fever in 1558 and became very weak. He died on 27 May 1564 and lies in an unmarked grave in Geneva.

eternal damnation for others: 'Every man, therefore, being created for one or the other of these ends, we say, he is predestined to life or death' (*Institutes of the Christian Religion* Bk3 Ch 21 s5).

This idea suggests that people have no free will as far as the consequences of their ethical decisions are concerned. It states that God makes his choice about who is to be saved independently of any qualities in the individual – God does not look into a person and recognise something good; nor does he look into the future to see who would choose him, but simply decides who will be saved because he can, and all the rest are left to go their natural way: to hell. So people do good only because God made them that way and put them in a certain environment; and the rest are just limited by their naturally sinful nature and can only choose to be sinful. Logically then, if we have no control over our actions, we have no responsibility for them.

Thought Point

Do we, as Einstein said, 'dance to a mysterious tune, intoned in the distance by an invisible piper'?

* From your own life and experiences list examples that show we are all determined. Can you think of other explanations for these events?
* Does hard determinism mean there is no point in the moral education of children?
* Does soft determinism overcome the problems of both hard determinism and libertarianism?
* If the future is determined, is God irrelevant?

ACTIVITIES

Here are some situations in which there is, in principle, freedom of action. Yet how free are we to choose? Consider the problems faced when the influences of the society in which we live are considered:

* *the influence of upbringing* – you need to lie to save a friend's reputation. You know it is the kindest thing to do but you also know that your face will give the game away. What do you do?

- *the influence of common politeness* – you find a lesson really boring and covering material you already know; there are still 30 minutes to go. You are free to walk out but . . .
- *the influence of convention* – you are going to your sixth-year ball. Everyone is dressing up in their ball gowns and dinner suits. You are free to turn up dressed in jeans – or are you?
- *the influence of social pressures* – you visit your boyfriend's or girlfriend's parents and they serve you your least favourite meal and then ask if you enjoyed it. What do you do?

Can you add to this list any situations in which in one sense you are free to act as you like, but in another sense your hands are tied?

REVIEW QUESTIONS

Look back over the chapter and check that you can answer the following questions:

1. Explain the roles of science, society and psychology in determinism.
2. Copy and complete the following revision chart on A3 paper:

Theory	Key scholars	Key ideas	Strengths	Weaknesses	Possible quotations
Hard determinism					
Predestination					
Soft determinism					
Libertarianism					

Islam might be viewed as deterministic because it teaches that nothing can happen unless it is God's will. However, humans, as vice-regents, have a duty to make the right decisions. As God's agents they have free will to choose how to act.

For the three Eastern religions, free will is associated with the principle of karma (kamma). Previous lives create the karma which affects the present life and this may therefore affect the freedom of the present life. However, if someone wishes to do good and live according to their dharma (dhamma) but cannot, it is the intention to act which then produces karmic (kammic) force.

Humans have far more freedom to act than other life forms and can choose to do what is right. Free will is essential if people are to create good karma.

Terminology

Do you know your terminology?

Try to explain the following key ideas without looking at your books and notes:

- Autonomous moral agent
- Compatibilism
- Determinism
- Hard determinism
- Incompatibilism
- Libertarianism
- 'Ought implies can'
- Predestination
- Soft determination

SAMPLE EXAMINATION QUESTIONS

(a) Examine the concept of free will, with reference to human actions and choices. (30 marks)

In your response you will be expected to explain, with examples, the concept of free will.

- You should use examples of actions or choices performed by humans.
- You might mention the part that genes and environment might play in decision-making processes; nature v. nurture, and the conflict of wills.
- In explaining free will, you might also explain determinism, but this is not essential.

(b) How far is it true to say that human actions and choices are free? (20 marks)

In debating this idea you should consider some of the following.

In favour:

- idea of choice
- idea of conscience
- the reality of reward or punishment as a consequence of behaviour or decisions
- the contrast between choosing and being forced into something.

Against:

- what part genes and people's environment play in the decision-making process
- the fact that no one is totally free; everyone is constrained (e.g. by laws, conscience, etc.)
- the reality of not doing things through fear of punishment.

Essential terminology

Aretaic ethics
Cardinal Virtues
Eudaimonia
Golden Mean
Intellectual virtues
Moral virtues
Phronesis
  (practical wisdom)
Vices
Virtue

12 Virtue Ethics

WHAT YOU WILL LEARN ABOUT IN THIS CHAPTER

- The principles of Virtue Ethics from Aristotle.
- Modern forms of Virtue theory from Anscombe, Foot and MacIntyre.
- The strengths and weaknesses of Virtue Ethics.
- How to apply Virtue theory to ethical dilemmas.

THE AQA CHECKLIST ✔

Virtue Ethics

- Aristotle's view: happiness (eudaimonia), moral and intellectual virtues, cardinal virtues and capital vices
- Modern Virtue Ethics: MacIntyre and Foot
- The application of Virtue Ethics to **one** issue of the candidate's choice **apart from issues in science and technology**.

ISSUES ARISING

- What are the strengths and weaknesses of Virtue Ethics as an ethical system?
- Is Virtue Ethics really different from deontological and teleological systems?

- What is the significance of a particular view of human nature for Virtue Ethics?
- How compatible is Virtue Ethics with a religious approach to ethics?

WHAT IS VIRTUE ETHICS?

Virtue Ethics goes back to Plato and Aristotle and focuses not on actions being right or wrong but on how to be a good person. It looks at what makes a good person and the qualities or virtues that make them good. Virtue Ethics is *agent-centred* morality rather than act-centred – it asks 'What sort of person ought I to be?' rather than 'How ought I to act?'

Our word 'virtue' sounds rather old-fashioned and religious, but the Greek word for virtue, *arete*, means excellence. So a virtuous person is one who does things excellently all the time. As we saw in Chapter 8 on Natural Law, a knife has excellence when it cuts sharply – *arete* is not only about people.

Virtue Ethics was re-examined and redeveloped in the twentieth century.

PLATO AND VIRTUE

Plato's moral theory is not one of judging particular actions. It centres on the achievement of a person's highest good, which involves the right cultivation of their soul (inner well-being) and the harmonious well-being of their life (*eudaimonia* or happiness). Happiness must be attained through the pursuit of virtue and actions are good when they help to achieve this. Plato seemed to consider certain virtues central: temperance, courage, prudence and justice (later called the Cardinal Virtues). Plato thought that when these virtues are in balance a person's actions will be good. However, there was not agreement among the Greek philosophers about which virtues were central, and Aristotle gives a very different account of the virtues.

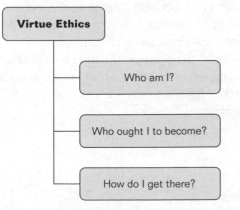

Virtue Ethics

- Who am I?
- Who ought I to become?
- How do I get there?

Virtue Ethics
The final goal of all human activity – happiness, well-being, human flourishing.

Virtue
Habitually doing what is right – being good requires the practice of a certain kind of behaviour.

Cardinal Virtues
Originated in Plato – prudence, justice, temperance, courage. Added to with three theological virtues of faith, hope and charity.

Eudaimonia
The final goal of all human activity – happiness, well-being, human flourishing.

ARISTOTLE AND VIRTUE

Aristotle sought to give an account of the structure of morality and explained that the point of engaging in ethics is to become good: 'For we are enquiring not in order to know what virtue is but in order to become good since otherwise our enquiry would be of no use' (*Nicomachean Ethics*, Book 1, ch. 2, 1103b27). Aristotle distinguishes between things which are good as means (for the sake of something else) and things which are good as ends (for their own sake only). He sees one final and overriding end of human activity, one final good – eudaimonia or happiness, human flourishing. Aristotle discusses the character traits of a person who is going to achieve eudaimonia.

Aristotle's ethical theory is known as Virtue Ethics or Aretaic ethics because at the centre of his description of the good are the virtues which shape human character and ultimately human behaviour. He suggests that human well-being and human flourishing result from a life characterised by the virtues. However, this good human life is one lived in *harmony* and *co-operation* with other people, since Aristotle saw people not only as rational beings but also as social beings. We live in groups (e.g. family, school, village) and he saw the well-being of the group as more important than that of a single member.

The Golden Mean

Virtue is to be found in the Golden Mean, which involves finding the balance between two means – this is the best way to live in society, as extremes of character are unhelpful (people who are too timid or too assertive can cause problems). Aristotle always said that virtue is to be found between two vices, each of which involves either an excess or a deficiency of the true virtue (e.g. courage is the mean – a coward does not have enough courage and the rash person just runs into danger).

Aristotle said that the difference between virtue and vice in both emotions and action was a matter of *balance* and extremes. However, the mean is not the same for everyone and depends on circumstance – you need to apply *phronesis* (practical wisdom) to decide on the right course of action in each situation. Phronesis is acquired as we grow up and move away from rules and the demands of authority figures to a more autonomous, person-centred and virtue-centred morality.

Acquiring virtues

Aristotle saw two types of virtues:

- intellectual virtues developed by training and education
- moral virtues developed by habit in the rational part of the soul.

There are nine intellectual virtues. The five primary intellectual virtues are:

- art or technical skill (*techne*)
- scientific knowledge (*episteme*)
- prudence or practical wisdom (*phronesis*)
- intelligence or intuition (*nous*)
- wisdom (*sophia*).

The four secondary intellectual virtues are:

- resourcefulness or good deliberation (*eubolia*)
- understanding (*sunesis*)
- judgement (*gnome*)
- cleverness (*deinotes*).

Moral virtues developed by habit

Aristotle argued that the best course of action falls between the vice of excess and the vice of deficiency. Here are the 12 moral virtues, with their corresponding vices:

Vice of deficiency	Virtue	Vice of excess
Cowardice	Courage	Rashness
Insensibility	Temperance	Intemperance
Illiberality	Liberality	Prodigality
Pettiness	Munificence	Vulgarity
Humble-mindedness	High-mindedness	Vaingloriousness
Want of ambition	Right ambition	Over-ambition
Spiritlessness	Good temper	Irascibility
Surliness	Friendliness/civility	Obsequiousness
Sarcasm	Sincerity	Boastfulness
Boorishness	Wittiness	Buffoonery
Shamelessness	Modesty	Bashfulness
Callousness	Just resentment	Spitefulness

Aristotle compares the virtues to skills acquired through *practice* and *habit*. He writes in his *Ethics*:

Aretaic ethics

Another name for Virtue Ethics, from the Greek word *arete*, which simply means any kind of excellence or virtue.

Intellectual virtues

Characteristics of thought and reason – technical skill, scientific knowledge, prudence, intelligence and wisdom.

Moral virtues

Qualities of character such as courage, friendliness, truthfulness.

Playing a musical instrument

We acquire virtues by first doing virtuous acts. We acquire a skill by practising the activities involved in the skill. For example, we become builders by building, we learn to play the harp by playing the harp. In the same way we become just by doing just acts, temperate by doing temperate acts and courageous by doing acts of courage.

To become virtuous then is rather like playing a musical instrument – it needs teaching and practice before it is possible to play well. We are all capable of being virtuous and need to get into the habit of acting virtuously from childhood so that we enjoy being virtuous. However, Aristotle believed that while all people have the potential to develop moral and intellectual virtues, only a few will actually achieve this – for Aristotle these were the gentlemen philosophers. Today we could say that this depends in part on *social factors*: where we are brought up and the environment in which we live.

Aristotle saw that a person who achieved eudaimonia was someone who used their reason well. He saw reason as the supreme human virtue, but by this he meant not only an ability to think but also a moral sense – reason included putting into action what you used your reason to judge as good. Reason is *practical* and involves both *understanding* and *responding*.

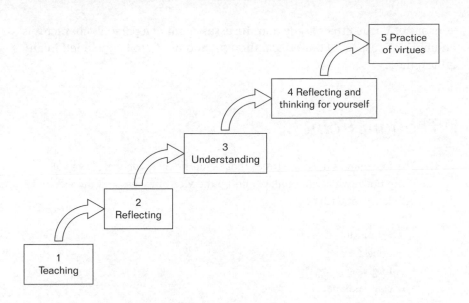

The example of virtuous people

As virtue is acquired through *doing,* one way to learn how to be virtuous is to follow the example of virtuous people. Most of us learn how to do things by watching others and imitating them. The lives of Socrates, Jesus, Gandhi, Martin Luther King Jr, Nelson Mandela and so on give us possible examples of moral excellence. They are not all 'perfect people' but they challenge us to go beyond the minimum, to aspire to 'moral heights' and to see what can be achieved.

There are many novels and films that show what happens when characters are destructive, such as Darth Vader in *Star Wars* or Dr Octopus in *Spiderman 2,* who sell out to the dark side and warn us of the consequences of losing our own integrity.

Golden Mean

The balance of extremes of virtues and vices. A balance between *excess* (having too much of something) and *deficiency* (having too little of something).

Vices

The direct opposite of virtues – habitual wrong action.

Phronesis (practical wisdom)

According to Aristotle the virtue most needed for any other virtue to be developed. Balancing self-interest with that of others. Needs to be directed by the moral virtues.

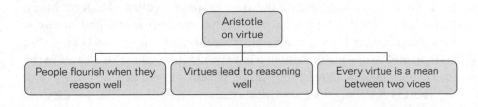

MODERN VIRTUE ETHICS

In the twentieth century there was a revival of interest in Virtue Ethics by philosophers who were unhappy with act-centred ethical theories. Modern

Phronesis

People flourish when they reason well. Virtues lead to reasoning well.

Aristotle on virtue

Every virtue is a mean between two vices.

versions of Virtue Ethics argue that the assessment of a person's character is an important aspect of our ethical thought and needs to be included in any ethical theory.

Thought Point

1. The following is a list of virtues that lie in the mean between two vices. Write down what you think would be the vice of excess and the vice of deficiency for each one:

    *   responsible
    *   honest
    *   forgiving
    *   compassionate
    *   patient

2. What virtues do you think are most important in the world today and what are their corresponding vices?
3. How does Aristotle's approach to ethics differ from other ethical theories you have learnt?
4. Does the Golden Mean imply that Aristotle supports mediocre people who do not take risks?
5. Aristotle implies that being virtuous depends a little on upbringing, environment and so on. Do you agree?

G.E.M. Anscombe (1919–2001)

G.E.M. Anscombe taught at Oxford and Chicago, and then took the Chair of Philosophy at Cambridge. She became a Catholic in 1940. In analysing actions she stressed reasons rather than causes and argued for a return to Aristotle's idea of virtue.

G.E.M. Anscombe and Virtue Ethics

In 1958 G.E.M. Anscombe published a paper called 'Modern Moral Philosophy' and put forward the idea that modern moral philosophy is misguided, asking if there can be any moral laws if there is no God – what do right and wrong mean without a lawgiver? She suggests an answer in the idea of eudaimonia, human flourishing, which does not depend on any God.

Neither Kantian ethics nor Utilitarianism depends on God, but they are still act-based and ignore the person who acts. Anscombe also thought that act-based ethics does not make sense because it ignores a belief people no longer hold, and in stressing the principle of autonomy it neglects the community aspect of morality.

Philippa Foot and Virtue Ethics

Philippa Foot attempted to modernise Aristotle's Virtue Ethics while still keeping the Aristotelian understanding of character and virtue. She recognises the importance of the person's own reasoning in the practice of virtue, claims that the virtues benefit the individual by leading to flourishing and stresses that the virtuous person does far more than conform to the conventions of society. Virtues are beneficial characteristics which one needs both for one's own good and for the good of others, so she argues that a wise person directs their will to what is good – and what is good must be both intrinsically and extrinsically good. However, a virtue does not operate as a virtue when turned to a bad end (e.g. when someone needs daring to commit a murder).

She also explains that virtues and skills are different things. We may make a deliberate mistake with a skill, but not damage our character or reputation, such as a teacher deliberately misspelling a word to draw the attention of the students to it. However, if you continually act in a non-virtuous way your reputation will suffer. Virtues are good for us and also help us to correct harmful human passions and temptations. Thus Foot characterises virtues as 'correctives', which means that we would not characterise something as a virtue unless there is some sort of natural tendency to act otherwise. She likens humans to planks of wood that are left out to season: wood naturally warps and needs continual straightening to make it straight. Virtues do the same for the human character.

However, Foot notes that there are 'degrees' of virtue – the person who shows great personal restraint in the face of great temptation shows greater personal courage than the person who is never tempted to do wrong. Does this make the first person more virtuous?

Alasdair MacIntyre and Virtue Ethics

In his book *After Virtue*, Alasdair MacIntyre claims that ethical theories have simply resulted in ethical disagreements. The result of this, he claims, is that people do not think there are any moral truths and consider one opinion to be as good as any other opinion. MacIntyre argues that most people's attitudes today are based on *emotivism* – moral statements are neither true nor false but simply express the feelings and attitudes of the speaker. He says that people often speak and act as if emotivism was true (racism is wrong: 'boo to racism', tolerance is right: 'hurrah for tolerance'). Do you agree with MacIntyre that 'people now think and act as if emotivism were true'?

MacIntyre looked at what has happened to ethical thought through history and concluded that the Age of Enlightenment, which gave rise to

Philippa Ruth Foot (1920–2010)

Philippa Foot was a British philosopher, best known for her works in ethics. She was one of the founders of modern Virtue Ethics, showing that it can compete with modern deontological and utilitarian ethics.

She was a tutor at Somerville College, Oxford, and later held the position of Griffin Professor of Philosophy at the University of California, Los Angeles.

Alasdair MacIntyre (1929–)

MacIntyre is a Scottish philosopher who is best known for his work in moral philosophy. He presents complicated and controversial philosophical arguments in simple narratives, often using ordinary storytelling to address complicated issues in philosophy.

MacIntyre is key to the recent interest in Virtue Ethics. He focuses on moral problems in making the most of an entire human life. He emphasises the importance of moral goods rather than ideas such as

continued

the obligation of a moral agent or the consequences of a particular moral act.

theories such as Utilitarianism and Kantianism, had lost sight of the idea of morality being people achieving their true telos – function or purpose. MacIntyre wants to restore the idea that morality should be seen in terms of human purpose, but he thought it would not be possible to restore Aristotle's theory of function and so he attempts to make human function, and so human virtue, depend on community. He says that the idea of the community, the 'polis', needs to be reinstated as a place where people had an identity based on specific roles within the community. It is this sense of identity that has been lost in the postmodern age which is concerned with the individual not the community; this has led to the 'dislocated self', and a community where there are three archetypal characters which embody characteristics desirable to sections of the community and who are seen as worthy of respect. These characters are:

- *The Bureaucratic Manager* – this is the dominant person in the world today, for whom profit is more important than principles. They are efficient at using resources and people to achieve their own aims and objectives. For the bureaucratic manager both people and resources are dispensable and all that is required is the greatest return from the resources that must be used efficiently.
- *The Rich Aesthete* – again dominant in our celebrity culture. This person lives for the pleasures in life and to the eyes of society they are admired, not for their personal qualities but for their wealth, lifestyle, thinness and clothes.
- *The Therapist* – this person is needed because someone has to deal with our failed aspirations and hopes. In a society where 'success' is enjoyed only by a few someone has to pick up the pieces. In a society where everything is sold to us to combat our stressful lifestyle we need therapists to help us pretend that our lives are not really empty and meaningless. MacIntyre suggests that chat show hosts are examples of people who engage in such therapy 'en masse'.

It is the shared practices of a community which help cultivate virtues. The word 'practice' MacIntyre uses in a particular way; he means any 'coherent and complex form of socially established cooperative human activity through which goods internal to that from of activity are realized in the course of trying to achieve those standards of excellence which are appropriate to, and partially definitive of, that from of activity' (MacIntyre, *After Virtue* p. 187). He goes on to explain that throwing a football, however skilfully, is not a practice but the game of football is, bricklaying is not a practice either but architecture is, so also is scientific enquiry, the work of the historian, painting and music. These virtues improve and evolve through time; there is a difference between the Homeric virtues such as strength, courage and honour, the Aristotelian virtues such as courage, justice and temperance, and the Christian virtues outlined by Aquinas. James Keenan S.J. suggests prudence, justice, fidelity, self-care and mercy. James Rachels suggests courage, honesty and loyalty to support friendship.

For MacIntyre virtues are 'any virtues which sustain the households and communities in which men and women seek for good together'. Thus, the virtues for MacIntyre are vital for everyday life; society needs people who organise sponsored walks, cake sales and other fund-raising activities for the local hospice, etc. Society, he says, depends for its very existence upon people who exhibit the virtues.

MacIntyre opposes much of the individualism of today, and argues that we all need to live a virtuous life, get into the habit of being moral and strive towards being virtuous. For MacIntyre the virtues are any human quality which helps us to achieve the 'goods' in life. MacIntyre says that we ask what it means to be a good manager, or a good parent or teacher, but fail to ask what it is to be a good human being. To do this we need to think of our life as a story, or as he calls it our life's narrative unity. When we discover what our story is about we can decide what our telos is and what practices we should and should not do. This also means that our virtues should remain consistent as 'our self' remains the same whatever community we are in at any one time; this enables us to make choices between different practices: should I go out with my friends or go to my grandparents' Golden Wedding party? Thinking about the narrative unity of my life will help me make the right decision. By choosing I recognise that both alternative courses of action lead to a real good. Practical reasoning, as for Aristotle, is in the judgement which enables the agent to pursue both their own good and that of the tradition.

So a true virtue is part of the whole life of the individual (narrative) and humanity as a whole (tradition). So the quest for the good life, which MacIntyre calls a narrative quest, will deepen a person's understanding and appreciation for human good. The virtues are those which sustain such a quest in the face of obstacles and which sustain societies; they are human qualities which make it possible to perform a practice well. Virtues are cultivated both for their own sake and as a means to the internal end of the practice. This is different from Aristotle as the telos can be confined to the practice. This means that there can be conflict between virtues as they come from many different practices and not only the agent's own character flaws. However, there does need to be one overriding telos which stops someone being destroyed by competing practices – MacIntyre sees this as 'purity of heart', which again only makes sense in the context of the whole life from birth to death.

MacIntyre's virtues are as follows:

- courage, which help us to face challenges in life
- justice, which is fairness – giving someone due merit

- temperance, which prevents us from acting rashly, for example, losing our temper
- wisdom, which is the ability to know the right way to act in different situations
- industriousness, which is the willingness to work hard
- hope, which is being optimistic
- patience, which is being willing to wait.

Living out these virtues needs a kind of society very different from that of bureaucratic individualism. The virtues must be underpinned by the good will of the person – to be virtuous must be voluntary. If a virtue is not intended then the act is not virtuous – which answers the final question raised by Phillipa Foot's approach. MacIntyre also use the idea of internal and external goods, such as is seen in Natural Law. An internal good or quality of character, which he calls 'goods of excellence', is specific to the act itself; for example, giving money to charity means that other people are helped and the giver has a sense of satisfaction. An internal good is an achievement of virtue and is also a good for the whole community who participate in the practice. An external good is a good that is not specific to the act; for example, giving to charity might influence other people to do the same. MacIntyre says that external goods are not bad in themselves, as without them there would be no development of internal goods –but they must not become the main aim or they could become vices.

He also warned that being virtuous does not prevent you from having vices: he uses the example of a great violinist who could be vicious, or a chess player who could be mean-spirited. These vices, he said, would prevent these people from achieving maximum virtue.

MacIntyre sees Virtue Ethics as affecting the whole of society, its institutions, businesses and organisations. The most important virtues for society are justice, courage and honesty, and excellence can be achieved only by practising all three. These core virtues will prevent institutions and organisations from becoming morally corrupt and spreading vices throughout society.

Returning to the archetypal characters: who are the people who take these roles in our society today? For Aristotle his *Ethics* lead directly to his *Politics,* and MacIntyre is going in a similar direction, but it will be impossible to complete MacIntyre's vision of a modern Aristotelianism without some sort of social and political theory.

FURTHER DEVELOPMENTS IN MODERN VIRTUE ETHICS

Rosalind Hursthouse and Virtue Ethics

Rosalind Hursthouse has a very Aristotelian framework for her Virtue Ethics, even though she does not agree with all of Aristotle's conclusions. Hursthouse defends a version of Virtue Ethics which claims that virtues are virtues because they help a person achieve eudaimonia, and so living a virtuous life is a *good* thing for a human being. Like Julia Annas she sees the virtues as shaping the virtuous person's practical reasoning in characteristic ways, and not simply as shaping that person's attitudes or actions. For Hursthouse being virtuous is the most reliable path to flourishing and she seems to think that no other path is as reliable. She also attempts to address the major criticism of Virtue Ethics: that it provides no guidance in moral dilemmas – not by telling us how a virtuous person would act, but by showing how a virtuous person would think about a moral dilemma.

> ### Rosalind Hursthouse (1943–)
>
> Rosalind Hursthouse is Professor of Philosophy at the University of Auckland, New Zealand, and is known for her work in Virtue Ethics. As well as theoretical work on Virtue Ethics, she has also written about the ethical treatment of animals in *Ethics, Humans and Other Animals* (2000).

Michael Slote and Virtue Ethics

Michael Slote describes Virtue Ethics as being mostly based on our commonsense ideas and intuitions about what counts as a virtue, and prefers to use the word 'admirable' to describe an action, rather than 'good' or 'excellent' which need qualifying and explaining. He sees the opposite as a 'deplorable' action, which can mean both foolish and careless and morally blameworthy actions. He describes virtue as 'an inner trait or disposition of the individual', so a virtue is a kind of balanced caring between those who are close to us, namely family and friends, and people in general. He goes on to say that morally admirable caring could, in some way, copy the sort of love we have for those to whom we are close and will always express balanced caring. However, Slote's view does seem to allow a wide range of actions by the person facing a moral dilemma, as a wide range of actions could be fitted into a life that showed balanced caring and does not seem to help very much when having to choose between a family member and strangers.

> ### Michael Slote (1941–)
>
> Michael Slote is Professor of Ethics at the University of Miami. He is a leading figure in the field of Virtue Ethics and argues that, in a particular form (the ethics of caring), it offers advantages over deontology, Utilitarianism and commonsense morality.

Perhaps the major contribution of Slote to the discussion of Virtue Ethics is his explanation of the difference between *agent-focused* and *agent-based* theories. Agent-focused theories understand the moral life in terms of what it is to be a virtuous person, where virtues are inner dispositions – Aristotle's Virtue Ethics is an example of this. On the other hand, agent-based theories evaluate actions according to the inner life and motive of the people who do such actions. He says there are many human traits we find admirable such as kindness and compassion, and we can identify these by looking at people we admire. Slote focuses on care and concern for others and empathy – he looks at the motives more than the community aspect of virtues.

Feminism and Virtue Ethics

> **Annette Baier (1929–)**
>
> Annette Baier is a moral philosopher focusing on Hume's moral psychology. She is a well-known feminist philosopher and is strongly influenced by her colleague Wilfrid Sellars.

Finally, it is worth looking briefly at one more modern version of Virtue Ethics as developed mainly by feminist writers such as Annette Baier. They claim that men often think morally in terms of justice and autonomy, which could be seen as 'masculine' traits, whereas women think morally in terms of caring, nurturing and self-sacrifice. Baier advocates a view of ethics that takes account of our natural biases (e.g. the love of a mother for her children and the importance of trust for people in lives and relationships). Writers who discuss the ethics of caring do not always make explicit links with Virtue Ethics, but much in their discussion of specific virtues, their relation to social practices, moral education and so on is central to Virtue Ethics.

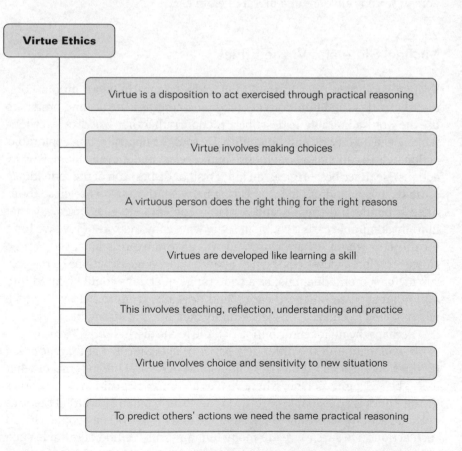

Virtue Ethics

- Virtue is a disposition to act exercised through practical reasoning
- Virtue involves making choices
- A virtuous person does the right thing for the right reasons
- Virtues are developed like learning a skill
- This involves teaching, reflection, understanding and practice
- Virtue involves choice and sensitivity to new situations
- To predict others' actions we need the same practical reasoning

Thought Point

1. What virtues do you think are important in the twenty-first century? Do you think they will still be important in the future?
2. Do you think Virtue Ethics is worth resurrecting? Why?
3. If we have little control over our personalities, our upbringing or our environment, can we be praised for our virtues or blamed for not possessing virtues?
4. What should someone do when faced with two different possible courses of action, both of which seem to express virtues?
5. How do modern versions of Virtue Ethics differ from the Virtue Ethics of Aristotle?

STRENGTHS OF VIRTUE ETHICS

*   Virtue Ethics avoids having to use a formula (e.g. 'the greatest good for the greatest number') to work out what we ought to do and focuses instead on the kind of person we ought to be.
*   Virtue Ethics understands the need to distinguish good people from legalists – obeying the law and following the rules does not make one a good person.
*   Virtue Ethics stresses the importance of motivating people to want to be good – it stresses the importance of education in showing that good actions are their own reward. It shows how we acquire and learn virtues by imitating others.
*   Virtue Ethics tells us how we learn moral principles and involves our entire life, as every moment, even the most mundane, is an opportunity for developing a virtue.
*   Virtue Ethics enables us to integrate many aspects of life – our emotions, commitments to others, our friends, social responsibilities – into our ethical reflection; it looks at what makes life worthwhile rather than looking at what is right or wrong in a particular situation or particular moment in our lives. It does not reject our emotions but includes them, and so is more in tune with how people naturally react to an ethical dilemma. It relates our ethical choices to the bigger picture.
*   Virtue Ethics sees it as good to be biased in favour of friends and family, unlike Utilitarianism or Kant which see impartiality as important.
*   Virtue Ethics does not pretend to be able to tell us what a good person would do in every possible situation but encourages us to be more like

such a person so that we will not need an ethical theory to make our decisions for us. It stresses the importance of character – after all, someone who helps the poor out of compassion does seem to be morally superior to someone who does it out of duty.

WEAKNESSES OF VIRTUE ETHICS

- One major difficulty is that of identifying the virtues. Are virtues culturally relative?
- How can Virtue Ethics be applied to moral dilemmas? This is the problem raised by Robert Louden ('On Some Vices of Virtue Ethics'): Virtue Ethics does not help people facing a crisis because it does not give any clear rules for action. It is difficult to work out what is the virtuous response to stem-cell research or abortion. Virtue Ethics does not give us any concrete answers and says only that it is a matter for the practical wisdom of the person facing the situation.
- Virtue Ethics seems to praise some virtues that we might see as immoral (e.g. soldiers fighting unjust wars may be courageous but that does not make them morally good).
- Louden also points out that it is difficult to decide who is virtuous, as acts which appear virtuous on the outside may not necessarily have good motives and vice versa.
- Virtue Ethics does not seem to have room for basic concepts such as rights and obligations, so as a theory of ethics it seems incapable of dealing with big issues – Virtue Ethics does not always have a view about what makes an act right or wrong.
- Virtue Ethics depends on some final end which gives shape to our lives: there may not be one, and being virtuous may not affect it anyway.

IS VIRTUE ETHICS DIFFERENT FROM DEONTOLOGICAL AND TELEOLOGICAL SYSTEMS?

Normative ethical systems are generally divided into deontological, teleological and Virtue Ethics. The first two are action-based ethical theories and focus on the actions of a person. When actions are said to be right in themselves or right in how well they conform to a set of duties, the ethical theory is deontological. When actions are judged to be right on the basis of their consequences, the ethical theory is teleological or consequential.

Virtue Ethics focuses on the character of the person doing the actions and looks at what actions would make a good person. There is much less emphasis on rules people should follow and more on helping people develop character traits which will help them make the right decisions later on in life. However, Virtue Ethics could be said to be more teleological as it focuses on the person's *telos* or end – eudaimonia or human flourishing.

HOW COMPATIBLE IS VIRTUE ETHICS WITH A RELIGIOUS APPROACH TO ETHICS?

At first glance Virtue Ethics involves personal responsibility and seems entirely secular – it is about developing qualities that will lead to eudaimonia. It, therefore, seems compatible with religion, but independent of it. However, recently in Christian ethics there has been renewed interest in the virtues, and it has been recognised that the thought of Aristotle had great influence on the Christian tradition, especially the work of Thomas Aquinas. Since the twentieth-century revival and the work of MacIntyre, Virtue Ethics has become important and influenced theologians such as Stanley Hauerwas and Jean Porter.

For most Christians what is important is following the life and teachings of Jesus. They do not understand their religious beliefs as following a code of conduct or a set of concepts. The life of Jesus as related in the Gospels is fundamental; though Paul in his writings often appeals to other values, it is always to the Gospel, to the death and resurrection of Jesus, that he turns when discussing any serious moral issue. Throughout the New Testament there is the constant call for Christians to be the sort of people they are called to become. This fits well into a Virtue Ethic approach which suggests following the examples of virtuous people in order to become virtuous people ourselves.

The appeal of Virtue Ethics is that it places a greater emphasis on being rather than doing – the kind of moral person one is to become, rather than goals or rules that must be followed. The focus of Virtue Ethics on motivation and transformation of character fits in well with the biblical teaching such as that found in the Sermon on the Mount (Matthew 5–7). Virtue Ethics also takes on the character of a particular culture, so that it can espouse particular Christian virtues such as mercy and agapaeic love. Christianity has also responded to the times, with each major upheaval bringing about a new way of living the Christian life: Benedictine monasticism in the Dark Ages, Franciscan and Dominican friars in the later Middle Ages, Protestant pietism in the eighteenth century and Blessed Mother Teresa's work among the poor in the twentieth century. Different times have seen the need for new virtues and new ways of living the Christian life.

Virtue Ethics does require practising the virtues in order to become virtuous, and from a Christian point of view this can seem a bit selfish – rather like helping the poor to get into heaven. But the relationship between human flourishing (eudaimonia) and virtuous activity does not neatly fit into a means-to-an-end category, as all human flourishing is about how we live – it is not an end state. For Christians the good life is to be found in communion with God and others.

So religious ethics does not need to mean unquestioning obedience to the commands of God, based on some private or particular revelation; it may also appeal to the natural (but God-given) moral insights and virtues of humans.

THE SIGNIFICANCE OF A PARTICULAR VIEW OF NATURE FOR VIRTUE ETHICS

In *Nicomachean Ethics* Aristotle asserts that humans by nature move towards a certain telos or end – eudaimonia. To achieve this, humans need to practise virtues such as friendship, magnanimity and phronesis. Over time philosophers have disagreed over what exactly the virtues are, but those who agree with Virtue Ethics would claim that we aim to be better than we are – the ideal has not been attained. Doing the right thing means simply the action that is done by the virtuous person. However, what if human life has no telos? This is the view of Iris Murdoch:

> There are properly many patterns and purposes within life, but there is no general and as it were externally guaranteed pattern or purpose of the kind for which philosophers and theologians used to search. We are what we seem to be, transient moral creatures subject to necessity and chance.
>
> (*The Sovereignty of Good* p. 79)

Virtue Ethics is thought to be naturalistic because its claims about our telos and virtues depend on a particular view of human nature. It is also based on developing our fundamental nature and so fulfilling our potential as human beings. This, however, does raise some important questions:

- Do we have a fixed nature or essence? Are there particular qualities we should all seek to express?
- Is our nature innate or does it depend on our environment or upbringing?
- If our nature is shaped by our culture, religion or upbringing, can we be held responsible for our virtuous actions?
- If virtues can be expressed in different ways, how does a virtuous person decide which is right; for example, one person might act out of love to help a person die, while another out of love might seek to prolong life at all costs.

Virtue Ethics has, however, shown that ethics is more than obeying rules and is concerned with the value and purpose of human life.

APPLICATION OF VIRTUE ETHICS TO AN ETHICAL DILEMMA – SEXUAL ETHICS

Virtue Ethics encompasses our entire lives, and sees every moment as a possibility for acquiring or developing a virtue, including sexual relationships. A virtue-based approach to sexual ethics does not give a choice of action from alternatives, nor does it tell us how to respond in a particular situation, such as when a person seems to go against a particular sexual moral norm. However, Virtue Ethics asks how a person acts virtuously over an extended period of time with regard to their sexual relationships. Virtue Ethics is not about decisions, but about the person making those decisions, and the skills and habits that enable the person to act rightly under pressure. As far as sexual ethics is concerned, Virtue Ethics aims to shape what we desire as well as what we do, and so presumes there is a right and wrong in sexual conduct – it is not just private choice.

Virtue Ethics would consider what kind of sexual practices would make a person more virtuous, and would consider that sex expresses human union – a sharing, giving and commitment. It would therefore see sexual practices that use others for one's own end, or that harm others, as not being virtuous.

Virtue Ethics implies that an action is right if it is what a virtuous person, who exercises the virtues, would characteristically do in a situation. Aristotle talks about practising virtues, and a mature person continually growing in virtues.

One approach to sexual ethics from the point of view of Virtue Ethics might consider the application of certain virtues, such as justice and fairness, in sexual ethics which treat each person with dignity. This could be used to discuss the commercialisation of sex, from prostitution to internet pornography, and the question of the equality of women.

Alternatively, Virtue Ethicists such as Michael Slote emphasise the ethics of care in relationships, and as far as sexual ethics are concerned this requires a sort of three-way balance: care for those who are near to us (intimate care); care for other people in general (humanitarian care); and care for our own well-being (self-care). This enables us to balance justice which asks us to treat all people with impartiality, with fidelity which asks us to consider our specific interpersonal relationships. Finally self-care allows one to be accountable for oneself, and not let oneself be taken advantage of in sexual relationships – responsible for ourselves as well as for others.

This view implies tolerance towards others' approaches to sexual ethics, while accepting that we are responsible for our character and the choices we make. Virtue Ethics also urges us to rediscover balance in human sexuality and in our sexual relationships.

❓ Examination Questions Practice

Unless the question specifically asks you about Aristotle's Virtue Ethics, you do not need to limit your answer just to his approach but may consider more modern approaches also. However, you need to remember the constraints on time in the examination.

REVIEW QUESTIONS

Look back over the chapter and check that you can answer the following questions:

1. Where did Virtue Ethics originate?
2. What is the difference between Virtue Ethics and other normative ethical theories?
3. Explain Aristotle's idea of the Golden Mean.
4. How did Aristotle say we acquired virtues?
5. How can Virtue Ethics help us in moral dilemmas?
6. Make a chart of the strengths and weaknesses of Virtue Sthics.

Terminology

Do you know your terminology?

Try to explain the following terms without looking at your books or notes:

- Aretaic ethics
- Eudaimonia
- Golden Mean
- Phronesis

The principles of Virtue Ethics can be found in the three Eastern religions of Buddhism, Hinduism and Sikhism. In Hinduism life is concerned with right conduct and living according to your dharma. The principal Buddhist virtue is compassion. Sikhism has five virtues which are necessary to work towards being united with God and help them develop compassion for all life. These five are: *Sat* (truth), *Santokh* (contentment), *Daya* (compassion), *Nimrata* (humility) and *Piare* (love).

SAMPLE EXAMINATION QUESTIONS

(a) Explain Aristotle's concept of eudaimonia. (30 marks)

In your answer you need to explain the concept of eudaimonia.

- You should establish that it means more than 'happiness' but a sense of well-being and an ultimate aim in life.
- In developing the concept, you should mention the Aristotelian virtues and the practising of these virtues.
- You might also mention Aristotle's views of characters who sought eudaimonia in the wrong ways.
- You may also use other Virtue Ethicists in your explanation.

(b) Assess how dependent the concept of eudaimonia is upon a particular view of human nature. (20 marks)

In your answer you need to consider the concept of eudaimonia in relation to human nature.

- What if eudaimonia is unattainable? Or invented?
- You might consider issues about the 'state' of human nature, and the 'nature v. nurture' debate.
- You might also consider the problem which can arise when eudaimonia is open to interpretation or conflicts with other 'virtues' and/or other ethical systems such as Utilitarianism which has different views about what makes people 'happy' or fulfilled.

Further information on world faiths can be found at: http://subknow.reonline.org.uk/.

13 Religious Views on Sexual Behaviour and Human Relationships

WHAT YOU WILL LEARN ABOUT IN THIS CHAPTER

- Religious approaches to sexual behaviour.
- The teachings of scripture on sexual behaviour.
- Church teachings on sexual behaviour.
- An understanding of the underlying principles and implications of these approaches for making decisions about the issues surrounding sexual behaviour – marriage, monogamy, polygamy, polyandry, premarital and extramarital sex, conception, love and family.
- How to assess the different approaches and to evaluate their strengths and weaknesses.

THE AQA CHECKLIST ✔

Religious views on sexual behaviour and human relationships

- Candidates will be expected to have studied the teaching of **one** of the six major world religions, but, where appropriate, may refer to more than one religion in their answers.
- Candidates should note that views should focus upon:

- scripture-based ideas which are rooted in text
- institutional-based ideas which have been developed by a particular religious institution
- individual-based ideas which will have been developed from individual conscience or interpretation of scripture or institutional-based ideas
- sexual behaviour outside marriage, including pleasure and pro-creation
- views on marriage as a sacred event or secular monogamy, polygamy, polyandry, adultery
- human relationships, respect and responsibility for others, the abuse of power
- concept of love (different styles: brotherly, physical, Christian agape), family and children.

ISSUES ARISING

- Because religious teaching is rooted in history, is it ever relevant to people today?
- Is sexual behaviour a matter that religion should concern itself with?
- Is modern society setting its own codes of behaviour, and is religion simply trying to adapt to them?

WHAT IS SEXUAL ETHICS CONCERNED WITH?

Sex is an enormously wide term covering a range of issues from homo-sexuality to marriage, from pornography to prostitution, to the relational dimensions which are expressions of love and pleasure. It is part of being human and involves above all the question of how men and women should treat each other.

In spite of the fact that, or maybe because, sex is so natural to us, we hedge it with rules. As Richard Holloway put it: 'Human sexuality is like a runaway car.' It can be destructive or creative, but we are never quite in control of it.

The Kiss, 1888–1898
(marble) by Auguste Rodin
(1840–1917)

© Musée Rodin, Paris,
France/Philippe Galard/The
Bridgeman Art Library

HISTORICAL VIEWS OF SEX

Originally the Greek philosophers saw sex as something weakening to the mind. The Pythagoreans, who influenced Plato, believed that humans should refrain from physical activities and live a more ascetic life. In this way the soul, which is imprisoned in the body, is freed to move to a new form. This dualism between the physical and the spiritual may be seen in Plato's model of the soul as the charioteer with his two horses: the beautiful white horse that is a model of self-control and responds to the spoken word, and the ugly black horse that needs controlling with a whip. There are in this many levels of interpretation as far as sexual desire/pleasure is concerned – the desire needs controlling but it is allowed to exist; after all, the charioteer needs both of his horses.

The Cynics, on the other hand, saw no point in controlling sexual desire or pleasure and saw no shame attached to the sexual act, even going so far as to perform it in public. The Stoics reacted totally against this and advocated overcoming any emotions that threaten self-control – the Stoics were the original 'stiff upper lips', and sex became linked to reproduction and the continuation of the human race.

So the early history of sexual ethics as far as philosophy was concerned was riddled with contradictions which have continued ever since.

The same contradictions may be discerned in early Judaism as found in the Old Testament and later in Christianity. However, for the Greeks sexuality is naturally excessive and so the moral problem is not whether it is right or wrong but how to control it. This did not involve laws which prohibited certain sexual acts, but required individual self-discipline.

THE OLD TESTAMENT APPROACH TO SEXUAL BEHAVIOUR

The Old Testament is a reflection of its times and does not seem to have one particular view on sexual ethics. It includes moving love stories, such as the story of Ruth and Boaz, and detailed accounts of incest, such as that concerning the two daughters of Lot in Genesis 19, whose incestuous relationship with their father has the intention of assuring his line: 'Come, let us make our father drink wine, and we will lie with him, that we may preserve offspring from our father' (Genesis 19:32). There are numerous tales of seduction and sexual revenge, such as the seduction of Bath-shua [Bathsheba] by King David and the murder of her husband, and the seduction of Tamar by Amnon which resulted in Amnon's death. Many of these are recounted in a factual way, without judgement. Sex is even celebrated in the Song of Songs.

> I am a rose of Sharon,
> a lily of the valleys.
> As a lily among brambles,
> so is my love among maidens.
> As an apple tree among the trees of the wood,
> so is my beloved among young men.
> With great delight I sat in his shadow,
> and his fruit was sweet to my taste.

He brought me to the banqueting house,
and his intention toward me was love.
Sustain me with raisins,
refresh me with apples;
for I am faint with love.
O that his left hand were under my head,
and that his right hand embraced me!
I adjure you, O daughters of Jerusalem,
by the gazelles or the wild does:
do not stir up or awaken love
until it is ready!

(Song of Songs 2:1–7)

In Genesis 1 and 2 there is an understanding that sex is created by God and meant for procreation. However, sex is seen not as wrong but as good; yet the contradictions also appear, as sex should not be practised in sinful ways. Sexual involvement with non-Israelites was forbidden, as it would lead away from God (e.g. 1 Kings 11:1–13), and adultery was forbidden: 'You shall not commit adultery' (Exodus 20:14). 'If a man commits adultery with the wife of his neighbour, both the adulterer and the adulteress shall be put to death' (Leviticus 20:10).

Adultery was seen as theft and punishable by stoning. This was a society in which women were not equal to men, but had to be part of the household of a man. Women should be virgins on marriage, but this was so the man could be certain that the children were his own and the line was assured.

In the Old Testament the stories and teachings show a number of different ways of having a sexual relationship from polygamy to concubines. David, held as the ideal king of Israel, was an adulterer who had a man murdered in order to marry his wife, though he did repent when found out (2 Samuel 11–12). However, there is a gradual shift to one man, one wife. This monogamy was confirmed by Jesus, and so became fundamental Christian teaching.

THE NEW TESTAMENT APPROACH TO SEXUAL RELATIONSHIPS

Jesus

Jesus himself said very little about sex; in fact he gave very few rules and instructions, but called his followers to live as part of the Kingdom of God, to reflect through their lives God's love for all people and to live justly with each other. As far as sexual ethics are concerned, Jesus seems to have left the issues open. Even in his teachings about marriage and divorce it is not possible to be sure what he said or what he meant. Jesus is quoted as saying: 'Whoever divorces his wife and (*kai*) marries another commits adultery (*porneia*) against her' (Mark 10:11b). The wording here is not easy to translate into English; the word 'kai' could mean 'in order to', not just 'and', and so, depending on what the word means, the understanding of what Jesus meant changes. Similarly with the word 'porneia' – it has three alternatives: it could refer to a woman who was not a virgin on marriage, in which case divorce would follow immediately after marriage; it could mean adultery, in which case a man could divorce his wife for her adultery, but she did not have the same right if he was adulterous; or it could mean 'fornication', which in the Old Testament means chasing after other gods – divorce is allowed if the partner is a non-believer. However, it is clear that Jesus is challenging the view of the wife as the man's property – he is talking more about equality than about sexual relationships. One thing is clear, however, and this is that Jesus is setting out an ideal and divorce falls short of it.

Jesus' teachings on adultery are all about the harming of relationships:

> You have heard that it was said, 'You shall not commit adultery.' But I say to you that everyone who looks at a woman with lust has already committed adultery with her in his heart. If your right eye causes you to sin, tear it out and throw it away; it is better for you to lose one of your members than for your whole body to be thrown into hell. And if your right hand causes you to sin, cut it off and throw it away; it is better for you to lose one of your members than for your whole body to go into hell.
>
> (Matthew 5:27–30)

He forgave the adulterous woman who was brought before him:

> Jesus straightened up and said to her, 'Woman, where are they? Has no one condemned you?' She said, 'No one, sir.' And Jesus said, 'Neither do I condemn you. Go your way, and from now on do not sin again.'
>
> (John 8:10–11)

He claimed that our intentions are the most important thing: 'For out of the heart come evil intentions, murder, adultery, fornication, theft, false witness, slander. These are what defile a person' (Matthew 15:19–20a).

Paul

As we have seen, the New Testament does not have a great deal to say on the subject, and much of Paul's writing is influenced by his expectation of the imminent return of Christ and the end of the world. There was not much point in giving a detailed ethic on sex, as all human relationships were soon to end. Paul, influenced by Greek thinking, attempted to move the Christian people away from the body towards the soul.

So he writes in 1 Corinthians 6:12–20 that Christians should not let their bodily emotions control them, that sexual activity is to be kept within marriage, that the body is a temple of the Holy Spirit and should be respected.

'All things are lawful for me,' but not all things are beneficial. 'All things are lawful for me,' but I will not be dominated by anything. 'Food is meant for the stomach and the stomach for food,' and God will destroy both one and the other. The body is meant not for fornication but for the Lord, and the Lord for the body. And God raised the Lord and will also raise us by his power. Do you not know that your bodies are members of Christ? Should I therefore take the members of Christ and make them members of a prostitute? Never! Do you not know that whoever is united to a prostitute becomes one body with her? For it is said, 'The two shall be one flesh.' But anyone united to the Lord becomes one spirit with him. Shun fornication! Every sin that a person commits is outside the body; but the fornicator sins against the body itself. Or do you not know that your body is a temple of the Holy Spirit within you, which you have from God, and that you are not your own? For you were bought with a price; therefore glorify God in your body.

This whole passage shows Paul attempting to move people away from bodily pleasures to a more spiritual realm. Marriage was not forbidden, but considered only for those with no self-control.

Paul's views on sex, marriage and women are also inconsistent. Sometimes he was positive about women – all are equal: 'There is no longer Jew or Greek, there is no longer slave or free, there is no longer male and female; for all of you are one in Christ Jesus' (Galatians 3:28). Yet elsewhere he argues that women should obey their husbands:

Wives, be subject to your husbands as you are to the Lord. For the husband is the head of the wife just as Christ is the head of the church, the body of which he is the Saviour. Just as the church is subject to Christ, so also wives ought to be, in everything, to their husbands.

(Ephesians 5:22–4)

Thus he returns to the Old Testament view of the wife as the property of the man. When he is positive about marriage and does not just consider it for the weak-willed, he compares marriage with the relationship between Christ and his Church:

'For this reason a man will leave his father and mother and be joined to his wife, and the two will become one flesh.' This is a great mystery, and I am applying it to Christ and the church.

(Ephesians 5:31–2)

Feminism
A way of thinking that seeks to emancipate women in society and give them equal opportunities.

However, this still seems to say that the man is the head of the household, just as Christ is head of the Church.

Paul's views do seem more rigid than the equality message of Jesus, but he was a product of his times, and his focus on the imminent return of Jesus limited his teaching to preparation for that day. Paul is credited with exerting great influence on the development of Christian thought, but he was also limited by his religious views and the attitudes of the times, especially on the value of celibacy and the inferior role of women. However, Platonic dualism and the views of the Greek philosophers were also important, as they stressed the spiritual above the physical – sex is part of the physical side of us.

AUGUSTINE AND SEXUAL RELATIONSHIPS

Augustine of Hippo lived in a world of multiple sects and 'heresies', some of which picked up on and emphasised the dualism of body and soul.

This dualism is found in Gnosticism, itself a mixture of the Greek traditions, with some from Judaism and Zoroastrianism. It was from Zoroastrianism, the religion of ancient Persia, that the extreme dualism sprang, along with a pessimistic fatalism. Central to Gnostic teaching was an intense dislike of the body and its needs, a total pessimism about sexuality which infiltrated the early Church. In this world, the views of Augustine were surprisingly liberal, and he considered that, far from abstaining from all sex, it was necessary for procreation, and that, as for Paul and the Greeks, sex was a necessary evil. Augustine taught, after his many sexual relationships, that sex was to be restricted to marriage, but it was still 'dangerous'. The devil uses women to lead men away from reason, and pleasure in sex leads men away from reason. For Augustine the problem, and the solution, dated back to creation and the Fall. Adam and Eve, he concluded, must have been made for procreation, though they would not have needed to procreate before the Fall, or at least would have experienced no desire or pleasure. However, God knew that Eve would take the fruit and so he prepared for the consequences.

For Augustine, then, sexual desire is a constant reminder of the human rebellion against God – it is our original sin. Augustine, unlike Pelagius, believed that we could not control sexual desire – he did not go in for 'muscular Christianity' like Pelagius, who thought that sexual desire could be controlled by the will. So, for Augustine, chastity was the ideal, but sex was allowed, so long as it was not enjoyed, within marriage.

Celibacy

Not having sexual relations with another person.

Attitudes such as those of Augustine have had great influence on sexual attitudes and practices in the Western world. Marriage was seen as the only way people could engage in sexual relationships without committing grave sins. Furthermore, sex within marriage was permitted only for the purpose of procreation, and it was this view that ultimately influenced the teaching of the Catholic Church, not only about marriage but also about couples living together, contraceptives and homosexual relationships. However, Augustine also had a more positive influence on Catholic teaching in that marriage is seen as a sacrament that should be the basis for a supportive, loving relationship that allows couples to be joined in union for life. Augustine was a major influence on the Catholic teaching that does not recognise divorce, but allows annulments to show that there was no marriage in the first place.

THOMAS AQUINAS AND SEXUAL RELATIONSHIPS

Thomas Aquinas' views on sexual relationships were accepted as right for Christians until they began to be questioned in modern times.

Aquinas based his thinking about sexual ethics on his understanding of Natural Law, in which he attempted to unite the thinking of Aristotle with Christian theology. Aquinas believed that human life had a purpose or telos; good acts developed our human nature and bad acts went against human nature. Aquinas assumed that humans shared a common human nature and so general principles could be applied to everyone, everywhere and at all times. Aquinas concluded that the purpose of the sexual organs and sexual activity was procreation, and any other use of sex was intrinsically wrong. Sex for Aquinas was to take place within the bounds of marriage, and must be open to the possibility of procreation. This became the view of the Catholic Church.

In the *Summa Theologiae*, Aquinas argued that sexual acts can be morally wrong in two different ways:

1. Sex is wrong when 'the act of its nature is incompatible with the purpose of the sex act [procreation]. In so far as generation is blocked, we have unnatural vice, which is any complete sex act from which of its nature generation cannot follow.' Aquinas gives us four examples: 'The sin of self-abuse' (masturbation), 'Intercourse with a thing of another species' (bestiality), acts with a person of the same sex (homosexuality), and acts in which 'the natural style of intercourse is not observed, as regards proper organ or according to other rather beastly and monstrous techniques' (foreplay?).

2. Sexual acts can be morally wrong even if natural; in these cases, 'conflict with right reason may arise from the nature of the act with respect to the other party'; for example, incest, rape or adultery.

Natural Law, however, raises two important questions:

1. Is an 'unnatural act' always wrong, even if it is consummated with mutual and informed voluntary consent?
2. Are there some non-procreative sexual acts that might be natural to human beings? Do we, in fact, share a common nature, but might God have created a variety of human beings with different forms of sexual expression?

MODERN INFLUENCES ON SEXUAL RELATIONSHIPS

Modern popular thinking, influenced by developments in psychology and sociology, began to question traditional views by asking such questions as: 'Why is sex within marriage for procreation more in accordance with human nature than sex outside marriage for pleasure?' and 'Why cannot sexual relationships be morally right if there is love, loyalty and intimacy?'

According to Sigmund Freud (1856–1939), each person's approach to sex and their sexual relationships is based on their upbringing and their relationship with their parents. He suggests that sexual personality may be found at the core of moral personality: how we behave towards sexual partners both influences and mirrors how we perceive and interact with people in general. So, the failure to learn to control the pursuit of sexual pleasure undermines the achievement of a virtuous character.

Freud says that we each have a super-ego, which is like an inner voice reminding us of the social norms inculcated in us by our parents and authority figures in society. We need this voice in order to live happily in a law-abiding society. Unlike Aquinas, Freud considers that being moral may not accord with our real natures at all and so it is not possible to base an ethical theory on what we essentially are.

Rules about sex and relationships have existed in every culture, as have disagreements about what is and what is not morally acceptable. Must morally permissible sex have only one function? Must it be heterosexual? Must it be limited to marriage? Does sex require love or just mutual consent?

Conditions in the modern world are changing rapidly and, as a result, modern opinions towards sex and relationships are also changing. This has influenced traditional religious teaching also.

Gender
Cultural and psychological characteristics that determine whether a person is male or female.

Queer theory
The idea that there can be no fixed rules about what is or is not a legitimate sexual relationship. Being queer is the freedom to define oneself according to one's nature.

Harm principle
The belief that an act or consequence is morally permissible if no harm is done.

THE DEVELOPMENT OF CHRISTIAN IDEAS ABOUT SEXUAL RELATIONSHIPS

Traditional Christian ethics about sex is based on the teachings of the Bible, Augustine and Aquinas. Marriage is seen as the norm and the purpose of marriage is seen as fidelity, union and procreation. The unitive role of love, as the couple becoming 'one flesh', is a comparatively modern element, and the role of sex in marriage as an expression of that love is also now recognised. Even sexual pleasure is seen as a gift from God – but only within the context of heterosexual marriage.

However, this view took a while to develop, and, as shown earlier, the Bible pays more attention to divorce than to the formation of marriage which is simply assumed, as it is through most of the early Christian period. For the early Christians, marriage customs, laws and practices were inherited from the Graco-Roman culture and from their Jewish background. The early Christians simply followed the customs of the time and moved in together, with or without a simple domestic ceremony. The differences for Christians were simple: it was the cohabitation of baptised people and they stressed sexual fidelity. There was no special ceremony for Christian marriage as there was for the Eucharist and for Baptism – marriage was simply not seen as needing to be blessed by a priest.

This position gradually changed as the power and influence of the Church grew and the principle of consent from Roman law and the emphasis of sexual consummation from Judaism gradually became an exchange of mutual consent. Marriage was seen as a process rather than an event and specific Christian ceremonies did not come in until well into the Middle Ages. It was only in the twelfth century that Pope Alexander III decided that mutual consent was the basis for a valid marriage and that it was an unbreakable contract. Since then the Roman Catholic Church has always held that a properly celebrated and consummated marriage cannot be dissolved.

As Philip Reynolds argues, getting married was a process rather than a simple act – marriage was initiated by betrothal and consummated by sexual intercourse. Any liturgical ceremony might occur at various points between courtship and betrothal.

This is a quite different understanding of marriage from the way it is seen today: marriage is a religious or legal ceremony taking about 30 minutes. This came about as a result of the Marriage Act of 1753 (Lord Hardwicke's Marriage Act [26 Geo. II. c.33]), which was intended to stop clandestine marriages into the aristocracy. This led to the end of the importance of betrothal, and the event of the wedding became all-important. Needless to say, this legislation was seen at the time as a massive intrusion by the state into people's personal lives. So our idea of marriage with a ceremony is a fairly recent and state-imposed understanding; previously cohabitation had been seen as marriage.

Today the Catholic Church teaches that marriage is a divine institution that cannot be broken, even by divorce. Marriage is seen as one of the seven sacraments, but harking back to the original understanding of marriage it is the only sacrament that is not administered directly by a priest, but which the husband and wife administer directly to each other. Vatican II describes marriage as follows:

> By their very nature, the institution of matrimony itself and conjugal love are ordained for the procreation and education of children, and find in them their ultimate crown. Thus a man and a woman, who by their compact of conjugal love 'are no longer two, but one flesh' (Matt. 19:ff), render mutual help and service to each other through an intimate union of their persons and of their actions. Through this union they experience the meaning of their oneness and attain to it with growing perfection day by day. As a mutual gift of two persons, this intimate union and the good of the children impose total fidelity on the spouses and argue for an unbreakable oneness between them.
>
> Christ the Lord abundantly blessed this many-faceted love, welling up as it does from the fountain of divine love and structured as it is on the model of His union with His Church. For as God of old made Himself present to His people through a covenant of love and fidelity, so now the Saviour of men and the Spouse of the Church comes into the lives of married Christians through the sacrament of matrimony. He abides with them thereafter so that just as He loved the Church and handed Himself over on her behalf, the spouses may love each other with perpetual fidelity through mutual self-bestowal.
>
> (*Gaudium et Spes* §48)

In general all Protestant Churches hold marriage to be ordained by God for the union between a man and a woman with the primary purpose of glorifying God by showing his love for the world, and then for intimate companionship, rearing of children and mutual support. Many Protestants usually approve of contraception and will allow the remarriage of divorcees. However, some Protestant groups such as the Religious Society of Friends (Quakers) accept homosexuality and are in favour of same-sex marriage.

In the Eastern Orthodox Church marriage is seen as a Sacred Mystery (sacrament), uniting men and women in eternal union before God. This Church also sees marriage as an icon of the relationship between Jesus and the Church – like the use of marriage as an analogy to describe the relationship between God and Israel by the Old Testament prophet Hosea. Unlike Western Christianity, Eastern Christians do not see the couple as giving each other the sacrament, rather it is seen as the action of the Holy Spirit acting through the priest and so only a priest or a bishop may perform the Sacred Mystery. Divorce is discouraged but sometimes out of *economia* (mercy) a marriage may be dissolved and couples may remarry, but only three times. Orthodox priests are allowed to marry before ordination, but if their wife dies they may not remarry and remain a priest. Bishops must always be monks and so are celibate.

Conditions in the modern world are changing rapidly and, as a result, modern opinions about sex and relationships are also changing. This has influenced traditional religious teaching also. The Catholic psychiatrist Jack Dominion argues, and has done for the past 30 years at least, not that sex is dangerous and needs marriage and procreation to protect it but rather that sex is so powerful and meaningful that justice can be done to it only in a continuous and enduring relationship. He does not see premarital sex, cohabitation or even one-off adultery as destroying this ideal and even considers that homosexual sex is fine within a permanent loving relationship. He sees society as moving forward and the Church as needing to rethink but not reject its fundamental truths.

This view is shared by the Anglican theologian Duncan Dormor, who suggests that for the majority of people today cohabitation is an integral part of becoming a couple and leading eventually to marriage for most. He says that the Christian Church needs to accept and welcome cohabiting couples and listen to their reasons, without just giving an uncritical idealised endorsement of marriage. He points out that people cohabit for a variety of reasons; sometimes they are trying out a relationship to see if it could become a permanent partnership or not. This means, he suggests, that the Church needs to help couples move from the wedding to the marriage as a life journey – this he says is a far greater moral issue than cohabitation and divorce. This view requires Christians to take a far more mature approach to sexuality so that sex outside marriage within a stable long-term faithful, but unmarried, relationship is not considered as sinful as the actions of the promiscuous hedonist. Dormor is not just saying that the Church should follow the morals of the time mindlessly, but he considers that the current approach of the Church means that it cannot make any useful contributions to the debate about current sexual issues which he sees as promiscuity, premature sexualisation and pornography.

HOMOSEXUALITY

One issue that has divided Christianity is that of homosexuality. Every religion is divided between fundamentalists and liberals, between what is revealed and what is discovered. In Christianity, the issue of homosexuality points up that division, with the literal interpretation of the Bible asserting that homosexuality is wrong, and the spirit of the New Testament holding that it is the quality of the relationships which matters. There are many other issues involved, such as homosexuality being not natural, as homosexual sex does not lead to the procreation of children, the question of the 'gay gene', and the actual translation of the words in the Bible.

The two Greek words that have traditionally been translated as 'homosexual' may mean 'loose living' or 'prostitute', so in the New Revised Standard Version of the Bible the word 'homosexual' has been omitted from Paul's letters. The story of Sodom (Genesis 19:4–11) is not about sexuality but about hospitality, and so the only specific references are in the codes of Deuteronomy (Deuteronomy 23:17–18) and Leviticus (Leviticus 20:13). The meaning of these codes was obviously important at the time they were written, but today laws about purity, including the types of animals and fish that could be eaten, which excluded shellfish, and about dress, which outlawed the wearing of garments made from more than one type of yarn, are just irrelevant to many people. One concept underlying the laws was the idea of the pure form of a man and a woman, which led to the prohibition of shaving in men so that they did not look like women, and also of cross-dressing and same-sex relationships. Almost all Christians ignore these prohibitions, except the one about homosexuality. So it seems as though the Bible is being used, as in the possible split in the Anglican Church over the ordination of gay bishops, to reinforce prejudices. As Richard Holloway points out, the impetus for social reform comes from society, not from within the Christian Church.

Within the Catholic Church the position is similar – there is no sin involved in having homosexual inclinations, only in putting them into practice. Following Natural Law, any sexual act that is not open to procreation is unnatural and wrong. Again the Catholic Church has done nothing to counteract prejudice against homosexuals.

SEXUAL BEHAVIOUR OUTSIDE MARRIAGE

Though there are exceptions, monogamous heterosexual marriage has been the norm for many cultures and civilisations throughout history. Many would argue that, as children are naturally conceived through heterosexual intercourse, the family, and so marriage, is based on biology not ideology or beliefs. Indeed, in 2001, the UK government stated: 'Marriage is the surest foundation for raising children and remains the choice of the majority of people in Britain.'

Many Christians would say that marriage is the only place that sexual activity is endorsed – using for justification Genesis 2:24: 'Therefore a man leaves his father and his mother and clings to his wife, and they become one flesh.' This passage is also quoted in the Gospels (Mark 10:6–8 and Matthew 19:4–5). Paul sees adultery and other forms of sex outside marriage as wrong:

> Do you not know that wrongdoers will not inherit the kingdom of God? Do not be deceived! Fornicators, idolaters, adulterers, male prostitutes, sodomites, thieves, the greedy, drunkards, revilers, robbers – none of these will inherit the kingdom of God.
>
> (1 Corinthians 6:9–10)

However, traditional Christian views and those of society at large do not always fit comfortably together; there is now no stigma attached to premarital sex. Sex is seen as an essential part of any relationship, it is an expression of love, part of life's experiences – it is just seen as fun.

Christian teaching sees sex differently and part of our relationship with each other. Sex is seen as something too important to just experiment with, and neither is it a form of entertainment, as it concerns people's bodies which are seen as sacred and not just as toys to be played with and discarded. Even within society at large premarital sex still has some rules: rape is seen as totally unacceptable as is paedophilia; there is still a stigma attached to prostitution and to high levels of promiscuity, and to some extent 'one-night stands'; a sexual partner also ought ideally to be single or 'separated'.

There is nothing in the Bible that explicitly bans sex before marriage, but all Christian arguments against it are based on the covenant of marriage as the correct place for sexual activity. There are, however, problems with linking sex and marriage too closely, as shown in Ian McEwan's novel *On Chesil Beach* (2007) in which a young couple in the 1960s fail disastrously to consummate their marriage on their wedding night, ruining their future. Most people do look for a meaningful relationship in which there is intimacy and mutual support; they may in fact have several of these before they get married. This means that they have tested a number of steady relationships and so they have a better idea of what marriage will entail, making their decision more mature. This seems a fairly practical approach to a lifetime commitment, and one which was recognised in medieval times when couples had full sexual relations after betrothal, but not one which is recognised or accepted publicly by the Christian Churches.

Thought Point

1.   Research the changing attitudes in history to sexual relationships.
2.   How far do you consider that religious teaching on sexual relationships should take account of changing views in society today?
3.   How far should we consider the religious views on sexual relationships in a multicultural society so that we do not unwittingly cause offence?

MONOGAMY, POLYGAMY AND POLYANDRY

Marriage is seen by Christians as sacred and monogamous. This view of marriage has developed over time. Polygamy, marriage to more than one spouse simultaneously, did happen in Old Testament times: Abraham had a child with Hagar, his wife's servant; Jacob was in love with Rachel but was tricked into marrying her sister Leah first; and David inherited wives from Saul and Solomon and was led astray by his many wives into worshipping other gods. It was not considered ideal, but it was a realistic and practical way of dealing with hard times such as famine, female infertility and widowhood. All wives were considered equal to some extent, and first-born sons should inherit. Technically the practice of a male marrying more than one female is polygamy, that of a woman marrying a number of male spouses polyandry.

For Christians polygamy was prohibited by St Augustine, who wrote that, although it was necessary to have children, polygamy was no longer acceptable as Christians should follow the Roman custom of monogamy. The New Testament authors also saw monogamy as the right way for church leaders to live: 'Now a bishop must be above reproach, married only once' (1 Timothy 3:2a). The Catholic Catechism 1993 teaches:

> However polygamy is not in accord with the moral law . . . because it is contrary to the equal personal dignity of men and women who in matrimony give themselves with a love that is total and therefore unique and exclusive.
>
> (§2387)

This view is also held by mainstream Protestant Churches. The only time polygamy is an issue for Christians is when there are tensions between traditional Christian teaching on marriage and traditional polygamy in some parts of Africa. However, there are individuals who promote polygamy.

THE CONCEPT OF LOVE

The word love can encompass a variety of expressions from 'I love ice cream' to 'I love my dog', from 'I love to dance' to the simple but meaningful 'I love you'. Within families and sexual relationships there are many layers of love and different expressions of it. To understand these best it helps to look at the origins of the word. The Greeks had several words to express different types of love:

- *Eros* is a word from which comes the English word 'erotica' – it is the love of sexual attraction and so is not deep and meaningful.
- *Storge* is the love found in families between the different family members. It is a much stronger type of love and involves commitment.
- *Philia* is what might be called brotherly love. This is not brotherly in the sense of family but in the sense of kinship – it is the type of love that makes us want to help others and see others as needing love.
- *Agape* is the highest form of love, an unconditional love for others in spite of their weaknesses. It is the love that puts the needs of others as a priority.

Within a Christian context the most familiar is the word agape which is specifically used of Christian love, often translated as charity, and even God as in the phrase 'God is love' in 1 John 4:8. 'This is my commandment, that you love one another as I have loved you. No one has greater love than this, to lay down one's life for one's friends' (John 15:12–13).

For most Christians the place where they learn to love is within the family, where children learn that love involves companionship and forgiveness, protection and support, so that family life is established as part of making a stable society. Pope John Paul II said:

> All members of the family, each according to his or her own gift, have the grace and responsibility of building day by day the community of persons making a family a school of deeper humanity. This happens where there is care and love for the children, the aged and the sick; where there is a sharing of goods, of joys and of sorrows.
>
> (*Familiaris Consortio* §21)

The New Testament teaches that Christians should show the same love that they have within the family to everyone:

> Do not speak harshly to an older man, but speak to him as to a father, to younger men as brothers, to older women as mothers, to younger women as sisters – with absolute purity.
>
> (1 Timothy 5:1–2)

Whoever does the will of God is my brother and sister and mother.

(Mark 3:35)

Agape remains the centre and ideal of Christian love from the time of Paul, who saw men and women as participating together in the love of God and in the common life (*koinoia*) so that love (agape) is given to others. According to the work of Francis Watson (Professor of New Testament Exegesis at the University of Durham), men and women are interdependent: 'Nevertheless, in the Lord woman is not independent of man or man independent of woman (1 Corinthians 11:11); they belong together within the Christian community and outside of it.'

RESPECT AND RESPONSIBILITY FOR OTHERS – THE ABUSE OF POWER

Bad sexual behaviour is usually associated with domination or violence, whereas a good sexual relationship is one of mutuality and equality. However, often sexual relationships echo the patterns of dominance in society. This is shown in the incident of the rape of Tamar (2 Samuel 13). Tamar is tricked into her half-brother's room and refuses to have sex with him because she says it is sacrilege. The Hebrew word used here shows that Amnon is acting in an un-Israelite way and is like a Canaanite. This reflects the fact that the author is writing for a community which considers sex between brother and sister forbidden as a pagan practice, but not completely so as before the act Tamar says that marriage between her and Amnon might be possible. What is interesting, as far as the abuse of power is concerned in the rape, is that her brother Absolom tells Tamar not to take the rape seriously, Tamar herself is inconsolable, whereas their father King David is angry but does nothing. There seems to be some sort of silence about the use of violence against Tamar, but, as Amnon's love (or lust?) for Tamar turns to hatred, Absolom hates Amnon and eventually murders him. Was this simply because Tamar, as a woman, was inferior, the property of her father, or was it that the rape of Tamar simply gave Absolom a reason for his hatred of Amnon, David's heir? It is not clear from the account, although the Hebrew does seem to show sympathy with Tamar.

However, the idea that women are inferior and the property of men can be inferred from stories such as the Levite's concubine in Judges 19. However, the New Testament offers conflicting ideas as women are told to remain silent and not teach (1 Timothy 2:11–14, 1 Corinthians 14:34) but husbands must love their wives as Christ loves the Church (Ephesians 5:28–9) and in Galatians 3:28 Christian men and women are considered equal. The difference in ideas about the role of women could most likely be seen as social and cultural rather than having any deep religious meaning.

However, the idea that women are inferior persisted: the Protestant reformer John Calvin wrote that woman is inferior to man as she was created for the sake of man and is therefore subject to him. Calvin advises women to accept their inferiority as a fact of creation. He writes: 'Let the woman be satisfied with her state of subjection, and not take it amiss that she is made inferior to the more distinguished sex.' This seems to be more a result of cultural influences than biblical teaching.

For Christians, it is true that, in the past, women were often seen as inferior because of the Bible account of Adam and Eve, where Eve is seen as sinful (1 Timothy 2:14). Today many Christians would interpret this story in a way that does greater justice to women – the story of the Fall can be interpreted as Adam and Eve sharing not only their sin and punishment but also God's love. However, there are still today some Christians such as evangelical Protestants who interpret the Bible literally and argue that women are primarily wives and mothers and should stay at home, following perhaps Ephesians 5:21. Also the position in the Catholic Church has changed only slightly. The 1995 'Letter to Women' (1995) by Pope John Paul II stresses the dignity and rights of women and the importance of their role in society, but still sees their role as mothers as the most important.

Others, however, take the view that men and women should have equal roles in the home as they were created equally.

The Bible teaches that women were created in the image of God in the same way as men.

> So God created humankind in his image,
> in the image of God he created them;
> male and female he created them.
>
> (Genesis 1:27)

God is understood as personal, and to be in the image of God is to be a person – so women as well as men are understood to be persons of value and worth. So as far as sexual behaviour is concerned this means that women should be treated as persons, not as sex objects. It is because cultural considerations – such as the giving away of the bride by her father in the marriage service as in the past she was her property under the law – have dominated that women are so often seen as the property of men, somehow inferior and not needing the same respect as men.

The same has applied to children, as consent is integral to any Christian approach to sexual ethics and children are deemed unable to give informed consent. For the same reason rape is also wrong in the eyes of both Christian ethics and the law as consent is not given. In addition, child–parent incest is also seen as wrong as it is an abuse of power and of a position of trust.

Buddhist views on sexual behaviour and human relationships

Unlike many other faiths, Buddhism does not stress the importance of procreation. Birth is seen as the entrance to a life of suffering.

For those people who cannot live a celibate life, marriage is recommended, but generally there is no marriage ceremony. This comes from a view that the married life of a lay Buddhist is not as spiritual as the celibate life of a monk, to an extent based on the life of Siddattha Gotama (the Buddha).

The third precept prohibits sexual misconduct, in particular adultery. Men and women are required to show each other mutual respect and honour in a marriage and these relationships should be conducted with right speech, right action and right livelihood.

As with most religions, Buddhism holds different opinions relating to homosexuality. Although Buddhism has no teaching about reproduction being the main purpose of sexual activity, nevertheless it teaches that the sexual organs must only be used in relation to procreative practices.

The Dalai Lama has recognised the dignity and rights of homosexual men and women but sees homosexual acts as an improper use of the sexual organs. He has, however, taught that, in time, these acts might become acceptable but to redefine a precept requires a collective decision by the sangha (Buddhist community).

The Triratna Buddhist Community (formerly Friends of the Western Buddhist Order) welcomes homosexual people, taking the view that different sexual practices are not the issue but it is sexuality itself which needs to be overcome in the quest for enlightenment.

Hindu views on sexual behaviour and human relationships

As with most issues, there is a very large diversity in Hinduism in relation to sex and relationships.

Traditional Hindu teaching is that people should marry within their caste: this is sometimes called a Brahma marriage. In this tradition, marriage is often arranged by parents. They seek partners from the same caste, language and geographical area. Some reformers have advocated love marriages and these are becoming more common.

In this traditional view, the role of a woman is seen as that of a householder, the second stage of samskara. This is also reflected in greater value and importance attached to a son in comparison to a daughter. Therefore a girl's education could be limited to household responsibilities. A positive consequence of this might be seen in the idea that worship in the home is the responsibility of the woman who leads the family individuals in following their dharma.

Western influence since the nineteenth century has been reflected in the appearance of woman as gurus and temple priests, who see models for their roles in the teachings of the Vedas and Upanishads. These teachings have also been used as justification for challenging some traditional practices such as *purdah* (preventing women from being seen by men), child marriage, *sati* (the burning alive of a widow on her husband's funeral pyre) and the state of a permanent widow. Both of the reforming movements of the twentieth century, the Arya and Brahmo Samaj, set up social organisations for women. The Brahma Kumari movement sought a change of family relationships through the use of yoga and abstinence. Following Indian independence the 1950 Constitution granted equality to women.

A different tradition is Taiva marriage, which ignores considerations such as caste and is instead based on mutual consent.

Tantra within Hinduism is supposed to offer techniques for sexual satisfaction and has become almost an obsession with some people from the West. The Tantric texts teach that sexual activity has a different purpose but its principal aim is liberation. In fact, however, there are very few Tantric groups in the subcontinent and generally they practise Tantric sex symbolically.

Jewish views on sexual behaviour and human relationships

Judaism contains different views on sex and relationships. Orthodox and Reform Jews have different views and there are distinctions between the purpose of sex as sensuality and unity or as a link to holiness.

Traditionally, marriage is viewed as a virtue and a duty. There are religious laws which require that sexual relationships must be between a man and a woman. Marriage with non-Jews is not permitted. However, sexual relationships within a Jewish marriage are a *mitzvah* (religious duty).

Sex is not permitted before marriage or with other partners during marriage. Nor is it allowed between a couple who are separating or when people are drunk. Nevertheless, it is common in many Western societies for Jews to cohabit.

The laws of *niddah* (purity) restrict sexual relations within a marriage from the beginning of a woman's period until she has taken a ritual bath at a *mikvah*, seven days after she has finished bleeding.

The traditional view of women is that marriage was a purchase and the woman became her husband's property. The woman could not seek a divorce or own property. Many people now reject these views and see that women and men are equal in relationships, which should be based on love, mutual respect and support.

A problem remains that divorce is permitted in Orthodox circles only when a man issues his wife with a *get*. Without this she is not free to remarry within the community. The Beth Din (religious courts) have sought to persuade husbands to grant a get but cannot dissolve a marriage without his consent.

Traditional views of women being subservient and having the primary purpose of procreation are still maintained within some communities.

Although many Reform and Progressive Jews recognise homosexuality, homosexual practices are seen as condemned by the scriptures and Rabbinic laws.

Muslim views on sexual behaviour and human relationships

According to Islamic teaching humans were created as sexual beings, and sexual activity is part of spirituality. Sexuality is therefore God's gift to create relationships between men and women. Sexuality can be seen as having a purpose other than creation – it also provides an indication of what life after death will be like.

However, although men should have their sexual needs fulfilled by their wives, some traditionalists do not hold that women should have the same rights.

It is important to consider what are the teachings of religion and what comes from culture and society. A bride's virginity is still held to be of great importance.

There are some legal rulings which seek to protect women who become pregnant outside of marriage. *Hila* (sleeping foetus) rules that a pregnancy can take five or up to seven years with the child being seen as the legitimate offspring of a dead or missing husband. Another ruling is the 'public bath'. This is based on the idea that a virgin who went to a public bath after a man could become pregnant.

The seemingly harsh punishments applied to women having sex outside of marriage are ameliorated by the need to have four adult witnesses to the crime.

The Qur'an permits a man to have up to four wives. However, it also requires that these wives must have complete equality. It could be considered that these laws were introduced not to promote polygamy but to limit it against the practice of society at the time.

Nevertheless, the Qur'an frequently stresses the equality of men and women. Women can own property, keep their own names, keep their dowry, run their own business and have the right to education.

All Muslims should be married if possible though it is seen as a contractual arrangement. Husbands can divorce their wives by formally saying 'I divorce you' three times. However, this is followed by a three-month waiting period to ensure that the woman is not pregnant. Women cannot institute divorce in the same way.

A *mut'oh* or *sigheh* is a Shi'ah custom of temporary marriage which involves a contract limiting the marriage to between an hour and 99 years.

Some liberal Muslims maintain that ahadith (sayings of the Prophet Muhammad ﷺ) may have been considerably influenced by the culture in which they were written.

Sikh views on sexual behaviour and human relationships

Sikhism teaches that marriage is a spiritual as well as a physical union. Many Sikhs do have an arranged marriage as the union is between two families as well as the couple themselves. However, the agreement of the couple is essential. Dowries were banned by the Gurus. Premarital sex is forbidden, and often unmarried Sikh girls are allowed out only with a chaperon. Adultery is forbidden and the *kachera* (white shorts) which are one of the 5Ks (the five physical signs worn by Sikhs) are seen as a reminder of purity and fidelity.

Whilst not encouraged, divorce is permissible on grounds such as cruelty and adultery. Heterosexuality is the expected norm but there is no specific teaching about homosexuality.

REVIEW QUESTIONS

Look back over the chapter and check that you can answer the following questions:

1. What does the Old Testament say about sexual ethics?
2. What does the New Testament say about sexual ethics?
3. Why and how did religious views about sex become linked with procreation?
4. List the strengths and weaknesses of a traditional Christian approach to sexual ethics.

Terminology

Do you know your terminology?

Try to explain the following key ideas without looking at your books and notes:

- Celibacy
- Feminism
- Gender
- Harm principle
- Queer theory
- Sex

SAMPLE EXAMINATION QUESTIONS

(a) Examine both positive and negative aspects of relationships between humans, from the perspective of religious teaching. (30 marks)

'Human relationships' is a broad topic, and therefore you can interpret the question broadly. However, you must be able to exemplify any aspect with teaching from religion(s). This can include scripture, leaders, organisations and interpretation.

You are asked to write about both positive aspects of human relationships (e.g. love, friendship) and negative ones (e.g. abuse, forgetfulness, adultery). Remember that you need to include both aspects in your answer to reach the highest levels.

(b) How far can it be said that religion sets the standards for acceptable relationships today? (20 marks)

Ideas you might use in support:

- Moral standards of what is considered acceptable.
- The concept of marriage, seen as a stable basis for society.
- Religious views which support what most might consider acceptable relationships.

Ideas you might use against:

- Religion is often opposed to homosexual relationships and unmarried people living together which many would see today as being acceptable relationships.
- Religion does not set standards; society does.
- Religious views are often seen as irrelevant for many people today.

Further information on world faiths can be found at: http://subknow.reonline.org.uk/.

14 Science and Technology

WHAT YOU WILL LEARN ABOUT IN THIS CHAPTER

- The benefits of scientific and technological advances.
- Experimentation and the role of ethics in decision making.
- The role of ethics in the control and use of scientific and technological advances.
- The conflict of human rights and technology.
- The Christian perspective on ethical issues in science and technology.

THE AQA CHECKLIST ✔

- Experimentation (animals and humans) and the role of ethics in decision making
- Inventions and the role of ethics in the control of their use (e.g. nuclear inventions)
- Scientific and technological advances and decisions about who benefits
- Human rights and the conflict with the use of technology, e.g. surveillance, data storage, cyber crime
- A religious perspective on these issues in science and technology

ISSUES ARISING

- Should science be controlled by ethics, and, if so, which ethical system?
- Is it better for ethics to be reactive – to respond to new scientific ideas?
- Can a scientific discovery be 'undiscovered'?
- How far should society allow religion to control scientific and technological development?

Modern scientific and technological advances move ahead at breakneck speed, and the ethics has to work hard to keep up. Just 50 years ago things that we take for granted such as test tube babies, microwave ovens, organ transplants were only just beginning to be thought of, and CCTV, iPhones and the ability to have our genome sequenced were still in the future. Science and technology have changed our world dramatically and in general we cope with the advances, but there are some scientific and technological changes that people find controversial and difficult to accept. The main problem areas used to include nuclear weapons, eugenics and experiments on animals, but recently the areas of contention have increased to cover much reproductive biology such as cloning, designer babies, stem cell research, human–animal hybrids and genetically modified organisms. Persuading people to accept some of these advances in science and technology shows up one vital difference in the way they see the world; it is only human to fear the unknown, but scientists spend their lives considering the possibilities and risks, so they tend never to say 'never'. Science sees itself as morally neutral, but needs to be aware of its responsibility, and understand the reactions of ordinary people, and try and find some way round the so-called 'yuck' factor (the 'Wisdom of Repugnance').

Mary Warnock, who chaired the committee that developed the early guidelines on embryonic research in 1984, said that it was important to take into account the reactions of ordinary people. She argued that:

> For morality to exist at all, there must be some things that regardless of consequences, should not be done because crossing the line leads to 'a sense of outrage . . . a feeling that to permit a practice would be indecent or part of the collapse of civilisation'.

Every new scientific and technological advance leads to some sort of popular outrage because the changes are human-directed, and many see these as making the world worse – leading to problems such as global warming. At the same time as human activity is vilified, nature is held in great esteem, and everything that is 'natural' is considered 'good'. This has also changed the way we see ethics: in one sense we are constantly being urged to be ethical, whether it be in the type of light bulbs we buy or even where we do our shopping; and in another sense questions of right and wrong are less deontological and more about our impact on the planet. Consequently scientific and technological advances that threaten to transform our relationship with nature are seen as unnatural and wrong.

This is shown clearly in the debate about cloning which has been ongoing since Dolly the sheep was born in 1996 in the Roslin Institute in Scotland. UNESCO declared that cloning humans was 'contrary to human dignity' and the European parliament said that it 'is a serious violation of fundamental human rights and is contrary to the principle of equality of human beings as it permits a eugenic and racist selection of the human race'. Is human cloning really immoral? If this technique is blocked, then the medical techniques, based on cloning methods which could save lives and lessen suffering, will also be blocked. Ethically cloning is objected to because it undermines human dignity and personal identity by creating exact copies, because it uses people as a means to an end and because it is seen as unnatural. However, any medical intervention from taking a cold remedy to open heart surgery is unnatural. This does not mean that new technologies do not raise important questions about society itself and what it means to be human; genetic engineering raises questions about health insurance, about individual rights and privacy.

This chapter will consider some of the types of modern scientific technologies that are in use today or are being developed.

GENETIC ENGINEERING

Genetic engineering
The technology involved in cloning, gene therapy and gene manipulation.

Genetics is about our genes, which are made of DNA and are the basic building blocks of life. Every cell has a full set of genes, carried in strands of DNA which are chromosomes. When new cells are replicated, each new cell has characteristics passed on by the DNA – genes are like a blueprint of life. In humans the genes decide the characteristics inherited from each parent.

It was in the mid-1970s that scientists first discovered how to move pieces of genetic material from one species to another – this came to be called genetic engineering. Some said that this was simply an extension of what breeders of plants and animals had been doing for hundreds of years and what nature did through evolution and natural selection, but others claimed that it was 'playing God' and was unnatural. Genetic engineering, however, continued to develop, and the technology was extended from plants to animals and finally to human cells. Today genetically altered crops, such as soybean and maize, are grown extensively, especially in the USA, and marketed all over the world. Scientists working for pharmaceutical companies

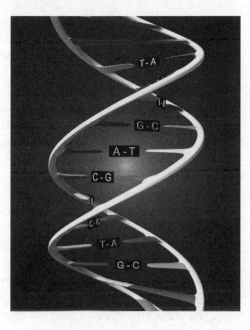

DNA helix – blue glow 2
(microscopic) Getty Images

use altered genes to produce 'designer' drugs, and research is gathering pace to treat certain inherited diseases by gene therapy.

The ethical questions first aired in the 1970s continue to be raised, both about the process itself and about the results. Others will say that humans have always altered their environment to benefit themselves, and this new biotechnology could help fight hunger and disease.

EMBRYO RESEARCH

Embryo research has as its aim to find cures for serious illnesses using tissue or cells from embryos. Most of this research concentrates on stem cells and the field of regenerative medicine – the repair of damaged organs and body parts. Stem cells can change into other types of cells such as heart cells, muscle cells, nerve cells or skin cells. The ultimate stem cells are the system cells in the early embryo because they can develop into every single cell type. There is very little debate over the use of adult stem cells which can be taken from body tissue without harming the patient; so far these are the only ones which have successfully helped patients. Embryonic stem cells are removed from early embryos in a process which destroys the embryo – this makes it inherently problematic as far as ethics is concerned. These embryonic stem cells may be taken from embryos left over from IVF treatment or created in a laboratory from donated sperm and eggs. At the present state of the science no cure has been achieved using embryonic stem cells, and they will always

Embryo
The developing bundle of cells in the womb up to eight weeks' gestation.

Stem cell
A 'master' cell that can become any kind of material.

Therapeutic cloning
A method of producing stem cells to treat diseases such as Alzheimer's.

Cloning
A form of genetic engineering by which a plant, an animal or a human is created with the same genetic identity as another.

cause problems, as they do not have the same genetic make-up as the patients and will be rejected unless anti-rejection drugs are used. So the best option, at present, is to make new embryos by therapeutic cloning – the same method as used to create Dolly the sheep. This of course gives rise to another problem – the potential of this development is limited by the supply of human eggs and possible exploitation if poor women are to be paid for eggs.

Reproductive cloning has been tried in animals and there have been some successes after many, many failures. The only dividing line between therapeutic cloning and reproductive cloning is the intention of the scientists.

In the UK the law is clear: embryos may not be experimented on past 14 days; a human embryo cannot be placed in an animal; human cloning is not allowed; the genetic structure of any cell cannot be altered while it is part of an embryo. The Human Fertilisation and Embryology Authority allows embryo research for the following purposes only:

- to promote advances in the treatment of infertility
- to increase knowledge about the causes of congenital disease
- to increase knowledge about the causes of miscarriage
- to develop more effective techniques of contraception
- to develop methods for detecting the presence of gene or chromosome abnormalities.

For the purpose of this book we will look at genetically engineered crops, genetic selection, genetic testing and screening, the alteration of human genes, stem cell research and whether the Human Genome Project understands humans primarily in terms of their genetic inheritance.

GENETICALLY ENGINEERED CROPS – 'FRANKENFOOD'?

The production of genetically modified (GM) crops has led to very strong reactions. In the UK press they were called 'Frankenfoods' after Mary Shelley's scientist and his manufactured monster.

These GM crops appear to have certain advantages: it is claimed that the food has better taste and quality and that the crops have a greater resistance to pests and diseases. They are also seen as environmentally friendly in that they do not require chemical pesticides and will conserve soil, water and energy. The most talked-about advantage is that these GM crops offer the world's best chance to end or at least greatly reduce hunger and malnutrition through greater yields and sturdier crops.

However, critics say that these GM crops threaten the environment and may cause havoc through cross-pollination. Genetically engineered crops could have as yet unknown effects on human health by causing unexpected allergic reactions and eventually reducing resistance to disease and transferring antibiotic resistance markers. A potentially more serious criticism does not concern the effects on the developed world, which can protect itself, but on the developing world: many poor farmers are encouraged to grow GM crops. Giant multinationals such as Monsanto and Novatis own patents on these altered crops and demand that farmers buy new seeds each year at great expense instead of reusing seeds from the previous year's crop.

One country that has stood out against this is Zambia, which does not have enough food of its own but refuses to import from the USA and rejects any seeds or foods that have been genetically modified. This decision is partly to protect its export of vegetables to Europe and partly a response to health warnings and damage to the environment; it is also concerned that this new biotechnology is part of a globalised system of agriculture which favours large producers; Zambians argue that it is more important to retrain small farmers to farm organically as they did in the past.

Finally, GM food cannot be seen as the sole solution to world hunger – that problem is far more complex, and questions of injustice in the social situations of today's world need to be examined.

SELECTING HUMAN GENES – 'DESIGNER BABIES'?

The ethical debate surrounding the selection of human genes is even more complex than that over GM foods. There are a number of reasons why embryos are selected: to screen for genetically inherited diseases such as Huntington's disease, Tay-Sachs and cystic fibrosis or for genetic conditions such as Down's syndrome; to create a healthy baby to treat a sick sibling; or to select the sex of the child (this is illegal in the UK).

In order to do this, embryos are created by in-vitro fertilisation and a single cell is removed from each for genetic testing; one embryo is selected for implantation and the rest discarded.

Case studies

In 2002 a British couple, Michelle and Jayson Whittaker, asked the Human Fertilisation and Embryology Authority if they could genetically select an embryo which would be a match for their son Charlie, who had a life-threatening blood disorder. They were refused permission and went to the USA for IVF treatment.

In 2003, however, the Hashmis, who also had a son with a rare blood disorder urgently needing a bone marrow transplant, were granted permission to select an embryo after many months of wrangling in the courts.

• Is this just a brilliant way of saving a child's life?
• Are scientists 'playing God'?
• What about the motivations of the parents?
• How could different ethical theories approach these situations?

Sex selection

Imagine a couple who have sons, but their only daughter died, and they want to use sex selection to have another daughter.

• If they want a daughter so badly, will they just want her to be like the daughter they had? Will this damage her?
• Can we even begin to know their motives?
• Would we feel differently if the sex selection was for medical reasons (e.g. to select a female to have a baby free from the haemophilia gene)?

Blastocyst
A fertilised egg at about four to five days of development.

Zygote
A 'proto-embryo' of the first two weeks after conception – a small collection of identical cells.

Genetic screening, and the idea of 'designer babies', involve destroying unwanted and unsuitable embryos. If the embryos are seen as persons from the moment of conception and, therefore, as having an intrinsic dignity and value that cannot be compromised in the name of other values, then any destruction of embryos would be opposed. However, fertilisation is a process that takes about 24 hours to complete and so there is no specific moment when personhood may be said to be conferred. Peter Singer points out that up to 14 days after conception the fertilised egg has the capacity to divide into two and become identical twins. In some cases it has been observed that such divided eggs blend back together into one blastocyst. If the egg is fertilised in vitro, one cell can be removed to have its genetic structure tested and the developmental process is unharmed. In fact, all the cells of the blastocyst can be separated and each has the capacity to become a whole human being – this is important as the blastocyst does not have true individuality. Without individuality it is difficult, according to Singer's argument, to see how the organism can be a person. However, even if the early embryo is not a person with full human rights, we do not yet have enough knowledge of early brain activity to know whether an early embryo feels pain.

Some people are concerned that the new-born baby will be subject to painful medical procedures to help a sibling, but, in fact, the necessary cells are taken from the umbilical cord. There are also concerns that, in an increasingly materialistic society, the baby is being treated as a commodity – just made to be a donor or to fulfil parental desires. As it is so difficult to assess the motives of others, some may say that embryo selection is the beginning of a 'slippery slope', with babies ultimately being chosen for eye colour or intelligence. However, we have been doing the same to animals for hundreds of years – would the selection or enhancement of humans be any different?

TESTING AND GENETIC SCREENING

Genetic testing

Scientists have created tests for various genetic diseases – for example, whether a patient is carrying the gene which produces breast cancer or sickle cell anaemia. Patients have to agree to the tests and understand the implications of the test should they prove positive. One of the main ethical questions is whether the tests should remain private or whether the results should be divulged to employers or insurance companies. If the government goes ahead with plans for an identity card which carries genetic information, it would be difficult to keep such information private and could lead to discrimination.

Genetic problems could also affect other family members – should they be informed if they have not given consent? Gene testing usually gives only a probability of developing the disorder and a limitation of all medical testing is the possibility of laboratory error.

Genetic screening

Genetic testing is done on sections of the population who are known to be at risk – this may be done on an adult, a child or a foetus. There are some advantages in knowing, in that the person can be encouraged to change their lifestyle to reduce the danger of developing the disease. However, it may lead to discrimination against certain groups, such as the wish of a Jewish committee in New York to prevent Ashkenazi Jews who carry the Tay-Sachs gene from marrying each other. It may also lead to aborting a foetus which has a genetic flaw, which may prevent the child from pain and suffering but which also raises questions about how we as a society define 'normal' and 'abnormal'. If, for example, scientists were to discover a gene for being born violent, should we test everyone to see if they are carrying the gene and then eliminate them to make society a safer place?

Gene therapy

A further problem involves the use of gene therapy to correct, alter or replace genes. This has proved successful in some areas but also causes problems, as in the case of sickle cell anaemia, which is prevalent among Afro-Caribbeans – this gene affects a few in a terrible way but it is the same gene which gives natural immunity from malaria.

There is also the issue of the allocation of health resources and how they are used. Can genetic screening be justified for a few individuals? Can it be justified if there is no cure available (e.g. for Huntington's disease)? How do we even know what to test for as more and more diseases are discovered to have genetic links?

THE ALTERATION OF HUMAN GENES

Human genome
A map of the human genes.

Germ line engineering
Changes in the parent's sperm or egg cells with the aim of passing on the changes to their offspring.

Somatic cell engineering
Changes in somatic (body) cells to cure an otherwise fatal disease. These changes are not passed on to a person's offspring.

Gene therapy aims to cure or ultimately prevent disease by changing genes. The science is only in its infancy and primarily experimental. Gene alteration can be targeted to somatic (body) cells, in which the patient's genome is changed, or to germ (egg and sperm) cells, in which the parent's egg and sperm cells are changed with the aim of passing on the changes to future generations. Germ line therapy is often confused with genetic selection, but it is not, in fact, being actively investigated in larger animals or humans.

Ethically this therapy is questionable, as it could ultimately change the whole of humanity and what it means to be human – we take charge of our own evolution.

The alteration of genes in a patient's somatic cells was first used successfully in 1990 – this type of genetic therapy raises the fewest ethical questions, especially when it is used to treat a life-threatening disease.

However, gene therapy given to a foetus before birth could again mean that we decide which genetic predispositions are to be altered – for example, at present conditions such as obesity, below-average intelligence and poor eyesight are seen as normal inheritable characteristics, but in the future may be considered to be grounds for alteration or even abortion. Some people feel that there is no difference between gene alteration to prevent a minor disability and paying school fees so that children get a first-class education. This may of course create a further ethical issue whereby a division is created between the genetically rich and everyone else.

However, most diseases involve the interaction of many genes and the environment. Many people who develop cancer not only inherit the disease gene but may also not have inherited particular tumour-suppressing genes. Diet, exercise, smoking and other environmental factors may all have contributed to their disease. Studies of identical twins show that individuals with the same genetic make-up do not develop the same diseases – environment plays a part.

STEM CELL RESEARCH

Stem cells are cells that can change into other types of cells – in the very early embryo they are *totipotent*: they can become any kind of body cell; in the adult they are *pluripotent*: they have the capacity to become a variety of cells, but not all. Adult stem cells can be taken from an adult, a child or even from the placenta of a new-born baby without harming the patient, but those removed from early embryos destroy the embryo. There are also foetal stem cells which are taken from aborted foetuses and are believed to have almost the same potential as embryonic stem cells.

Scientists hope that stem cells can be used to cure many disorders such as Parkinson's disease, diabetes, spinal cord injuries, heart disease and cancer – but all this is a long way off, decades in the future. In 2006 it was reported in the *Lancet* how, five years previously, patients' own cells had been used to grow and replace bladders in seven children who suffered from spina bifida. These were not stem cells, but more specialised cells which can grow only into bladder cells. This has improved the lives of these children beyond measure, and they do not have to take anti-rejection drugs, as the bladders are made from their own cells. A bladder is a much simpler organ than a liver or a kidney, but scientists are now testing kidneys successfully in cows. This is a very different situation from the use of embryonic stem cells, which necessitates the destruction of embryos for the benefit of others, which goes against the teaching on the sanctity of life.

However, research continues apace, and trials have already started to use stem cells to repair the breasts of women who have had cancerous lumps removed. The treatment uses stem cells from stomach fat which is injected into the breast. This gives stomach reduction and breast enlargement, and so will probably lead to the use of stem cells for breast enlargement instead of using implants in cosmetic surgery.

British scientists have also developed a stem cell therapy using embryonic stem cells to cure the most common cause of blindness by making replicas of the missing cells.

Embryonic stem cell research is the threshold of cloning – first developed at the Roslin Institute by Ian Wilmot in 1997, when Dolly the sheep was cloned. Human cloning is illegal in the UK, but several rogue scientists have attempted it elsewhere. Scientists simply say that it is unsafe for the cloned child, as, from the experience of cloning other mammals, producing one child might need hundreds of pregnancies and many abnormal late-term foetuses could be produced. Others oppose human cloning on the grounds

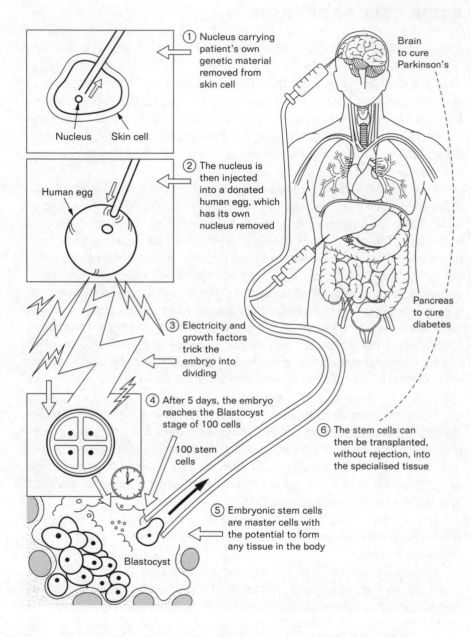

① Nucleus carrying patient's own genetic material removed from skin cell

Nucleus   Skin cell

② The nucleus is then injected into a donated human egg, which has its own nucleus removed

Human egg

③ Electricity and growth factors trick the embryo into dividing

④ After 5 days, the embryo reaches the Blastocyst stage of 100 cells

100 stem cells

⑤ Embryonic stem cells are master cells with the potential to form any tissue in the body

Blastocyst

⑥ The stem cells can then be transplanted, without rejection, into the specialised tissue

Brain to cure Parkinson's

Pancreas to cure diabetes

Two diagrams of stem cell research

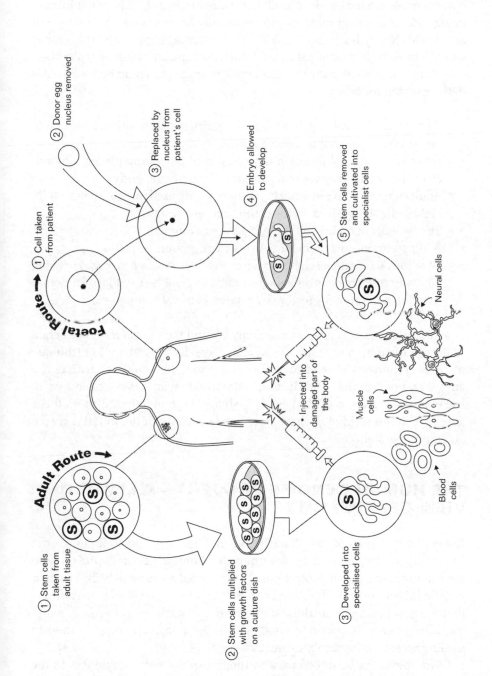

Foetal Route

① Cell taken from patient

② Donor egg nucleus removed

③ Replaced by nucleus from patient's cell

④ Embryo allowed to develop

⑤ Stem cells removed and cultivated into specialist cells

Neural cells

• Injected into damaged part of the body

Muscle cells

Blood cells

Adult Route

① Stem cells taken from adult tissue

② Stem cells multiplied with growth factors on a culture dish

③ Developed into specialised cells

that it would produce confusion in family relationships and encourage parents to see cloned children as objects rather than as independent human beings. However, the problems will eventually be overcome and many will argue that cloning is a possible solution for infertile couples, and that clones would simply be like identical twins, which are natural clones of each other.

Many scientists now say that it is unnecessary to use embryonic stem cells in their search for cures:

- Embryonic stem cells are very 'plastic', which means they can be unstable and become malignant, causing cancer.
- Adult stem cells are found in umbilical cord blood and placenta blood, as well as virtually every major organ of the human body.
- Adult stem cells have already been successfully used in treatments, while embryonic stem cells are still at the theoretical stage.
- The benefits of embryonic stem cells are a long way off.
- Adult stem cells overcome the problem of immune rejection.
- With the rise of animal rights activists and the problems involved in using adults to test drugs, it is likely that embryos will be used less for actual research and more for testing by pharmaceutical companies.

Recently scientists have found a way around the ethical issues attached to the use of embryonic stem cells as they have discovered a safe technique to reprogramme skin cells to embryonic form. It would seem that the advantages of this and of adult stem cells would mean it is not necessary to use embryonic stem cells; however, it should be remembered that all the advances in this technology have been made because of the initial research on embryonic stem cells.

THE HUMAN GENOME PROJECT – A LIMITED VIEW OF HUMANITY?

Robert Song (Head of the Department of Theology and Religion at the University of Durham) asks whether the human genome project and the resulting advances in biotechnology simply reduce human beings to their genetic inheritance. He does not criticise the science itself, nor does he say that the new genetics is intrinsically reductive in itself. He sees the developments in genetics as shaped by what he calls the 'Baconian Project' – the aim to eliminate suffering and maximise choice.

This view may be traced back to the rise of the natural sciences in the seventeenth century (and also follows Francis Bacon's emphasis on the necessary social use of scientific knowledge), the Utilitarianism of the eighteenth century and the Romantic emphasis on individual fulfilment and autonomy.

The result of this is that all suffering is seen as pointless (the rise in a desire to legalise euthanasia could follow from this), which has brought about an increase in the number of medical interventions and an understanding of our bodies as things to be changed according to our individual tastes through plastic surgery and so on. The human genome project has given us not just the knowledge of the 'basic building blocks' of the body and how it is constructed but also the knowledge of how it may be reconstructed.

CHRISTIAN PERSPECTIVES ON GENETIC ENGINEERING AND EMBRYO RESEARCH

The sanctity of life is a key theme with which to approach the questions of genetic engineering and embryo research. The Bible teaches that God created the human in his image and so human life has intrinsic value. Using an embryo for the sake of another human is wrong, as the embryo has intrinsic worth. Any technology that creates spare embryos to be used or discarded is wrong. However, there are not the same objections to using adult stem cells or to the modification of animals or plants.

Catholic ethics are based on Natural Law and so are positive about advances in science that improve human life, but never at the expense of human life, which is sacred from the moment of conception.

The Catholic Church also expresses concern about who is investing in the research and who will benefit from it. However, the Catholic Church recognises the need for humans to use their God-given intelligence to transform and humanise the world. This was the view of Pope Pius XII when he justified the use of painkillers: 'Man preserves, even after the Fall, the right of dominating the forces of Nature, of using them in his service, and of employing the resources so offered to him to avoid or suppress physical suffering.'

Catholics claim that certain actions are intrinsically evil, as they go against what it is to be human. Evil is seen as falling short of what humans are intended to be and is a result of free will. They make a distinction between *doing evil* and *suffering an evil*. Humans who are physically impaired (e.g. are blind or have Down's syndrome) are suffering an evil because they fall short of what it is to be fully human. Correcting these impairments is therefore a good thing – but the use of genetic engineering to achieve this is still ruled out. There is also concern that too much stress is placed on being physically perfect and the spiritual side of what it means to be human is neglected.

The Catholic Church rules out embryo research as being unnatural and destroying life, but it approves of genetic engineering which respects human life and human rights on the basis of its help for the individual and society.

Other Christian churches may take a different view and follow a Situation Ethics line based on agape. An action is good if it is based on love and bad if it is based on selfishness. Two influential Protestant writers on bioethics were the Episcopalian Joseph Fletcher and the Methodist Paul Ramsay.

Fletcher saw a human being as 'a maker and a selecter and a designer' who acts morally when in control of genetics. He was not opposed to IVF, concluding that embryo research is the most loving thing to do with spare embryos when the only other option is to destroy them, especially when such research could lead to cures for terrible diseases. However, creating embryos for the direct purpose of stem cell research is difficult to justify as being the most loving action.

Ramsay opposed separating procreation from conjugal love and was pessimistic about our attempts to 'play God', but his arguments were always teleological and looked at the benefits for humanity of genetic engineering. He approved of genetic screening as doing 'more good than harm' and said it was important that 'the benefits from any course of action must be weighed up against any risk'.

Christians in general seem to look favourably at genetic medicine, while acknowledging both the risks and the limits that should be imposed on research in terms of respect for human life.

TRANSPLANTATION AND XENOTRANSPLANTATION

Transplants save many lives each year, but donor organs are scarce and there are not enough for everyone who needs them. This shortage has led scientists to search for new ways to help patients needing transplants. Xenotransplantation, the transplantation of organs from animals into humans, is a possible solution to the problem. Recent scientific developments mean that the problem of rejection of tissue transplanted between species can be overcome. However, there are complex ethical and safety issues which need to be addressed:

- the ethics of using animals to make 'spare parts' for humans
- the ethics of producing genetically modified pigs containing human genes
- the suffering of the animals
- the protection of patients
- the cost to the NHS of animal to human transplants.

It is true that there is something unnatural about putting a pig's heart into a human, but the question to ask is whether it matters or not. Very often it is the immediate 'gut-reaction', the so-called 'yuck' factor, that guides the ethical thinking, or it may be that we consider that the natural boundaries are being abused by technology without considering the consequences for either humans or animals. Some argue that people oppose xenotransplantation simply because it is new and unfamiliar; arguing that there is little difference between killing an animal to eat and killing it for its organs, but we are more familiar with one than with the other. Human to human transplants no longer cause us any problem but education, time and familiarity do not always work to dispel the 'yuck' factor, as is shown by the public reaction to nuclear power. However, as Mary Warnock pointed out, the issues of public perception in biotechnology need to be considered.

The ethical treatment of the animals to be used for the transplants and the possibility that they may bring diseases to humans also need to be considered. Joyce de Silva, director of Compassion in World Farming, said:

> An increasing focus of our work is in animal sentience. We are finding out more and more about the way animals think and feel. In this context, it is unlikely that any acceptable way of using them as spare-part factories will be found. Animals used to grow organs for humans would have to be kept in bio-secure surroundings and would have their own immune systems suppressed. They would also feel pain and fear even before they were operated upon.
>
> (*Times Higher Education Supplement* 26 March 2004)

CHRISTIAN PERSPECTIVES ON XENOTRANSPLANTATION

The Bible teaches that humans are responsible for others before God – so any decision about xenotranplantation without considering the society as a whole cannot be justified. From the Judaeo-Christian viewpoint the innate value of the animals must also be considered, so that they are not simply exploited instrumentally or perceived only as their utility value. The welfare of humans and the welfare of animals need to be weighed up. Christian ethics would also consider the value of humans and how we see our bodies. Does xenotransplantation simply see the human body mechanistically? Christians would also consider whether we are placing economic interests above the welfare of humans and animals; raising questions about the fair distribution of organs and whether such an expensive technology should be used in helping a few people live longer when so many countries in the world lack basic medical care.

THE ETHICAL ISSUES IN HUMAN EXPERIMENTATION

Scientific testing on human volunteers is essential to finding new or improved treatments and discovering how diseases work. Human experiments must be performed ethically and governed by safeguards and controls. Medical experiments can be divided into two main categories: therapeutic research aims to find ways of curing disease or disability, and non-therapeutic research tries to improve the ability to diagnose the disease or to understand how the disease works.

Participants in experiments should be volunteers and understand what they are doing. They should not be offered large financial inducement, they should be aware of the risks and be free to leave the experiment at any time they wish – this is what is involved in informed voluntary consent.

There must always be a control group which receives no treatment. Then, because some patients' symptoms will improve simply because they believe they are being given a treatment, some people in a second group receive the drug being trialled whilst others receive a dummy treatment called a placebo. To make sure that the researcher and the volunteer avoid all bias in the results, experiment codes are given so no one knows what treatment is given until the end of the experiment. However, the use of placebos leads to further ethical issues – as the person receiving the placebo is being deceived. This needs to be explained carefully at the beginning of the experiment and again informed consent obtained.

However, problems arise with vulnerable minorities especially in gaining informed consent – these vulnerable minorities include:

- embryos, foetuses and children
- ethnic minorities
- poor people in developing countries
- groups who could be 'forced' or open to inducements, such as prisoners, members of armed forces, students and employees
- old or dying patients
- pregnant women
- people with genetic diseases.

The issue of vulnerable minorities has become more important in recent years as, though Edward Jenner tested the smallpox vaccine on his own son and neighbourhood children, the testing by the Nazis and the Japanese on prisoners and inmates of concentration camps and public health tests in the USA led to the World Medical Association Declaration of Helsinki in 1964 and all recent amendments to give ethical guidelines for all research on humans.

Another major ethical issue is transparency and honesty; for example, children's organs should not be kept without their parents' consent. All results should be published – even negative ones – and it is not permitted to take a Utilitarian stance to sacrifice present sufferers for the sake of those who may come in the future. Risks must always be weighed against benefit.

CHRISTIAN PERSPECTIVES ON HUMAN EXPERIMENTATION

The Bible can help with the ethical issues involved in using humans for experimentation. The Golden Rule of treating others as you would wish to be treated means that researchers must always put the needs of the volunteer before their own interests and the experiment.

As all human life is considered sacred because people are made in God's image (Genesis 1:17) it is wrong to use someone as a means to an end, however good that end may seem. Nobody should be forced to take part in an experiment, and the aim of all experimentation on humans should be to restore to health.

Christians believe that all creation and their knowledge of it is given by God. Humans are God's and so are not ours to manipulate for our own or others' gains – even if the research aims to improve the well-being and health of humans.

THE ETHICAL ISSUES IN ANIMAL EXPERIMENTATION

Animal experimentation normally refers to experiments or tests on live higher animals, usually mice and rats, and not the use of material from animals or studies on lower animals like insects. Experiments on animals are used to understand how the body functions or disease occurs, to develop new medicines and to test for the safety of a variety of products. The ethical issues surrounding this topic involve the problem of the suffering and pain for the animals, the reduction of their quality of life and their inability to give consent. The scientists who experiment on animals do consider these ethical problems and try to use as few animals as they can and make their experiments as humane as possible. They also avoid using animals if alternative methods provide equally valid results.

Those who support animal research and testing say that the benefits that they produce for humans and companion and domesticated animals outweigh the harm to the animals used for the studies. This approach sees animals as of instrumental rather than intrinsic value. However, scientists are encouraged to reduce the numbers of animals they use, and to minimise the impact on the animals by improving their experimental techniques and keeping the suffering involved to a minimum. They try to use techniques which are less invasive, give the animals as good a life as possible and, where possible, replace experiments using live higher animals with ones using animal tissue, cell cultures, bacteria, computer models or, if safe, human volunteers. They also try to avoid unnecessary duplication by sharing the results of their research with other scientists.

Many people argue that banning animal experiments would mean an end to advances in understanding of disease, and development and testing of new drugs. However, animal tests cannot show how safe and useful new drugs are for humans but can show only that they are potentially effective and safe enough to be tested on people. If a drug passes the animal test programme, it is then used on a small group of human volunteers in tightly controlled and regulated conditions before a large-scale clinical trial takes place.

Whether one considers that these experiments are right or wrong depends on whether one considers that animals have rights which are being violated or not. The Utilitarian approach would not consider the question of rights as it would say that the benefits to humans would justify the suffering of the animals. This recognises that there is a range of benefits and a range of suffering and would consider that considerable benefit is needed to justify higher levels of suffering. Conversely, only low levels of suffering may be considered ethical in those experiments on animals done to advance understanding of how the body works, where any benefit for humans may be well into the future. The Utilitarian view gives greater moral value to a human than to an animal. The problem here is that the harm done by experimenting on animals is weighed against the harm done to humans by not experimenting. Both the harm done to the animals by experimenting and the potential harm done to the humans by not experimenting can be estimated (though the former is more easily quantified), but experimenting may not be morally equivalent to failing to experiment. This is the question raised by James Rachels – whether deliberately acting is worse than omitting to act.

Another Utilitarian approach would be to consider the economic cost of experimenting on animals – the purchasing, feeding, housing, treating animals with drugs in a controlled environment is not a cheap option, and this use of resources should be weighed against the likely benefit from the work.

Peter Singer suggests that scientists should ask themselves whether they would be prepared to use a brain-damaged human being at a similar mental level to the animals. There would be no ethical issue involved if the humans are normal and able to give free informed consent. Singer and many followers of the Animal Liberation Movement see humans as just one among many species with no reason to claim dominance; to do so is to be guilty of speciesism. There is further information on Peter Singer in Chapter 10 on the environment.

CHRISTIAN PERSPECTIVES ON ANIMAL EXPERIMENTATION

The Bible does not say anything directly about experimenting on animals, but the idea of dominion in the first creation story – Genesis 1:28 – has been interpreted by many Christians as saying that humans have authority over animals, so many Christians would consider that the medical knowledge gained through animal testing makes it justifiable. Human life is seen to have greater value than animal life, but animals should still be treated with respect and care. Scientific research should not result in animals being made to suffer unnecessarily, and must contribute to caring for or saving human lives.

Recently there has been much writing by Christian philosophers and theologians about the ethics of animal testing which has challenged the assumptions that humans are superior to animals and raised questions about their status and treatment. The use of animal experimentation makes people question the relationship between animals and humans, whether animals have moral standing, whether we have direct or indirect duties to animals and whether human benefit always outweighs animal suffering. Some theologians such as Andrew Linzey and Celia Deanne-Drummond (see Chapter 10, p. 149) have also raised questions about this.

In the USA, Donna Yarri (Associate Professor of Theology, Alvernia University, Texas) also studies this question. She points to the similarities between humans and animals and argues that these are differences of degree rather than kind so that animals' cognition and sentience together mean that animals do have rights. Yarri makes the case for restricting animal experimentation, as well as making sure that it is more humane.

THE CONFLICT BETWEEN HUMAN RIGHTS AND SCIENTIFIC AND TECHNOLOGICAL PROGRESS

The growing ability of people to manipulate the natural world and influence almost every aspect of human life leads to a tension between ways of understanding the world, and seems to give the power to a few: the scientists. This affects our sense of what it means to be human, our values and beliefs, and our freedom to make our own autonomous decisions. The idea of human rights is the formal expression of these values and blends together two ethical traditions: the principle of utility, which says that we must maximise the happiness or welfare of the majority, of the community; and the necessity to see the individual as possessing certain inalienable rights, which the individual can waive for the benefit of others, but which cannot be taken away by a majority. In recent years some UN members have proposed more general rights such as the right to peace, to development and a healthy environment.

The main causes of tension between science and technology and human rights are clearest in two areas: biological issues; and privacy. Each of these can be found in literature: Aldous Huxley's *Brave New World* anticipated genetic selection; and George Orwell's *Nineteen Eighty-Four* presented a vision of a state conducting perpetual and punitive surveillance on its citizens.

Potentially we could have the same situation that Huxley suggested, as the use of biotechnology could threaten our right to life, our right not to be subjected to medical or scientific experimentation. At the same time the expansion of exercising surveillance over individuals, including tracking their movements and intercepting their conversations and private emails and rapidly distributing all sorts of data about individuals, threatens the right to privacy and free speech. However, such knowledge also enhances our welfare and security.

At present an embryo can be experimented on up to 14 days when the primitive streak develops – embryos are then discarded, as are unwanted ones from IVF: without this cut-off point discarding these 'spare embryos' could be considered murder, as the most fundamental of all human rights is the right to life. However, on the other hand, many would argue that women also have the right to avail themselves of the new reproductive technologies including IVF and surrogate mother contracts, but at present this is limited to those who have the ability to pay once the limited number of treatments available from the NHS have been exhausted.

The advances that may come in the future could lead to even more problems in this area with the possible creation of artificial sperm and eggs or even artificial wombs in which foetuses can grow outside of human mothers – are these attempts to 'play God' or are they advances to help the infertile? What are the human rights of these foetuses?

As far as the use of new technologies for the collection and distribution of information is concerned, George Orwell certainly saw the evil potential of these technologies. Governments worry about the loss of control, and private citizens worry about an excess of control over their behaviour. In the eighteenth century everybody's private papers were either in their house or in their place of business – now they are on computer disks which are lost by government employees. It is the banks, insurance companies, employers who know everything about us, and we have little control over how they use that information. On the other hand, governments will argue that this sort of information is what gives us protection against terrorists.

Surveillance covers a variety of technologies, many of which can distribute private information around the world in an instant:

- Email is a quick, instant form of communication, but international ECHELON screens emails for key words in the name of national security. This is done without our consent – it would seem that information is considered more important than people.
- Security cameras are now common in most town centres and even in some small villages, businesses and schools. Their obvious use is to help the police solve crimes and to deter antisocial behaviour. However, are we again leaving the responsibility for society to those who watch the security screens?
- ID cards are used in many countries, in the armed forces, in schools and universities, etc. to allow legitimate access to buildings and information. Biometrics such as fingerprints or the eye's retina are now being used more often. However, these cards, as they carry more and more information, can leave us open to identity theft.
- The internet is an extraordinary resource, but websites use forms of surveillance to find out about their users.

Cyberveillance can alter our lives in ways so subtle we do not notice – for instance, cameras are used to monitor shoppers, and check-out computers and loyalty cards gather information about our purchases to alter stock and the way it is placed on the supermarket shelves to catch our eye and subtly control our purchases.

It can also be used by businesses to make good investments and assess the future, but equally people's health, criminal record and credit ratings can also be used by companies – the knowledge may not be accurate: it may have been somebody who previously lived at the same address as you who gave you a bad credit rating, but you do not know until you find you are unable to borrow money.

With the increasing use of technology to control our lives we need to consider whether privacy is of greater value than the needs of the state or national security. John Stuart Mill defined liberty as autonomy and considered it to be the most important attribute. He said that the state should not interfere within the private lives of individuals unless it is to protect them from harm. So knowledge of an individual is necessary only for that individual's well-being. In contrast to this, the totalitarian Marxist view rejects any private ownership of property, including rights over one's own body. Perhaps we need to move to a point in between these two opposing views. We have allowed data to be used – companies will pass on our addresses and telephone numbers to other companies unless we expressly ask them not to. We know that in many circumstances easy access to data is very useful – for example, the new National Health Service computer will make treating patients easier and potentially save lives. However, what of the increasing biometric data and DNA held by the police, even of those people who have committed no offences?

The increasing use of surveillance and the new technologies make us question what it means to have any sort of personal identity, and also make us consider what sort of society we wish to have. We do, therefore, need to take a more active role in the use of surveillance if we do not wish to be totally manipulated by others so that we almost turn from autonomous people into passive consumers. However, unlike the Big Brother state depicted by George Orwell, the UK has no central authority but rather a variety of interested groups building up and exchanging information about us through many worldwide technologies. In addition, the way data are analysed just ends up reinforcing social class and divisions according to race and sex. David Lyon, Professor of Sociology at Queens University, Canada, has written extensively on the surveillance society and in his YouTube talk (21 September 2007) stresses that surveillance is about social sorting, so that different groups of people can be treated differently; whether as a higher risk or threat level after '9/11', or for insurance or simply by postcode so that 'suitable' spam is sent to that address. He says that surveillance is about predicting the future: this means that we do not need to see the use of the new technologies as a necessarily evil, but we should not see them as neutral either as they have the most severe consequences for those who are already marginalised by society. We need to consider whether we want to welcome all sorts of people into society or just exclude them because of electronically controlled data, and ask whether the Utilitarian or capitalist approaches to surveillance are necessarily right.

Whatever our position in society, whether we are comfortable middle classes protecting our privacy in affluent societies, or whether we lead an impoverished life in the developing world trying to claim food, land and shelter, human rights give everyone a shared respect for each individual as unique. Human rights issues resulting from the advances in science and technology can be seen as trivial from the viewpoint of those who are struggling to simply survive.

THE ROLE OF ETHICS IN THE CONTROL AND USE OF INVENTIONS

Much of the development of inventions and scientific discoveries has, in recent times, been attributed to the declining Influence of superstition and religious ethics. This has led to a materialistic and reductionist view of nature which gives science and technology the view that there are no limits to its knowledge, discoveries and exploitative capabilities. Sustaining the world's population, while at the same time competing for economic success, has had a corrosive effect on the natural world. Many economically successful inventions have led to a far greater price being paid in environmental terms – for example, the depletion of the ozone layer as a result of chloro-fluorocarbons and even more direct pollution as a result of technological waste and by-products of inventions such as the petrol engine. Technology has not always led to totally positive results.

Ethical responses to some of these problems have led to initiatives such as conservation and recycling but they do not seem to be enough, and one of the major ethical issues facing humanity is to get the scientific community to work on a long-term view and focus on developing technologies that are less harmful to the planet. This is beginning in industry with the introduction of social responsibility programmes that promote the welfare and dignity of humans and are respectful of the planet and its finite resources.

Too often scientific inventions have forged ahead and the ethics has trailed behind, but in order for the human race to survive it is now being recognised that a greater ethical dimension needs to be applied to scientific research. This will be difficult, as has been shown in the work forging ahead on human cloning, in spite of attempts to control it.

Wherever research goes it is certain to influence our lives in the future as machines become faster and smarter with the development of silicone-based electronics. The future is uncertain and the technological revolution cannot stop. We will have new problems in the future and human inventiveness and ingenuity will try to solve them. The question is whether ethics will lead the way or continue to trail behind.

CHRISTIAN RESPONSES TO INVENTIONS

The world is moving at a fast pace. New inventions, new technologies and new lifestyles persistently outdate what was previously considered as traditional and, while they point to the future, they indirectly compel us to forsake our past. It seems as though there was never a yesterday, that traditions are no longer necessary in a hectic world and that all that matters is living according to the latest trend.

In this fast-moving world, values seem at stake. Morality is apparently subject to the fluctuating demands of the rat race. The dominant worldview is secular: life is short, so work hard and play hard. In this scenario, religion unfortunately becomes just another type of commodity that can be bought and used whenever it pleases and when it is not demanding. However, most Christians would welcome any inventions that would help people or even improve evangelisation; for example, many Christian churches make good use of modern means of communication.

However, some inventions, such as weapons of mass destruction, are not looked upon so favourably. In his 1963 encyclical *Pacem in Terris*, Pope John XIII wrote:

> 110. The production of arms is allegedly justified on the grounds that in present-day conditions peace cannot be preserved without an equal balance of armaments. And so, if one country increases its armaments, others feel the need to do the same; and if one country is equipped with nuclear weapons, other countries must produce their own, equally destructive.
>
> 111. Consequently, people live in constant fear lest the storm that every moment threatens should break upon them with dreadful violence. And with good reason, for the arms of war are ready at hand. Even though it is difficult to believe that anyone would dare bring upon himself the appalling destruction and sorrow that war would bring in its train, it cannot be denied that the conflagration can be set off by some unexpected and unpremeditated act. And one must bear in mind that, even though the monstrous power of modern weapons acts as a deterrent, there is nevertheless reason to fear that the mere continuance of nuclear tests, undertaken with war in mind, can seriously jeopardize various kinds of life on earth.
>
> 112. Justice, then, right reason and consideration for human dignity and life urgently demand that the arms race should cease; that the stockpiles which exist in various countries should be reduced equally and simultaneously by the parties concerned; that nuclear weapons should be banned; and finally that all come to an agreement on a fitting program of disarmament, employing mutual and effective controls. In the words of Pius XII, our Predecessor of happy memory: 'The calamity of a world war, with the economic and social ruin and the moral excesses and dissolution that accompany it, must not be permitted to envelop the human race for a third time.'

The Anglican Church has also discussed the use of nuclear weapons many times, In 2003 the Synod of the Church of England said:

> The debate on nuclear weapons needs to be conducted with much greater honesty and consistency. If certain countries retain their nuclear weapons on the basis of the uncertainty and potentially violent volatility of international relations, on what basis are the same weapons denied to other states? The non-nuclear weapon states need to be presented with rather more convincing arguments and incentives than they have been up to now as to why it might be in their best, long-term interests not to go nuclear.

Television, radio and computers are widely used and accepted by most Christians; indeed many Churches have their own websites and the World Wide Web is seen as a major tool for evangelisation. However, many Christians do have concerns about the way in which the Web is used and some of the material available. These modern inventions do pose problems for Christian groups such as the 'Exclusive Brethren' (a branch of the Plymouth Brethren). The following is taken from a paper written in 1990 by Dr Stephen Bigger of the University of Worcester and published in the *Journal of Beliefs and Values.*

The media, and especially television, is regarded as potentially corrupting so parents ask for their children to be excused from lessons involving video (although to listen but not watch is considered acceptable).

Computers

The last century has seen great strides in human achievement. Humans are capable now of great good, but also of evil on a monstrous scale. The key to much of this 'progress' is the computer. 'Progress' is accompanied by pride, as people seek to create a new world, and to sweep aside the old, as it were to emulate God himself. Further, the computer represents an assault on individual freedoms as unchecked data accumulate. Computers have no values, but make decisions mechanistically, having no regard for issues which should be central – moral dilemmas, intrinsic worth and human concerns. In short, the computer represents the greatest danger, physically as well as spiritually, to humankind. It makes global annihilation possible, and can be a powerful tool of social control.

Yet humanity puts great store by computers, tying up their hopes and aspirations in a form of technology to which moral and spiritual values are irrelevant. The computer is thus seen as an immensely anti-Christian force, an agent, so to speak, of the Devil himself. Therefore, 'Exclusive' Brethren do not use computers in any form, and do not wish their children to learn how to use them in school.

The Exclusives' strong objections are thus theologically central. In our present 'dispensation' (that is, the period of time immediately before the second coming of Jesus) possible association with anti-Christian forces takes on for Exclusives renewed meaning, as the struggles described in the Book of Revelation between the forces of Christ and Antichrist unfold in real history. To associate today with the forces of Antichrist presents a greater than usual threat to spiritual purity.

The UK government's insistence on computer awareness being a compulsory part of the National Curriculum seems to have no easy resolution, since 'Exclusives' neither wish to leave state schooling nor are as a body able to set up their own schools. It is not ideal, but may be possible as an interim measure, to learn about computers using suitable written material, without having 'hands-on' experience. Pupils may be demonstrably able to meet the relevant attainment targets, even though they are unwilling to put these into practice. Such material would need to be acceptable both to 'Exclusives' and educationalists (Stephen Bigger, '"Exclusive" Brethren: an Educational Dilemma').

This attitude to modern technology is shared by some other Protestant Christians such as the Amish, Mennonites, Hutterites and the Bruderhof. Members of these Christian communities are characterised by their separation from the outside world as shown by their dress, their use of horses rather than cars, etc. However, interestingly the Bruderhof (Darvell Community) of Robertsbridge in East Sussex do not use televisions, computers, etc. for their own recreational use, but have the latest in Japanese computer technology for their multi-million-pound factory which makes toys and aids for the disabled:

> The foreman, Francis Marsden, sees nothing wrong with computerised routers, automated drill presses or anything else that will keep their business ahead of the game. 'We need to be able to compete to earn our living,' he says. 'It's not incompatible with our simple lifestyle. In fact, it's used to produce equipment that enhances the Christian life.'
>
> But the business is a means to an end. What drives it is a timeless Christian ethic: concern for one's neighbour. This stretches beyond the community gates. Bruderhof members are active in social welfare projects, from emergency relief during recent floods in East Sussex to inner city programmes to help the homeless and unemployed in New Jersey.
>
> (*The Times* 25 September 2004)

Technological inventions move forward today at such a pace that our mobile phones and computers, for example, are often outdated before the warranty on them expires. This can lead people into a world of materialistic consumption which, in a world of finite resources, obscene poverty, widespread human suffering due to disease (much of which is curable and/or preventable) and conflict prompt many Christians to say that our continued consumption and quest for ever more technological advances needs to be assessed in light of Christian teaching about concern for the poor and oppressed.

REVIEW QUESTIONS

Look back over the chapter and check that you can answer the following questions:

1. Explain the differences between therapeutic and reproductive cloning.
2. How could genetic engineering be used to alleviate world hunger? What are the problems with this?
3. Explain the difference between adult and foetal stem cells – why is this important ethically?
4. Take a current newspaper article about any form of genetic engineering or foetal research. Stick it on a piece of A3 paper and write brief notes around it on the ethical problems that arise from the issue.
5. List some of the ethical problems with genetic engineering, foetal research and xenotransplantation.

Terminology

Do you know your terminology?

Try to explain the following key terms without looking at your books and notes:

- Blastocyst
- Cloning
- Germ line engineering
- Somatic cell engineering
- Xenotransplantation

SAMPLE EXAMINATION QUESTIONS

(a) Explain the issues behind the use of technology and the perceived abuse of human rights. (30 marks)

Obviously your answer will depend on which aspects of technology you choose and you can interpret this quite widely. An obvious choice might be the use of information technology (mobile phones, computers, etc.), and the perceived abuse of human rights would then include lack of privacy, phone-bugging, cyber-bullying, computer-hacking, altering of Facebook entries, etc.

(b) How far can it be said that technological advances do abuse human rights? (20 marks)

Arguments that you might use in support:

- People do not want their privacy invaded, and that is much easier on a mobile phone than on a landline.
- Facebook entries can easily be altered.
- People's computer details can be checked (by police, teachers, etc.).

Arguments that you might use against:

- People could be more discreet in their use of mobile phones.
- Firewalls and other preventive measures can be taken to protect one's entries on Facebook, etc.
- Surely we want the police, etc. to be able to monitor computer/or mobile phone activity by would-be terrorists and/or child abusers?

UNIT 4C

15 Ways of Moral Decision Making

Essential terminology

Brain death
Developed economies
Developing countries
Embryo
Emerging economies
Life support systems
Macro-economics
Micro-economics

WHAT YOU WILL LEARN ABOUT IN THIS CHAPTER

- Religious teaching and guidance on making moral decisions.
- The role of religious traditions in making moral decisions.
- Ethical theories that are predominately religious.
- Religious views on the conscience.
- Ethical issues in medical research and developments.
- Ethical issues in business practice and economics.

THE AQA CHECKLIST ✔

- Religious and moral decision making. The use of religious law(s) both from scripture and from religious institutions. Religious teaching and guidance about behaviour and how to determine good and bad, right and wrong. The use of religious conscience for allowing an individual to determine how to make decisions. The role of religious tradition in determining behaviour.
- The application of religious ethical teaching and systems to one of the topics below, either A or B.
- Ethical systems, both deontological and teleological, and how these can be used to assist people in making moral decisions; consideration of which style might be more suitable or have fewer weaknesses. Consideration of hybrid styles of ethical systems and whether these are more suitable for moral decision making in twenty-first-century societies.
- The application of ethical systems to **one** of topics A **or** B, below.

Candidates should study **one** of the topics (A or B) below to support their answers:

(A) Medical research and medical developments

The use of embryos, human cells, medical trials on humans. The use of animals for medical research. Brain death, life support systems, limitation of the availability of drugs or medical services for people.

(B) Business practice and economics

Moral management of national economies (macro). The moral management of individual companies (micro), ethical investment. The developed economies versus the Third World developing economies. Approaches to emerging economies, including China and India.

HOW DO CHRISTIANS MAKE ETHICAL DECISIONS?

There is no easy answer to this question, as there is so much diversity within Christianity. Some Christians will base their ethical decisions solely on the Bible and its teachings, others will base their ethical decisions on the biblical teachings but also on Church tradition and Natural Law, others will follow a Situation Ethics approach and others will look to their conscience as a guide. As a result of this diversity, Christians have different responses to ethical issues, whether it is in the field of medical research and developments or business practice and economics. It is important to understand not only what Christians think on different ethical issues but also why they think as they do and the basis of their ideas.

In many ways Christian ethics does not look at right and wrong actions, but at the sort of person Christians are called to become. The Bible teaches that humans are created by God in his image and called to live free and responsible lives, but sin and ignorance have led us to misuse this freedom. In many ways, therefore, Christian ethics has more in common with Virtue Ethics than with any other ethical theory.

The Jewish roots of Christian ethics

The early Church brought into Christianity much that belonged to Judaism, and many today would still claim that we can obtain absolute moral rules from the Bible: the Ten Commandments are rules that must be followed without exception, and in the Bible we can find many acts such as homosexuality and divorce that are utterly condemned. However, it is clear that Christianity left behind the Jewish ethic of law as a divine command made known in a comprehensive legal code and interpreted by lawyers into many ritual requirements and practices. Christians attempted to drop the legalism

Moses and the Ten Commandments. *Moses receives the Tablets of the Law from God on Mount Sinai* (colour litho) by French School (nineteenth century)

© Private Collection/Archives Charmet/The Bridgeman Art Library and keep the law, especially the Ten Commandments, which were seen as an important part of God's revelation and good guidelines for human existence and human flourishing, in accordance with the human nature which they believe God gave to humanity. Jewish ethical teaching, at its core, is based on relationships: our relationship with God and all our many and varied relationships with other people.

The basis of Christian ethics in the Bible

The use of the Bible, both the Old and New Testaments, in Christian ethics is not as straightforward as some would believe; some passages need careful exegesis which is beyond the scope of this book. The Bible is a collection of writings put together over a long period of time and reflecting many different cultural contexts. It is important that this fact is borne in mind and that its diversity is recognised. There is no biblical morality or even New Testament teaching that can be followed in every detail, as it all needs to be understood in its cultural context. Christian denominations have always chosen the Bible teachings that back up their particular take on Christianity, such as the Catholic use of Mark's teaching on divorce (Mark 10:2–12) and total disregard for Matthew's exception clause (Matthew 5:32), or the Lutheran misuse of Romans (7:14–20):

> For we know that the law is spiritual; but I am of the flesh, sold into slavery under sin. I do not understand my own actions. For I do not do what I want, but I do the very thing I hate. Now if I do what I do not want, I agree that the law is good. But in fact it is no longer I that do it, but sin that dwells within me. For I know that nothing good dwells within me, that is, in my flesh. I can will what is right, but I cannot do it. For I do not do the good I want, but the evil I do not want is what I do. Now if I do what I do not want, it is no longer I that do it, but sin that dwells within me.

However, some Christians do believe that biblical ethics are a consistent and uniform act of revelation. The following section will necessarily take a broad-brush approach and follow general themes.

The ethics of Jesus

Although Christian ethics carries with it the Ten Commandments, it is of a totally different mindset from a law-based ethic. It was, from the beginning, attempting to reply to the philosophical questions of *happiness* and *salvation*. Therefore the most concentrated body of ethical teaching in the Gospels, the Sermon on the Mount, begins with the Beatitudes: 'Blessed are the poor . . .' (Matthew 5:3).

The Sermon on the Mount may seem to be a set of impossible commands, but, although its teaching is challenging, underlying it all is the commandment of love. However, it is not always easy to see what is meant by 'love': for Jesus in the Synoptic Gospels it is love of God and love of neighbour; for Paul it is mostly love of neighbour, especially Christians; John's Gospel seems to speak of love in an even narrower sense. It may be summed up as follows:

> 'You shall love the Lord your God with all your heart, and with all your soul, and with all your mind.' This is the greatest and first commandment. And a second is like it: 'You shall love your neighbour as yourself.'
>
> (Matthew 22:37b–39)

or: 'In everything do to others as you would have them do to you' (Matthew 7:12a). The ultimate Christian ethical teaching seems to centre on love: 'Love is the fulfilling of the law' (Romans 13:10b). This New Testament ethical teaching is part of the relationship with God – what makes Christian ethics different is the 'faith' element; Christian ethics comes from a need to interpret, understand and respond to ethical issues from the point of people's particular relationship with God.

This idea of the special relationship with God is carried on in the idea of the *Kingdom of God*. What the Kingdom of God actually means has been debated endlessly, but it seems to be a state which has arrived, but not yet – a little like a visitor who has arrived at a friend's house and rung the doorbell, but the door has not yet been opened. The problem is how this paradox is to be maintained as far as ethics is concerned. Jesus' ethics can be connected with the idea of the Kingdom of God only by seeing entry into the Kingdom as a result of responding to the appeal to the desire to be children of God; a joyful acceptance of forgiveness and a desire to do God's will. This is no blind obedience, nor is it a morality of law, command, duty and obligation; it is motivated not by the promise of reward in heaven or punishment in hell, but by a desire to follow God's will – the love commandment.

Thought Point

Look up some of the following texts to see how Jesus' ethics is based on, yet seems to reinterpret, the Jewish law:

Matthew 5–7
Mark 2:23 to 3:6
Mark 7:1–23

The ethics of Paul

The other source of biblical Christian ethics is found in the Epistles of Paul. He wrote at a time when the early Christians were attempting to interpret the teachings of Jesus and apply them to a variety of new situations. Paul stresses the importance of Christian freedom, but to be free from the law means to be united with Christ and with one another in love and service. It is *life lived in the Spirit*:

> Live by the Spirit, I say, and do not gratify the desires of the flesh. . . . But if you are led by the Spirit, you are not subject to the law. . . . If we live by the Spirit, let us also be guided by the Spirit.
>
> (Galatians 5:16, 18, 25)

For Paul, the whole law may be summed up in *love of neighbour*, and this love is limitless, as is shown in the great hymn to love in his first Letter to the Corinthians. Paul also calls the Christians to imitate the virtues of Jesus in their daily lives: meekness; gentleness; humility; generosity; mercy and self-giving love. However, the words and life of Jesus could not be made into a blueprint for Christian ethics in the early Church without becoming legalistic, and so it was recognised that following Christ depended on the gift and guidance of the Holy Spirit which was given to the *community* of believers. Paul's list of virtues is called 'the fruit of the Spirit' (Galatians 5:22– 3) and love is the greatest sign of the presence and activity of the Holy Spirit (I Corinthians 13).

Christian ethics in this developing Church could be called a *community ethic*: the ethic of a community guided by the Holy Spirit, rather than by law or tradition.

> If then there is any encouragement in Christ, any consolation from love, any sharing in the Spirit, any compassion and sympathy, make my joy complete: be of the same mind, having the same love, being in full accord and of one mind. Do nothing from selfish ambition or conceit, but in humility regard others as better than yourselves. Let each of you look not to your own interests, but to the interests of others.
>
> (Philippians 2:1–4)

However, there is no explicit concern with changing society as a whole. The main attitude towards rulers was that of obedience, as their authority was given by God, but, if the commands of the state and those of God conflict, then the Christian should obey God. According to Paul the barriers between slaves and free men and women had been broken, both marriage and celibacy were seen as gifts, and wealth was to be shared with those in need. However, there is no evidence of struggling for justice, as it was believed that God would soon intervene in history and establish his kingdom, apart from which Christians were few in number with no political clout. The teaching of love for one's neighbour, however, did eventually lead Christians to exercise greater social responsibility.

Love

This distinctive moral teaching based on love continued to dominate the work of Christian thinkers:

> Love, and do what you will. If you keep silence, keep silence in love; if you speak, speak in love; if you correct, correct in love; if you forbear, forbear in love. let love's root be within you, for from that root nothing but good can spring.
>
> (Augustine, *Epistola Joannis* 7.8)

Love, according to Thomas Aquinas, is the reason why we were made; it unites us with God and to love is to share his life. Without love no virtue is possible, and love alone leads to happiness and fulfilment.

AUTHORITY AND TRADITION IN CHRISTIAN ETHICS

Although Aquinas followed the early Christian idea of morality as love and grace, not law, it is true that legalism has justifiably been associated with Christian ethics, both in theory and in practice. Peter Singer criticises this legalism and accuses Christianity of obscuring the true nature of morality: human fulfilment – happiness. He thinks that the end of the Christian influence on our moral standpoints will open up a 'better way of life for us', and the Judaeo-Christian ethic is 'an empty shell, founded on a set of beliefs that most people have laid aside'. Christian ethics has been seen as deontological and authoritarian, with an emphasis on certain acts as being either right or wrong.

The issue of authority and tradition is treated differently by the different Christian churches. Some Protestants see the Bible as the sole authority in every matter and this is more important than the role given to tradition in Catholicism. Catholics would argue that scripture does not give guidance on many important matters and so tradition is important, as interpreted by the *magisterium* (the Pope and the bishops). This teaching does not claim to be absolutely accurate or infallible, but is teaching on behalf of the community of the people of God. It can become authoritarian, especially when the issues are new or there is no consensus of views among the episcopacy or the Catholic community – for example, the teaching of *Humanae Vitae* (1968) which banned artificial contraception and has been totally ignored by many Catholics.

This idea of the 'agreement of the faithful' has been further developed by many free churches, which have built their forms of church government on congregational lines – this is going back to Paul's idea of attempting to discern the will of God by the Holy Spirit working in the Christian community. However, many Christian legalists would argue that Christians should keep rules because God has revealed them – is this why Christian ethics has become so irrelevant?

DIVINE COMMAND THEORY

If God's will is taken as arbitrary, then this does not give any satisfactory explanation for why anyone is morally bound to follow it. If God commands something for good reasons, then it is these reasons which are the source of moral obligations, regardless of God or any religious law.

Does religion give people a reason to be moral? Is there any meaning to life that would make it even possible to talk about morality? In Dostoyevsky's *The Brothers Karamazov*, Ivan contends that, if there is no God, everything is permitted – so does God give a reason to be moral? In Albert Camus' *The Stranger*, the issue of meaning is a central theme – Mersault does not condemn any action as wrong and, when he ends up shooting a complete stranger, he is sorry only that he got caught – killing someone has no more meaning than any other action. However, we do make judgements about what is right and wrong, and many people do so without seeing any involvement from God.

The whole problem of doing something because God commands it was examined by Plato in what has become known as the Euthyphro Dilemma. Plato asks: 'Is X good because God wills it or does God will it because it is good?'

The first option says that certain actions are good because God commands them – it is the command of God that makes something good or bad. This means that if God commanded 'Make a fat profit', then it would be right – this makes God's commands arbitrary. Leibniz in his *Discourse on Metaphysics* sums this up:

> So in saying that things are not good by any rule of goodness, but sheerly by the will of God, it seems to me that one destroys, without realising it, all the love of God and all his glory. For why praise him for what he has done if he would be equally praiseworthy in doing the contrary.

The idea that moral rules are true because God commands them is called the Divine Command theory. In many ways the laws of the Old Testament may be seen as a good example of this theory (e.g. 'Thou shalt not commit murder'). This view of Christian ethics goes completely against the morality of love and grace, but it was held by many Christian thinkers such as Duns Scotus, William of Ockham and Descartes as well as many conservative Protestants today. If we do good acts simply out of obedience to God, are we being good for the right reasons?

The second option says that God commands things because they are right or wrong in themselves. Murder is wrong in itself and that is why God forbids it. God can see that it destroys life and makes people unhappy, and so it is unlikely that he would ever command it. However, this option seems to be arguing that there is a standard of right and wrong which is independent of God and which influences his commands. James Rachels argued that it is unacceptable for religious belief to involve unqualified obedience to God's commands as it means abandoning personal autonomy – the rightness of an action must come from the fact that the action is right in itself.

Thought Point

1. Do we need God to give meaning to life?
2. Do you agree that 'without God everything is permitted'?
3. Explain the difference between 'X is good because God wills it' and 'God wills X because it is good'.
4. Read the Euthyphro Dilemma and work out the key criticisms of the argument.
5. Can morality ever be founded on authority?
6. How do you decide what is good or bad? Justify your view.

SITUATION ETHICS

Situation Ethics presumes that it is not necessary to abandon moral autonomy, nor is it necessary to allow everything (antinomianism) or to be totally legalistic. In any situation people need to avoid subjectivism and individualism, and to use in each situation the moral rules of the community, but they should also be prepared to set these aside if love is better served by doing so. Reason, then, is to be used, but based on the Christian principle of agape. This centralisation of love is explained most clearly by Joseph Fletcher in his book *Situation Ethics* (1966) – nothing is intrinsically good except love.

Rules can help us, but they cannot tell us what to do – they are subservient to love. Love wills the good of neighbours, whether we like them or not; love is to be the only motive for action, and consequences need to be taken into account and only the end justifies the means.

Situation Ethics has been criticised for being Utilitarian and simply sub-stituting love for pleasure, and Fletcher is thought to be rather vague; values and situations are so variable that we cannot easily see all the ramifications, past, present and future. Can Situation Ethics be considered Christian? As we saw in Chapter 3, it certainly puts love at the centre, but there are many differences among Christians about what exactly love is and how it is shown. Fletcher's examples are all exceptional cases: Mrs Bergmeier; the last blood plasma to be given to a skid-row drunk or a mother of three; the resistance fighter priest who refused to surrender in spite of the death of hostages. Fletcher's idea of love is not exactly the same as that of Jesus, who individ-ualised love; take, for example, the woman with the haemorrhage, or the healing of the centurion's servant – not a very popular act of love. Fletcher either reinterprets Jesus' actions or dismisses them, so it is hardly surprising that in later life religion played no part in his life and he ceased to describe himself as a Christian Situationist.

Thought Point

1. Do you think Fletcher's ethics are Christian?
2. Analyse Fletcher's view that 'the end of love justifies the means'.
3. Is Situation Ethics a useful guide for everyday ethical decisions?
4. Are moral rules totally useless in moral decision making or can you see a role for them?
5. Is the choice for Christian ethics just between legalism and situationism?

NATURAL LAW

A full treatment of Natural Law may be found in Chapter 3. Natural Law is often seen as centred on law, and so on obligation, and Aquinas himself speaks of the Natural Law. However, by this he meant that our nature is objectively knowable and our reason will help us to understand what is meant by it. Ethics is a matter of our common humanity, not a set of principles from which we make moral decisions, and its purpose is to enable us to become complete and whole humans and to achieve our desires.

Morality is rooted in the desire for happiness, but, for Aquinas, Natural

Law is not enough if we are to attain final happiness – for this God's grace is needed.

Natural Law has come to be seen as deontological and authoritarian with its application of the primary precepts, but Aquinas said that the primary precepts were always true, as they point us in the right direction; however, different situations require secondary precepts and if our reasoning is faulty these may be wrong – we need to discern what is good and what will help us to become complete and whole human beings. Intention is important, but in Natural Law it is not possible to say that the end justifies the means, although there is certainly flexibility in the Natural Law approach. Aquinas wrote: 'the more you descend into the details the more it appears how the general rule admits of exceptions, so that you have to hedge it with cautions and qualifications'.

However, Aquinas is certain that there is an absolute Natural Law and this has led the Catholic Church, following Aquinas, to emphasise reason as a tool for showing that certain acts are intrinsically right or wrong, as they go against our true purpose; certain absolutes, such as the sanctity of life, cannot be changed by the circumstances.

CONSCIENCE

A full treatment of conscience may be found in Chapter 11. Catholics consider that conscience plays an important part in Christian ethical decision making. Here conscience is not seen as some inner voice or oracle which will point us in the right direction – conscience is not about feelings but about reason and judgement. Aquinas saw conscience as reason making moral decisions. But conscience as the 'voice of God' can easily become what we mean by 'right' and 'wrong' – so people persecute 'heretics', slaughter enemies and become suicide bombers in the name of God.

MEDICAL RESEARCH AND DEVELOPMENTS

Use of embryos is discussed on p. 253; of human cells on on p. 253; of animals in medical research on p. 265. Brain death and life support systems are discussed on p. 92.

Medical trials on humans

One of the most difficult problems facing medical professionals is how to apply ethical principles to real decisions affecting patients. Is it ethical to ask patients to take part in trials? Is it ethical to experiment on people who are probably dying anyway? How do you assess consent?

Those who support research would say that no new drug should be offered outside a controlled trial, so that the treatment's efficacy can be measured, not only for the patient's benefit but for that of future patients as well. The treatment of childhood leukaemia side-effects is a good example of the benefits of research on humans. There is now a national research programme so that most children with leukaemia (with parental consent) are allocated randomly the latest proven and tested treatment or the latest experimental treatment. The result of this experimentation has lowered the mortality rate from 100 per cent to 50 per cent. This was not the result of some amazing discovery like penicillin, but of slow, painstaking research over many years.

Using humans in drug trials means that doctors need to be aware of the research, aware of the relevant results and statistics, but also remembering their duty of care to their patients and the fact that the patients might see themselves as being used as guinea pigs. Also for trials to be successful there needs to be a randomness by which the patients are allocated to the trial, so it is not the doctor who decides what is the best treatment for a patient but a computer. However, if the doctor decides this is not in the patient's best interests then the patient should not be entered into the trial. There needs to be clear communication with the patients at all times, and the doctor/patient relationship needs to be based on trust so that the patient's own wishes are considered.

Thus in using humans for drug trials there are three main areas of ethical concern:

- What is valuable in research? What will give a good result – a teleological approach.
- The doctor has an obligation to do the best for his or her patients – a duty of care approach.
- The wishes and needs of the patient need to be taken into account – the research subject's autonomy.

Therefore, it is not sufficient to take a Utilitarian approach to medical research on humans and simply concentrate on maximising happiness.

The availability of drugs or medical services

People today increasingly see themselves as consumers who can access diagnostic and treatment services other than through their GP. The internet is used both by private companies wishing to sell services such as DNA profiling and by patients wishing to acquire information about health matters or even to buy drugs. This leads to both benefits and disadvantages – it means that criminals can profit from health issues and worries, it means that untested drugs are given to unsuspecting members of the public, but it also means a greater availability of over-the-counter medicines. There are also obvious ethical issues with a consumer-led approach to medical services as people may take drugs they do not need and those who cannot afford to pay will remain sick.

Ethical conflicts may also arise when doctors are asked to make decisions about the use of resources and patient care, when the needs of the individual patient and the needs of all patients cannot be both fully met. Doctors are generally guided to consider allocating resources in a way that best serves the majority of patients – but they still need to consider the care of their patients. This makes for a difficult ethical decision. This is why the National Institute for Clinical Excellence or NICE was set up in 1999 to cover such issues in England and Wales. It is supposed to provide a guide to 'best practice': however, its own guidelines do not solve the dilemma of the individual patient versus the majority of patients as they say:

> Once NICE guidance is published, health professionals are expected to take it fully into account when exercising their clinical judgment. However, NICE guidance does not override the individual responsibility of health professionals to make appropriate decisions according to the circumstances of the individual patient in consultation with the patient and/or their guardian or carer.
>
> (*A Guide to NICE* 2005 p. 6)

Funding of treatments is also an issue, and since 2002 the NHS has been responsible for funding any NICE recommendations. For example, NICE recommended that the NHS should fund three attempts at fertility treatment for those couples who met specific criteria, but this has not been implemented because of the cost implications. There have also been concerns raised by doctors over NICE's refusal to license drugs for the treatment of Alzheimer's in spite of doctors raising their concerns about the need of patients being of greater importance than the cost implications. There will be no answer to this dilemma as there is an infinite amount of suffering in the world and a finite amount of money to mitigate it. In the real world the doctor cannot always put the individual patient first, as priorities always need to be juggled and one person's treatment is another person's denial of treatment, and the duty to one patient cannot be considered in isolation from the duty to all other patients.

BUSINESS PRACTICE AND ECONOMICS

Business ethics considers the ethical relationship between businesses and consumers, between businesses and their employees. It also considers the impact of globalisation on the environment, and on society at large.

Ethicists do not always agree about the purpose of business in society – some see the main purpose of business as being to maximise profits for its owners or its shareholders. So only those activities which increase profits are to be encouraged as this is the only way that companies will survive – this was the view of the economist Milton Friedman. Others consider that businesses have moral responsibilities to their stakeholders; including employees, consumers, the local community and even society as a whole. Other ethicists have adapted social contract theory (based on the ideas of John Rawls in his *A Theory of Justice* 1971) to business, so that employees and other stakeholders are given a voice as to how the business operates. However, this view is criticised on the grounds that businesses are property, not means of distributing social justice.

Times have changed, however, and ethics in business and corporate social responsibility are becoming crucial. There are many reasons for this, driven by the social, political and economic developments in the world. Consumers have shown their dissatisfaction through taking to the streets, and there have been riots from Genoa to Seattle, bringing together many different types of activists and protestors campaigning on a variety of business-related issues from globalisation and human rights to Third World debt. Stakeholders, and especially consumers, are becoming increasingly empowered and vocal, forcing businesses to review their strategies.

Organisations like The Body Shop and the Co-operative Bank have led the way and brought business ethics and social responsibility into the public eye and on to the business agenda, championing key issues such as human and animal rights, fair trade and environmental impact. Consumers now expect businesses to be socially responsible, and businesses are increasingly thinking about what they can achieve by putting the power of their marketing behind some key social issues so that they can help make a positive social difference.

However, business ethics is not as simple as it looks, as there is no longer one agreed moral code and multinationals operate in different parts of the world, employing and serving people from different cultures. Profit will still be the main motivating factor for businesses and this affects all the people who work there, generating its own culture with its own standards, so it becomes difficult for individuals to resist the need to fit in and stand up against any attitudes and decisions they disagree with.

Modern technologies also create ethical dilemmas for businesses that never existed until quite recently – such as medical products and gene technologies: should parents be allowed to alter the genetic profile of their unborn child, and should businesses sell products to do this?

All these issues pull businesses in different directions, so that many now set up their own ethical committees. Businesses that are caught acting unethically are publicised in the press, and pressure groups that oppose the activities of certain businesses are better organised, better financed and so better able to attack such businesses. An extreme example of this is Huntingdon Life Sciences in Cambridge, where the Animal Liberation Movement set up a splinter group called SHAC (Stop Huntingdon Animal Cruelty) which, in turn, started an international campaign to close the company down, often using ethically dubious methods: threatening employees, as well as employees of shareholders and banks. The opponents of this business understand business and its weak points very well as the company nearly went bust. However, it changed tactics, the public reacted against the extreme methods of SHAC, and in 2007 it reported a 5 per cent increase in profits, leading the managing director to plead with the financial services industries to no longer treat the business as 'radioactive' (*Financial Times* 16 September 2007).

The moral management of national economies (macro)

Morality is central to economic functioning and underpins the market economy. In business, morality is seen as behaving with integrity and honesty, treating others fairly and expecting the same treatment in return. At the macro level this involves cultural and political considerations, whilst at the level of the individual company (micro) it concerns the degree to which managements take responsibility for the development of ethical considerations within their organisations and in their market dealings.

Today many national economic considerations are global and all economies affect each other. Downturns and upturns in one economy affect what is happening elsewhere: this is globalisation. It promotes the free movement of labour, capital, goods, services, technology and management in response to markets around the world.

Globalisation means the reduction of the difference between one economy and another, so that trade all over the world, both within and between different countries, becomes increasingly similar. This has been going on for a long time, and used to be quite a slow process, but in recent times it has speeded up. The reasons for the increase in the pace of globalisation are:

- technological change – especially in communications technology
- transport – faster and cheaper
- deregulation and increase in privatisation – countries can now own

businesses in other countries (e.g. some UK utilities which were once government-owned are now owned by French businesses)

- removal of capital exchange controls – money can now be moved easily from one country to another
- free trade – many barriers to trade have been removed, sometimes by grouping countries together as with the EU
- changing consumer tastes – consumers are now more willing to try foreign products
- emerging markets in developing countries.

All of this means that businesses are now freer to choose where they operate from, and can move to countries where labour is cheaper. This has meant, for example, that much manufacturing has moved to countries such as Indonesia, and many call centres such as the Microsoft® Corporation have moved some of their work to India.

National borders are becoming less important, as markets stretch across them and multinationals have taken advantage of this. Consumers are alike, but not the same, in different countries, and businesses have needed to consider local variations.

However, globalisation also brings problems – especially those of justice towards poorer countries. Trade between countries is not totally fair, and some of the richest countries, such as the USA, have very strong trade barriers to protect their national interests. It could be said that globalisation means that the interests of the shareholders are more important than the interests of the employees or the consumers, and it means that the poorest 20 per cent of the world's population have just 1.4 per cent of the global income. The gas tragedy at Bhopal in India in 1984, the world's worst industrial catastrophe, is a prime example, as the chemical companies concerned continued to deny responsibility for a long time, and some survivors still await compensation. Toxic waste still pollutes the environment.

Anti-globalisation movements campaign against the bad effects of globalisation:

- Amnesty campaigns for a global human rights framework for business based on the UN Norms for Business.
- The World Council of Churches campaigns for responsible lending and unconditional debt cancellation.
- There are also campaigns for ecological farming practices, and against the imposed privatisation of public services, especially water.

In his book *One World: The Ethics of Globalization* (originally published in 2002) Peter Singer lists the various global problems that we face and challenges us to develop a system of ethics and justice that can be accepted by all people, regardless of their race, culture or religion.

The moral management of individual companies (micro)

The moral management of companies involves the business approach to two main groups of people: the customers and the employees.

Customer rights – quality, safety, price and customer service – were once the most important ethical concerns in business. Now consumers influence business ethics, and have been instrumental in bringing about change: consumers expect businesses to demonstrate ethical responsibility in its widest sense – affecting the treatment of employees, the community, the environment, working conditions, etc. Some companies have been the focus of consumer criticism and forced to change their practices – Shell over Brent Spar and Ogoniland; Monsanto over GM food; Nike and Gap over child labour. Shell bowed to consumer pressure and did not sink the Brent Spar, and Nike now monitors its factories following the BBC *Panorama* programme (2000).

One of the first ethical businesses was The Body Shop, pioneered by the late Anita Roddick. The company became a great success in the mid-1980s, following a change in consumer awareness in how beauty products were tested, and began to look for alternative ways. It was later bought out by L'Oréal but according to its website it is still a beacon of ethical practice. However, an ethical business does not need to be at the level of The Body Shop, as even small gestures like participation in community events or collections for charities can improve a company's appearance to consumers.

Consumer action, therefore, can be very effective, as if enough consumers stop buying from a business then the business will be forced to change or go bust. Ethical business practices will give a better image to the consumer and better sales.

Many employer/employee relationships now entail working together. In 1978, in the UK, the Advisory, Conciliation and Arbitration Service (ACAS) was set up to try and create good and harmonious working relationships. It negotiates in disputes, and has been very successful, as there have been few major employment disputes, and ACAS has been able to suggest guidelines for better relationships in most situations.

For employer/employee relationships to be successful there has to be a balance of interests: the employer wants to plan for the future of the business, make profits and keep employees motivated; the employee wants the best possible conditions and living standards. If employees are unhappy there will often be high turnover of staff, poor timekeeping and much absenteeism – as a result of this discontent profits will suffer.

However, relationships between employers and employees do not always work out. The internet now allows for rapid sharing of information across the world – and multinationals operate across the world. There are now a multitude of websites that publicise and discuss the behaviour of businesses.

Whistleblowing is now more acceptable – access to secret information is now better and it is even protected by law in some countries. From 'Deep Throat', the person who leaked the Watergate scandal in the 1970s, to Dr David Kelly, who was accused of passing material on the Iraq War to a journalist, whistleblowers have risked their jobs and sometimes their lives to tell what they perceive to be the truth and to make organisations accountable. Whistleblowers have even gained the respectability of being the subject of a television drama series.

The question of whether or not it is ethical for an employee to blow the whistle, especially in the public domain, raises questions of confidentiality and loyalty – there is no simple answer to cover all cases. However, neither confidentiality nor loyalty should simply override the necessity for the unethical conduct of others to be reported, especially when product safety or the severe financial hardship of others is concerned. Whistleblowers often risk dismissal and may find it difficult to find similar employment in the future; they may be frozen out or ostracised. There are now organisations to protect whistleblowers such as Freedom to Care, which promotes our 'ethical right to accountable behaviour from large organisations' and says that employees have an 'ethical right to express serious public concerns' in the workplace and if needed to go public.

Thought Point

1. 'Businesses exist to make a profit.' Is it society's task to protect those who are badly affected in the process?
2. Do you think standards of integrity in business are declining or not? Give reasons and examples.
3. Do you think workers should participate in management?

Case Study 1

There are three area managers in a company: Tom, Steve and Tim. Tom was the latest to join the company and has learnt from Tim and from his own observations that Steve is not to be trusted. Steve seems to have no morals and his only goal seems to be his own advantage. He 'manages upwards' always trying to please the director, he lies to cover up difficulties or shortfalls, he tells his staff to take no notice of established policy – but never in writing and never to more than one person at a time. At the same time Steve gives the impression of a straight-talking man of the people.

Tom finds this really hard to deal with but is unsure how to respond. Sinking to Steve's level would not be acceptable, but just putting up with it like Tim does, and his own staff do, really goes against the grain and all that Tom holds dear. But how do you accuse a colleague of dishonesty?

- What are the choices facing Tom?
- What principles do you think are relevant when dealing with a colleague of this sort?

Case Study 2

The head of a department in a medium-sized company with a good profit record is 55 years old and has worked for the company for 20 years. He is married with two children at university. His life is his work. However, he is becoming less effective and no longer inspires those who work for him. Several of the brightest young people in his department have left because of the situation. If you were his boss would you:

- declare him redundant with compensation?
- retire him prematurely on a full pension?
- transfer him to an advisory post?
- take corrective action and leave him in his job?
- transfer him to a new executive position on the same pay until he is 60?
- do nothing or take some other course of action?

Ethical investment

Can people invest money with a clear conscience and still expect to make money? One of the main reasons that people choose to invest ethically is so that their money does not fund something they consider wrong such as gambling or arms, or to invest in something they consider right such as protecting the environment.

This is often a minefield for the investor as there are so many funds available that claim to be 'green' or 'fair', and companies have different approaches to defining 'ethical'. Most companies have ethical policies and give information about their business practices and activities, but they still want investors so they can grow and make a profit.

Managers can select their stocks in a variety of ways:

- *Negative criteria* – some funds will actively screen out companies that are involved in businesses such as tobacco production, deforestation, animal testing, etc.

- *Positive criteria* – some funds look for companies which actively do things to help the environment such as sustainable energy.
- *Engagement* – other funds 'engage' with companies to push for changes in the way the business deals with human rights, environmental issues, etc.

All ethical companies perform well or they would not attract investors, and there is now a National Ethical Investment Week in November to give investors information about their various options.

Approaches to emerging economies

The economies of China, India and Latin America are likely to be the main competitors in the future. Their success can be attributed to lower costs, especially labour costs, ambitious leaders, good products and modern facilities. They are competing with the multinationals as they are helped to their success by the fast-growing markets in their own countries and they can compete at home as they provide the goods that customers who cannot afford expensive products will buy.

However, one of the most important areas of debate concerning these emerging economies is the climate change debate. Emerging economies fear that the industrialised nations will use it to limit the growth of developing countries and for trade protectionism. These countries are still dependent on fossil fuels for energy, but this means that, if helped, they could be in the forefront of energy efficiency and clean coal technologies. However, this means real dialogue between the industrialised nations and these emerging economies, which are very different in character and method of government.

Other issues that need to be discussed concerning these emerging economies are issues of human rights, safety at work and safe products. In China sweatshop conditions are reported in many factories, with poor working conditions and low pay – this is an issue that contributes to low production costs.

One of the emerging industries in both China and India is the field of biotechnology. India's IVF clinics have long been a source of embryos for experimentation. However, as the technology moves quickly it is important that the ethical standards are in place, and enforced, if these countries are to be accepted global players in biotechnology. If this does not happen then scientists such as Geeta Shroff can publicise her treatment of cases of spinal injuries, paralysis, etc. and receive simultaneous praise from the Indian Health Minister and condemnation from Western stem cell scientists. India and China are making a contribution to biotechnology and challenging Western views, but negative publicity may mean less cooperation from other countries.

One of the main benefits for a business of behaving ethically is that a better image is given to the world at large, and especially to consumers, resulting in greater profit. It can also mean that expensive and potentially embarrassing public elation disasters are avoided. As far as employees are concerned, if the business is seen to behave ethically, for example, with regard to the environment, it will recruit more highly qualified employees, and this leads to better employee motivation as the employees are proud of their jobs.

Being ethical can increase costs for emerging economies (e.g. they have to pay reasonable wages to all employees). So if a Western importer of goods from these countries is truly putting its ethics into practice it will have to pass on the same standards down the supply chain and this will mean no longer doing business with suppliers who are not prepared to meet the same standards.

However, businesses are products of the society in which they operate, and, if society does not always have clear standards, it is not always easy for a business to decide what to do. For instance, some people in our society are completely opposed to employing child labour, but others would argue that it is all right for a business to do so if it benefits the local economy.

Sometimes a business may need to consider that its role is to make a profit, provide jobs and create wealth for society as a whole, and it may consider that ethical practices are good if they help achieve these aims, and to be ignored if they do not.

THE RELIGIOUS APPROACH TO BUSINESS PRACTICE AND ECONOMICS

For the purpose of this book a Christian approach will be followed. The Bible gives guidelines that can easily be applied to the ethical issues surrounding business. The Old Testament contains laws and injunctions about the fair treatment of employees (e.g. Leviticus 19:13) about justice, honesty and fairness in business – 'Do not steal' – and laws about just weight (e.g. Deuteronomy 25:13–15) – giving the full amount for fair payment. The prophets, especially Amos, spoke out about the unfair treatment of the poor by the rich. People are told to treat others as they would be treated – and in the New Testament Jesus was concerned with not amassing wealth for the sake of it, and sharing with those in need.

In the Middle Ages just price, usury, property and work were the only ethical approaches to business, and it was some time before Christian ethics looked at the real ethical problems facing modern businesses.

Protestant social teaching pulled in two different directions. First was the individualistic approach, concerned with the individual's calling and personal integrity, so people in business could be praised for their charity. Second was the the concern about the competitive individualism of capitalism and the great social inequalities caused by capitalism, so social solutions were offered.

Catholic thought was never very individualistic and very early on addressed the problems of modern industrial life. The encyclicals *Revum Novarum* in 1891, through to *Populorum Progressio* in 1967 and *Centimus Annus Laborem Exercens* in 1991, all recognised the needs of workers, and argued for trade unions and for the protection of the needs of poor countries to correct the defects of the world market. The idea of the common good, of solidarity, is a basic value in Catholic social teaching and has led the Catholic Church to criticise both communism and free market capitalism which acts against the poor and leads to the selfish pursuit of wealth.

Christian Churches have increasingly, as organisations and as individual Christians within those Churches, monitored and corrected the harm done by the businesses in which they are shareholders. This has led to changes in behaviour in areas such as environmental impact and marketing practice in the developing world. This role of the ethical investor is not new – in the eighteenth century the Quakers refused to invest in companies that were involved in the slave trade.

APPLYING ETHICAL THEORIES TO BUSINESS PRACTICE AND ECONOMICS

Utilitarianism

Utilitarianism considers the majority affected by a certain action – general welfare is important, and this is often seen as good business policy: the general good of the organisation is more important than that of individuals. So, for example, an employee, though qualified for a certain position, will have to give way to another, so that the interest of the business as a whole can be preserved. A farmer may have to give up some of his or her land for a dam project, because it will provide irrigation for lots of farmers and generate electricity for the whole community. However, the best business transactions are the ones in which the best result is achieved, when both business and consumer, employer and employee, shareholders and stake-holders are considered and benefited. This means that, when making business decisions, all alternatives need considering – no one can act just on intuition if they wish to maximise utility.

Economically Utilitarianism would seem to be a good ethical approach to business; however, in many cases it is not simple and clear-cut. For example, closing a polluting factory may be good for the environment, but not for the local community which may need the jobs. Whatever the business does it is going to upset one group of people or another. Utilitarianism does not always help here.

Kantian ethics

Kant does not talk about business, but his ethics can be applied to business practice. Kant believed that morality in all spheres of human life, including business, should be grounded in reason. His categorical imperative held that people should act only according to maxims that they would be willing to see become universal norms, and that people should never be treated as a means to an end. Kant's theory implies the necessity of trust, adherence to rules and keeping promises (e.g. contracts). Kant argued that the highest good was the good will – the importance of acting from duty: so, for example, if a merchant is honest in order to gain a good reputation, then these acts of honesty are not genuinely moral. Kant's ethics are ethics of duty rather than consequence: a business behaving morally in order to impress consumers is not truly moral according to Kant. Kant's ethical theory applies well to both employees and consumers as it does not permit people to be treated as means to an end – even if that end is profit. Kantian ethics would also see a business as a moral community – employers and employees, stakeholders and shareholders, standing in a moral relationship with each other which would influence the way they treat each other. This seems to require that the work that employees are given should be meaningful, and that businesses should be organised more democratically.

Kant's universalisation means that business laws would have to be universal (e.g. no bribery or corruption), and this would have a beneficial effect on international business. But Kantian ethics has far more to offer to international business ethics as it shows how business can contribute to world peace. N.E. Bowie quotes Kant as saying:

> In the end war itself will be seen as not only so artificial, in outcome so uncertain for both sides, in after effects so painful in the form of an ever-growing war debt (a new invention) that cannot be met, that it will be regarded as the most dubious undertaking. The impact of any revolution on all states in our continent, so clearly knit together through commerce will be so obvious that other states, driven by their own danger, but without any legal basis, will offer themselves as arbiters, and thus will prepare the way for distant international government for which there is not precedent in world history.

If business (commerce) brings people together then the chance of peace among nations improves. Bowie considers that Kantian ethics has rich implications for business ethics.

Virtue Ethics

Virtue Ethics from Aristotle shows that business cannot be separated from society – everyone is part of the larger community, the 'polis', the corporation, the neighbourhood, the city, the country or the world, and our virtues are defined by that larger community. Business is part of that community. Virtue Ethics focuses on the character and motivation of the agent and on the agent's ability to pursue eudaimonia. Virtue is also learnt through observation of others' behaviour – as far as business is concerned an individual can be ethical not in a vacuum, but always as part of the ethical community. This applies to the employers as well as the employees who must show the virtues of character such as honesty, prudence, fairness and courage.

The virtues of cooperation seem to triumph over competition, but does this mean that the virtuous person in business will be the good corporate citizen rather than the high flyer, the wheeler-dealer or the entrepreneurial innovator?

Virtue Ethics is interested in the most general traits that make a harmonious society possible, so the traits that make for good business must be the same as those of a good society; the virtues of a successful businessman and those of a good citizen must also be the same. In business, as in society, trustworthiness and cooperation are essential; even the most devious business dealings presuppose an atmosphere of trust; competition is possible only (as in sport) within a context of general cooperation. Business is an essential part of society, not separate from it, and, as in society living together is central, making a profit is just a means.

REVIEW QUESTIONS

1. In what ways might a business be said to be ethical?
2. How might Virtue Ethics be applied to business, particularly in relation to developing countries?
3. Explain how decisions might be made about the treatment of brain-dead patients.
4. Explain the arguments for and against medical trials on humans.

Terminology

Do you know your terminology?

Try to explain the following key ideas without looking at your books and notes:

- Brain death
- Developed economies
- Developing countries
- Embryo
- Emerging economies
- Life support systems
- Macro-economics
- Micro-economics

SAMPLE EXAMINATION QUESTIONS

(a) Explain how religious views can be used to guide and control human behaviour. (45 marks)

Human behaviour can be interpreted widely and you can answer this section from the stance of one or more religions, but you should be able to substantiate any claim you make with religious teaching from scripture, religious leaders, organisations, individual conscience or interpretation.

Focusing your answer is very important in this section, and thus it may help you to be clear how you are intrepreting the words 'guide' and 'control'.

This is the synoptic unit, and you should try and bring in your other areas of study from both AS and A2 in answering the question. However, the examiners just need to see evidence of synopticity; they do not have a checklist in front of them by which to penalise you.

(b) Assess the view that non-religious ethical systems are more appropriate than religion in guiding human behaviour. (30 marks)

You will need to decide which non-ethical systems you are going to evaluate (this will depend on which other units you have studied).

As this is the first time you have written about non-religious ethical systems, you will need to explain the principles behind them before you start evaluating them. Remember, you do not have to write about more than one non-religious ethical system, just as you do not have to write about more than one religion, but you do have to write enough.

Once again, you need to be focused and so you must be clear what you understand by the term 'appropriate' in this question (i.e. for whom? for what end? on whose judgement?).

Glossary

A posteriori

Used of a statement which is knowable after experience.

A priori

Used of a statement which is knowable without reference to any experience.

Abortion (procured abortion)

The termination of a pregnancy by artificial means.

Absolute

A principle that is universally binding.

Absolutism

An objective moral rule or value that is always true in all situations and for everyone without exception.

Act Utilitarianism

A teleological theory that uses the outcome of an action to determine whether it is good or bad.

Active euthanasia

The intentional premature termination of another person's life.

AI (artificial insemination)

The injection of sperm into a woman.

Anthropocentrism

An approach to the environment that places human interests above those of any other species.

Apparent good

Something which seems to be good or the right thing to do but which does not fit the perfect human ideal.

Aretaic ethics
Another name for Virtue Ethics, from the Greek word *arete*, which simply means any kind of excellence or virtue.

Assisted dying/suicide
When a person takes their own life with the assistance of another person. When the other person is a doctor, it is called physician-assisted suicide.

Authoritarian conscience
Our sense of moral right and wrong formed in us by authority figures whom we want to obey.

Autonomous moral agent
Someone who can make a moral decision freely; someone who is totally responsible for their actions.

Autonomy
Self-directed freedom, arriving at moral judgement through reason.

Benevolence
Butler saw this as wanting the well-being of others.

Biocentrism
An approach to the environment that considers the biological nature and diversity of the Earth to be of supreme importance.

Biodiversity
The variety of living things on Earth.

Blastocyst
A fertilised egg at about four to five days of development.

Cardinal Virtues
Originated in Plato – prudence, justice, temperance, courage. Added to with three theological virtues of faith, hope and charity.

Categorical imperative
A command to perform actions that are absolute moral obligations without reference to other ends.

Celibacy
Not having sexual relations with another person.

Cloning
A form of genetic engineering by which a plant, an animal or a human is created with the same genetic identity as another.

Compatibilism
The belief that it is possible to be both free and determined, as some aspects of our nature are determined, but not our ability to make moral decisions.

Conscience
Our sense of moral right and wrong.

Conscientia
The actual judgement or decision a person makes which leads to a particular course of action based upon those principles.

Consciousness
Awareness of self as an independent being, the ability to feel pain and pleasure.

Consequentialism
The belief that the rightness or wrongness of an act is determined by its consequences.

Conservation ethics
The ethics of the use, allocation, protection and exploitation of the natural world.

Copernican Revolution
The discovery by Copernicus that the solar system revolves around the Sun, not around the Earth. Kant's analysis is often referred to thus metaphorically, as its implications for us are just as vital

Cultural relativism
The belief that what is right or wrong depends on the culture.

Deep ecology
An approach to environmental ethics that sees all life forms as of value and human life as just one part of the biosphere. It rejects anthropocentrism.

Deontological ethics
Ethical systems which consider that the moral act itself has moral value (e.g. telling the truth is always right, even when it may cause pain or harm).

Determinism
The view that every event has a cause and so, when applied to moral decisions, we do not have free will.

Divine Command theory
The view that actions are right or wrong depending on whether they follow God's commands or not.

Divine Law
The Bible – this reflects the Eternal Law.

Doctrine of double effect
An action where the main intention is to do good, but which may have a bad side-effect. The good intention makes the action right.

Dominion
The Judaeo-Christian idea that humans have a special place in the natural world and have responsibility for it.

Duty
A motive for acting in a certain way which shows moral quality.

Ecosophy
A word formed by contracting the phrase 'ecological philosophy'. It refers to philosophies which have an ecocentric or biocentric perspective such as deep ecology.

Embryo
The developing bundle of cells in the womb up to eight weeks' gestation.

Emotivism
A theory which says that moral statements are just expressions of feelings.

Ensoulment
The moment when the soul enters the body – in traditional Christian thought this was at 40 days for boys and 90 days for girls. The Church now believes that life begins at conception.

Eternal Law
The principles by which God made and controls the universe which are only fully known by God.

Eudaimonia
The supreme good for humans.

Euthyphro Dilemma
The dilemma first identified by Plato – is something good because God commands it or does God command it because it is good?

Feminism
A way of thinking that seeks to emancipate women in society and give them equal opportunities.

Foetus
An organism in the womb from nine weeks until birth.

Gaia hypothesis
A theory of James Lovelock.

Gender
Cultural and psychological characteristics which determine whether a person is male or female.

Genetic engineering
The technology involved in cloning, gene therapy and gene manipulation.

Geocentric
An approach to the environment which considers the geological nature and diversity of the Earth to be most important.

Germ line engineering
Changes in the parent's sperm or egg cells with the aim of passing on the changes to their offspring.

Golden Mean
The balance of extremes of virtues and vices. A balance between *excess* (having too much of something) and *deficiency* (having too little of something).

Good will
Making a moral choice expresses a good will.

Hard determinism
The belief that people do not have any free will and that all moral actions have prior causes. This means that nobody can be held morally responsible.

Harm principle
The belief that an act or consequence is morally permissible if no harm is done.

Hedonic calculus
Bentham's method for measuring the good and bad effects of an action.

Hedonism
The view that pleasure is the chief 'good'.

Hippocratic Oath
Written in the fifth century BCE, it became the basis for doctors' ethics. Other promises now replace it, but it is specifically against abortion.

Holistic
Used of an approach to the environment that considers a range of factors, including the importance of balance within the ecosystem.

Human genome
A map of the human genes.

Hypothetical imperative
An action that achieves some goal or end.

Incompatibilism
The belief that determinism is logically incompatible with free will. Thus some incompatibilists will say that determinism is a fact and so we are not free, but most take the opposite view that free will is a fact and so determinism is false.

Instrumental value
The view that something's value lies in its usefulness for others.

Intellectual virtues
Characteristics of thought and reason – technical skill, scientific knowledge, prudence, intelligence and wisdom.

Intrinsic value
The concept that something's value lies in itself.

Intrinsically good
Used of something which is good in itself, without reference to the consequences.

Intuitionism
A theory that moral truths are known by intuition.

Involuntary euthanasia
This term is used when someone's life is ended to prevent their suffering, without their consent, even though they are capable of consenting.

IVF (in-vitro fertilisation)
The procedure by which sperm and eggs from a couple are fertilised in a laboratory dish (in vitro = in glass; test tube babies).

Jus ad bellum
Justice in the decision to wage war.

Jus in bello
Justice in the conduct of war.

Jus post bellum
Justice in the ending of the war.

Just War theory
The belief that war is morally justified if it meets certain criteria.

Kingdom of Ends
A world in which people do not treat others as means but only as ends.

Law
Objective principle, a maxim that can be universalised.

Libertarianism
The belief that determinism is false and people are free to make moral choices and so are responsible for their actions.

Maxim
A general rule in accordance with which we intend to act.

Meta-ethics
The analysis of ethical language.

Moral virtues
Qualities of character such as courage, friendliness, truthfulness.

Natural Moral Law
The theory that an eternal, absolute moral law can be discovered by reason.

Naturalistic fallacy
The claim that good cannot be defined.

Normative ethics
A term used to describe different moral codes of behaviour; rules by which we make moral decisions (e.g. Utilitarianism, Natural Moral Law, Kantian ethics, Virtue Ethics).

Ordinary and extraordinary means
According to Natural Law moral duties apply in ordinary situations. A patient may refuse certain treatments on the grounds that they are 'extraordinary' (i.e. over and above the essential).

'Ought implies can'
The idea that someone cannot be blamed for what they could not do, but only for what they were capable of doing but did not do.

Pacifism
The belief that violence is wrong.

Passive euthanasia
Treatment is either withdrawn or not given to the patient in order to hasten death. This could include turning off a life support machine.

Personhood
Definition of a human being as a person – having consciousness, self-awareness, ability to reason and self-sufficiency.

Phronesis (practical wisdom)
According to Aristotle the virtue most needed for any other virtue to be developed. Balancing self-interest with that of others. Needs to be directed by the moral virtues.

Predestination
The belief that God has decided who will be saved and who will not.

Preference Utilitarianism
The idea that moral actions are right or wrong according to how they fit the preferences of those involved.

Primary precepts
The fundamental principles of Natural Moral Law.

Proportionality
In war, the belief that weapons should be proportionate to the aggression.

Purpose
The idea that the rightness or wrongness of an action can be discovered by looking at whether or not the action agrees with human purpose.

PVS (persistent vegetative state)
When a patient is in this condition, doctors may seek to end that person's life. The relatives have to agree and usually the patient must be brain-stem dead.

Qualitative
Looking at the quality of the pleasure.

Quality of life
The belief that human life is not valuable in itself; it depends on what kind of life it is.

Quantitative
Looking at the quantity of the happiness.

Queer theory
The idea that there can be no fixed rules about what is or is not a legitimate sexual relationship. Being queer is the freedom to define oneself according to one's nature.

Real good
The right thing to do – it fits the human ideal.

Relativism
The belief that nothing may be said to be objectively right or wrong; it depends on the situation, the culture and so on.

Rule Utilitarianism
Establishing a general rule that follows Utilitarian principles.

Sanctity of Life
The belief that human life is valuable in itself.

Secondary precepts
These are worked out from the primary precepts.

Self-love
Butler thought of this as wanting the well-being of self or enlightened self-interest, not selfishness.

Sentience
The ability to feel pleasure and pain.

Shallow ecology
The concept that Earth is cared for to make conditions better for humans.

Situation Ethics
The morally right thing to do is the most loving in the situation.

Slippery slope
A concept used to suggest that when one moral law is broken others will also be gradually broken and there will be no moral absolutes.

Soft determinism
The belief that determinism is true in many aspects, but we are still morally responsible for our actions.

Somatic cell engineering
Changes in somatic (body) cells to cure an otherwise fatal disease. These changes are not passed on to a person's offspring.

Stem cell
A 'master' cell that can become any kind of material.

Stewardship
A way of interpreting the use of dominion, which sees humans as caretakers of the natural world.

Subjectivism
The belief that each person's values are relative to that person and so cannot be judged objectively.

Summum bonum
The supreme good that we pursue through moral acts.

Super-ego
Freud's idea is that the super-ego reinforces ideas of correct behaviour implanted in us when we were young.

Synderesis
Aquinas' idea of what he termed 'right' reason by which a person acquires knowledge of basic moral principles and understands that it is important to do good and avoid evil.

Teleological ethics
The belief that the morally right or wrong thing to do is determined by the consequences.

Therapeutic cloning
A method of producing stem cells to treat diseases such as Alzheimer's.

Universalisability

The belief that, if an act is right or wrong for one person in a situation, then it is right or wrong for anyone in that situation.

Utilitarianism

The belief that only pleasure and the absence of pain have utility or intrinsic value.

Utility

The theory of usefulness – the greatest happiness for the greatest number.

Viability

Where a foetus is considered capable of sustaining its own life, given the necessary care.

Vices

The direct opposite of virtues – habitual wrong action.

Virtue

Habitually doing what is right – being good requires the practice of a certain kind of behaviour.

Voluntary euthanasia

The intentional premature termination of another person's life at their request.

Zygote

A 'proto-embryo' of the first two weeks after conception – a small collection of identical cells.

Bibliography

PUBLICATIONS

Ahluwalia, L. *Foundation for the Study of Religion*, London, Hodder & Stoughton Educational, 2001.

Anscombe, G.E.M. 'War and Murder', in *Moral Problems*, Palmer, M. (ed.), Cambridge, Lutterworth Press, 1991.

Aquinas, T. 'Summa Theologiae', in *Basic Writings of Thomas Aquinas*, Pegis, A.C. (ed.), Hackett, IN, Random House, 1997.

Aquinas, T. *Summa Theologiae II–II q.40* (Dominican translation), London, Burns & Oates, 1936.

Aristotle. *Nicomachean Ethics: An Introduction to Aristotle*, McKeon, R. (ed.), Ross, W.D. (trans.), New York, Random House, 1947.

Ayer, A.J. *Language, Truth and Logic*, London, Penguin, [1936] 2001.

Baelz, P. *Ethics and Belief*, New York, Seabury Press, 1977.

Barclay, W. *Ethics in a Permissive Society*, London, Collins, 1971.

Bellioti, R. *Good Sex: Perspectives on Sexual Ethics*, no place, University Press of Kansas, 1993.

Benson, J. *Environmental Ethics*, London, Routledge, 2000.

Bentham, J. *Introduction to the Principles of Morals and Legislation*, Harrison W. (ed.), Cambridge, Cambridge University Press, 1948.

Bentham, J. and Mill, J.S. *Utilitarianism and Other Essays*, London, Penguin, 1987.

Bigger, Stephen, '"Exclusive" Brethren: An Educational Dilemma', *Journal of Beliefs and Values*, 11/1 (1990): 13–15.

Blackburn, S. *Being Good: A Short Introduction to Ethics*, Oxford, Oxford Paperbacks, 2002.

Blackburn, S. *Ethics: A Very Short Introduction*, Oxford, Oxford University Press, 2003.

Blackburn, S. *Lust*, Oxford and New York, Oxford University Press, 2004.

Bolt, R. *A Man for All Seasons*, London, Methuen, [1960] 1996.

Bowie, N.E. *Business Ethics: A Kantian Perspective*, Oxford, Blackwell, 1999

Bowie, R. *Ethical Studies* (2nd edn), Cheltenham, Nelson Thornes, 2004.

Brandt, R.B. *A Theory of the Good and the Right*, Oxford, Oxford University Press, 1979.

Butler, J. *1726 Fifteen Sermons*, London, Bell, 1964.

Calvin, J. *Institutes of the Christian Religion* (1536 edn), no place, Wm. B. Eerdmans Publishing Company, 1995.

Carson, R. *Silent Spring*, Boston, Houghton Mifflin, 1962.

Catechism of the Catholic Church, London, Geoffrey Chapman, 1994.

Coates, A. *The Ethics of War*, Manchester, Manchester University Press, 1997.

Condit, C.M. *Decoding Abortion Rhetoric: Communicating Social Change*, no place, University of Illinois Press, 1994.

Cook, D. *The Moral Maze*, London, SPCK, 1983.

Coppieters, B. and Fotion, N. (eds) *Moral Constraints on War*, New York and Oxford, Lexington Books, 2002.

Crisp, R. and Slote, M. *Virtue Ethics*, Oxford and New York, Oxford University Press, 1997.

Davies, B. *Philosophy of Religion: A Guide and Anthology*, Oxford, Oxford University Press, 2000.

Davies, B. *An Introduction to the Philosophy of Religion* (3rd edn), Oxford, Oxford University Press, 2003.

Deane-Drummond, C. (ed.) *Brave New World*, London and New York, T. & T. Clark, 2003.

Deane-Drummond, C. *Genetics and Christian Ethics*, Cambridge, Cambridge University Press, 2005.

Deidum, T. 'The Bible and Christian Ethics', in *Christian Ethics: An Introduction*, Hoose, B. (ed.), London, Cassell, 1998.

Devall, B. and Sessions, G., *Deep Ecology: Living as if Nature Mattered*, no place, Gibbs Smith, 2001.

D'Holbach, Baron. *The System of Nature*, vol. 1 (1770), no place, Kessinger Publishing Co., 2004.

Dominian, J. *Passionate and Compassionate Love: A Vision for Christian Marriage*, London, Darton, Longman & Todd, 1991.

Dormor, D. *Just Cohabiting? The Church, Sex and Getting Married*, no place, Darton, Longman and Todd, 2004.

Drengson, A. and Inoue, Y. (eds) *The Deep Ecology Movement: An Introductory Anthology*, Berkeley, CA, North Atlantic Books, 1995.

Finnis, J. *Natural Law and Natural Rights*, Oxford, Clarendon Press, 1979.

Fletcher, J. *Situation Ethics*, Philadelphia, PA, Westminster Press, 1963.

Fletcher, J. *Situation Ethics: The New Morality*, London, SCM, 1966.

Fletcher, J. *Situation Ethics: The New Morality*, Intrp. by James F. Childess (2nd edn), Philadalphia, PA, Westminster Press, 1997.

Foot, P. *Virtues and Vices*, Oxford, Blackwell, 1978.

Frederick, R. *A Companion to Business Ethics*, Oxford, Blackwell, 1999.

Gensler, H. *Ethics: A Contemporary Introduction*, New York and London, Routledge, 1998.

Gensler, H., Earl, W. and Swindal, J. *Ethics: Contemporary Readings*, New York and London, Routledge, 2004.

Gill, R. *A Textbook of Christian Ethics*, London and New York, T. & T. Clark, 1995.

Glover, J. *Causing Death and Saving Lives*, London, Penguin, 1990.

Glover, J. *Humanity: A Moral History of the Twentieth Century*, New Haven, CT, Yale University Press, 2000.

Graham, G. *Living the Good Life*, New York, Paragon House, 1990.

Graham, G. *Evil and Christian Ethics*, Cambridge, Cambridge University Press, 2001.

Graham, G. *Eight Theories of Ethics*, London, Routledge, 2004.

Grayling, A.C. *What Is Good? The Search for the Best Way to Live*, London, Phoenix Press, 2004.

Grisez, G. and Boyle, J. 'The Morality of Killing: A Traditional View', in *Bioethics: An Anthology*, Kuhse, H. and Singer, P. (eds), Oxford, Blackwell, 1999.

Gula, R. *Reason Informed by Faith*, no place, Paulist Press, 1989.

Hare, R.M. *The Language of Morals*, Oxford, Oxford University Press, 1952.

Hare, R.M. *Freedom and Reason*, London, Clarendon Press, 1963.

Hare, R.M. *Essays on Bioethics*, Oxford, Clarendon Press, 1996.

Harman, G. and Jarvis-Thomson, J. *Moral Relativism and Moral Objectivity*, Oxford, Blackwell, 1995.

Hick, J. *Evil and the God of Love*, London, Palgrave Macmillan, 2010.

Hinman, L. 'Ethics Updates', available online at http://ethics.acusd.edu/.

Hodge, R. *What Is Conscience for?*, London, Daughters of St Paul, 1995.

Holloway, R. *Godless Morality*, Edinburgh, Canongate, 1999.

Holmes, R. *On War and Morality*, Princeton, Princeton University Press, 1989.

Holy Bible: New Revised Standard Version (anglicised), Cambridge, Cambridge University Press and Oxford, Oxford University Press, 1996.

Honderich, T. *How Free Are You?*, Oxford, Oxford University Press, 1993.

Hoose, B. (ed.) *Christian Ethics: An Introduction*, London, Cassell, 1998.

Hope, T. *Medical Ethics: A Very Short Introduction*, Oxford, Oxford University Press, 2004.

Hughes, G. 'Natural Law', in *Christian Ethics: An Introduction*, Hoose, B. (ed.), London, Cassell, 1998.

Hume, D. *Treatise of Human Nature*, London, Penguin, [1740] 2004.

Hume, D. *An Enquiry Concerning Human Understanding and Concerning the Principles of Morals*, Oxford, Oxford University Press, [1748] 1975.

Hume, D. *Dialogues Concerning Natural Religion*, London, Penguin, [1779] 1990.

Hursthouse, R. *On Virtue Ethics*, Oxford, Oxford University Press, 1999.

Hursthouse, R. 'Virtue Theory and Abortion', in *Ethics in Practice: An Anthology*, Lafollette, H. (ed.), Oxford, Blackwell, 2002.

Jarvis Thomson, J. 'A Defense of Abortion', in *Bioethics: An Anthology*, Kuhse, H. and Singer, P. (eds), Oxford, Blackwell, 1999.

Jones, R. 'Peace, Violence and War', in *Christian Ethics: An Introduction*, Hoose, B. (ed.), London, Cassell, 1998.

Kant, I. *Lectures on Ethics*, Heath, P. and Schneewind, J.B. (eds), Cambridge, Cambridge University Press, 1997.

Kant, I. 'Groundwork of a Metaphysics of Morals', in *The Moral Law*, Paton, H.J. (trans.), London, Routledge, 2005.

Keenan, J. 'Virtue Ethics', in *Christian Ethics: An Introduction*, Hoose, B. (ed.), London, Cassell, 1998.

Kirkwood, R. 'Ethical Theory', in *Dialogue*, Special Issue.

Kuhse, H. 'Why Killing Is Not Always Worse – and Sometimes Better – than Letting Die', in *Bioethics: An Anthology*, Kuhse, H. and Singer P. (eds), Oxford, Blackwell, 1999.

Kuhse, H. and Singer, P. (eds) *Bioethics: An Anthology*, Oxford, Blackwell, 1999.

Lafollette, H. (ed.) *Ethics in Practice: An Anthology*, Oxford, Blackwell, 2002.

Leopold, A. *A Sand County Almanac*, Oxford and New York, Oxford University Press, 1968.

Leopold, A. 'The Land Ethic', in *Ethics in Practice: An Anthology*, Lafollette, H. (ed.), Oxford, Blackwell, 2002.

Linzey, A. *Christianity and the Rights of Animals*, London, SCM Press, 1987.

Louden, R. 'On Some Vices of Virtue Ethics', in *Virtue Ethics*, Crisp, R. and Slote, M. (eds), Oxford, Oxford University Press, 1997.

Lovelock, J. *Gaia: A New Look at Life on Earth*, Oxford, Oxford University Press, 1979.

Lovelock, J. *The Revenge of Gaia: Earth's Climate Crisis & The Fate of Humanity*, no place, Basic Books, 2007.

MacIntyre, A. *A Short History of Ethics*, London, Routledge, 1968.

MacIntyre, A. *After Virtue*, London, Duckworth, 1985.

MacIntyre, A. *A Short History of Ethics (Routledge Classics): A History of Moral Philosophy from the Homeric Age to the Twentieth Century*, London, Routledge, 2002.

Mackie, J.L. *Ethics: Inventing Right and Wrong*, London, Penguin, 1990.

Macquarrie, J. and Childress, J. *A New Dictionary of Christian Ethics*, London, SCM, 1986.

Maguire, D. *The Moral Choice*, New York, HarperCollins, 1979.

Maguire, D. *Death by Choice*, New York, Image Books, 1984.

Mahoney, J. *Seeking the Spirit: Essays in Moral and Pastoral Theology*, London, Sheen & Ward, 1981.

Marshal, A. *The Unity of Nature*, London, Imperial College Press, 2002.

Merton, T. *Elected Silence: The Autobiography of Thomas Merton*, no place, Hollis & Carter, 1949.

Mill, J.S. *Utilitarianism*, Indianapolis, Hackett, [1861, 1863], 2002.

Moore, G. 'Sex, Sexuality and Relationships', in *Christian Ethics: An Introduction*, Hoose, B. (ed.), London and New York, Cassell, 1998.

Murdoch, I. *The Sovereignty of Good* (2nd edn), London, Routledge, 2001.

Naess, A. 'The Shallow and the Deep, Longrange Ecology Movement', *Inquiry* (Oslo), 1973.

Niebuhr, R. *Moral Man and Immoral Societies*, New York, Scribner, 1932.

Norman, R. *Ethics, Killing and War*, Cambridge, Cambridge University Press, 1995.

Norman, R. *The Moral Philosophers*, Oxford, Oxford University Press, 1998.

O'Connell, T. *Principles for a Catholic Morality* (revised edn), New York, HarperCollins, 1990.

O'Neill, O. *Autonomy and Trust in Bioethics*, Cambridge, Cambridge University Press, 2002.

Palmer, M. *Moral Problems*, Cambridge, Lutterworth Press, 1991.

Palmer, M. *Moral Problems in Medicine*, Cambridge, Lutterworth Press, 1999.

Pearce, D.W., Markandya, A. and Barbier, E.B. *Blueprint for a Green Economy*, no place, Earthscan Ltd, 1995.

Peters, T. *Playing God? Genetic Determinism and Human Freedom*, London, Routledge, 1997.

Plato. 'Euthyphro', in *The Last Days of Socrates*, Tredennick, H. (trans.), London, Penguin, 1969.

Plato. *The Republic*, Lee, D. (trans.), London, Penguin, 2003.

Pojman, L.P. *Ethical Theory*, Toronto, Wadsworth, 1989.

Pojman, L.P. *Ethics: Discovering Right and Wrong*, Toronto, Wadsworth, 2002.

Preston, R. 'Conscience', in *A Dictionary of Christian Ethics*, Macquarrie, J. (ed.), London, SCM, 1967.

Rachels, J. 'Active and Passive Euthanasia', in *Bioethics: An Anthology*, Kuhse, H. and Singer, P. (eds), Oxford, Blackwell, 1999.

Rachels, J. and Rachels, S. *The Elements of Moral Philosophy*, New York, McGraw-Hill, 2007.

Ramsay, I. *Christian Ethics and Contemporary Philosophy*, London, SCM, 1966.

Rawls, J. *A Theory of Justice*, Cambridge, MA, Harvard University Press, 1971.

Ridley, M. *The Red Queen: Sex and the Evolution of Human Nature*, London, Penguin, 1994.

Ridley, M. *Genome*, London, HarperCollins, 2000.

Robinson, J. *Honest to God*, London, SCM, 1963.

Rosenstand, N. *The Moral of the Story* (5th edn), New York, McGraw-Hill, 2006.

Ross, W.D. *The Right and the Good*, Oxford, Clarendon Press, 1930.

Ruland, V. *An Ethics of Global Rights and Religious Pluralism*, San Francisco, CA, University of San Francisco Press, 2003.

Sacred Congregation for the Doctrine of Faith. 'Declaration on Euthanasia', in *Bioethics: An Anthology*, Kuhse, H. and Singer, P. (eds), Oxford, Blackwell, 1999.

Sardar, Sant Singh Khalsa *Siri Guru Granth Sahib*, Tuscon, Ariz., Hand Made Books, n.d.

Schumacher, E.F. *Small Is Beautiful – Economics as if People Mattered*, no place, Harper Torchbooks, 1973.

Scruton, R. *Kant*, Oxford, Oxford University Press, 1982.

Scruton, R. *Animal Rights and Wrongs*, London, Continuum, 1996.

Sidgwick, H. *Methods of Ethics*, Indianapolis, Hackett, 1981.

Singer, P. *Practical Ethics*, Cambridge, Cambridge University Press, 1993.

Singer, P. (ed.) *A Companion to Ethics*, Oxford, Blackwell, 1994.

Singer, P. *Rethinking Life and Death*, Oxford, Oxford University Press, 1994.

Singer, P. *Animal Liberation* (4th edn), London, Pimlico, 1995.

Singer, P. 'All Animals Are Equal', in *Ethics: The Big Questions*, Sterba, J. (ed.), Oxford, Blackwell, 1998.

Singer, P. *One World: The Ethics of Globalization*, New Haven, CT, Yale University press, 2004.

Slote, M. *Morals from Motives*, Oxford and New York, Oxford University Press, 2001.

Smart, J.J.C. and Williams, B. *Utilitarianism: For and Against*, Cambridge, Cambridge University Press, 1973.

Solomon, R.C. *Ethics and Excellence*, New York, Oxford, Oxford University Press, 1993.

Song, R. *Human Genetics: Fabricating the Future*, London, Darton, Longman & Todd, 2002.

Stevenson, C.L. *Ethics and Language*, Oxford, Oxford University Press, 1945.

Stroll, A. *Did My Genes Make Me Do It?* Oxford, Oneworld Publications, 2006.

Swinburne R. *Is there a God?* Oxford, Oxford University Press, 1996.

Taylor, P. 'The Ethics of Respect for Nature', in *Ethics: The Big Questions*, Sterba, J. (ed.), Oxford, Blackwell, 1998.

Thompson, M. *Ethical Theory*, London, Hodder Murray, 2005.

Thompson, M. *Teach Yourself Ethics*, London, Hodder Arnold, 2006.

Tillich, P. *Systematic Theology*, London, James Nisbet and Company Limited, 1968.

Van Inwagen, P. *An Essay on Free Will*, Cambridge, Clarendon Press, 1983.

Vardy, P. *The Puzzle of Sex*, London, Fount, 1997.

Vardy, P. and Grosch, P. *The Puzzle of Ethics*, London, Fount, 1999.

Walker, J. *Environmental Ethics*, London, Hodder & Stoughton, 2000.

Ward, K. *The Development of Kant's View of Ethics*, Oxford, Blackwell, 1972.

Ward, K. *God: A Guide for the Perplexed*, no place, One World Publications, 2003.

Ward, K. *Why There Almost Certainly Is a God: Doubting Dawkins*, London, Lion Hudson plc, 2008.

Warnock, M. *An Intelligent Person's Guide to Ethics*, London, Duckworth, 1999.

Warren, K. 'The Power and Promise of Ecological Feminism', in *Ethics: The Big Questions*, Sterba, J. (ed.), Oxford, Blackwell, 1998.

Warren, M.A. 'Abortion', in *A Companion to Ethics*, Singer, P. (ed.), Oxford, Blackwell, 1991.

Warren, M.A. 'On the Legal and Moral Status of Abortion', in *Ethics in Practice: An Anthology*, LaFollette, H. (ed.), Oxford, Blackwell, 1997.

Watson, F. *Agape, Eros, Gender: Towards a Pauline Sexual Ethic*, Cambridge, Cambridge University Press, 2000.

Westermann, C. *Genesis 1–11: A Commentary*, Augsburg, Fortress, 1984.

White, L.T., Jr. 'The Historical Roots of Our Ecologic Crisis', *Science*, Vol. 155 (Number 3767), 10 March 1967, pp. 1203–7.

Wilcockson, M. *Issues of Life and Death*, London, Hodder & Stoughton, 1999.

Wilcockson, M. *Sex and Relationships*, London, Hodder & Stoughton, 2000.

Williams, B. *Morality: An Introduction to Ethics*, Cambridge, Cambridge University Press, 1993.

Williams, B. *Ethics and the Limits of Philosophy*, London, Routledge, 2006.

Wink, W. *Jesus and Nonviolence: A Third Way*, Minneapolis, Abingdon Press US, 2003.

WEBSITES

http://www.angelfire.com/ms/perring/baier.html
http://www.bbc.co.uk/religion/ethics/
http://www.en.wikipedia.org/
http://www.erg.ucd.ie/arupa/references/gaia.html
http://www.faithnet.org.uk
http://www.gadfly.igc.org/e-ethics/Intro-ee.htm
http://www.hkbu.edu.hk/~ppp/Kant.html
http://www.importanceofphilosophy.com
http://www.jcu.edu/philosophy/gensler/et/
http://www.justwartheory.com/
http://www.newadvent.org/

http://www.newmanreader.org/works/grammar/chapter5-1.html
http://www.newmanreader.org/works/grammar/index.html
http://www.nobunaga.demon.co.uk/htm/kant.htm [Kant's works online]
http://www.online.sfsu.edu/~rone/Environ/Enviroethics.htm
http://www.oup.co.uk/academic/humanities/philosophy/viewpoint/hursthouse/
http://www.pbs.org/wgbh/questionofgod/ownwords/future2.html
http://www.plato.stanford.edu/
http://www.religion-online.org/
http://www.religioustolerance.org/
http://www.rep.routledge.com/article/DB047
http://www.rsweb.org.uk/ [Useful for all A level RS – Newman on conscience]
http://www.srtp.org.uk/
http://www.uri.edu/personal/szunjic/philos/util.htm
http://www.utilitarian.org/utility.html
http://www.utilitarianism.com/mill1.htm
http://www.victorianweb.org/philosophy/utilitarianism.html

Index

Note: **bold** page numbers denote glossary references.

a posteriori 107, 117, **306**
a priori 104, 106, 107, 109, 117, **306**
abortion 63–84, **306**; beginning of life question 64–7, 75–6; Buddhism 81; Christian ethics 75–6; definition of human life 78–9; doctrine of double effect 128; genetic screening 257; Hinduism 81–2; Islam 82–3; Judaism 82; legislation 77–8; life of the mother 67–8, 70–1, 76, 82, 83; population control 165; quality of life 71–5; sanctity of life 68–71; Sikhism 83
absolutes 23, 29, 31, 104, 108, 291, **306**
absolutism 81, 104, 109, 122, 128, **306**
Act Utilitarianism 11, 15, 16–18, **306**
active euthanasia 86, 90, 93, 98, **306**
Adam and Eve 45, 139, 156, 200, 233, 244
adultery 230, 231, 235, 240, 248
aesthetic experience 132
agape 4, 24, 30–4, 37, 242–3, 263–4, 289–90; *see also* love
agent-based/agent-focused theories 217
al-Ash'ari 57–8
Alexander III, Pope 236
Ambrose of Milan 52
Amish 50, 276

animals 43, 165, 167; animal rights 149–51, 268, 269; Buddhism 169; experimentation on 2, 267–9, 295; extinction of species 153, 169; human dominion over 140; Judaism 169–70; wild 150–1; xenotransplantation 264–5
Annas, Julia 217
Anscombe, G.E.M. 212
anthropocentrism 150, 152, 155, 156, 160, **306**
anthropomorphism 156
antinomianism 29, 30, 289
apparent good 126–7, **306**
applied ethics 3
Aquinas, Thomas: animals 140; Aristotle's influence on 221; conscience 185–6, 188, 190–1, 291; ensoulment 75; free will 46; human dominion 155; human nature 44, 130, 131; love 287; Natural Law 122, 124–8, 130, 290–1; sexual ethics 234–5, 236; suicide 93; Virtue Ethics 215; war 52
Aretaic ethics 208, 210, **307**
arete 207
Aristotle: ensoulment 75; Forms 137; happiness 8–9; human dominion 155; human nature 44; influence on Christian ethics 221; Natural Law 122–4; Virtue Ethics 207, 208–11, 214–15, 216, 222, 223, 224, 225, 304

artificial insemination (AI) 38, **306**
assisted dying/suicide 87, 88, 94, **307**
atheism 191–2
atman 55, 56, 81, 97
Augustine of Hippo: biography 189; conscience 37, 188; creation 137, 142; evil 139; free will 46, 178–9; human nature 44; love 287; original sin 45; polygamy 241; predestination 201; sexual ethics 233–4, 236; violence 52
authoritarian conscience 182, **307**
authority 287–8
autonomous moral agents 199, **307**
autonomous morality 182
autonomy 94, 95, **307**; act-based ethics 212; 'Baconian Project' 262; feminist Virtue Ethics 218; Kantian ethics 106, 112–13; medical ethics 292; Mill on 271

Bacon, Francis 67, 262
Baier, Annette 218
balance 208
Ball, John 48
Barclay, William 34
Barth, Karl 44, 49, 131
basic goods 131–3
behaviourism 196–8
benevolence 186, 187, **307**
Bentham, Jeremy 8, 9–11, 17; biography 9; comparison with Mill 13, 15; comparison with Sidgwick 16; exploitation of

minorities 22; view on religious ethics 23, 24
Berkeley, George 104
Bible: basis of Christian ethics 284; beginning of life question 65; Bentham's rejection of 23; business ethics 301; divine law 126; dominion 269; environmental ethics 155; equality and difference 46–7; ethical decision making 282; homosexuality 239; human experimentation 267; human nature 43; intrinsic value 117, 156, 263; role of women 47, 243–4; sanctity of life 68–9; sexual ethics 229–33, 236, 240; Situation Ethics 29, 34; xenotransplantation 265; *see also* New Testament; Old Testament
Bigger, Stephen 275
biocentrism 159, **307**
biodiversity 149, 152, 168, **307**
biofuels 154
biotechnology 270, 300; *see also* genetic engineering
birth, life begins at 67
Blasi, Augusto 183
blastocysts 256, 260, **307**
Blood, Diane 39
blood transfusions 118
body: Christian ethics 44; Gnosticism 233; Hinduism 56; Plato's body-soul dualism 228–9; Sikhism 61
The Body Shop 294, 297
Bowie, N.E. 303
Boyle, Joseph 91
Brandt, Richard 19, 21
Brown, Gordon 164
Brown, Louise 38
Bruderhof Brethren 50, 276
Buddhism 54–5; abortion 81; environmental ethics 169; euthanasia 96–7; self-sacrifice 62; sexual ethics 245; uncreated world 142–3; Virtue Ethics 225
business practice 282, 294–304; emerging economies 300–1; ethical investment 299–300, 302; globalisation 295–6; Kantian

ethics 303; moral management of companies 297–9; religious approach to 301–2; Utilitarianism 302–3; Virtue Ethics 304
Butler, Joseph 186–8

Calvin, John 201–2, 244
Camus, Albert 288
cancer 69–70
capitalism 301–2
Cardinal Virtues 207, **307**
caring: balanced 217; feminist Virtue Ethics 218; sexual ethics 223
Carson, Rachel 159
caste 55, 56–7
categorical imperative 109–13, 115, 120, **307**; abortion 79; business ethics 303; Christian ethics 117; euthanasia 95; genetic engineering 118, 119
Catholicism: authority and tradition 287–8; beginning of life question 64, 75–6; business ethics 302; conscience 189, 291; criticism of Situation Ethics 36; euthanasia 90–1, 92; genetic engineering and embryo research 263; homosexuality 239; inclusivism 49; IVF and the right to a child 38; marriage 236, 237; Natural Law 30, 129, 131, 291; pacifism 51; polygamy 241; proportionalism 37; role of women 47, 244; sanctity of life 69; sexual ethics 234
causality 124, 194; determinism 195–6, 199; libertarianism 180
celibacy 233, 234, 245, 286, **307**
character 220, 221
charity 108
chastity 233
children: child development 182; experimentation on 266, 267
China 300
Christian ethics: abortion 75–6; animal experimentation 269; authority and tradition in 287–8; business ethics 301–2; comparison with Kantian ethics 117–18; conscience 184–5, 189,

190, 191, 291; creation 140–2; Divine Command theory 288–9; environmental ethics 155–9, 160, 165; equality and difference 46–9; ethical decision making 282–7; euthanasia 90–2; free will and fatalism 45–6; genetic engineering and embryo research 263–4; human experimentation 267; human nature and the human condition 43–5; inventions 273–6; IVF and the right to a child 38–9; Jewish roots 283–4; libertarianism 193; predestination 200–2; revelation 186; sanctity of life 68–71; self-sacrifice 62; sexual ethics 229, 230–3, 236–44; Situation Ethics 29–30, 31, 34, 35–6, 290; Utilitarianism 23–4; Virtue Ethics 221–2, 282; war and peace 49–52; xenotransplantation 265; *see also* Catholicism; Protestantism
Church of England (Anglican Church): abortion 76; homosexuality 239; nuclear weapons 274; Oxford Movement 188; *see also* Protestantism
climate change 147, 148–9, 154, 162–3, 164, 300
cloning 252, 254, 259–62, 273, **307**
cohabitation 238, 246
community 214, 304
community ethic 286
compassion 95, 96, 120; Kantian ethics 106; Virtue Ethics 217–18, 220, 225
compatibilism 176, **307**
computers 275–6, 278
conception 64–5, 69, 70, 75, 81, 83, 256
conditioning 197
conscience 184, 291, **308**; abortion 76, 78; Aquinas on 185–6; biblical teaching 184–5; Butler's approach 186–8; formation of 191; Freudian theory 181–2; Islam 57; modern understandings of 189–90; as a moral guide 190–1; Newman's approach 188;

problems with 191–2; Situation
Ethics 36, 37–8; as voice of God
188, 189, 191, 291
conscientia 185, **308**
consciousness 44, 73, 81, **308**
consequentialism 8, 9, 15, 21, 220,
308; Act Utilitarianism 11, 17;
animal rights 151; Finnis's
critique of 132; Preference
Utilitarianism 20;
proportionalism 37; Rule
Utilitarianism 18
conservation ethics 149, 151–3,
308
contraception 165, 234, 237, 288
co-operation 208, 304
Co-operative Bank 294
Copernican Revolution 104–5, 106,
308
corporate social responsibility 294,
297
courage 215, 216, 304
creation 136–45; best of all possible
worlds 137–9; Buddhism 142–3;
environmental ethics 156;
Hinduism 143; Islam 143–4;
Judaism 143; Sikhism 144; status
and duty of humankind 140–2
cultural relativism 4, 131, **308**
customer rights 297
Cynics 229

Dalai Lama 81, 245
Darrow, Clarence 177, 179, 196–7
Darwin, Charles 71, 130, 197, 198
Davies, Brian 139
Dawkins, Richard 198
Deane-Drummond, Celia 155, 269
Declaration of Human Rights 115
deep (dark green) ecology 159,
160–1, 163, 165, 168, **308**
deep green theory 161
deforestation 148, 154
deontological ethics 3, 8, 220, **308**;
abortion 79; Christian ethics 23,
287; Kantian ethics 104; Natural
Law 291; Rule Utilitarianism 18
Descartes, René 23, 105, 289
determinism 176, 194–202, **308**;
behaviourism 196–8; causality
principle 195–6; hard 176, 196–7,

310; Islam 204; rejection of 179,
180; soft 176, 199–200, **314**
Devall, B. 168
developing world 154–5, 255, 266,
272, 296
Diggers 48
Dignitas 87
dignity: abortion debate 71; arms
race 274; cloning controversy
252; euthanasia 90, 92; genetic
engineering 118; Islam 57, 58;
Judaism 60; Kantian ethics 113,
115; preservation of life 133;
sanctity of life 71
disability 47–8; abortion 68, 77–8,
81; Buddhism 55; hospices 89;
Sikhism 61
discrimination: abortion 77–8; data
collection and use 272; principle
of 52
disease 255, 257, 258–9, 266–7,
268, 276
Divine Command theory 3, 4,
288–9, **308**
divine law 125, 126, 185, 188, **308**
divorce 234, 236, 237, 283; Eastern
Orthodox Church 238; Islam
247–8; Jesus on 231; Judaism
246–7; Sikhism 248
Dolly the Sheep 252, 259
dominion 140, 143, 155–6, 157,
158, 169, 269, **309**
Dominion, Jack 238
Dormor, Duncan 238
Dostoyevsky, F. 288
double effect, doctrine of 67, 70, 76,
90, 128, 129, 134, **308**
Doukhobors 50
Down's syndrome 77–8, 255
dualism, body and soul 228–9, 233
Duncan, Gordon 36
Duns Scotus, John 289
Dutch Reformed Church 46–7
duty 22, 23, 220, **309**; abortion 79;
Kantian ethics 108–9, 111, 114,
115, 116, 120, 303; not to kill 92;
ordinary and extraordinary means
70; Ross's theory 116–17; sanctity
of life 71

Eastern Orthodox Church 47, 237–8

eco-holism 161–3
economics 167–8, 282, 295–6
ecosophy 160, **309**
ectopic pregnancy 69, 70, 76, 128
ego 181
Einstein, Albert 180, 202
email 271
embryos 66, 70, 74–5, **309**; embryo
research 25, 118, 251, 253–4,
259–62, 263–4, 270; genetic
selection 255, 256–7; human
experimentation 266; Kantian
ethics 118; stem cells 253,
259–62
emerging economies 300–1
emotionality 73
emotions: biological basis of 198;
conscience 192; Kantian ethics
106, 115; Stoics 122; Virtue
Ethics 219
emotivism 213, **309**
empiricism 23, 24, 104, 195
employer/employee relationships
297–8
end-time theology 158–9
enlightenment 54, 55, 61, 97
Enlightenment, Age of 44, 213–14
ensoulment 70, 75, **309**
environmental ethics 146–72;
animal rights 149–51; Buddhism
169; climate change 148–9;
conservation of the living
environment 151–3; definition of
147–8; developing world 154–5;
genetically modified crops 254–5;
Hinduism 169; human
responsibility 165–6, 172; impact
of scientific inventions 273; Islam
144, 170; Judaism 169–70;
philosophical approaches to
159–63; religious approaches to
155–9, 169–70, 172; science and
technology 251–2; Sikhism 170;
wealthy nations 163–4
Epicureans 8, 10
Epicurus 10
equality: animals 150, 167;
Buddhism 55; Christianity 46–9;
cloning controversy 252;
Hinduism 56–7; Islam 58;
Judaism 59; Sikhism 61

eternal law 125, 126, 127, 129, **309**
ethical investment 299–300, 302
ethics, definition of 1–2
eudaimonia 8, **309**; Natural Law
123; Plato 207; Preference
Utilitarianism 20; Virtue Ethics
208, 210, 217, 221, 222, 225,
304; *see also* happiness
euthanasia 85–100; active 86, 90,
93, 98, **306**; beliefs about 2;
Buddhism 96–7; definition of
86–7; Hinduism 97; hospices
88–9; involuntary 86, 90, 96, 97,
311; Islam 98; Judaism 98;
legislation about 87–8; Natural
Law 133–4; non-voluntary 86;
passive 86, 90, 93, 98, **312**;
religious approaches to 90–2;
right to choose when to die 93–5;
Sikhism 98; voluntary 86, 87, 90,
92, 94, 97, 98, 133–4, **315**
Euthyphro Dilemma 288, **309**
evil 11, 138–9; Buddhist view of
142; Catholic view of 263; free
will defence 193; Jewish view of
59
evolution 198
'Exclusive Brethren' 275–6
exclusivists 49
existentialism 29, 178, 180
Exodus 82
external goods 216
extinction 153, 169

facts 3, 4, 130
fairness 23, 304
the Fall 45, 139, 140, 157, 200, 244
fallacies 2; is-ought fallacy 3;
naturalistic fallacy 130;
Utilitarianism 15
family, love for 242
fatalism 199; Buddhism 54–5;
Christianity 45–6; Hinduism 56;
Islam 57–8; *see also* determinism
feminism 77, 218, 233, **309**
Finnis, John 131–3
Fletcher, Joseph 29–37, 41, 289;
biography 29; criticism of 290;
embryo research 264; euthanasia
92; IVF and the right to a child
39; on justice 24

foetuses 78–9, **309**; abortion law
64; beginning of life question
64–6; doctrine of double effect
70; personhood 72–3, 74–5;
quality of life 71; religious
teachings on abortion 81, 82;
right to life 67–8, 80; rights of 80;
viability 74
Foot, Philippa 213, 216
free will 193–4, 205; Buddhism
54–5; Christianity 45–6; conflict
of free wills 178–9; constraints to
177–8; definition of 176; genetics
and 177; Hinduism 56; Islam
57–8; Judaism 59; karma 204; *see
also* libertarianism
free will defence 139, 193
freedom 94, 180–1; illusion of 195;
Kantian ethics 106–7, 114, 199;
New Testament 193;
predestination 201
freedom of religion 23, 48–9
Freedom to Care 298
Freud, Sigmund 181, 235
Friedman, Milton 294

Gaia hypothesis 161–3, **309**
Galatians 24, 44, 47, 286
Gandhi, Mohandas 51, 56, 143, 211
gender 235, **309**; Buddhism 55;
equality 47; Hinduism 57; Islam
58; Judaism 59; sex selection of
children 82; *see also* women
gene selection 255–7, 270
gene therapy 253, 258
Genesis: Adam and Eve 45; creation
137, 142, 143, 156;
environmental ethics 157; the Fall
200; gender 59; human dominion
140, 155, 158, 269; image of God
43, 58, 244; sanctity of life 68–9;
sexual ethics 229, 230, 239–40
genetic engineering 118–19, 252–3,
263–4, **309**
genetic screening 255, 256, 257,
264
genetic testing 257
genetically modified (GM) crops
119, 254–5
genetics, free will and 177
geocentrism 161, **310**

germ line engineering 258, **310**
Gilkey, Langdon 44
global warming 147, 148–9, 162–3,
164, 251
globalisation 294, 295–6
Glover, Jonathan 67, 75
Gnosticism 233
God: beginning of life question 76;
Christian love 31; conscience
coming from 37, 186–8, 189, 190,
191, 291; creation 137–9, 140–2,
156; Divine Command theory
288–9; environmental ethics 156,
157, 158; equality before 47;
euthanasia 91, 98; exclusivist and
inclusivist views 49; free will 46,
178–9, 193; image of 43–4, 49,
58, 68, 80, 124–5, 140, 244, 267;
Islam 57–8; Judaism 60; Kantian
ethics 114, 117–18; knowledge of
God's will 29–30; morality
dependent on 212; Natural Law
122, 125; obedience to 286;
original sin 45; predestination
176, 178, 200–2; relationship
with 285; sanctity of life 68–9;
sexual ethics 232; Sikhism 60;
suicide as rejection of 93; as
sustainer 145
Golden Mean 208, 211, **310**
Golden Rule of Jesus of Nazareth
15, 24, 115, 117, 132, 267
Golding, William 161
good: apparent 126–7, **306**;
intrinsic 32, 39, 129, **311**;
Judaism 59; Kantian ethics 114;
real 126–7, **313**; Utilitarianism 8,
11
good will 32, 107, 109, 114, 120,
150, 303, **310**
Gospels 221, 240, 284–5
Greatest Happiness Principle 12, 17,
27
Greeks, ancient 44, 122, 228–9,
233; *see also* Aristotle; Plato
Grisez, Germain 91, 133
Grosch, P. 131
guilt 181–2
Gula, Richard 189
Guru Gobind Singh Ji 61, 62
Guru Nanak Dev Ji 56, 61, 170

Hagee, Pastor John 158–9
happiness: Aquinas on 290–1; Christian ethics 284; Greatest Happiness Principle 12, 17, 27; Kantian ethics 114; love leading to 287; Natural Law 122, 130; universalisability 14–15; Utilitarianism 8–9, 11–12, 14–15, 17, 21, 22; *see also* eudaimonia
hard determinism 176, 196–7, **310**
Hare, R.M. 19, 20, 21, 112, 151
harm principle 235, **310**
Harris, John 43
Hashmi family 256
Hauerwas, Stanley 221
health care 21, 292–3
hedonic calculus 9–10, 23, 25, **310**
hedonism 8–9, 10, 11, **310**
Heisenberg, Werner 180
Helsinki Declaration (1990) 164
heteronomous morality 182
heteronomy 106
Hick, J. 139
Hinduism 55–7; abortion 81–2; creation 143; environmental ethics 169; euthanasia 97; self-sacrifice 62; sexual ethics 245–6; Virtue Ethics 225
Hippocratic Oath 64, **310**
Hobbes, Thomas 177
Holbach, Paul-Henri Thiry d' 195, 196
holistic approach 161, **310**
Holloway, Richard 29, 227, 239
Holy Spirit 286, 288
homosexuality 129, 234, 237, 238–9, 245, 247, 248, 283
Honderich, Ted 180, 195–6
honesty 216, 295, 301, 303, 304
Hoose, Bernard 36
hope 216
Hospers, John 196
hospices 87, 88–9, 100
Hughes, G. 128
human experimentation 266–7, 291–2
Human Fertilisation and Embryology Act (1990) 65, 75
Human Fertilisation and Embryology Authority (HFEA) 25, 254, 255

human genome 258, **310**
Human Genome Project 254, 262–3
human life, value of: Buddhism 55; Christianity 38, 49–52; euthanasia 90, 91, 93; Hinduism 55; Islam 58; Judaism 60; Natural Law 133; self-sacrifice 62; Sikhism 61; universality 133; Utilitarianism 25; Virtue Ethics 223; *see also* abortion
human nature: Buddhism 54; Christianity 43–5; conscience and 186–7, 188; eudaimonia and 225; Hinduism 56; Hume's ethics 107–8; Islam 57; Judaism 58–9; Mill's approach 15; Natural Law 122, 124, 127, 130, 131; Sidgwick's approach 16; Sikhism 60; Utilitarianism 24; Virtue Ethics 222–3
human rights 115, 269–72, 278, 294, 296, 300
Hume, David: biography 108; human nature 107–8; interpretation of events 194; is-ought fallacy 3; Kant's rejection of 106; knowledge 104, 105
Huntingdon Life Sciences 295
Hursthouse, Rosalind 217
Hutterites 276
Huxley, Aldous 270
hypothetical imperative 109, **310**

id 181
ID cards 271
identity: based on community 214; moral 183
image of God 43–4, 49, 58, 68, 80, 124–5, 140, 244, 267
immanence 141
immortality 114
incest 82, 229, 235, 244
inclinations, natural 126–7
inclusivists 49
incompatibilism 177, **310**
India 296, 300
individualism 215, 216, 289, 301–2
industriousness 216
information technologies 270–2
informed consent 266
instrumental value 149, **311**

integrity 22, 23, 295
intellectual virtues 209, 210, **311**
interests 20
internal goods 216
internet 271, 275, 292–3, 297
intrinsic goodness 32, 39, 129, **311**
intrinsic value **311**; creation 140; environmental ethics 155, 156–8, 160, 163, 168; genetic engineering and embryo research 263; Kantian ethics 117; Utilitarian rejection of 22, 24
intuitionism 16, 188, **311**
inventions 272–6
investment, ethical 299–300, 302
involuntary euthanasia 86, 90, 96, 97, **311**
Inwagen, Peter van 179
Irenaeus of Lyons 43, 139
Isaiah 140, 157
Islam 57–8; abortion 82–3; creation 143–4; determinism 204; environmental ethics 170; euthanasia 98; self-sacrifice 62; sexual ethics 247–8
is-ought fallacy 3
IVF (in-vitro fertilisation) 38–40, 118, 255, 264, 270, 300, **311**

James, Daniel 87
Jenner, Edward 266
Jesus of Nazareth 15, 24, 211, 221, 284–5; agape 30; anti-racist teachings 47; conscience 37; creation and 141; ethics of Paul 286; healings by 47; love 36, 50, 290; mercy 92; monogamy 230; pacifism 50; on rules 117; sexual ethics 230–1
Jim and the Indians story 22
Job 48, 69
John 69, 141, 193, 231, 242, 285
John Paul II, Pope 76, 242, 244
John XIII, Pope 274
Judaism 58–60; abortion 82; creation 143; environmental ethics 169–70; euthanasia 98; Jewish roots of Christian ethics 283–4; marriage 236; self-sacrifice 62; sexual ethics 229, 246–7

jus ad bellum 52, **311**
jus in bello 52, **311**
jus post bello 52, **311**
just authority, principle of 52
just cause, principle of 52
Just War theory 49–50, 52, **311**
justice: arms race 274; business ethics 301; environmental ethics 164; Rawls 23; sexual ethics 223; Sidgwick's approach 16; Situation Ethics 24, 32; Virtue Ethics 215, 216, 218

Kant, Immanuel/Kantian ethics 3, 4, 103–20, 165, 212; abortion 79; animal rights 150; biography 104–5; business ethics 303; categorical imperative 109–13; 'Christian Kantianism' 133; Copernican Revolution 104–5; determinism 199; duty 108–9; freedom 106–7; genetic engineering 118–19; good will 32, 107; hypothetical imperative 109; impartiality 219; personal autonomy 95; religious ethics 117–18; Ross's theory 116–17; strengths of 115; three postulates of practical reason 114; value of life 71; value of people 31; weaknesses of 115–16
karma (kamma) 54, 55, 56, 62; abortion 81; euthanasia 96; free will 60, 204; rebirth and 142–3; suffering 98
Keble, John 188
Keenan, James 215
King, Martin Luther, Jr. 51, 211
Kingdom of Ends 112–13, **311**
Kingdom of God 157, 230, 285
knowledge: as basic good 132; embryo research 25; Kantian ethics 104–5
Kohlberg, Lawrence 182
Koterski, Joseph 133
Kuhse, Helga 72, 93
Kyoto Protocol 152, 154, 159

LaBossiere, Michael 153
labour standards 301
Lake District 152–3

Laplace, Pierre 195
Lasagna, Louis 64
last resort, principle of 52
Latin America 300
law: abortion and the 64, 65, 68, 77–8; euthanasia 86, 87–8; judgement of conscience 36; suicide 93; universal 109, 110–12, 113, 120, **311**
Law of Nature 110
Lawrence, T.E. 35
legal cases 68, 77
legalism 29, 30, 219, 283–4, 287, 288
Leibniz, Gottfried Wilhelm 105, 106, 288
Leopold, Aldo 160, 166–7
Leopold, Nathan 177, 196, 197
leukaemia 292
Levellers 48
liberalism 23
libertarianism 176, 179–84, 193–4, **311**; *see also* free will
life: as absolute value 134; as basic good 132; beginning of life question 64–7, 75–6; intrinsic value 160; right to 67–8, 70–1, 72–5, 80, 92, 100, 270
Linzey, Andrew 149–50, 269
Locke, John 104, 195
Loeb, Richard 177, 196, 197
Louden, Robert 220
love: environmental ethics 157; genetic engineering and embryo research 263–4; of God 37; importance of 287; Jesus's idea of 36; marriage 38–9, 237; of neighbour 286, 287; Sermon on the Mount 285; sexual ethics 236, 242–3; Situation Ethics 24, 29–34, 37–8, 39, 41, 289–90; towards enemies 50
Lovelock, James 161–3
Luther, Martin 44
Lyon, David 272

MacIntyre, Alasdair 115, 213–16, 221
MacNamara, Vincent 189
Maguire, Daniel 91, 133–4, 190
Mahayana Buddhism 81

Mahoney, Jack 192
Mandela, Nelson 183, 211
Mark 284
marriage 38–9, 231, 236–8, 286; Augustine on 234; Buddhism 245; Hinduism 245, 246; Islam 247–8; Judaism 246; monogamy 241; Paul on 232–3; sex outside 238, 239–40, 246, 247; Sikhism 248
Marshall, Alan 159
martyrdom 94, 97, 98
Marxism 271
Matthew 47, 50, 156, 221, 231, 240, 284, 285
maxims 104, 109, 110, 112, 303, **311**
McDonagh, Enda 192
McEwan, Ian 240
means and ends: abortion 79; Kantian ethics 112, 117, 118, 303; ordinary and extraordinary means 70, 90, 92, **312**; Situation Ethics 31, 33; Utilitarianism 11, 23, 25; Virtue Ethics 208
medical ethics 282, 291–3; abortion and the right of the child 63–84; euthanasia 86; human experimentation 266–7; refusal of medical treatment 92; *see also* science and technology
Mennonites 50, 276
mercy 92
Merton, Thomas 51
meta-ethics 3, **312**
Mill, John Stuart: application to embryo research 25; on Bentham 23; environmental preservation 153; freedom from state interference 271; personal autonomy 94; Utilitarianism 9, 12–15, 18, 23–4
'Millennium Village' 164
minorities 22, 115
monogamy 230, 241
Moore, G.E. 130
moral agency 73
moral development 182
moral virtues 209, 210, **312**
Muhammad (pbuh), Prophet 58, 170
murder 35, 62, 289; abortion as 76,

78; commandment against 50; embryo research as 270; euthanasia as 98; Judaism 60; sanctity of life 69
Murdoch, Iris 222

Naess, Arne 160–1
National Institute for Clinical Excellence (NICE) 293
Natural Law 3, 4, 121–35, 290–1; a posteriori nature of 117; abortion 79; Aquinas 124–8; Catholic following of 30, 263; comparison with Utilitarianism 23, 24; definition of 122; doctrine of double effect 128; ethical decision making 282; euthanasia 90, 133–4; Finnis's approach 131–3; natural inclinations 126–7; 'New' 91; ordinary and extraordinary means 70; origins of 122–4; practical reasonableness 132–3; primary and secondary precepts 127–8; proportionalism 36–7; purpose of human beings 124–5; sanctity of life 69; sexual ethics 234–5, 239; strengths of 130, 135; summary of 129; weaknesses of 130–1, 135
Natural Moral Law 122, 125, 133, **312**
natural selection 71, 130, 198
naturalistic fallacy 130, **312**
Neilsen, Kai 131
Netherlands 86, 87, 93, 94
New Testament: basis of Christian ethics 284, 285; business ethics 301; conscience 37; creation 141; disability 47, 48; homosexuality 239; libertarianism 193; love 242; monogamy 241; role of women 243–4; sexual ethics 230–3; Utilitarianism as incompatible with 24; Virtue Ethics 221
Newman, Cardinal John Henry 188
Newton, Isaac 180, 195
nirvana (nibbana) 54, 55, 56
'Noble Eightfold Path' 54
non-violence 51, 169
non-voluntary euthanasia 86

normative ethics 3, 220, **312**
nuclear energy 163
nuclear weapons 274

O'Connell, Timothy 190
Old Testament: business ethics 301; creation 137; disability 47; Divine Command theory 289; God's will 138; polygamy 241; sexual ethics 229–30; on women 232
omniscience 46, 179, 200
ordinary and extraordinary means 70, 90, 92, **312**
original sin 44–5, 233
Orwell, George 270, 272
'ought implies can' 199, **312**
'ought' statements 3, 105, 130
Oxford Movement 188

pacifism 49–51, **312**
pain 9, 21, 23, 90, 92
passive euthanasia 86, 90, 93, 98, **312**
patience 216
Paul: conscience 37, 184–5; creation 137, 141; equality 47; ethics of 285, 286–7, 288; God's authority 51; human nature 44; life of Jesus 221; love 243; predestination 200–1; sexual ethics 231–3, 240
Paul VI, Pope 64–5
Pavlov, Ivan Petrovich 197, 198
peace 303
Pearce, David 153, 167–8
Pelagius 201, 233
perfection 125, 137, 139
persistent vegetative state (PVS) 90, 91, 92, **313**
personalism 31–2, 37
personality 181–2, 235
personhood 25, 43, 72–3, **312**; beginning of life question 66, 74–5, 256; euthanasia 90, 91
Peterson, Gregory R. 44
Philippians 286
Phillips, Kay 177
phronesis (practical wisdom) 208, 211, 212, **312**
physics 180, 195, 198, 199
Piaget, Jean 182

Pinker, Steven 198
Pius XI, Pope 64
Pius XII, Pope 34, 90, 263, 274
placebos 266
Plato: Euthyphro Dilemma 288; Form of the Good 137; happiness 8; human nature 44; the soul 228–9; Virtue Ethics 207
play 132
pleasure: origins of hedonism 8–9; quality of 13–14; Sidgwick's approach 16; Utilitarianism 8, 9–10, 11, 15, 21, 22, 23, 152–3
pluralism 49
pollution 152, 154, 163, 273, 296
polygamy 230, 241, 247
population growth 154, 161, 163, 165
Porritt, Jonathon 165
Porter, Jean 221
positivism 31
poverty 154
practical reason: Kantian ethics 105, 109, 112–13, 114, 115, 199; Virtue Ethics 210, 215, 218
practical reasonableness 132–3
pragmatism 31
predestination 46, 60, 176, 178, 200–2, **312**
Preference Utilitarianism 19–21, 80, **312**; animal rights 150, 151; environmental ethics 153
Priestley, Joseph 8
prima facie duties 22, 116–17
primary precepts 127, 128, 133, 291, **313**
primitive streak 66, 270
privacy 270, 271–2, 278
private utility 10
probability of success, principle of 52
process theism 138
promise-keeping 110–11
proportionalism 36–7, 91
proportionality, principle of 52, **313**
Protestantism: attitudes to technology 276; authority and tradition 287; business ethics 301–2; IVF and the right to a child 38–9; legalism 30; marriage

237; polygamy 241; role of women 47, 244; war and peace 52; *see also* Church of England
psychoanalysis 181
psychology 182
public utility 10
punishment 196, 198, 199
purity of heart 215
purpose 122–3, 124–5, 214, **313**
Pythagoreans 228

Quakers 48, 50, 237, 302
qualitative, definition of **313**
qualitative Utilitarianism 11, 15, 22, 23, 153
quality of life 71–5, **313**; environmental ethics 163, 168; euthanasia 90–2, 93, 94, 100, 134; hospices 89
quantitative, definition of **313**
quantitative Utilitarianism 11, 15, 22, 23, 152–3
quantum physics 180, 198
queer theory 235, **313**
Qur'an 57, 58, 98, 144, 247

Rachels, James 93, 215, 268, 289
racism 20, 46–7
Rahner, Karl 49, 141
rainforests 152, 154, 163
Ramsay, Paul 29, 38–9, 264
rape: abortion in cases of 79, 81, 82, 83; sexual ethics 235, 240, 243, 244
Rapture 158–9
rationalism 104, 105
Rawls, John 22, 23, 294
real good 126–7, **313**
reason 3, 23; Aristotle on 123, 124; conscience and 185–6, 192; Kantian ethics 95, 104–7, 109, 112–13, 117; Natural Law 122, 127–9, 131, 134, 290, 291; personhood criteria 73; Virtue Ethics 210, 212; *see also* practical reason
reasonableness, practical 132–3
rebirth 54, 56, 57, 60, 81, 142–3
reflection, principle of 187
relativism 4, **313**; Act Utilitarianism 17; cultural 131, **308**; Rule

Utilitarianism 18; Situation Ethics 31
religion, as basic good 132
research 266–7, 273, 291–3; *see also* science and technology
resources 148, 163, 169, 170
responsibility: conscience 188, 190, 192; determinism 176, 200, 202; environmental 165–6, 172; free will 176, 194; Judaism 59; New Testament 193; soft determinism 199; Virtue Ethics 221
restorative justice 32
revelation 186, 201, 284
Revelation, Book of 158, 275
Reynolds, Philip 236
right intention, principle of 52
rights: animal 149–51, 268, 269; beginning of life question 64; Christian ethics 24; customers 297; euthanasia 92, 93–5; human rights and scientific progress 269–72, 278; individual 22; Kantian ethics 104, 115; of mothers 67–8, 77, 80; personhood and 43; right to life 67–8, 70–1, 72–5, 80, 92, 100, 270
Robinson, Bishop John 29, 33, 34
Roddick, Anita 297
Roe v. Wade case (1973) 77
Romans 51, 137, 184–5, 201, 284
Ross, W.D. 22, 116–17
Rousseau, Jean-Jacques 23, 108
Ruland, Vernon 189
Rule Utilitarianism 15, 16–17, 18–19, 21, **313**
rules: Act Utilitarianism 17; antinomianism 30; Divine Command theory 288–9; Kantian ethics 117, 303; Rule Utilitarianism 15, 18–19; sex 235; Situation Ethics 289–90

samsara 55, 56, 57, 97
sanctity of life: abortion 68–71, 75; definition of **313**; euthanasia 87, 90, 91, 100; genetic engineering and embryo research 263; Natural Law 291; Singer on 93
Sartre, Jean-Paul 178, 180

Saunders, Dame Cicely 89
Schumacher, E.F. 166
science and technology 130, 141, 250–78; animal experimentation 267–9, 295; business ethics 294–5; Christian ethics 263–4; embryo research 25, 118, 251, 253–4, 259–62, 263–4, 270; environmental problems 147–8; gene selection 255–7, 270; gene therapy 253, 258; genetic engineering 118–19, 252–3, 263–4, **310**; genetic screening 255, 256, 257, 264; genetic testing 257; genetically modified crops 119, 254–5; human experimentation 266–7, 291–2; Human Genome Project 262–3; human rights and 269–72, 278; inventions 272–6; xenotransplantation 264–5
Scruton, Roger 150–1
secondary precepts 127–8, 133, 291, **313**
secularism 273
self, concept of 72
self-awareness 73, 178, 199
self-care 223
self-defence 79, 92, 98
self-determination 94
self-interest 15
self-love 110–11, 186, 187, **313**
self-sacrifice 30, 52, 62, 94, 218
Sellars, Wilfrid 218
sentience 25, 43, 73, 149, 265, **314**
Sermon on the Mount 284–5
Sessions, George 160, 168
sex selection of children 82, 256
sexual ethics 129, 223–4, 226–48; Aquinas on 234–5; Augustine on 233–4; Buddhism 245; Fletcher on 30–1; Hinduism 245–6; historical views 228–9; Islam 247–8; Judaism 246–7; love 242–3; modern thinking on 235; New Testament 230–3; Old Testament 229–30; polygamy 241; role of women 243–4; sex outside marriage 238, 239–40; Sikhism 248

shallow (light green) ecology 152, 159–60, 163, 165, **314**
Shroff, Geeta 300
Sidgwick, Henry 16, 93
Sikhism 56, 60–1; abortion 83; creation 144; environmental ethics 170; euthanasia 98; self-sacrifice 62; sexual ethics 248; Virtue Ethics 225
Silva, Joyce de 265
sin 157, 201, 202
Singer, Peter: animal experimentation 268; animal rights 149–50, 151, 165; biography 20; criticism of legalism 287; embryo research 25; equality of species 71, 167; euthanasia 93; fertilisation process 256; global problems 296; human dominion 157; Preference Utilitarianism 19, 20–1; preservation of the environment 151–2, 153, 155, quality of life 72; sentience 43
Situation Ethics 3, 4, 28–41, 289–90, **314**; Christianity and 35–6; comparison with Utilitarianism 24; ethical decision making 282; euthanasia 92; genetic engineering and embryo research 263–4; proportionalism 36–7; role of conscience 37–8; six fundamental principles 32–3; strengths of 33; weaknesses of 34
situationism 30
Skinner, Burrhus Frederic 197, 198
slippery slope argument 2, 93, 95, 257, **314**
Slote, Michael 217–18, 223
sociability 132
social contract theory 294
Socrates 211
soft determinism 176, 199–200, **314**
somatic cell engineering 258, **314**
Song, Robert 262
Song of Songs 229–30
soul 44, 73; ensoulment 70, 75, **309**; Plato's model of the 228–9
South Africa 32, 46–7
speciesism 43, 71, 149, 269

Spinoza, Baruch 195
Spirit 286, 288
St Francis of Assisi 156
stem cells 253, 259–62, **314**
stewardship 140, 143, 144, 157, 158, 160, 169, **314**
Stoics 122, 124, 229
Stokes, Robert and Jennifer 87
subjectivism 289, **314**
suffering: animals 169–70, 268; Buddhism 54, 81, 142; Catholic view of 90, 263; disability and 47, 48; disease 276; elimination of 262–3; euthanasia 92, 95, 96, 97; evil and 138–9; God's 138; Hinduism 56; Sikhism 98, 144
suicide 2, 93–4, 95, 133
summum bonum 114, 120, **314**
super-ego 181, 182, 235, **314**
surveillance technology 270–2, 278
Swinburne, Richard 139
Switzerland 87
Sylvan, Richard 161
synderesis 185, **314**

Tantra 246
technology *see* science and technology
teleological ethics 3, 8, 220, **314**; abortion 79; Utilitarianism 17, 23; Virtue Ethics 221
television 275
temperance 216
Temple, William 29
Ten Commandments 23, 283–4
therapeutic cloning 254, **314**
Thomson, Judith Jarvis 73–4, 79
Tillich, Paul 29, 31
transplantation 264
Tutu, Desmond 32
Twain, Mark 184
twins 74, 75, 177, 256, 258–9

uncertainty principle 180
universalisability: definition of **315**; Kantian ethics 106, 110–12, 114, 115, 117, 303; Utilitarianism 14–15, 20, 21
universe 141–2
Utilitarianism 3, 4, 7–27, 117, 212, **315**; abortion 79–80, 81; Act 11,

15, 16–18, **306**; animal rights 151, 268; 'Baconian Project' 262; Bentham's approach 9–11; business ethics 302–3; embryo research 25; environmental ethics 152–3; euthanasia 91; Finnis's critique of 132; human experimentation 267; impartiality 219; love and justice 32; medical ethics 292; Mill's approach 12–15; origins of hedonism 8–9; Preference 19–21, 80, 150, 151, 153, **312**; religious ethics 23–4; Rule 15, 16–17, 18–19, 21, **313**; Sidgwick's approach 16; strengths of 21; weaknesses of 22–3
utility, principle of 8, 10, 16, 17, 24, 269–70, **315**

values: environmental economics 167–8; moral reasoning 190; Natural Law 129, 130, 134; proportionalism 37; universal 16
Vardy, Peter 131
vegetarianism 149, 150, 151
viability 65, 74, 80, **315**
vices 209, 211, 216, **315**
violence 50–1, 61
virtue, definition of 207, **315**
Virtue Ethics 4, 206–25, 282; abortion 81; Anscombe 212; Aristotle 208–11; Buddhist 'Noble Eightfold Path' 54; business ethics 304; conscience 189; definition of 207; feminism and 218; Foot 213; human nature 222–3; Hursthouse 217; MacIntyre 213–16; Plato 207; religious approaches 221–2, 225; sexual ethics 223–4; Slote 217–18; strengths of 219–20; weaknesses of 220
virtuous people 24, 114, 211, 213, 217–18, 219–21
Voltaire 23
voluntary euthanasia 86, 87, 90, 92, 94, 97, 98, 133–4, **315**

Wałęsa , Lech 51
war 49–52, 274, 303
Ward, Keith 44, 138

Warnock, Mary 251, 265
Warnock Committee 74–5, 251
Warren, Mary Anne 67, 73
Watson, Francis 243
Watson, John Broadus 197
weapons of mass destruction 274
well-being 21, 208
Westermann, C. 45
whistleblowing 298
White, Lynn 155
Whittaker, Michelle and Jayson 255–6

William of Ockham 289
Williams, Rowan 163–4
Williams, Sir Bernard 22, 23
Wilmot, Ian 259
Wink, Walter 52
wisdom 216
Wolpert, Lewis 66
women: Buddhism 55; Hinduism 57, 245–6; inferiority of women in the Bible 47, 243–4; Islam 58, 247; Judaism 59, 246, 247; Paul on 232; right to abortion 77;

sexual ethics 230; Virtue Ethics 218
World Council of Churches 296
world heritage sites 151–2

xenotransplantation 264–5

Yarri, Donna 269

Zambia 255
Zoroastrianism 233
zygotes 256, **315**